Mary Heaton Vorse

The Life of an American Insurgent

American Civilization
A series edited by Allen F. Davis

Mary Heaton Vorse

The Life of an American Insurgent

Dee Garrison

 Temple University Press – Philadelphia

Temple University Press, Philadelphia 19122
Copyright © 1989 by Dee Garrison. All rights reserved
Published 1989
Printed in the United States of America

∞ The paper used in this publication meets the minimum requirements
of American National Standard for Information Sciences—Permanence
of Paper for Printed Library Materials, ANSI Z39.48-1984

Library of Congress Cataloging-in-Publication Data
Garrison, Dee.
    Mary Heaton Vorse: the life of an American insurgent / Dee
Garrison.
        p.   cm. — (American civilization)
    Bibliography: p.
    Includes index.
    ISBN 0-87722-601-6 (alk. paper)
    1. Vorse, Mary Heaton, 1874–1966—Biography.   2. Authors,
American—20th century—Biography.   3. Journalists—United States—
Biography.   4. Feminists—United States—Biography.   5. Labor and
laboring classes—United States—Historiography.   I. Title.
II. Series.
PS3543.088Z68 1989
818'.5209—dc19
    [B]   88-29386
                                                                    CIP

For Lora Tennessee,
who first had the dream,
and for Clara Mae and Ruth Jeanne
who nurtured it

Contents

Preface

Mary Heaton Vorse is one of the most compelling and representative figures in the history of American radicalism. That she has been slighted in its annals shows the effect upon scholarship of sexism and the Cold War. She spent fifty-four years of her life in active struggle for libertarian socialism, feminism, and world peace. This union of ideas was far too radical for most of her contemporaries to consider—another reason for the scholarly inattention paid her life.

As the foremost pioneer of labor journalism in the nation, and as a correspondent covering international events from 1912 through the late 1940s, her impassioned reporting pulled her audience to a wider vision of democracy. Millions of Americans were agitated and informed by her interpretation of world events, war and peace, labor battles, and feminist demands. Along with many other Americans of her time, she protested the social and political conditions created by the advance of industrial capitalism. Her life also spanned the period when significant numbers of middle-class women found work and purpose in the public arena. The issues raised by economic inequality and gender conflict compose the core of her thought and address the fundamental questions of her age.

She had many audiences. Vorse provided the news coverage that could bridge the communication gap between union leadership and the general reading public. Unlike most labor journalists, Vorse was often a strike participant. Her inside knowledge of union strategy, combined with her fervent commitment to accurate reporting, brought uncommon depth and feeling to her work. Her measured, knowledgeable accounts found easy entry into major journals like *Harper's*, *Scribner's*, and the *Atlantic*, outlets that were normally closed to writers closely identified with the left, and thus labeled "propagandists" by the mainstream press. But Vorse also wrote for intellectuals and reformers in the *Masses*, the *Nation*, and the *New Republic*, and for the workers themselves in her hundreds of dispatches for union newspapers, newsletters, and broadsides for the union press. Her appeal to every class of readers was a call for common-sense application of traditional national ideals—liberty, equality, justice—all carefully placed within the global context of the socialist movement.

Always, her writing recreated the human drama within a context of factual detail. Under her hand, the workers' determined faces, rough clothing, and excited speeches become visible and noisy. One feels the fear on the picket line as the armed goons or awesome mounted police approach. The defiant strength of hundreds of marching unionists, or suffragists, or farmers, or unemployed, is evident. We absorb the memory of the work-reddened hands of the miner's wife resting lightly on her son's shoulders, or the gray silence of the crowd of thousands in the Russian famine area, or the anguished French mother with three sons dead shaking her fist at the beribboned soldiers parading outside her door.

Vorse's unique contribution to the journalism of her time is her consistent attention to the special concerns of women. The immigrant wife, the Serbian orphan, the mean tenement home, the starved children, the courage of girl pickets—these are the core of her material. Through Vorse's eyes, we see the contribution of women to labor's advance.

Mary Heaton Vorse wrote sixteen books, two plays, and hundreds of articles and stories in major journals, newspapers, and magazines. For several decades she was one of the most popular writers of women's fiction in the United States. She wrote short fiction only to support her three children and to finance her political work. Yet her stories of women's lives so appealed to the concerns of her age that in 1906, although she had been writing only two years and had not yet published her first book, her work was included in a composite novel written by a group of distinguished American authors that included William Dean Howells and Henry James.

In 1930, at age fifty-six, Vorse purposely renounced her comfortable literary reputation and income, determined to concentrate her effort on labor reporting. After that, it was only when she literally ran out of money, and that was often, that she would hole up to dash off another "lollypop" to pay her way for a few more months. Yet despite her disrespect for it, much of her popular fiction rises above formula to provide stunning apparitions of female unity and discontent.

But perhaps Mary Heaton Vorse's most remarkable achievement was her ability to sense the moment and find the center where action would occur. "There was always an easy rule for locating her in time and space," Murray Kempton wrote, "whenever you read across forty years about an event in which men stood in that single, desperate moment which brings all past, all present, and all future to one sharp point for them, you could assume that Mary Vorse had been there." Her uncanny ability to move to crucial places at critical moments took her to major strikes, international conflicts, and radical and women's meetings in Europe and the United States. She appeared in Lenin's Moscow and Hitler's Germany, at sophisticated literary salons, and on dangerous picket lines, at luncheons with Senators or with impoverished sharecroppers, at feminist rallies and at CIO strategy sessions.

Far more than most thinkers of her time, Mary Heaton Vorse was dominated by the great social movements that operate under the surface of events. She caught the rising tide of radical revolt, of unionization, of feminism, and was moved by all its retreats and advances. Intrigued by her valor, John Dos Passos took her life as symbol for an era, using her as counterpart for Mary French, one of the twelve main characters in his classic trilogy, *U.S.A.* Later, in his right-wing period, Dos Passos returned to Mary Vorse as model for his portrait of Anne Comfort in his semi-autobiographical novel, *Chosen Country*, where Dos Passos interpreted Vorse's experience to express his theme of womanhood defeated by ancient circumstance.

When Mary Heaton Vorse died in 1966 at age ninety-two, her passing was only briefly noted by the mass-circulation media. In a quick and guilty bow to an honored but slightly intimidating past, *Time* and *Newsweek* ran short obituaries. The New York *Times* noted her exit under a two-column headline: MARY HEATON VORSE, A NOVELIST AND CHAMPION OF LABOR, DEAD, FIGURE OF MAJOR STRIKES OF 20s AND 30s—REPORTED FROM EUROPE BEFORE THE WAR. Since most of her friends were long dead, Walter Reuther was the only notable who issued a press release. "She was one of the great labor writers of all time. . . ." he said. "This magnificent woman . . . was . . . of invincible spirit and fearless courage. . . . Hers was a life that brought richness and beauty to all mankind."

Essentially, however, she had outlived her own reputation. With the end of the labor wars in the 1930s, her literary standing faltered. With the beginning of the Cold War, her style of political expression was quieted. With the ascendance of the Feminine Mystique, her generation of fighters lay largely forgotten.

But even at the moment of her death, a new feminist movement was stirring toward birth, a new radical generation was arising. In the eighties, her books and articles were reprinted, her fiction featured in *Ms.*, and a vignette of her life presented as part of the series "American Portraits" on CBS television.

This would not have surprised her. Mary Vorse thoroughly understood the momentary extinction of her work—for all her life and all her writing had centered on the relationship between individual and society. Times were sure to change, she knew, even in her last years. She was confident that her experience contained lessons to teach another generation. She fully expected to be studied and understood. Her life had carried exceptional impact. Her ideas would endure.

Born into a wealthy New England family in 1874, Vorse first was inspired by the social ideal of the New Woman of the time. Vorse rejected her mother's demand that she follow the familiar path to marriage and maternity. This, her premier and most difficult rebellion, led to Vorse's escape to Paris and New York City as an art student in the 1890s.

In Greenwich Village, she was happily situated at the center of the social revolution that began in 1912. An editor of the *Masses* and a charter member of the Liberal Club, she was both a conduit for the younger men and women entering the world of the avant garde and a core participant in the ongoing revolt. Due in part to her influence, Provincetown, her home since 1906, became a kind of summer suburb for the New York intelligentsia. The famed Provincetown Players were born in 1915 on her fish wharf. In these same years Vorse helped to found that Greenwich Village nursery of modern feminism, the remarkable Heterodoxy Club.

Vorse came late to the support of labor's cause. She was a thirty-eight-year-old mother of two when the Lawrence textile strike of 1912 altered the course of her life. "I leaped lightly to my fate one morning when I got up and went out to get an order to go to Lawrence," she wrote in 1926.

> I entered into a way of life I never yet have left. . . . Before Lawrence, I had known a good deal about labor, but I had not felt about it. I had not got angry. In Lawrence, I got angry. . . . Some curious synthesis had taken place between my life and that of the workers, some peculiar change that would never again permit me to look with indifference on the fact that riches for the few were made by the misery of the many.

Until World War I she continued her important alliance begun at Lawrence with the radical union, the Industrial Workers of the World, or Wobblies, as they were known.

Later, on her tour of the war zones, Vorse ignored the political and diplomatic events of the time and reported the effect of war on the ordinary people of Europe, especially women and children. One of the few American reporters to visit Bela Kun's short-lived Communist government in Hungary, her June 1919 mission was marked by embroilment in political intrigue. On her return to the United States, she worked as publicist for the Great Steel Strike of 1919 and organized women shirtmakers in Pennsylvania. Reaching the Soviet Union several weeks before the male reporters from the great American dailies were admitted, she was Moscow correspondent for the Hearst papers during 1921. Hounded all the way by agents of the Department of Justice, she returned home to report the campaign to free American political prisoners incarcerated during the Red Scare.

Vorse returned to labor work as publicity director for the Passaic, New Jersey, textile strike of 1926. The revolutionary publicity tactics she developed at Passaic would set the pattern for the successful techniques that marked the labor uprisings of the next decade. Vorse was a firstcomer at the southern textile war in Gastonia, North Carolina, in 1929, and at Bloody Harlan County in Kentucky in 1931, where her group, which included Edmund Wilson and Malcolm Cowley, was expelled from Kentucky by nightriders. That same prescience took her in the thirties to unemployed marches, the farmers' strike, the Scottsboro Boys' trial, and to early New Deal Washington, D.C., where she worked at the Indian Bureau under the controversial reformer John Collier. While in Washington, she was for a time associated with what would come to be called the Ware group, a network of radicals later fated to receive wide attention for its connection to the Alger Hiss case.

She was, of course, present at the pivotal struggle of the CIO at Flint, Michigan in 1937, and went on to report CIO battles across the nation. In the 1930s, she recorded the rise of Hitler in Germany and the rule of Stalin in the USSR. During World War II, she was perhaps the oldest official American war correspondent. After the war, she served in Italy with the United Nations Relief and Rehabilitation Administration.

In the 1950s Mary Heaton Vorse lived in semiretirement in her beloved beach house in Provincetown, Massachusetts. But she continued to write —of Mafia-connected union chiefs, of migrant workers, and of civil rights work in the South. Her last big story to receive national attention was the 1952 exposé of crime in the waterfront unions, published in *Harper's* when she was seventy-eight. In her eighties and nineties, the scope of her battleground shrank to Cape Cod. She helped to organize a Provincetown protest against offshore dumping of nuclear waste. At age ninety-one, she began her last crusade. She backed Provincetown's young Episcopalian minister, one of the first to march against the Vietnam War.

Just as Lawrence shaped her social outlook, her experience at Heterodoxy and at the Women's International Suffrage convention held in Budapest in 1913 determined her feminist vision. Vorse's work in the suffrage movement led to her appointment as the delegate from the New York City Woman Suffrage Party to the peace congress held at The Hague in 1915. In Germany and France, Vorse saw troop trains filled with soldiers who were laughing and drinking from bottles, happy young men en route to the places where they would be killed. "There is that which makes man his own enemy and every woman's," she wrote in her diary then. "Man takes passionate joy in risking his own life while he takes the life of others. When women's understanding of this becomes conscious, it is called feminism."

Twice widowed, in 1910 and 1915, Vorse was a single mother most of her life. In Paris in 1919, she fell in love with Robert Minor, the famous American cartoonist and anarchist. One year later, Minor converted to communism. In 1922 her affair with Minor ended disastrously when, four-months pregnant with his child, she suffered a miscarriage, and he deserted her for a younger, more politically compliant woman. As a result of her medical treatment after the miscarriage, Vorse was for some years addicted to morphine.

In the 1920s, with the labor movement quieted, the feminist movement crushed, a Republican government in power, Vorse returned home to be a mother. During that dark decade, her massive depression centered around her conviction that she must pay whatever price necessary to compensate for what she believed to be the negative effect on her children of the years spent away from her family. For seven torturous years, she placed her work second to the presumed needs of her children.

"My story wouldn't be important if it were the story of one woman," she wrote in 1922. "My failure is that of almost every working woman who has children and a home to keep up, whether she scrubs floors, or works in mills, or is a high-priced professional woman. It's nearly impossible to do both jobs well. So most women fail in either or both. Their energy and thoughts are divided. . . . Don't housewives deserve a sabbatical year? . . .

I have never wanted to write as much as I do now. On the other hand I have never realized my children's needs so clearly and have never wanted so much to fill them. Are the two things possible? Must there always be a double failure?"

Forty years later, at age eighty-eight, Vorse was absorbed in the task of arranging her papers for preservation in Detroit's new library of labor history. She sorted through the mass of letters, clippings, manuscripts, and diaries, the memories of husbands, lovers, children, and friends. She paused now and then to add marginal comments to the documents, to correct, deny, or elaborate on a previous statement. She spoke to the future inquirer—a last attempt to give coherence to the imperfect documents spread before her.

"You must understand," she wrote, "that when I was very young, Life said to me, 'Here are two ways—a world running to mighty cities, full of the spectacle of bloody adventure, and here is home and children. Which will you take, the adventurous life or a quiet life?'

'I will take *both*,' I said.'"

The choice seemed to be between love, security, warmth—and ambition, creation, risk. Both were defined and separated for her by the weight of her entire culture. Her words speak to the decision peculiarly pressed upon women. And here, encapsuled for us, does lie the explanatory core of her living. Modern women will instantly recognize the common links between Vorse's desperate shuffle and their own everyday effort to balance love and work, home and job.

Few women writers suffered more from lack of self-permission, space, quiet, and leisure to write than Mary Heaton Vorse. Tillie Olsen, Joanna Russ, and others have written about the deterrents to women authors. They describe the fear of impropriety, the lack of female models or a female literary tradition, the inclusion of only extraordinary women writers in the literary canon, and the devaluation of women's experience and consequent attitudes, values, and judgments as less representative or less important than male experience. Foremost among these discouraging obstacles to women writers through the ages, the simple lack of time in which to write is surely the most common and the most heartbreaking handicap. Most of us appreciate the difficulty of being full-time writer, full-time housekeeper and mother, full-time breadwinner. To add labor activist and reporter is to strain the imagination. Yet Vorse managed it all, usually well, sometimes badly, at times just barely. Like many of her generation of talented and ambitious women, she would know more defeats than victories.

Surely Mary Vorse would have been more honored had she been more conventional. She fit nowhere in the shifting political groups of the 1920s and after. She had long laid down the illusion of some liberals that reasoned appeals alone could cancel the capitalist-fueled repression of radicalism. Nor did she share the faith of the Communists. She learned the failure of the Communist promise in Hungary and Moscow, at Passaic and Gastonia. It was the Bolshevik massacre of Soviet peasants, which began in the late twenties, that she could not forgive or forget. She learned earlier than many of her socially engaged friends, and her popularity fell victim to her premature awareness.

But she also balked at the point where liberals and democratic socialists turned right. She refused to bait the Communist rank and file in the trenches, for she knew they often served justice with more constancy and courage than most. Vorse never confused embattled labor activists, many of whom were women, with the Communist Party functionary or the carping bystander, most of whom were men.

She cared little for political abstraction. Her attention veered inexorably to the concrete. She judged people by what they did, not by what they said, by their action, not their theory. She did not admire those inactive on the sidelines who felt compelled, with righteous fervor, to continue beating the dead horse of American communism. More than that, she shamed those who did. Her usefulness to many literary and political figures lessened accordingly.

Not liberal, Communist, or anti-Communist, she eluded categorization. Even though Communist officials considered her unreliable and unreasonable, she was harassed for over thirty years by private and federal spy hunters. In 1944, the FBI placed her on the list of dangerous citizens to be jailed immediately on presidential order. To ensure her rapid arrest, the agency maintained an up-to-date record of her location for at least another twelve years—until she was eighty-two years old. This distinction may have earned her a place as some sort of record holder among the targets of federal intelligence agencies.

Yet the legacy of another's life can never be complete, for it must be spun and edged from fragments. Mary Heaton Vorse understood the dilemma. "Life, as it happens," she wrote in 1914, "fails often to have a recognizable pattern—for you may bleed your heart out and die of the wound, and yet the pain of which you die, the drama which caused your heart to bleed, will have had neither logical beginning nor definite end, and in the whole course of it, though it has been life and death to you, there will have been none of those first aids to the reader—suspense, dramatic contrast, or plot. You have suffered and died but it may not make a story."

It is the task of the biographer to present that story. Assiduously collected from oral testimony and a clutter of paper, the life-telling facts can be placed methodically in order. But the biographer must also search for the reality behind the subject's public pose—to find what Leon Edel has called "the figure under the carpet, the evidence in the reverse of the tapestry, the life-myth of a given mask." It is the unwritten and unstated construction —the inner personal myth we all create in order to function—that gives breath and meaning to an individual's life. And it is this interpretation that is so difficult for the biographer to glimpse—in subject as in self.

For Mary Heaton Vorse, the reverse of the tapestry is the mirror opposite of the outward pattern. What seems to be excessive mother love conceals furious resentment. Militant feminism is accompanied by traditional romantic dreams. Brave adventures are undertaken to avoid self-knowledge. Frenetic movement masquerades as purpose. These are the contradictions in Vorse's useful and creative life. Taken together, they can be seen as an individual adjustment to a personal past, as well as part of a collective response to an inequitable society and to the fast-changing position of women within it. Vorse's struggle to resolve these contradictions gives her life its greatest poignancy.

Her front-row view of the momentous clashes in American labor history provides a striking perspective on one of the most consequential social transformations in national life. Her intimate knowledge of the world of socially involved intellectuals is filtered through the critical intelligence of the natural outsider—the achieving woman of the period—to enrich the flavor of American radicalism and to increase our awareness of its evolving boundaries. Her story is in large part a recital of those changing environs, especially the relation of American rebels to the worldwide socialist movement.

Although Vorse very early on rejected the denial of civil liberties and the subordination of society to state that marked Soviet-style communism, she also knew that for many thousands of American citizens, those far removed from the rigid doublespeak of party leadership, the American Communist movement in the late twenties and thirties often seemed the only organization on the left that effectively linked a Marxist class analysis to combative daily action, not only on the labor front, but also among the poor and unemployed. And she understood that the virulent Cold War strain of anticommunism, which ignored the crimes and derelictions of the capitalist democracies, was, like its predecessor in the post–World

War I period, the dominant weapon used by conservatives to stem the radical pressures for change generated by both wars. From 1921 on, Vorse assumed a lonely stance. She stood in opposition not only to American conservatives, but also to the American Communist leadership, and, later, to Cold War–convulsed democratic socialists and liberals as well. Her prophetic anticipation of today's most pressing issues of world peace and revolutionary change connect us to this often overlooked but highly significant lineage within American radical history.

Yet as a woman, Vorse was perceived by some not as a radical, but as a bleeding heart. What commentators called steadfastness or vision in a male, is often judged naïveté or idealism in her. The political journalist Marquis Childs, in his introduction to one of her books, tried to capture in his description that complete sense of love of freedom, which everyone noted as such a strong trait in her, almost embarrassing to some, so simple and strong and steady was her belief. It was the same lack of concern for immediate realities that moved her in the 1960s, when she received her small amounts of money, much of it donated to her by friends who had little to spare, to send at once a large portion of the tiny sum on to César Chavez and the farmworkers in California or to various civil rights groups in the South. For the world was in motion again, and it was her fight, too —had always been.

Above all else, her life carried passionate conviction. Her own radical generation was forged in bohemian Greenwich Village, transformed by the world's first great socialist upheavals, and buried by the witch hunt that followed World War II. Whatever its political mistakes, misplaced visions, and moral failings, it had a kind of glory that always made it more right than wrong, more heroic than foolish. And whatever her errors along the way, Mary Heaton Vorse had been there, from start to finish, an unrepentant rebel to the last. Hers is a rich bequest, to our present as much as to our history.

Acknowledgments

My debt to three people is enormous. With the fearless, loving spirit of their mother, Mary's children, Heaton Vorse and Joel O'Brien, and daughter-in-law Jill O'Brien, opened their homes, hearts, memories and records to me, with no restrictions, knowing that their judgment of events might not be mine.

My deepest intellectual and personal debts are to those friends and scholars who gave of their time and expertise to read part or all of the manuscript or to provide guidance and encouragement. I am especially grateful to Rosalyn Baxandall, Sue Cobble, Wayne Cooper, Caroline Coughlin, Susan Crane, Sue Gal, Judy Gerson, Linda Gonzalves, Gerald Grob, Mary Hartman, Ed Hartman, Evelyn Hu, Kathy Jones, Suzanne Lebsock, Phyllis Mack, John Marin, Art Miller, Lynn Miller, William O'Neill, David Oshinksy, Carol Petillo, Jim Reed, Sue Schrepfer, Judith Schwarz, Will Weinberg, Deborah White, and Virginia Yans. I remain grateful to Betty M. Unterberger whose inspired teaching and committed scholarship first led me to the study of history.

The entire staff at the Walter Reuther Library at Wayne State University, Detroit, and especially Dione Miles, served my needs with remarkable skill and kindness. My research and writing have been supported in part by the Rutgers University Research Council. The meticulous professionalism of the personnel at Temple University Press transformed the publishing process into a personal pleasure.

As always, the constant and loving support of John Leggett is precious beyond measure.

Part One: 1874–1910

I love my golden wings and I want to fly right into the sun
until they are all draggled and battered.

—MHV, 1896

Chapter One

Amherst

Mary Heaton Vorse's story properly begins with the mansion on a hill in Amherst, Massachusetts, although she was not born there, and fled from it as soon as she was able. In 1879, when Mary was five, her parents bought the twenty-four-room house on Amity Street, pronounced "a-mighty street" by the local wits in note of the prominence of the families who resided there. Even before she reached her teens, Mary's girlhood home had assumed the shape of an expectant trap in her imagination. In Amherst she forged her most basic self-definition—the affluent outsider in rebellion against polite mores.

Mary's position as the youngest child in the Heaton household further set her apart, but did not ensure maternal attention. Her mother was too preoccupied with the supervision of five teenage children from her first marriage to attend to the tasks of raising a small child. From her birth, Mary's daily care was assigned to a procession of nurses and housemaids. As the foreign, late arrival to her mother's brood, Mary often felt ignored, even victimized, in a household of heedless adolescents naturally a bit jealous of their mother's new child.

Prompted by her parents' ridicule of the town elite, Mary also felt an alien in Amherst society. She soon learned that beneath Amherst's peaceful exterior lay the feuds of long duration, the lives cramped by religiosity, the fearful hearts of comfortable folks who seldom dared to question much or to risk impudence. Amherst women and Amherst proprieties symbolized the antithesis of all she would be and all she would cherish: "Amherst was not my home spiritually. I never accepted it anymore than it accepted me."[1]

Outwardly, Amherst in the 1880s looked to be a sheltered spot. Its gentle folk seemed untouched by severe deprivation; its social relations appeared as contented and orderly as its quiet streets. One hundred miles from Boston, the small farming community long remained an economic and cultural backwater, untroubled for years by either liberal Unitarianism or the influence of the mercantile centers. Amherst lacked the water power to support the factories that grew up in nearby towns like Northampton, Holyoke, or Springfield. Aside from the railroad, gas, running water, concrete sidewalks, and public sewer system in place by the 1890s, the industrialization transforming American life hardly touched Amherst. Nor did the wrenching gap between rich and poor, dramatically apparent in the eastern cities by the late nineteenth century, taint Amherst's ideal of social order. Amherst was set apart from the modernizing world, yet the genteel conformity that apparently ruled town society was actually a remnant of spiritual antiquity, a precariously balanced cultural tradition under attack.[2]

Despite the town's relative seclusion, the new intellectual and social concerns sweeping the nation reached Amherst as well. Many men and women of intellect who grew up there found it stifling. "I fail to recognize any bliss in vegetating in that humdrum, old foggy hamlet of Amherst," as the poet Eugene Field put it. The town's most creative resident, Emily Dickinson, reported that the Amherst men and women she knew "talk of Hallowed things, aloud, and embarrass my dog." High-spirited Mabel Loomis Todd, who arrived in Amherst in 1881, also found town women lacking: "estimable ladies of quiet tastes dressing in dark colors, having their suppers at six o'clock, not playing cards, nor dancing." But it was Dickinson who best skewered the female notables of Amherst, as she immortalized their decorative characteristics in verse:

> What Soft-Cherubic Creatures
> These Gentlewomen are—
> One would as soon assault a Plush—
> or violate a Star—[3]

When Mary Vorse was twenty, she noted in her diary that the greatest difference between herself and Amherst women was "that they think I talk of serious things lightly and I think they talk of light things ponderously. There is an awful gulf."[4] Like many other intellectuals of her time, she reacted against the disintegrating Victorian culture that could no longer sustain her and learned withdrawal early in order to examine life on her own terms. She did so partly because in Amherst—still in so many ways a Bible-centered Puritan village—the moral and social contradictions of the time were especially apparent to a questing mind, and partly because her parents encouraged her difference through their own proudly maintained distance from respectability. At home one could venture widely, promote any theory. It was only among the stolid townspeople that one edited. Yet Vorse realized, "if I in my high spirits did things which made me 'talked about' my mother didn't care one whit."

In truth, it did not require much to alarm the town. The pace of social change in Amherst made the steady turn of the seasons of the year seem recklessly swift in comparison. Among Mary's peers, one of the most anticipated events of the spring came when they joined a group of adults whose idea of a party was to gather in the parlor and sit up till the wee hour of 11 P.M.—all in order to observe the flowering of a night-blooming cereus placed in a bowl of ice on a center table.[5] Amherst's numbing odor of sanctity, as well as its lack of economic opportunity, drove the young away.

Mary's father probably agreed to move to Amherst because the town's college faculties provided associates with whom he could indulge his interest in American history, or because the setting reminded him of his rural childhood at Stockbridge, fifty miles away. Mary's mother stuck to Amherst because it was large enough to offer a society life of sorts, yet small enough to allow her talent for deviation considerable notice. As one of the wealthiest women in town, Ellen Heaton's status in community life could hardly be dismissed, no matter how peculiar her ideas. In Amherst she could indulge her need to pose on high as the cosmopolitan lady shocking the provincial natives of a New England village. This was a stance that Mary would adapt for her own purposes.

Mary's mother held the power position in the Heaton household. This was not simply a result of her forceful nature; it was her money that sustained the family life style. Ellen Heaton could trace her English ancestry back to the first settlement of the New England colonies in the 1630s. Ellen's father, a grocery merchant, settled in Burlington, Vermont. In 1852, Ellen lifted herself from middle-class obscurity by capturing the heart of a fabulously wealthy visiting seafarer. Captain Charles Bernard Marvin had made his fortune in the China trade and as a liquor merchant serving the thirst of hopefuls who created the San Francisco boomtown during the 1849 Gold Rush. He and Ellen were married within a few weeks of meeting. He was thirty-nine; she was eighteen.

To provide his catch with a proper setting, Captain Marvin purchased the finest house in Burlington—the old governor's mansion on upper Main Street. Marvin paid $12,000 for the property and hired an artist for $10,000 to do the decorating. The Marvins frescoed the front rooms in a design of garlands and cupids, and added marble mantels, bronze chandeliers, and European statuary. Ellen adjusted easily to her sudden elevation in Burlington society. She bore five children in fifteen years, while greatly expanding her experience of the world by sojourns in Europe, San Francisco, and Brooklyn. Widowed in 1871 at age thirty-seven, Ellen enjoyed a comfortable income from her husband's estate.[6]

Within two years, Ellen remarried. Seven years her junior, her new husband, Hiram Heaton, was a slight, rather passive man with a delicate look. Hiram's English ancestors had passed through Canada, where several generations of Heatons, preferring town life to farm labor, served as innkeepers and barmaids to trappers and travelers. His hotel-keeper family had come from Ticonderoga, New York, to Stockbridge, Massachusetts, in 1851. At the time of Hiram's marriage to Ellen, he was helping his mother and brother-in-law run the fashionable Stockbridge House, better known today as the Red Lion Inn. When the newly widowed Ellen arrived at the inn as a summer guest, "chaperoned" by her ailing aunt, she decided at once that the shy Heaton boy, with his interest in books and art, would do her just fine. He was sufficiently malleable, yet a nice change from Captain Marvin, who had indulged her high spirits and taught her worldliness, but whose cultural knowledge extended no farther than the opera house. With no difficulty, Ellen convinced Hiram to join her in a life of travel and leisure. Twenty-two months later, on October 11, 1874, Mary was born at the family's East 40th Street house in New York City.[7]

The Heaton family trio, and the older Marvin children, spent the winters in New York until Mary was ten. After that they were more likely to be in California, Vienna, or Paris during the winter season. Before she was fifteen, Mary learned to speak and write French, Italian, and German. All the Marvin children were educated at home. Mary attended two private schools and the high school in Amherst for a brief time, but the bulk of her education came through travel and private instruction. Her father insisted that she make all the appropriate bows at the cultural sites of western Europe, from the catacombs to Westminster Abbey. But religious training was perfunctory. If Mary longed to be among the much discussed pioneers who composed America's first generations of college women, she never mentioned it. Most likely, Mary recognized that she would find the prudishly monitored halls of Wellesley, Vassar, or Smith as constraining to the agnostic spirit of Ellen Heaton's daughter as were the parlors of Amherst.

Ellen's "triumph and sureness" dominated the lives of her older children, Mary later wrote, remembering that only she among Ellen's daughters escaped the maternal mold. During Mary's early years, Ellen was consumed in channeling her five fatherless children into appropriate avenues—economic endeavors for the boys, secure marriages for the girls. The two Marvin daughters especially required Ellen's attention. There must be dresses selected, parties planned, hair styles considered, social training acquired, husbands captured. If Ellen's organizational skill and energy were oppressive, they were also awesome. Within two days of the family's arrival in Paris or Vienna, Mary recalled, "my mother would have found an apartment, engaged three servants, hired a piano, had the trunks unpacked and the establishment running as if we had always lived there, complete with the flowering plants she liked."

Influenced by her father's perception, Mary early recognized the personal catastrophe that smoldered beneath Ellen's superficial gaiety: "My mother's life was tragedy. She had a fine mind and great executive ability and all this dynamo was idle."[8] Ellen's intelligence and energy found little outlet in late Victorian America. The weary problem of how to cope with leisure afflicted the lives of many middle- and upper-class women of the day. Barred from serious commitment to any sort of work, trained to shun public activity as the affair of men, women like Ellen were sentenced to fill the long hours of every day as best they could. Many women facing this dilemma simply went to bed, permanently, or lingered on in the twilight of the curious female nervous disorder known as neurasthenia. Other women turned to social reform or women's causes.

Despite her discontent, Ellen remained bound to the notion of woman's limited domestic sphere. Throughout her life she opposed women's suffrage on the grounds that "too many fools are already voting." Ellen preferred to see suffrage curtailed rather than extended. She favored rigid property qualifications and would forbid immigrants the vote unless they had an American education.[9]

Ellen channeled her quest for meaning into what she called "Housekeeping as a Fine Art," which meant careful direction of her five servants. Haunted by her lost youth, an inheritance that Mary would assume, Ellen was obsessed with spontaneity and pursuit of "fun." "Games and more games filled my mother's hours," Mary wrote. "I was taught [very young] to play cards and was often called in from play to make a fourth."[10] Clothes interested Ellen, but true to her rebel self-image, she disdained fashion. Long after the demise of its popularity, she refused to forsake the bustle. Ellen was a proponent of the women's dress-reform effort, but believed women's clubs should drop their literary and historical studies and consider more serious matters—like the paucity of reliable domestic help. Other than distributing an occasional food basket during the depression of the mid-nineties, Ellen felt no need to perform social service, paid or unpaid.

Although no one was allowed to penetrate her inner core, Ellen was probably less guarded with Mary than with anyone else. Ellen often confided to Mary her disappointments with the Marvin children or revealed the problems they presented to her. But Ellen's message to her youngest child was designed to produce distance, not to encourage closeness. Hearing her mother's confessions taught Mary "the firm resolve never to give my mother a moment of trouble." Only when Mary experienced severe marital crisis in her twenties did she break her reticence and come to Ellen for comfort. Ellen's advice was that Mary repress her anxiety and never reveal it to anyone else, including Mary's husband. "My mother told me, 'Never let him know how you feel.' I have the impression she really had little to tell me," Vorse remembered bitterly.[11]

During Mary's girlhood, she watched her mother's lonely adjustment to the limitations of age. For the thirty-five years of life remaining to her after Mary's birth, Ellen continued her time-filling quest. To fill the empty hours, and perhaps with an eye to publication, Ellen wrote pages of instructions to housewives on training cooks and selecting menus, and sometimes tried her hand at fiction. After the youngest Marvin child left home, her mother had sighed heavily and said to Mary, "Now [I must begin] these ghastly women's meetings again." Decades later Mary wrote, "Here the woman was living in an environment chosen by her, in a beautiful home, and she couldn't fill her own life at all. I felt, I remember, coldly repelled by this."[12] Determined to escape Ellen's plight, and to forsake the feminine ideal that closed the domestic trap and condoned mind-deadening triviality, Mary also idolized her distant, audacious mother. She admired Ellen's confident direction of household affairs, her role as adventuress, and her open contempt for New England sanctimony. Perhaps Ellen's domineering ways were sufficient to breed resentment in a daughter who was also pampered by a slyly subversive father, himself yearning for a somewhat wider range of decision. The misleading veneer of Amherst society, which so early repulsed Mary, resembled the hypocrisy drawn over her own family drama, with its patterned cheerfulness and hidden demons.

Ellen trained Mary as a nonconformist, but it was Hiram Heaton's adoration of Mary that strengthened her ego to the extent that rebellion became possible. As a child Mary knew herself to be a special person— special because she was of the privileged class, special because she was the baby of a large household, but most favored because she was her father's only child. Hiram and Mary formed a natural alliance, both shadowy additions to the already existent Marvin family. Hiram was her parent teacher, companion, and escort. Unlike Ellen, he offered easy familiarity and enjoyed a variety of close and long-lasting friends. Whereas Ellen was a remote figure shimmering on the horizon, Hiram was the immediate guardian who could be counted upon to hear Mary's problems and, with a word to the servants, set her world aright. Gentle Hiram served as buffer —although he eventually proved to be an unreliable one—against Ellen's rushing power.

The unusual freedom given to Mary as a child both enriched and frightened. Yet she suspected that her lack of supervision was due to parental inattention. "There was no doubt about it. I was, in a certain way, not neglected, but the household was so big that no one noticed [my absence] . . . I was raised like Topsy. There were long years . . . when no one knew what time I came or what time I went to bed, what I read or how I spent my days or with whom, when I had anything but the normal life of a young girl. I had not been reared within the conventions of a community. I heard formal education laughed at, and perhaps rightly, but my parents did nothing much to replace such education."[13] Mary's solution to the feelings of insecurity she experienced as the unattended and intimidated youngest child was to "act out in a wild desire to be different." Her siblings teased her: "You are a COI—a Creature of Impulse." Mary assumed the identity of the family daredevil. Thus in one stroke she attracted notice, found an expression for repressed tensions, and won her mother's secret approval.

Sidney, the youngest Marvin child, was Mary's one sure ally. Perhaps sympathetic to Mary's desire to overtake his sisters in matters of social success, Sidney taught Mary how to attract the opposite sex. "You're not pretty or witty," he told her, "so you'd better learn how to get along with men." Mary was intensely grateful for Sidney's attention. She remembered how she jogged to keep up with Sidney's fast walk, as she listened intently to his lessons in social skills.

The days spent with Sidney were valuable excursions into the wider world of the male. Like so many future feminists of her generation, Mary was a self-identified "tomboy." Rejecting society's gender-role demands, she enjoyed the psychological satisfaction and bodily joy of physical exertion. In Amherst, Mary sought in vain for a female friend willing to walk with her for over a mile. As an adult, Mary was a devoted hiker. In her eighties, she won renown in her Cape Cod home for her long daily swims.

As to all tomboys, there came that moment of girlhood, never to be forgotten, when many of her same-age male friends, once her equal in physical strength, surpassed her in muscular development. Slowly but steadily, the old wrestling games and tests of strength became a series of humiliating defeats. Mary suffered from the experience. Recovering, she decided that "I didn't need to compete; I was a girl." The decision delayed overt repudiation of her mother's feminine ideal and marked Mary's introduction into puberty, with its self-conscious recognition of the opposite sex.

"I can remember no time in my life when I was not acutely conscious of boys and young men," Vorse wrote when in her sixties. Her first memories were of competition for the attention of her mother whose interest was centered on the entertainment of suitors for the Marvin girls. Her active girlhood years while in Sidney's tow made her feel comfortable with male friends and convinced her that boys' activities were of more interest than the restrictive play of girls. And surely her adored and adoring father shaped her positive attraction to men.[14]

Still, her sensuality was remarkably advanced for a well-bred female born in the 1870s. Young Mary had little difficulty in winning any male she set out to capture. Her desirability often puzzled her, for she knew she was not particularly beautiful by the standards of her day. Yet she rarely lacked attention and hardly suffered those moments of uncertainty common to adolescent girls. As an adult, she relished the sport of romance and the physical pleasure of love, both casual and committed. Indeed, her only sexual defeat came so late in life that the unfamiliar experience of rejection shattered her spirit.

Perhaps no incident so well expresses Mary's assured sexuality as the scene aboard a train that she recorded in her diary when she was in her early eighties.

> There's a curious thing about people who belong to one. When I was young I recognized instantly the men who belonged to me . . . always there was the curious knowledge which came unheralded. I

would find the eyes of my man and we would look at each other. It had been so with lesser lovers and with my husbands. Sometimes I knew the man as a friend before the moment of illumination came. . . . Now I am very old and I thought these things were behind me. Then today . . . I never knew why I turned around to look at the young officer sitting behind me on the train. There he was, a man who belonged to me . . . his eyes, his kind mouth. We smiled at each other as though we were old friends. It was the old recognition.[15]

Here was Mary, a child of the post-Civil War Reconstruction Period, flirting with a young stranger during the late Eisenhower Era. A rare moment.

As an adult, Mary Vorse usually covered her sensual power with a pose of gentility. She seemed a quiet-spoken New England lady at first meeting. Malcolm Cowley spoke of her "soft, old-family New York voice." But her friends realized the volcanic strength that lay beneath her air of elegant reserve. "In conversation," Art Young said of Mary, "she took her time, pausing to light her cigarette with a slow, sinuous curve of her arm, taking an indifferent puff, then lazily saying something that was neither brilliant nor very interesting." At first, he said, Mary seemed "pallid, unassuming, no one would guess on slight acquaintance that she was gifted or distinguished." Louis Untermeyer captured her essence when he dubbed her "the intransigent Mary Heaton Vorse, that quiet firebrand."[16]

Her habitual mode of restraint was a conditioned response to the demand of her otherwise permissive parents that she contain negative feelings. Her father's only anger toward her came when she made too much noise or otherwise betrayed his sense of good manners. At home, one must look pleasant and sound pleasant, even if one did not feel pleasant. Messages like these reinforced Mary's fear of parental inattention. To break the social surface was to pester preoccupied adults. She traced her "early fatalistic acceptance of disagreeable things" to her childhood "feeling that protest did no good." As a mature woman, Vorse most often fled from unpleasant personal encounters: "Mary," a friend in the labor movement later told her, "you are a good comrade but a poor fighter."[17]

Struggle as she would to escape, Mary wore her mother like an inner skin. Ellen's resentful neglect of the maternal role was concurrent with her powerful dominance over her family. Mary's similar struggle to escape motherhood in pursuit of personal goals would be coupled with her jealous need to maintain centrality in her children's lives. Ellen's restless activity would be repeated in Mary's lifelong flight from place to place in order to avoid conflict and self-insight.[18] And if Ellen refused to notice or to ponder anything more important than the surface of her life, so too would Mary deny her innermost pain.

Infrequently, but periodically, Mary would pause to note her marked refusal of self-discovery, as in 1934 when she was writing her autobiography and her editor and close friends were urging her to present a truthful account of her loves and sorrows. But Mary ignored their appeal. She wrote instead a tale of action almost entirely free of personal detail. And when the reviewers bemoaned the loss of who she was and how she felt and what she had learned from it all, Mary scoffed at their remarks, and, in defense, asked herself: Was she not one of the best reporters in the country and did not the interest of her story lie in that excellence, and in events rather than self? Beyond the defense lay the memory: Ellen, groomed, distant, writing intently every evening while seated at her mahogany bedroom desk, working on short stories or diary entries, the meticulously chosen words shot out onto paper to conceal the abysmal failure of her thought; young Mary, equally entranced with the music of language, also filling page after page with carefully penned prose, intently aware of her mother's void, yet observing the formalities of compliance in order to please.

It is not surprising that a girl of Mary's intelligence and social class found comfort in words and books. At eleven, Mary's mental ability and personal ambition were further developed by her encounter with two gifted women. Emma and Vryling Buffum ran a small school in the home of a local Amherst minister. Vryling Buffum was an early New Woman, symbol of a new age, following one of the few occupational avenues open to intellectual women in the late nineteenth century. She graduated from Wellesley in 1881, attended Columbia University, and eventually became a librarian at a Massachusetts teachers' college. The Buffum sisters, Mary said, opened her eyes "to the multiform magnificence of the world." The educators also provided Mary concrete evidence of the possibilities open to deviant women who sought public roles.[19]

Her father shared Mary's joy in learning. Hiram, who filled his leisured days with more rewarding activities than did his wife, was interested in history and geography. When he was not working in his garden, or conversing with his faculty friends, he allowed Mary to help him compile the many scrapbooks filled with newspaper clippings and mementos of cultural events with which he busied himself. Nearing fifty, Mary Vorse recalled the "two secret hidden lives" she led as a child. One, "the physical life . . . animal like . . . food, movement, warmth of sun, wind in face." The other, the "hidden life of secret subjective, that dazzling fertile place where I wandered alone, absorbed, self-sufficient. My father had it too. Our eyes would meet in sympathy. This was nothing my mother could share. She lived on events or activities."[20] Hiram Heaton's intellectual interests were haphazardly formed, but he clung to the notion of the value of work. Mary knew both her parents were underoccupied.

By her teen years, reading was Mary's most compelling pastime. Experiences and ideas locked away in books beckoned to a world more vast than she could ever know, even as a member of the traveling Heaton household. She began to fill notebooks with dialogue and description of New England society. When she was sixteen, she published a few light fiction pieces in the Springfield Journal. But Mary found no certain goal. She longed to escape both her mother's vacuous life and Amherst's decorum. The precise means of doing so she could not yet fathom.

One can imagine the excitement in the Heaton household in 1891 when New England Magazine accepted Ellen's only published piece, an event that also reflects the rivalry between mother and daughter, as Mary had published her first story the year before. Ellen's story portrayed upper-middle-class life in a small New England town. There were all the stock characters: the religious fanatic, the philosophical physician, the frivolous society dame, the Harvard hero, the mean-spirited businessman. Against these respectables were the harbingers of the new age—the social gospel minister and the socially concerned heroine. This young woman longed for meaningful existence. Ellen's main theme was the ennui of privileged women and their struggle to escape it. Her solution was the totally expected one. The heroine of the story transferred maternal love, in quick succession, from dead brother to slum waif to Harvard hero. Young women could have a fling at social work so long as they understood that true happiness lay in marital service to a financially secure male.[21] As discerning a reader as Mary could hardly have missed the significance of the appearance in the next issue of New England Magazine of Charlotte Perkins Gilman's "The Yellow Wall-Paper," the now classic horror tale of one woman's failure to escape boredom.

Mary was enmeshed in a series of painful contradictions. Raised as a polite eccentric, she was expected to assume a conventional female role. Trained as an outsider, she was encompassed by class-bound wealth. Encouraged to reject societal controls on behavior, she was taught subordination to maternal demands. Ellen believed in self-expression, but channeled hers into the pursuit of pleasure. Mary's love of liberty was rooted in her rebellion against her mother's idleness and dominance. Mary sought release to make of herself what she wanted. Yet her thwarted mother could not give her a blessing to be different. It was an ancient tale. Her love for her mother was blurred by contempt and guilt. Her mother's lack of choice became an injury to her daughter.

The form of Mary's early rebellion took root in her time. She came of age in the 1890s, that period the historian Henry Steele Commager called the watershed of American history. The term stuck, so aptly did it describe the crucial slippage between modern industrial America and the rural past. The decade set the problems every succeeding generation of Americans has been required to confront. The nineties were years of vivid, often violent, social protest. Workers, women, farmers, and intellectuals rose in full-throated rebellion against the old order. Among the chief issues of the period was the question of women's changing status. When the first organized feminist movement in the United States began to crest, the "woman problem" was fully as disturbing to the status quo as the great class conflict of the time.

In 1874, the year of Mary's birth, there occurred that most puzzling of historical phenomena, the sudden and unexpected, seemingly spontaneous, emergence of a massive protest movement. It began in December 1873 in the small town of Hillsboro, Ohio. There a tiny band of women set out to invade saloons and close down the liquor traffic. The idea spread like a prairie fire. Within four months, temperance leaders in Philadelphia claimed to have 25,000 women on the streets. The Woman's Christian Temperance Union, formed soon after, mushroomed to exceed in size any previous women's organization. Under the direction of Frances Willard the WCTU moved far beyond the temperance issue, championing women's suffrage and social reforms. By 1893, the WCTU and its auxiliaries had well over 200,000 members, dwarfing the 33,000 combined membership of the other two powerfully influential women's groups, the General Federation of Women's Clubs and the reunited National American Woman Suffrage Association.[22]

These groups motivated middle-class and generally conservative women to leave their homes and assume a wide variety of political activity in support of women's and reform causes. Single-sex groups provided women unfettered opportunity to express their identity, speak in public, learn the techniques of mobilization, run charity organizations, and heighten their social and gender consciousness. Their activity helped to create the mass center among American women from which the Progressive and the suffrage movements could later take off.

This vocal minority of women hacked at the foundations of idealized femininity, at the same moment widening its base. The coalescing women's movement redefined the concept of motherhood to justify both its assumption of new political responsibilities and its attack on abuses of industrial society. Maternal virtue, women leaders taught, would dissolve entrenched evil and guide the state into a righteous course. As the historian Mari Jo Buhle has noted, women activists made claims for the female comparable to those orthodox socialists made for the proletariat. Aroused females, the women said, were the agents of history who would purify society. Mobilized women would end war, political corruption, and economic inequality, to bring a reign of peace and happiness to earth. This concept of womanhood was a powerful rallying point, for most women could see easily enough how thoroughly males had botched the creation of civilization. A second compelling tenet was held by many organized women of this time. They substituted for class consciousness an alternative analysis —their faith in the collective female bond. Networks of loving female friends commonly sustained the feminist achievers and social activists of the late nineteenth century, who rediscovered the wondrous contentment of female separatism their grandmothers had known. As the call for the International Council of Women—held in Washington, D.C., in 1888— put it: "Much is said of a universal brotherhood, but . . . more subtle and more binding is universal sisterhood."[23]

By 1890, when Mary reached sixteen, tens of thousands of American women had been touched by feminist ideas. Middle-class American women had a generation of experience of political action and social reform behind them. A decade later, they had witnessed the growth of the largest social protest movement since the Civil War. The outcry of labor's eight-hour campaign, the agrarian resistance of populism, the birth of both an orthodox and a Christian socialism, the discontent of women— all this for a time seemed to challenge the ongoing consolidation of corporate capitalism. Their organizational ties and related activities made it evident that thousands of conservative and radical women alike hoped to use government at all levels to create a more humane society.

Mary's mother's peers, the same mothers who had formed women's clubs and joined the WCTU, also gave birth to the New Woman—their daughters, who repudiated their mothers' ways. The New Woman, wrote the historian Peter Filene, was "a minority of the female minority, but disproportionately conspicuous." Denunciations and defenses of the New Woman first appeared in popular fiction and genteel journals. By the 1890s she had become the subject of serious novels. The New Woman was usually leisured and middle class. She was above all educated, either through wide and uncensored reading, or, more commonly, by the new colleges open to women. She was also athletic, with tanned cheeks and a most unwomanly stride. She was at ease with men (no more the adoring, trembling Lady of lowered eyes) and conversed freely with them on every topic. The New Woman was apt to be economically self-supporting. Born of some curious symbiotic relationship between her mother's discontent and her society's economic shift, the New Woman became a popular metaphor for social disorder and change.[24]

Mary Vorse reached maturity at a time when female insurgence was rapidly restructuring the aspirations of middle-class women. The generations of American women that immediately preceded her own "were the real revolutionaries," Vorse realized. "They majored in college, kicked out chaperons, clamored for economic independence, entered professions and occupations hitherto forbid women . . . shattered convention, belled sacred cows, and tweaked the beards of stuffed shirts." Vorse's peers would carry on the battle in their fight for social regeneration, birth control, suffrage, and the end of war. But it was women in the generations before her, Vorse knew, who left a more spacious world for their daughters and granddaughters. Of her own cadre, Mary Vorse wrote: "We were the crop, not the seed."[25]

Chapter Two

La Bohémienne

In the 1890s, Mary Vorse knew that only determined resistance would alter the preordained course of her life. She was expected to enter a conventional existence as wife and mother. The one way to expand that limited future, she decided, was through devotion to work.

For a woman whose parents could afford to support her indefinitely, the natural choice of occupation was study in the arts. Yet that choice was circumscribed as well. Vorse had little musical ability. Polishing literary skills might keep her long years at home, still subject to parental demands. The best option would be to work as an artist; her half-brother was already studying painting abroad. Thus, in 1893, at age nineteen, she persuaded her parents to enroll her in a Parisian art school, the Academy Delecluse.

Art students, poets, and writers from all over the world came to the Parisian Latin Quarter in the nineties, lured by its relaxed morals, cheap lodging, and famous salons. The legendary Bohemia of the Paris of the 1840s had largely disappeared, but its memory still inspired an international army of able and defiant young. In the last decades of the nineteenth century, hundreds of women of polite heritage appeared in Paris to study art. But whereas young bourgeois male students could still find good opportunities for sin on the Left Bank in the 1890s, the women students, segregated in female art classes, were more hard put to engage in perilous adventure.[1]

The few women artists who had achieved notice before the nineteenth century were almost without exception related to better-known male artists, for women were otherwise denied access to studios and formal art training. By the mid-1800s the growth of the middle class had brought a corresponding explosion of demand for works of art. This stimulated the formation of public art schools and cleared room at the top for some women artists. Yet the famed Ecole des Beaux-Arts, the national art school run by the Académie Royale, remained closed to women through most of the nineties. Still, women who could afford the price of tutelage were admitted to the private ateliers of the French masters as early as the 1870s.

At these private academies, men and women were not only physically separated, but also were accorded quite different treatment. The female students, generally composing about one third of the total student body, were charged fees two to three times higher than those paid by men. Women were presumed to be both inferior artists and fickle dilettantes, and thus a drain on the master's time. Whereas male students were given two criticisms a week, the women received a weekly visit from the master, who—running from seat to seat—attempted to comment on as many as 250 female-produced works within a space of two hours.

But the hardest struggle fought by aspiring women artists in the late nineteenth century—and the main reason for their delayed entry into art training—was the battle over the nude. Woman's presumed delicacy forbade her the sight of a nude model, especially a male. At a time when the most esteemed genre of art depended on the artist's ability to portray the human body accurately, life drawing classes were closed to women. Deprived of the opportunity to create works of "genius," women were shunted into the "minor" schools of portraiture, landscapes, still life, and animal scenes. In the 1870s, women first were allowed to sketch nude females, and then later, children. In transition to the dreaded, though fig-leafed male, women were for a time offered unclothed sheep and cows as models in the academies. When at last women were allowed full privileges as art students, commentators assured the public that females who gazed on the male body remained chaste and sane.[2]

Of course Ellen insisted on accompanying Mary to Paris. Despite all the protective mechanisms her mother devised for her, Mary felt a wicked release. Certainly attendance at a Parisian art school was confirmation of her deviance. She had never known such discipline or talked with so many women of different cultures. She relished her reckless devotion to work, a preoccupation that she knew set her apart from other women of her age. Again, she was allowed wider liberty than most young ladies of her background. Once a shocked family friend found her alone with a young man sipping tea in an outdoor Parisian cafe. Vorse's delighted memory of this scandalous breach of propriety reveals as much about the limited nature of her revolt in Paris as it does about the expectations imposed upon women of her class.[3]

While in art school, Mary enjoyed her first romance. She was courted by Robert MacCameron, a twenty-seven-year-old midwesterner studying art at the Ecole des Beaux-Arts under the master Jean-Léon Gérôme. MacCameron, who would later achieve some recognition as a portraitist before his early death in 1912, was often on the verge of starvation during his student days in Paris. When Mary returned briefly to Amherst in 1893, he wrote her lengthy, self-serving letters in which he discussed his perception of her strengths and weaknesses, as well as his "low vile" exploits with fisher-girls. He professed his overwhelming need for her, yet also his inability to need anyone, including Mary.

MacCameron claimed to admire her independent spirit. He encouraged her determination "not to become a housewife and nothing else," her "wish to speak to the world of intellect as well as passion." When he experienced her "powerful spirit, struggling within . . . its effeminate prison," he wrote her, "I feel like weeping with you that the gods have not made you a man." Nevertheless, her undue self-sufficiency threatened his virility. "I rejoice in your weaknesses," MacCameron reassured himself. "Each cry you utter of freedom is softened and subdued by a magical charm. . . . You have one great sin that will always be with you. . . . You fight it, but though you live 200 years, never will a beard grow upon your face."

During their brief encounter, Vorse's letters to MacCameron were composed, her tone no doubt affected by his final admission that "strong women are repulsive to me. . . . Let a woman be educated. . . . Let her be talented above men . . . but never let her gain that power when she will say, 'We need no men to protect us.'" Unsatisfactory as MacCameron was, his acceptance of her career hopes was encouraging. Hence Mary continued the correspondence, addressing him as a wiser kindred spirit to whom she could reveal her self-doubts and career ambitions. "My common sense tells me that all I wish is impossible," she wrote him in 1896, "but there is that which tells me I will succeed, that I cannot fail. I threw away all my toys today, that my hands may be free to stretch toward the moon."[4]

The skirmish between Mary Vorse and her first serious suitor illustrates several recurrent themes in her relationships with men. She seemed drawn to strong-minded, even dominating and insensitive masculinity, proclaiming all the while her determination to remain free of any man's controls. Her tension sprang from the contradictory convictions that then dominated much of her thought. Vorse's partial allegiance to femininity bound her to an ideal that she was personally unable to realize. She wished to stand as a model of selfless womanhood; she simultaneously wanted to act as an autonomous individual. Vorse sought to actualize in her early fiction the ideal concept of the relationship of the sexes, but her stories written in the nineties are riddled with the negative strains of her real-life perceptions. Her first writings are a testimony to the female experience, to the modes of entrapment, betrayal, and exclusion devised for spirited, intellectual women in late-Victorian America.

Whisked home to Amherst by her parents after her short stint in Bohemia, Mary savored her home-town reputation as a New Woman. Her mutiny, still more imagined than actual, was directed against the meager concerns of New England gentility. "Amherst never changes," she wrote upon her return. "The town was definitely split into cliques, along church lines. . . . It is an awful thing to live in a town of admirable women, and when they aren't admirable, then they're capable." As her mother told the subdued neighbors, "Mary will probably marry young, as most of the women in our family do. If she doesn't have fun now, she never will." Mary hardly needed this reminder of impending domestic shackles. She shrank anew from her mother's "petty cares of material existence" and held to "windy ideas of independence and career."

The inevitable clash between Mary's needs and Ellen's demands could no longer be postponed. Mary had plans for further art study before finding employment. Within forty-eight hours of returning home, Mary wrote, "instead of a brave spirit starting out in life," she had been made to feel "like a bad and preposterous little girl." Her parents did not oppose her desire to work. They simply ignored it. Ellen let silence smother her daughter's "visionary little scheme."

Worst of all, gentle Hiram also failed Mary. Although she sensed a perfect understanding between herself and her father, she at first feared to approach him about her wish to work. She was stopped "by a certain look of fragility which had come over him in recent years." Finally Hiram advised her not to defy Ellen, teaching Mary at last that his relationship to her mother "was not as to an equal, but as to the Queen of Persia."

Mary imagined herself as having been pushed into "the army of the defeated," girls like herself, "whose parents had been stronger than they, who had settled down to wait for marriage, forever desiring that they might have had their try in the world. Why should it be allowed so freely to boys and not to girls?" she brooded. Ellen's unwillingness to lose her to a career, Mary knew, was more than equaled by her willingness to lose her via the role of marriage. "One was natural and right, and the other was unnatural and wrong, not only in my mother's eyes, but in the eyes of the entire community."

Mary's ultimate "desertion" of Ellen was a bitter scene. Twenty-two and determined, Mary induced her parents to enroll her in a New York City art school, but only after Mary threatened that she would go with or without her mother's blessing. Mary had joined another host, "a smaller force, the army of women all over the country," who are "out to hurt their mother, who have to, in order to work," the "strange army of all the girls who in my mother's time would have stayed at home and I wonder what necessity sent us all out?" Mary wrote. "More and more and more of us coming all the time, and more of us will come until the sum of us will change the customs of the world, and as we change the world, the world is going to change us." Mary paid a price for her victory. Ellen's attitude toward her underwent a subtle, but permanent, change. It was as though Mary had turned out to be such a different person from the daughter she had always imagined that Ellen turned away, not in anger, but in dismissal. Ellen never forgave Mary her elopement into adventure.

Sent to the city to room with a family friend, Mary Vorse was free for the first time from direct parental supervision. "I am an escaped bird, flying through the clear air of heaven," she crooned. Her passion for exploration drove her from the Parisian Latin Quarter to the nearest pale imitation of Bohemia in America—the Art Students' League of New York City.[5]

In the United States, the first group to call itself bohemian had gathered about the leading personalities who met in the 1850s at Pfaff's, a German beer cellar on lower Broadway in New York. Here Walt Whitman came to be admired by literary men who cherished their reputation as erotic sinners, free of both middle-class morality and money madness. They honored Edgar Allan Poe, their patron saint, and Henry Clapp, the founder of the pioneer American Bohemia, who deliberately died of drink. The real end of the Pfaffians came with the Civil War, just as the later Bohemia of Greenwich Village would dissolve with World War I. Soon there were only a few survivors of the once romantic assemblage.

Until the nineties there was no distinctive New York group of artistic rebels visible enough to elicit envy and fear from the staid. It was then that James Huneker inspired his circle of musicians, writers, painters, and newspapermen to attend the midnight parties at Luchow's Restaurant, and to turn these festivities into something of a media event. Huneker first sought release from conformity as a music student in Paris, before moving to New York in 1886, where he became the city's leading music and drama critic. Van Wyck Brooks claimed Huneker taught the young what they were forbidden to learn in college. Henry L. Mencken, no piker himself at shocking the public, said of Huneker, "If a merciful Providence had not sent James Gibbons Huneker into the world, we Americans would still be shipping union suits to heathens, reading Emerson, sweating at Chautauquas and applauding the plays of Bronson Howard. In matters exotic and scandalous he was our chief of scouts, our spiritual adviser."[6] Huneker's racy publication, *M'lle New York*, and its successor, the *Criterion*, openly questioned the intelligence of New York's elite. Huneker introduced French literature and art to the deviant intelligentsia, and hobnobbed with anarchists and immigrants. Thus, by 1895, bohemianism, a city product, breathed again, not only in New York, but in Chicago, Boston, Philadelphia, and San Francisco. Youthful American literati gleefully shook loose their Victorian bonds.

The rebellion was only mildly libertarian, in comparison with the Parisian model of the past or the 1912 Greenwich Village that was to follow. The 1890s revolt was naive and pretentious, the pose of young native thinkers who were, for the most part, as sexually prim and unquestioningly patriotic as the respectable society they claimed to oppose. Lacking a firm socialist or feminist component, the Bohemians of the McKinley era chiefly busied themselves with literary heresy, heavy drinking, and intellectual snobbery. Yet here can be found the beginnings of the cultural and political left of the early twentieth century. Influenced by East Side immigrants and serious social workers, groups like Huneker's established the milieu in which New York artists and writers could gather encouragement for their future assault upon literary and political bastions.

In 1896 Mary Vorse gained entry into this exciting world of the art gentry when she began her studies at the Art Students' League, located on West 57th Street near Eighth Avenue. The league was established in 1875 by young men with advanced art theories in protest against the conservative establishment, which ruled at the National Academy of Design. By 1894, five of the league's eleven officers were women, and women composed the majority of its over eleven hundred pupils. In sex-segregated day and evening classes, men and women studied sketching, modeling, and painting. No less than eleven classes worked from the nude or draped model. Worried parents were told that the league's classes were never "scenes of riotous fun and horse-play, such as still occasionally break out at [the] . . . studios in Paris. . . . There is no instance recorded of anything happening at the League which would tend to disgust women students. Care is taken to have as models the most respectable persons in the profession, and the antecedents of the pupils are inquired into before they are accepted."[7]

William Dean Howells, then the chief of American literature, ridiculed the female students of the Art Students' League in his 1893 novel, *The Coast of Bohemia*. Howell's heroine, Charmian Maybough, compensates for her deficiencies as an artist by her decorous attempts to be radical. Her pretensions include heroic efforts to smoke cigarettes and to clutter her studio with appropriate abandon, although her mother's maid is sent to clean the apartment each morning. Maybough lives her double life in innocent disorder.[8]

Howells's interest in the changing ideal of womanhood was characteristic of the period. In 1894, with the publication of Constance Cary Harrison's novel *The Bachelor Maid*, the Bachelor Girl began to replace the New Woman as the target for Victorian concern. Whereas the New Woman had been granted grudging admiration by many authors, the Bachelor Girl—a woman who *preferred* the single life—had gone too far. A spate of articles and novels hysterically reported that the Bachelor Girl was a mere transitory phenomenon, for surely women could not live without love, and could not find love without marriage. Hardly anyone had ever met a New Woman, Vorse observed satirically in an unfinished manuscript written in the mid-nineties, although people sometimes heard that someone's sister was a lawyer, or a reformer, or attended suffrage meetings. Conversely, "everyone in a large city knows a Bachelor Girl, although they do not speak of themselves that way."

Godey's Magazine reported the worrisome number of female bachelors near Washington Square in a series of articles in 1895 and 1896. Looking much like mannequins, women artists and writers were shown propped up in studios excessively furnished with pillows and stuffed monkeys. The *Arena* in 1898 hopefully predicted that "feminine Bohemianism" would be a failure. These pathetic females "weary of the endless struggle and the bitter disillusionment of [their] Bohemian existence," and longing "for the sweet repose of home," fell easy prey to unprincipled men, the *Arena* warned.[9]

Vorse's understanding of the Bachelor Girl was more practical. Although admitting the difficulty of a woman's battle to earn a living, Vorse argued in 1897 that the Bachelor Girl found a life of uncertainty preferable to the controls of home, where she was apt to be treated as a little girl, while her brothers were being defined as men. Self-support, Vorse wrote, was women's only road toward "liberty and a chance to work out their own individuality. After four years of comparative freedom at college, where a girl has perhaps been at the head of her class, it is humiliating to go home and to be told by one's mother, 'Mary, go and put on your rubbers at once.'"[10] From her own experience Vorse learned tht conventional mothers often bred their own antithesis. Ambitious young women like Vorse emigrated to the city to opt for the single life of freedom, and for the destruction of lineage ideals.

Through 1897 Vorse continued her studies at the league. She was under the tutelage of Frank Moore Colby, with whose family she roomed. Colby, whom her parents had known as a history professor at Amherst College, moved to New York University in 1895 as a professor of economics. Colby squired Vorse into the world of newspapermen and artists gathered within Huneker's circle. Huneker's talented second wife, Clio, was also a friend at the Art Students' League. "I am part of the avant garde," Vorse rejoiced. "I have overstepped the bounds!"[11]

Just beneath the surface of her exultation, however, lay a strong disquiet. After four years of devotion to art, Vorse could not blind herself to the unexceptional quality of her work. Her surviving sketches show lifeless peasant girls and sharp-nosed women, as stolid as they are still. As the wayward daughter of wealthy parents, her limited artistic ability could be indulged both by academic teachers who needed her patronage and by observers who expected her fancy would be ended by a responsible marriage.

Coerced into accompanying her parents on a summer and fall tour of France and Switzerland in 1897, Mary mourned the difficulty of work amid the dislocation of travel. Her isolation during this period enabled her to confront her art with more honesty: "When I come into my room and see my work lying around," she wrote in her diary, "my sense of my own futility overwhelms me. After so much work, that is all I can do." By September she had decided to give up painting: "I don't like to think even to myself how great a reevaluation this means. . . . I cry all night." But a paying job still seemed the only escape from maternal domination. Mary reached the joyless decision to seek work as an illustrator when she returned home.[12]

The displacement of energy from dreams of artistic success to the practical reality of finding a job with a living wage apparently increased her awareness of men, stoking her desire "for impossible and forbidden" things. Mary considered the "certain reckless irresponsibility that a woman of bad life must feel." She concluded "that would be worth paying a large price for." Mary was twenty-three in 1897. Her parents and her friends were beginning to worry, as Colby frequently reminded her, that she might never marry and find her place.

Mary was ready to fall in love. In the early winter of 1898 she met Albert White Vorse, a thirty-two-year-old newspaperman and aspiring author. After his graduation from Harvard in 1889, Bert Vorse had worked with the Children's Aid Society in Boston, then briefly tried his hand at business with the Pennsylvania Railroad in Philadelphia. In 1892, as editor of the Philadelphia *Press*, he was chosen to go on the relief expedition to Greenland in search of the explorer Robert E. Peary. The expedition would prove to be handsome Bert's highest adventure, one he wrote and talked of for years. Even his later activity as a charter member in the Explorers' Club and Aero Club seemed anticlimatic after the arctic odyssey of his youth. Travel to an exotic land and the hospitable Eskimo culture, with its notorious matrimonial infidelities, was an enlightening experience for the son of a Massachusetts minister. In September 1897, he moved to New York to take a job as dramatic editor of the *Illustrated American* and to join Huneker's coterie.

Bert was much like Mary. He fancied himself a Bohemian, and in important ways did defy the rules of his conventional upbringing. Yet he was thoroughly middle class. His Harvard classmate Hutchins Hapgood remembered him as "a dark vivid man with a lively temperament, more sensuous than mental, with a passion for boats and the sea." Like Mary's father, Bert was a gregarious fellow, and unorthodox enough to win Mary's attention. Yet his easygoing charm sprang from a self-indulgence that together with his concept of manliness would eventually strain the emotional bond between them.[13]

Bert and Mary were married secretly after a five-week courtship. Bert recalled his proprietary delight at finding Mary—despite Parisian art training—still a virgin: "From our first walk on the pier . . . and then that afternoon at Riverside Park . . . afterwards the few days of doubt and then the famous Friday, then the ferry ride and the Hungarian restaurant and after that the little moment in the parlor and in the passageway where you hesitated and I pushed you . . . and then, and then, my surprise, for I was surprised the next morning when I saw certain things. An exquisite feeling of preciousness. . . . I am so proud that I may write you this without reserve, my darling. . . . It is my right as well as my privilege to say it."[14]

Afire sexually, she reveled in the bliss of her "first studio latch key."[15] They lived together for a month in New York before she returned to Amherst in the spring, where she would pretend to be awaiting marriage in October. Mary had been rash enough to marry secretly, but she was unwilling to disturb her parents with the news of her hasty decision. Amherst ethics required a long engagement, partly to quiet any possible rumors of pregnancy, but, more important, to ensure that the union was based on adequate acquaintance. In those days, marriage was most often forever.

From Amherst, Mary wrote Bert of her thwarted desire to work. He consoled her: "Suppose you had worked in the teeth of your parents. You would have cared more for your work than for me. You would rather hold me highest, wouldn't you dear? Please say so, for I am so happy in believing it." Mary's reply was not reassuring: "If I had worked in the teeth of my parents, as you say, they would respect me more and I would be independent now and would stay where I chose most of the summer. As for my caring more for work than for you, it would have made no difference only I would have been able to do more and you would be prouder of me." [16]

Bert Vorse was slight, mustached, and masterful. His fiction often betrayed his fondness for women with "soft, clinging hands" who were both submissive and daring, willing to serve as backdrop for his dashing maleness.[17] Bert believed himself a lover, a maverick, and a writer. He would enjoy real success at the first two endeavors.

During the six months that Mary awaited him in Amherst, Bert attempted free-lance writing, sold a few stories, and lived in romanticized poverty. Sleeping with her topaz necklace in his hand, he fought sexual frustration through hard-drinking nights with other newspapermen like Hutchins Hapgood and Lincoln Steffens from the *Commercial Advertiser*. Bert's correspondence to her was loving and sensual. Mary scoffed at her mother's opinion that sex twice a week was excessive. She wrote Bert that she was "horribly scared to think to what frightful excess we had gone, and all my fault."

Mary told her parents of her engagement on the day the Spanish American War began. Bert volunteered for combat duty with Theodore Roosevelt. He "couldn't do less," he wrote her, "for how should you feel if someone should ask in years to come if your husband fought for his country, and I hadn't? . . . It's better if one is going to fight to be among the first." Mary was terrified. She begged him not to go. A long series of letters followed in which he chided her for her lack of courage and she finally agreed: "The worst would be if my love had caused you not to be a man." Bert must have enjoyed the exchange. He failed to inform her that Roosevelt had meanwhile refused Bert's offer to join the Rough Riders.

Awaiting formal entry into matrimony, Mary was, as usual, conflicted. She longed to be with Bert and wished she were prettier. She felt affronted at the thought of losing her own name, and then gloried in its loss, for "I belong to you," she wrote him, "and so absolutely. . . . *Our* name is what is dear to me." Yet she also intended to be free of wifely duties and woman's role: "I don't want to belong to . . . any institution or a church. I want the whole world to play in and be free to come and go, without a by-your-leave to anyone."[18]

Bert arrived in Amherst with a new hat, new clothes, and seven dollars. They were married by his father, in Mary's home, on October 26, 1898.

One can be sure that Mary's mother was modishly attired for her daughter's wedding. She might have urged Mary—probably without success—to heed the Amherst newspaper's advice to women "to wear gloves, with sweet oil inside, at night to whiten the hands." The Amherst press that week advised ladies that false hips and bustles were offered in the dry goods store to "supply the curve of the hip which fashion now demands," while an adjacent article by Senator H. W. Blair claimed that Frances Willard's life proved that the "long-time serf relationship" of women to men was a thing of the past. There was also a gleeful report of an Indian uprising put down by U.S. troops in Minnesota—with dozens of the redskins slaughtered—alongside a complete account of the local Sunday School lesson. War-lust news was prominent, at the same time that striking miners in Illinois were denounced as murderous savages. For the fashionable, the newspaper noted that gowns of heavy black knotted silk with deep fringed edges were in vogue for evening wear. Grapes, cherries, and bows were preferred trimmings for millinery. "Cuban Red" was the most popular color for hats, perhaps to complement the bloodshed at San Juan Hill.[19]

During her first marriage, Mary Vorse would come of age as an author, while painfully moving toward a more realistic assessment of matrimony and of her relationship to a world that set such formidable blocks in the path of intellectually aggressive women. But at this point in her life, Mrs. Mary Heaton Vorse was as inharmonious a brew of old and new as the society of the 1890s reflected in the Amherst press. She was at once a compliant wife, an adoring daughter, and a woman who dreamed of fame and unfettered achievement.

Chapter Three

Completed Circle

For their first home, Mary and Bert Vorse chose an eighth-floor Greenwich Village apartment with queer, pie-shaped rooms opposite the park on Sheridan Square. By 1898, Greenwich Village was fast becoming the abode of the artistic and intellectual young. Set amid the evenly aligned thoroughfares of New York, the Village's maze of crooked streets and narrow alleys was also the habitat of that fascinator, the Bachelor Girl. The journalist Hutchins Hapgood was one of the first to marvel at the new womanhood developing there. When the world began to change, these women would be the main fount of the cultural oasis to be known as Greenwich Village. But in the late 1890s Hapgood found them "still deeply held by the traditions of womanly restraint." This grip included the notion that marriage should precede any sexual encounter.[1]

As often as they could afford, Bert and Mary visited the most genuine bohemian meeting place in the Village. Maria's was a basement restaurant on MacDougal Street. There, at what Vorse remembered as "one of the first green shoots of the Village that was to be," guests sat around one large table, actually spoke with strangers, contributed music, poetry, and speeches, and got a good Italian meal with red wine for fifty cents. Sudden altercations among the sensitive sometimes sent plates of spaghetti swirling through the air. One writer rhapsodized that Maria's late Saturday night suppers brought "two hundred Bohemians in one large lump," while an "additional one hundred more verging Bohemians, Philistines and the curious" gazed on the imbroglio.[2]

It was a grand thing to be young, to pioneer a new century. The "forerunners of a new world," Bert and Mary dubbed themselves. She dared to wear only one petticoat and no corset at all when dining at the Hotels Lafayette and Brevoort—already in their prime and just two blocks from her apartment. In the cellar of the Brevoort, Vorse and her friends, following the example of George Sand, lit cigarettes in defiance of the house rules, which forbade women to smoke. Told to put them out, the women soon relit them. "Time and time again," Vorse said, "[we] went through the ritual, with the air of those performing a public service."[3]

They lived an ideal of youth, gaiety, and sophistication, with a certain daring born of middle-class comfort. Bert was then literary adviser at G.P. Putnam's, a promising position for young writers who hoped to launch their career through the creation of valuable connections. He earned $20 a week, and sometimes sold an article to bring in another $50. After heat, food, and entertainment were provided for, there was one dollar available for savings and six for extras.

When Mary became pregnant in 1901, they moved to a larger apartment on Waverly Place, one block from Washington Square. As an economy measure, Mary wrote occasional book reviews for the *Criterion*, where Bert had a new job. Most of the staff were friends of Huneker's. This group embraced ideas and authors that the staid weeklies and monthlies of the day ignored. The magazine quickly declined after Bert became associate editor, although it survived until 1905.

In December, Mary's first son, Heaton, was born at home. Attended by a woman doctor, Mary had an easy birth. Only the horrified protest of the nurse kept Mary from immediately beginning work on her book reviews. Mary found a simple way to avoid maternal interference during her pregnancy. She falsely informed her mother that the baby was not due until February.[4] First, a secret marriage; now, a secret birth. (In her second pregnancy, six years later, Mary would not tell her mother of the birth until after it had occurred.)

At about this time came the first indication that Bert was overstepping the bounds of monogamy. He reassured Mary, as he would so often in the future, that he was faithful to her. During the summer of 1902, when she summered in Amherst with the baby, their letters to one another decidedly stiffened in tone.

Before long Mary knew her suspicions justified, even though she could not badger him into direct confession. At first she cried a great deal, mourning all her lost dreams of marital bliss. Bert chafed under what he chose to interpret as Mary's excessive need for his attention. "I made a great mistake to cry and bore you with tears. . . ," she wrote him, "you talk so much about tyranny." When tears failed, she tried scolding. Life narrowed into an anxious wait for his comings and goings, which she met with swollen eyes or angry accusations. Nursing their separate hurts, the dreadful tension between them took shape and grew, until Mary felt she could actually see it, a great, gray box, square and closed, absorbing her world.

Finally, in defeat, even seeking and following her mother's advice, she opted to accept his philandering in the approved female fashion—with sacrificial passivity. She formed a theory that it was only Bert's failure to succeed as a writer that made him compensate with "a new personal success" now and then. She would soothe his dissatisfaction with himself by her own calm, she decided. Nevertheless, as Mary commented about one of her fictional heroines who was in the same fix: "Something so awful had happened that she couldn't comprehend it yet. But she did know that life as she had known it, that little restricted life that seemed so safe and so secure, was shattered forever, and that never in the big, unchancy world would she ever feel so safe again."[5]

Of course she was furious at Bert—so full of a masculine importance she could never know, so slyly supported by the barely concealed understanding of his male world. She dreamed of escape and violent revenge. She loathed her moroseness, and dripping nose, and self-pity. She had given up her youthful dreams, had traded them for the promised joy of marriage and motherhood. Now she was left without an income, without internal illumination, tied to a child and his care and protection, alone and miserable, unable to imagine herself unmarried and *not* miserable. The greatest cruelty that Bert imposed on her was his denial of the circumstance that poisoned their union, his lies and evasions, which were designed to leave her unsure of her deeply felt certainty. The greatest cruelty she fastened on herself was her fearful acceptance of those deceits. Erecting a shaky pile of hope and "love," she bravely endured, as good wives and mothers were meant to do.

Meanwhile, encouraged by the lukewarm reception given to his book of arctic tales, Bert continued to write, laboriously grinding out each sentence. He sold a disappointing number of adventure stories, or of romances in which the hero prevailed over the brief, meek defiance of his bride-to-be. Bert's writing style reflected his plodding effort.[6]

Mary continued to publish a few book reviews, but still very much her mother's daughter, she thought of her writing as a kind of "selfish pastime." Careful to keep both herself and her work in its place, she earned only enough money to indulge frivolous needs: "to buy an extra hat, an ornament for the house." She was even willing to take the blame for Bert's literary failure. It was his forced daily labor in an office in order to support his family, she claimed, that prevented him from perfecting his writing skills.

In the winter of 1903 Mary and Bert came to a crucial decision. In order that Bert might quit his job and thus have the chance to develop his writing, they would move to Europe where living was cheaper. It was agreed that Mary would also write, but only temporarily, to augment their income. Her earnings, their savings, and a small stipend sneaked them by Mary's father would theoretically suffice until Bert made good. The unstated motivation behind their move was Mary's, and perhaps even Bert's, desire to begin again, to avoid old haunts—and old lovers.

In France, Bert's and Mary's mutual confinement to create two writing careers in one small apartment only compounded marital stress. To escape tension, Mary traveled with her nurse and her two-year-old son to Fiesole where she stayed through the spring. Her first lengthy separation from Bert was a joyful experience. Even though she was thirty years old, it was the first time, except for trips between New York and Amherst, that she had traveled any distance without father or husband. Twenty years later she still savored those single days in Fiesole. There she was able to write with zest, freed from "criticisms and demands." She told her father, "this time I shall always look on as an oasis in my life . . . all care and worry seem to have slipped from me."

To her surprise, Mary's love stories sold easily to the women's magazines and the genteel journals. Her fiction caricatured the rigid etiquette that constricted middle-class sex relations. Mary's stories often pictured a tomboylike heroine whose direct approach wrests the prized male from the simpering belle. But even her more traditional women, on the surface trusting and childlike, barely concealed a determination that lifted them far above the dulling routine of marital life.

Although Mary and Bert were reunited in the summer of 1904, the difference in their mode of literary production became too apparent for either's comfort. Bert wrote in a slow agony. Mary said, "I reel off stuff like a regular phonograph. . . . I slap down and let her go which is the way for me to have fun." Bert wrote long into the night. Mary worked only when she felt like it. Bert sold almost nothing. Mary sold almost everything she produced.

Yet while Mary was "truly pleased with the Comfortable Little Income" she earned, she assured her parents that Bert was following the best and only road to "becoming a writer of note."[7] Her self-disparagement was sincere, not designed simply for parental consumption or to save Bert's pride. It was at this time that she wrote a revealing set of articles published in the *Atlantic Monthly*. They brought her some minor fame and were eventually compiled to form her first book, published in 1908.

The Breaking in of a Yachtsman's Wife describes a bride's introduction to the world of sailing by her overbearing husband. Marjorie and Stan purchase their twenty-foot sloop in the first summer of their marriage (just as Mary and Bert purchased a boat with Lincoln and Josephine Steffens in the summer of 1899). Stan allows Marjorie to prove her love for him by assisting him in the toilsome stripping and painting of his new boat, all the while accusing her of a lack of interest and feminine ineptitude for the task. Marjorie learns to sail well. She loves the thrill of danger and the sense of physical competence. Alas, her achievement also damages Stan's sense of superiority. Marjorie finally concedes that "it is so much against the usual for a woman to sail a boat as to seem almost against nature, and so I say . . . no yachtsman's wife should learn to sail, for no grown woman can learn to handle a boat and not be puffed up with pride. . . . The world over, a man should be the skipper of his boat." While the ending was conventional, one cannot miss the scorn for childish males implicit in Marjorie's renunciation.[8]

The dilemma of the yachtsman's wife was Mary's own, as she and Bert wrestled with the meaning of her disturbing literary triumphs. Years later, in 1938, Mary sourly commented that this "mealy-mouthed" story of women keeping their place was "dated as a bustle. . . . It belongs to another civilization."[9] But in 1904, tied to a marriage that frustrated her ambition and eroded her happiness, her denial of self was real enough, an exercise in female survival.

That year she and Bert settled for a time in Venice. There she received her baptism into the labor movement that she would later serve with over half a century of her life. In her autobiography written years later, she presented an overly dramatized version of the scene. Mary claimed that the Italian general strike, which she and Bert observed from Venice, riveted her imagination as nothing before ever had. Above all else, she said, she learned the potential power of workers who act in unity.

In Venice, Bert and Mary, through their gondolier, met the secretary of the sandola guild. Their new friend took Mary to her first labor meeting. Later, in a procession of two thousand people, Mary, made giddy by what she called the "peculiar, beautiful contagion" of mass solidarity, marched arm in arm with two girl workers down the Merceria to the Grand Canal.

At Venice, "for the first time," she later insisted, "I felt . . . the people marching and singing together for a high conscious aim. I was caught up and carried along by these marching, singing people who had so much power and yet had such discipline."[10] Throughout her long career as a labor writer, nothing thrilled her more than the sound and sight of masses united in protest. For Mary Vorse mass action would always be felt as a mystical "flame of creation," personally igniting her repressed fury, searing her inhibitions, expanding timidity into invincible certitude.

Mary's political enlightenment proceeded parallel to Bert's literary failure. After two years in Europe he had all but lost faith in his artistic power. Consoling himself with a conviction that Mary's work required his firm editorial hand, he told her parents that with his help it was Mary who would "become the family genius. . . . If she isn't a truly eminent novelist in a few years, I miss my guess."

Despite his proclaimed respect for her work, Bert blamed her for neglect of home and family and for not providing him with the essentials of life —like clean underwear. In one of his many unpublished articles, entitled "The Husband of a Celebrity," he wrote:

> She wanted to make her own pin money, and so long as she didn't let the household go wrong, I had no objections to offer against that. . . . [But] her new realization of her increasing greatness has quietly changed all our relations. For example, nowadays I do not like to disturb her if I don't find fresh underclothing in the mornings. And this brings me to the great point of change—our whole life has had to be adjusted to meet her engagements. She hasn't time to keep house. . . . She is not concentrated on our purpose as I am.

In her articles entitled "Working Mother" and "Failure," Mary retaliated:

> I had . . . insensibly altered our relations over a period of years, and did it without realizing it. . . . He let himself procrastinate getting back into life. The more I worked, the less he did. What did my success do to him? It dimmed life in some way. It tapped some vital force in him. There he was, suddenly no longer needed. . . . And his sickness with himself reacted on me.
>
> Not many men will forgive their wives for supporting them. Inevitably they visit their bitter defeat upon their wives.[11]

In Europe, a "little wondering question" took shape in her mind. There came a moment when instead of feeling that work was keeping her from him, in "some odd way the situation was shifted." She felt definitely that he was keeping her from her work. At first she had been apologetic for the hours away from him. She seemed to be always excusing herself, always accounting for her time spent on work, rather than on family. Finally she knew herself enslaved, and felt it as something humiliating.

From denial of unseemly ambition, Mary moved to open resentment of his inability to accept her strengths: "Neither the fruits of the spirit nor the amenities of social life can evolve where one person is either consciously or unconsciously lording it over others." Mary wrote:

> In the hearts of men for a long time must have lurked the suspicion that they were not made of such very different clay from their wives. From this suspicion must have sprung the irritable vanity of the old fashioned husband. He knew that the tenure of his position as head of the household was insecure, and he bolstered it up, sometimes with loud blusterings, oftener in subtler assumptions of masculine superiority.[12]

Soaring sales of her work brought a new sense of self-worth. When Lincoln Steffens read one of her early stories, he wrote her, "Remember that the mind that can write the good piece can write innumerable good pieces. You have made your place now . . . as a writer in whom I can believe." Mary felt, if "not smug, at least sure that this business of women's co-operating in wage-earning was the solution to domestic life." How much better for children "to have a live mother abreast of the time" and for a "husband to have a helpmeet instead of a millstone. . . . It seemed to me all the things the feminists had promised with the cry of economic independence had come true."[13] Feminist hope crashed on Bert's intractable demands. She focused her fury on all "men who are small enough to want to feel superior."

Mary's anger erupted in one of her most powerful short stories, published in the *Atlantic Monthly* in 1907. "The Quiet Woman" is about an aged mother whose sad, reclusive nature is a reaction to the restrictions placed on her by her patronizing husband, now dead. Her son continues in the same tradition as his father, smothering the mother with insensitive control. Katherine, the young narrator of the story, seems as powerless as the mother to resist the domineering son. Katherine is dissuaded from marrying him only by his mother's warning that he will humiliate and bruise Katherine's spirit: "You would try and try, and then you would see that neither patience nor submission nor love could change him." He and his father "are the men with no women in them." Men such as these demand that women serve them and then scorn the passivity they create. In the "quiet woman," Mary portrayed her own loneliness and need for a supportive mother, as well as her new assessment of women's obligation to please men: "Often I have seen on a woman's face a look of anger or fear or cunning, and I knew that here was another of me. There are more of us than you think, and we use in self-defense, [either] guile, or flattery, or affection or submission, according to our natures."[14]

When Bert gave up his hope for a literary career, he sought, and failed to find, a job as a diplomatic consul. They returned to Amherst in April 1905. In July he was refused a place in Admiral Peary's expeditionary force, another blow to his self-esteem. Through the summer and fall they lived apart, as Bert, supported by Mary's writing, searched for work in New York City. His eye for women soon led to what Mary later termed her "first severe sexual defeat." By the end of the year their marriage was near collapse.[15]

Again, Mary suffered the whole familiar gamut of pain. In succession came self-righteous hurt, then fear, self-blame, fury, the tortures of the rejected lover. Her first settled reaction, however, was guilt. She decided that she had strangled his spirit with too many demands. She had demanded perfect unity between them with a "devouring ego which demanded graspingly that her man should be hers, all of him."[16] She once more opted to ease his suffering through maternal solicitude. She would be as endlessly sweet and tireless as a mother with a sick child. Her determination to be "perfectly good" carried them through another winter in New York. During the summer, they rented a house at Provincetown, Massachusetts. Here they snuggled in to nurse their mutual sores.

The first time Mary Vorse saw Provincetown she came down from Boston by boat, skirting remote shores inhabited only by colonies of sea gulls. Provincetown was the loveliest of spots, a small village with jutting gray wharfs and huge willow trees. The garden beds were lined with white shells and ornaments of whale's vertebrae. Ox teams dragged low-hung wagons with wide wheels through the sand of the main street.

That summer marked the beginning of her love affair with the fishing village on the tip of the Cape. Mary's Provincetown house, purchased in 1907, was her treasured base, her one sure anchor, for the next fifty-nine years. As illusions dissolved, along with her marriage, her need for stability grew. After a life of international mobility, broken only by inland stays in Amherst and the easy vagabondage of Greenwich Village and Europe, she longed for permanence. "At first sight," Mary wrote, "I was invaded by the town and surrounded by it, as though the town had literally got into my blood."

Provincetown's beach circled the harbor like the gold setting of an emerald. The bay, seen from her workroom window, constantly changed color and mood, as the fog bell beat a steady tone.

Like many before her who found Provincetown, Mary Vorse felt "the sense of completion that a hitherto homeless person has on discovering home." Provincetown had been a lawless, godless settlement for over two hundred years. Boston ministers and magistrates had often expressed their dismay at the roisterous smugglers, Indians, and squatters who clustered at the land's end. Mary believed it was the Portuguese fishermen and their families who arrived in the mid-1800s who made Provincetown unique. Their relation to the sea—as a source of both nourishment and sudden death—bred an impassioned, prideful people. She had discovered the direct opposite of Amherst: "The blight of gentility and pseudo-culture that crept over English-speaking countries in the nineteenth century never spread over us [in Provincetown] as it did inland."

Her one-hundred-year-old house on the sandy main street fronting the harbor, with its wide floorboards and hand-wrought nails, became her lifelong passion. She wrote of it, spoke of it, loved it, fumed against it, as though it lived. A house was a female shell, "one's defense against the world." A woman without a house had no sanctuary: "To any woman who has not a house I would say to 'Go and buy one if it be but two rooms.'" The female need met—a room of one's own. More important—a room purchased with one's own earnings.[17]

While in Provincetown that first summer of 1906, Mary and Bert utilized the classic ploy of the unhappily married couple to stitch together their unwinding lives. By September, Mary was pregnant.

They left the Cape to winter in New York, a pattern Mary Vorse would follow for much of her life. She and Bert joined sixteen other people at A Club, a cooperative housing venture at 3 Fifth Avenue, a few blocks from Washington Square and across the street from the Hotel Brevoort. Succeeded in 1913 by the famed Liberal Club, the A Club was the first organized group to express the revolt of the Villagers in the years before the war. A Club harbored writers and painters, lawyers, clergy, settlement workers—"everybody a Liberal, if not a Radical—and all for Labor and the Arts," as Mary wrote. A Club was named when Howard Brubaker said, "Oh, just call it a club." The newspapers called it the Anarchist Club and predicted that B, C, and D clubs would be formed. A New York reporter was sent to investigate the subversives. All he found was four-year-old Heaton Vorse, who offered to play ball with him in the hall.[18]

A Club was an intellectual jolt. For the first time Mary lived alongside men and women of sparkling intellect "who questioned the system under which they lived." At A Club, "even Bert had a new consciousness," she noted. The array of talent there was astounding. Most of the members were destined for prominence as writers, reformers, radicals, or social critics of the Progressive era. Women residents included Anna Strunsky, her sister Rose, and the writers and social activists Midge Jennison, Miriam Scott, Martha Bruere, Bertha Carter, and Charlotte Teller Hirsch. The men included William English Walling, Walter Weyl, Ernest Poole, Paul Wilson, Howard Brubaker, Leroy Scott, Arthur Bullard, and Robert Bruere, most of them social workers associated with University Settlement.

Mark Twain dropped by almost every day to smoke his long cigars and spin his tales. Frances Perkins, Rose O'Neill, Dolly and John Sloan, and William Glackens were in and out. Everybody at one time or another came to A Club, as Mary remembered it, including such different types as Mother Jones and Theodore Dreiser. Ernest Poole recalled of A Club: "With most of us writing books, stories, or plays and all of us dreaming of reforms and revolutions of divers kinds, life in that house was a quick succession of intensities, large and small, from tremendous discussions about the world to hot little personal feuds and disputes; but through it all ran a broad fresh river of genial humor and relish in life." For Mary, A Club was above all "a completely successful and civilized experiment in communal living."

A Club functioned as a kind of American press bureau for the 1905–1907 Russian revolution. Political refugees "arrived from Russia with ours as the only American address," Mary Vorse remembered. A Club members became national news in 1906 when they gave sanctuary to the Russian radical Maxim Gorky, after he was evicted from several New York hotels. Gorky's trip to the United States to raise funds for the Russian revolutionaries had at first elicited the support of the literary lights of New York —until Gorky publicly supported William "Big Bill" Haywood, the militant American labor leader then held on a trumped-up murder charge in Idaho.

The staff at the Russian embassy incited the newspapers to create a scandal about the illicit relationship between Gorky and his common-law wife who had accompanied him to America. The press exploded with denunciations of Gorky's sex life. Gorky's welcoming dinner was canceled, as gentlemen like Richard Watson Gilder and William Dean Howells ran for cover. Meanwhile, President Theodore Roosevelt vowed that Gorky would never enter the White House. Gorky and his female companion, widely denounced as monstrous evils, were ejected from several hotels, including even the Hotel Lafayette in the Village. For several days Gorky hid in the A Club rooms, while the moralists outside raved of dangerous foreign influences on the American family. Undaunted, the A Clubbers continued their support of the Russian dissidents. During Mary's first months there, they sheltered a Russian gunrunner who purchased ammunition and stored it at A Club in boxes marked "Soap." [19]

The winters spent at A Club, in 1907 and 1908, were a period of rapid political and professional growth for Mary Vorse. She finished her first book there, *The Breaking in of a Yachtsman's Wife*, and wrote most of her next two books, including *The Story of a Very Little Person*, a description of the infancy of her daughter, Ellen, who was born in 1907. Mary was notorious at A Club for plastering warning notes on her closed door: "I am working! Do not enter!"—a revealing sign of her new pride in self.

Looking back twenty years later, Mary Vorse admitted that although those at A Club had a high level of purpose and activity, talk was really their main occupation—"talk which led many of the members into joining the Socialist Party." [20] Most of the A Club members called themselves revolutionaries. They were really nothing more than liberal reformers, "natural-born New Dealers" Mary would later call them, part of the movement of well-heeled, inspired young into settlement houses at the turn of the century. Mary Vorse was younger than the other residents of A Club. Even though her experience there had a moderating influence on her political thought, her intellectual progression would follow a far different course from her friends at A Club, most of whom finally settled for Wilsonian idealism, or "government controlled" corporate growth. Her time at A Club marked the beginning of her radicalization and not its apex.

Meanwhile, after two winters at A Club, Mary's marital frustration reached an intolerable level. More and more, a slackness crept into Bert's life. The book he planned remained unwritten. His faith in himself bled away. Mary suffered from continuous nervous headaches. Her anxiety heightened when she learned that she was again pregnant. She remembered the summer of 1908 in Provincetown as one of the worst periods in her life. It was the "awful summer" when she discovered that Bert was involved in an affair with her stenographer.

Once, in a state of high agitation, Mary set out to find Bert and his new conquest. Mary hired the teenage boy next door to drive her in a wagon out Snail Road to search for the wayward duo in the back country.

Mary and her driver surprised her sandpiper Bert and his embarrassed companion emerging from the dunes. Dapper in his customary white ducks, Bert attempted humor. "Ah, such is the way of the world," he shrugged. Sickened by jealousy and anger, Mary claimed to have lost her child through miscarriage. She spent most of her time that summer lying on the couch, attempting to write as tears rolled down her cheeks in a seemingly endless stream. Once again, Bert promised to reform.[21]

In the winter of 1909, Bert and Mary toured Europe with the children. They were accompanied by Bror Nordfeldt, a Swedish etcher of some note, and his fiancée. Young Wilbur Daniel Steele, a distant cousin of Bert's and then an unrecognized author, joined the group in Italy. The trip was enlivened by Vorse's discovery of Steele's writing skill. He showed his first story to her and she pronounced him "a born writer."[22] In the spring, she and Steele returned with the children to Provincetown, where he boarded at Mary's house during the summer of 1909. Bert remained in Europe; he would never again return to their Provincetown home.

After eleven years of marriage, something more than her affection for Bert had ended. She was also free of her need to please and pamper him. After eleven years, "revolt, absolute and complete . . . I thought I will kill this thing or it will kill me." She transcended that self that practiced perfect goodness in perfect fraud. Something that had long been gestating was given birth. "Never again was I so enslaved. . . . I loved Wilbur and I was happy. . . . It was now that I began to have the men I cared for serve me."[23]

That summer in Provincetown Mary Vorse refurbished and launched her twenty-three-foot dory, the *Molasses II*. She scraped and sandpapered the bottom, reworked the mast and the bowsprit, puttied all the seams, and painted the inside of the boat ocher. Strangers and fishermen stopped in the sun to talk, and helped to paint. She wet the halyards and coiled and recoiled them to prevent a kink. Finally, there it was, body white as a gull, bottom glassy green. Mary rubbed up all the brasswork, the pin, the blocks, as she polished the name *Molasses* on its side and its stern. With pride, "I finally launched her—paid out her sheet, saw her sail catch, and floated off on the shining surface of the bay."

The "Yachtsman's Wife" had herself broken free.

She stayed outside as much as possible that summer, blueberrying with eight-year-old Heaton, a handsome, mischievous boy of intelligence. Sneaker-footed, they explored the golden ponds and trails and desolate, beautiful stretches of the outside shore, gathering spicy bayberries, beach plums, and wild grapes and roses. There was a cosmic quality to her pleasure, nourished by the sea and woods, the companionship of her son, gigantic meals. Her baby, Ellen, was "soft and milky." Mary's sails alone were joyous.

"I knew that I would never be quite so happy again," she wrote. "For a moment, a few brief weeks, I had recaptured the happiness I had as a girl, and yet I had the freedom of a woman. I had my house and my children, and yet I had the gaiety that comes only, as a rule, with the irresponsibility of youth." Mary Vorse made a tremendous discovery—"how grand a life can be without continually having someone as it were continually over you." There was no one "to find fault with me, to nag, to be superior. I liked living alone, I was out of love with Bert. I had had enough." Mary had not written since that terrible summer of 1908. She began to write again, experiencing such strength that she could "work all day and then walk four miles to the outside shore and back for sheer joy."[24]

Since 1906, her earnings had supported the family. As early as 1907, she brought home about two thousand dollars a year, almost as much as Bert had earned in his heyday of 1902, and her income rose each year. Between 1906 and 1911 she published three well-received books and over sixty articles and short stories in major journals and popular magazines. Her work was eagerly sought by the high-paying women's journals like *Woman's Home Companion* and *Good Housekeeping*, as well as by the more general interest magazines like *McClure's*, *Scribner's*, *Harper's*, *Atlantic Monthly*, and *Outlook*. So rapid was her success that she was selected in 1906 to contribute a chapter to a novel written by twelve important American writers, among whom were William Dean Howells and Henry James.[25] While she was working hard at learning her craft, it seemed that almost every word she wrote found a ready market.

Mary Vorse's work sold so readily because it expressed the turmoil that characterized the sexual relations of her chiefly female and middle-class audience. Although her fiction spoke best to women's concerns, it sparked the interest of male readers who were forced to adjust, not only to restive mates, but to urban business society with its competitive demands. Mary's was a generation of adjustment. In the early twentieth century, the nuclear family, already stripped of much of its economic function, lost much of its educational, religious, and nursing functions to outside agencies. Privileged women, even though they enjoyed greater leisure and more years free of childbearing, were channeled exclusively into care of children and husband. As women's economic and biological functions waned, their emotional and psychological role in the family increased. At the same time the growth of industry curtailed men's participation in family life. Direct patriarchal authority within the family declined as a result of the father's absence from the home. In a society characterized by sexual inequality, the changes in the organization of production placed tremendous structural strains on marriage and domestic life. As Mary's discontent, rooted in her experience as wife, mother, and female achiever, grew, it shaped the content and tone of her written expression. Like much best-selling fiction of the day, her work chipped at the idols of Masculinity, Womanhood, and Gentility.[26]

She dramatized the tough-minded thesis that the adored wife–child of the past was hopelessly outdated. Her stories swarm with these pitiful creatures. Inevitably, their husbands grow bored, avoid coming home, and turn, with relief, to the sensible world of business and men. Preoccupied with sunny sentiment, these women seek to remain the emotional center of their husbands' lives, long past the natural limits of the period of first love. Their efforts to keep a keen edge on romance are as dangerous to their happiness as having "an infantile disease late in life," she wrote.[27] A woman whose purpose in life begins and ends with pleasing her man eventually is left high and dry emotionally. Her answer to the problem is that women must learn to "stand on their own feet," "broaden their interests," and "not expect too much," although the details of realizing these homilies are left exceedingly vague.

Mary concluded that the great game of marriage was a terribly unequal one. Yet "women are too courageous, for the most part to tell the truth, even to themselves; they accept the inevitable and tell themselves and others that things are for the best."[28] Mary highlighted the predicament of the economically privileged wife, pinned to stereotypical ideals of woman's proper role, isolated emotionally and physically from the public world, and destined to lose, in the end, even the glamor of romance. This defeat sounded a common chord in the experiences of many of Mary's readers during the first decade of the new century.

Contemporary women found in Mary Vorse's fiction both consolation and explanation for their disappointment with True Womanhood. The source of their problems as women, Mary believed, was the unfortunate training of the male. Childish, selfish, egotistical—even when well-meaning and warm-hearted, the men in Mary's stories are rarely admirable. She habitually sketched three types. The first is the effeminate genteel, so trapped in sexual repression that he is unable to do much more than flutter, ineffectually, near the desired, but never conquered, more lively female. Another is the business-oriented autocrat who is wholly baffled by the sensitivity of his wife to human concerns. In his struggle to behave in proscribed fashion as a "good provider" and a "faithful husband," he remains an emotional cretin whose unconscious deprecation of women and children stems from his belief that he must be served by these lesser beings.

The third version of manhood in Mary's writing is more complex in structure, as well as more prevalent in her work. This creature is powerfully rapacious. His lips curl, eyes burn, muscles ripple, and voice booms. His mouth is invariably sensual and cruel. His appearance both frightens and entrances the women he encounters. They respond either by narrowly escaping, only through great self-control, his magnetic charm, or, more commonly, by imperfectly subduing his magnificent sexuality through his love for them. In either case, the male animal is triumphant, although ego-dependent on the reflection of himself in the woman he dominates. Even after 1900, women's popular fiction still relied on the old poetic forms of male power and female passivity, with the common theme of women's dependency, investing it with bliss and horror, interweaving it with dreams of submission and escape.

Regardless of the variation in her male characters, Mary emphasizes that their personality characteristics are produced by early socialization. If men seem generally weak, insensitive, vainglorious, and even silly, it is not their fault so much as it is the creation of society itself. Women are forced into dependence on the undependable.[29]

The role of modern women, Mary counseled, was patiently to nurture and instruct man, despite the male's boyish strutting and selfish demands. In essence, much of Mary's work in this period is an early development of the core ideology of feminist-based pacifism, which would surface within a decade. The popular ideal of woman's selfless, maternal love is thus transformed in Mary's fiction—from its late nineteenth-century form as illustration of women's superiority, to its twentieth-century use as demonstration of men's inferiority.

A related theme is Mary's exposé of married existence. She stressed that "the perfect hour" when love was new and all-consuming would inevitably pass during the first years of marriage. In her stories, it is sometimes replaced by a distant, friendly understanding between man and wife, but more often by a one-sided yearning of the wife for a return of emotional unity. Left without similar resources and interests, the wife must nonetheless adjust to her husband's natural desire to have every legitimate freedom of action.

Nor could women turn, as their mothers had promised, to happy absorption in home and children. Mary's writing exposed this myth as relentlessly as her work stripped away romantic notions of marriage. She ridiculed the novels where mothers were always seen as loving saints, eyes full of holiness, sewing little clothes. In her work, mothers frequently feel incompetent, tired, and angry with their lovely new babies. They are frustrated by their limited experience.

Her pages describe the children who have been made rebellious and unpleasant by their mother's old-fashioned denial of self. Women who sacrifice all for their children, in line with the ideal, create "beautiful soulless monstrosities . . . indifferent minotaurs who eat their mothers alive." They produce daughters who are as reluctant to grow up as their mothers are. "The child becomes a victim of her mother's immolation; the mother a victim of the child of her own raising. . . . Unselfishness breeds a perfect selfishness." And fathers are no help at all in Mary Vorse's fictional world. Wholly absorbed in money making, fathers, when they appear, are distant, inaccurate assessors of family problems.[30]

By shrouding it in just enough conventionality to make it marketable, Mary found a fictional formula that worked. It was popular because it told women what they could no longer endure and what they did not know how to change. In a real sense the combatants in Mary's early fiction are Mary versus her mother, and women versus men. The conflict echoed in the homes of millions of her readers.

In the fall of 1909, her interest sparked by pieces written by A Clubber Arthur Bullard, Mary asked the editor of *Harper's Monthly Magazine* to send her to Morocco to write a series of travel stories. It was her first foreign assignment as a journalist.[31] She bid her young lover Wilbur Daniel Steele an amiable goodbye and sailed for Europe.

With $200 on hand, and an additional stipend of $100 a month from *Woman's Home Companion*, Mary was now responsible for the support of five people—the two children, the again-penitent Bert, and the nursemaid and secretary who accompanied her. In the spring Bert returned to New York alone, while Mary and the children remained in Europe. At their parting, Heaton watched in wonder the uncommon sight of his mother sobbing without control. She realized this separation was more final than the rest, and she mourned the lost dreams now dead. "It's odd," Bert wrote from New York. "We have not told anyone of our difference, but everyone here seems to surmise something is wrong. I take a simple and natural tone, but last night when I suggested to Paul [Wilson] that I might engage a house for a year, in view of the fact that you might want to take a house next winter, Paul looked at me with derision and then laughed outright."[32]

On June 15, 1910, a phase of Mary's life ended abruptly. On that date, aboard an ocean liner and ultimately bound for Provincetown, she received word that both Bert and her mother were dead.

Bert died on June 14 of a cerebral hemorrhage while on an unexplained visit to Staten Island. He was found unconscious in a hotel room in the morning—alone. Mary's mother, after hearing of Bert's death, died of heart failure in Amherst the next day.[33]

There is little evidence of the immediate effect on Mary of this news. Even after the lapse of many years, she avoided all discussion of the deaths. There are fragments of horror to be found in several letters written to a friend.

> [Bert] hated so the thing he was. . . . It was not any great viciousness that killed him. It was his small daily indulgences. . . . I have a curious haunted feeling tonight as though the one I used to be was there in the room somewhere with the one he used to be. Do you suppose I will always have to bleed for him as I do now, drop by drop of blood and the strength of me goes. . . . I cannot bear that he should have died in the dark without me and I cannot bear that he died without seeing his children again. They asked me in the hospital if he had some great nervous shock lately. There are other things too that I can't very well write about yet, and I don't think ever.[34]

It is likely though, that Mary Vorse spoke best through her fiction, when she described the feelings of a widowed woman whose marriage had also chilled long before her unfaithful husband died. Mary wrote, "It wasn't grief I felt—it wasn't loss. In some ways it is worse to feel nothing than to feel pain."[35]

Part Two: 1910-1915

[I was one of] all the gay, warmhearted girls who had [en-tered] the nineties in their teens, or who turned twenty early in the century. And [who] felt it was up to them to be doing something about saving the world . . . and in the world in which we lived proudly, real things were positive and not relative. We were unbitten by reality, psychoanalysis or war. We came to maturity in what was really for women a golden age. Since we had the feeling that we were important civic factors who could put in a thumb almost anywhere and pull out a plum, ranging from votes for women to a fine new building law . . . me with my youth spent in the Vanguard, and thinking of myself as immensely up to date.

—MHV, 1934

Chapter Four

Crossroads

Vorse worked every day during the summer of 1910 at Provincetown, only to destroy all she had written. During that summer her moods fluctuated from depression to an ecstatic sense of freedom. Her Provincetown house seemed even more a haven. To balance the fears she felt as a thirty-six-year-old widow liable for the sustenance of so many, she built a determination out of past success and grit. That summer of adjustment, of knowing that she was now the only person responsible for a young family's welfare meant an entire shift, she wrote, "a slow revolving on its axis of my whole approach to existence."[1] She need no longer pretend that writing was something she could take up or put down when she wanted. For the rest of her life, concern for work must—could at last—be placed first.

Vorse never wavered in her resolve to support her family through free-lance writing. This was a momentous decision, for the cushion of the Marvin fortune was lost to her. Ellen's will provided one thousand dollars a year to Mary's father, already growing senile. After Ellen's death, Hiram lived with Mary for a year before his admission into McLean Hospital where he died in 1914. The remainder of the Marvin inheritance was divided equally among Mary's five half-brothers and half-sisters. As a final reproof of Vorse's willful life style, her mother left her not a penny.[2]

In the fall of 1910 Vorse returned to Greenwich Village where she moved the children and her father into an apartment near Sheridan Square. Her stories began to sell easily once more. In the pleasantly shabby neighborhood, with its vital mix of immigrants, artists, and reformers, she reshaped her goals. The next two years marked a crucial turning point in her life. Three intense emotional experiences of that period increased her awareness of the lives of poor women and inspired her lasting commitment to radical politics. Vorse outgrew the last vestiges of habit and thought that characterized the often-indulged daughter of a privileged family.

The first transforming experience came that winter when Vorse joined with other middle-class women in a crusade against infant mortality in New York City, where poor, mostly immigrant, mothers often were required to work long hours for subsistence wages. They suffered poor health and were unable to nurse their babies during the working day. When breast feeding is impossible, pure milk assumes central importance in infant survival.

Yet most of the milk sold to working-class mothers in New York City before 1912 was produced in unsanitary conditions. Unsterilized and insufficiently chilled before sale, it was often contaminated by bacteria that produced scarlet fever, diphtheria, typhoid fever, tuberculosis, infant diarrhea, and intestinal infections. During the summer months when temperatures rose, the infant-mortality rate skyrocketed in the immigrant sections of the city. Watered milk, although illegal, was common. Large-scale milk producers and distributors knew that profits realized from selling dirty milk far outweighed the nominal penalties imposed by law. In the crowded working-class sections of American cities, sewerage was inadequate, disease rampant, and the water supply scanty and often contaminated. Human life was cheap for many workers in the industrializing countries, the lives of their children cheapest of all.

In 1910, the wealthy Mrs. J. Borden Harriman formed the New York Milk Committee and waged a year's campaign to raise funds for milk depots to distribute free or low-cost pasteurized milk. The city agreed to take over these new depots at the end of the year if the women's New York Milk Committee could show that the infant-mortality rate had been appreciably lowered. The results of the Harriman-led campaign amazed even the most sanguine. Seventy-nine depots were opened in 1911, some sponsored by the New York Health Department and some by private sources. In 1911 the infant mortality rate fell 8 percent. In 1912 the rate fell another 5 percent.[3]

Vorse joined as a district leader in the drive launched by the New York Milk Committee. She solicited funds and supervised their collection in her area. As a member of the writing section of the committee, she publicized the need for pure milk. Many commentators of the time blamed the high death rate of infants of the poor not on polluted or watered milk, but on the neglect of children by ignorant immigrant mothers, on inherent ethnic traits, or on urban congestion. Vorse wrote an angry rebuttal of these alleged causes. Through the presentation of statistical data, she showed that the children of working mothers frequently died from drinking contaminated milk. The wealth of a few, she charged, was "paid for all over the world by the lives of little babies."

That judgment shook her world view so completely that it forced her to rethink her entire political outlook. As a well-fed member of society, she had been aware of an underclass among which she moved and which she sometimes encountered in person, but knowledge of working-class poverty had not before touched her so directly. Her new position as a widow, alone responsible for the care of two children, determined her response. She was now a female wage earner, decidedly an anomaly among the women of her class, not just in philosophy, as previously, but in actual economic standing as well. "A society that allowed children to die because their parents didn't make enough money," she wrote, "seemed senseless and vicious. . . . I was the sole support of my children. I saw myself poor, and my own wanted and beloved children dying because I couldn't make enough money."[4]

One other event in 1911 stands out as preparation for the realignment of Vorse's life. One late March afternoon she heard women shrieking on the street below her Village apartment. She descended the stairs and ran with the crowd eight blocks to the Asch building, a ten-story structure off Washington Square. Here about five hundred garment workers, most of them young Italian and Jewish immigrant women, were struggling to escape the fire consuming the three top floors where the Triangle Shirtwaist Company was located.

The firemen were helpless. Their ladders reached only to the sixth floor. The building's single fire escape, eighteen and one-half inches wide, had collapsed, grotesquely deformed by the weight of the throngs that tried to descend it. By the time the firemen unrolled their lines, the Triangle workers were jumping the nine floors from the inferno to the street below. Only four minutes after the firemen arrived, the fire hoses were almost completely buried under the multitude of bodies. Spectators, many of them relatives and friends of the trapped workers, joined firemen and policemen holding up huge fire nets. The jumping garment workers drove the nets into the sidewalk with such force that the men holding the nets turned somersaults over onto the bodies.

Inside the building, cloth and barrels of oil fed the flames, which ran within the fireproof walls. The terrified workers could not escape through the eighth- and ninth-floor doors. It was company policy to keep the doors locked. This illegal action had forced workers to leave by the elevator exits where handbags could be checked daily for possible stolen materials. In flight from the flames, the women forced several doors, all of which opened against the flow of the panic. One hundred and twenty-five workers sought to pass down a thirty-three-inch-wide stairway. Trampled bodies soon jammed the flow from above. The women clawed the clothes off each other in their rush to get through. As a black porter worked in the basement to keep the elevator motors going, the elevator operators, in blinding smoke, made desperate, random guesses as to where the floor openings were. The elevators managed a few trips down before the bodies of women jumping in terror jammed the elevator shaft from above.

In less than forty-five minutes after the fire began, 146 workers were dead.

Standing in the dense crowd near Washington Square Park, Vorse heard people ahead of her crying, "Another's jumped! Another's jumped! All on fire!" She watched as four women, their dark skirts aflame, sprang from the high windows in headfirst dives to the ground. Within a few hours almost twenty thousand people had assembled in the streets near the Asch building, among them sobbing relatives and friends of the Triangle's workers. The people stood vigil throughout the night as the dead were counted and identified.

Vorse realized that political corruption and official neglect killed the Triangle women. She also remembered the outcome of the 1909 "Uprising of the 20,000" and the role the Triangle Shirtwaist Company had played in that struggle. In that year, the immigrant garment workers had walked out in protest against severely exploitative working conditions. Through hunger and cold, through beatings and incarceration, the young women workers had maintained an unparalleled unity. The Triangle management had attempted to smash that unity by hiring local gangsters to attack the pickets—a common practice, but refined in this case. Triangle also hired prostitutes and pimps to attack as many as ten pickets in one day. The pickets had then been arrested for "assault" by the waiting, watching New York police. Vorse knew that many of the policemen she saw restraining the crowds about the Asch building on the day of the fire had only two years before used their clubs on the Triangle pickets. The Triangle Shirtwaist Company was one shop that had refused to yield to a critical demand of the 1909 strikers—the improvement of safety conditions.

The tragedy of the Triangle fire engendered massive outrage among East Side garment workers, middle-class reformers, and diverse radicals. Protest meetings helped set the tone for the dramatic funeral parade:

120,000 marched in silence. This demonstration brought added pressure on officials to enforce and to strengthen factory laws and safety regulations, although it was to be four years before the new state and city industrial codes were wedged into law and many years more before they were adequately enforced. Vorse could not forget the words the garment worker Rose Schneiderman used to memorialize the Triangle victims: "I would be a traitor to those poor burned bodies if I came here to talk good fellowship. We have tried you good people of the public and we have found you wanting. . . . The life of men and women is so cheap and property is so sacred. There are so many of us for one job it matters little if [we] . . . are burned to death. . . . Too much blood has been spilled. . . . It is up to the working people to save themselves."

After the fire, the owners of the Triangle firm were acquitted of a charge of negligence. They soon reopened their shop in a condemned building, and again proceeded, with official cooperation, to defy the safety "laws" of New York. Triangle's new shop held an extra row of sewing machines that blocked the outside exit.[5]

Vorse's understanding of the brutal handicaps suffered by working women led her to a new political stance. This shift occurred when she reported the famed 1912 textile strike in Lawrence, Massachusetts. Vorse's path to Lawrence had been prepared by her presence at the Venetian general strike in 1904 and by the activating effect of A Club. She had shared the vulnerable anguish of working mothers. She had reacted against the heedless rich, made wealthy by the sale of contaminated milk that killed the babies of the poor. She had understood the cause of the Triangle tragedy—and she was ready to reorient her life.

Nineteen twelve was to be a banner year for progressives. The combined presidential votes given to Theodore Roosevelt, Eugene Debs, and Woodrow Wilson buried the supporters of President Taft. Feminism became a prime subject for discussion. Alice Paul, fresh from the militant Pankhurst suffrage movement in England, returned to the United States to shake up the lethargic image of American suffragists. American Bohemianism came to a boil in Greenwich Village. Socialist sentiment was widespread in the nation, and at the polls. The muckraking movement was at its height. An increasing number of young people at Ivy League colleges were certain that progress lay in denouncing their parents' world; labor radicals were turning to dynamite in the West. When the Industrial Workers of the World came east to organize the workers in Lawrence, Massachusetts, the Greenwich Village intellectuals had a first-hand chance to learn about class warfare.

Situated thirty-five miles north of Boston along the Merrimac River, Lawrence was founded by a group of manufacturers in 1845. Its textile employees were at first chiefly native New Englanders and the new immigrants driven to the United States by the potato blight in Ireland. Beset by disease, death, industrial accidents, and nativist hysteria, the miserably poor Irish built the dam, canal, and giant factories in Lawrence in the 1850s.

In the 1890s the character of the working population in Lawrence underwent a sharp change, as Italians, Poles, Russians, Syrians, and Lithuanians replaced the native Americans and western Europeans in the textile industry. By 1911, seventy-four thousand of the eighty-six thousand inhabitants of Lawrence were first- or second-generation immigrants, with one-third of these southern and eastern Europeans. Most of the new immigrants were Italian, living within a one-mile radius of the Lawrence mills. There, by 1912, twenty-five separate nationalities spoke fifty different languages. This diversity went far to explain the difficulty of organizing the new American working class.

The influx of southern and eastern European immigrants provided an enormously profitable source of cheap labor for the mill owners. Although profits and living costs rose, wages declined, partly because the employers had effectively crushed union organization in their Lawrence plants before 1912. Indeed, the somnolent American Federation of Labor craft unions had shown little interest in organizing the impoverished "Dagos" and "Hunkies" in Lawrence. In 1912 the little capitalist utopia in Lawrence fattened upon the lives and labor of these men, women, and children, whose average work week was fifty-six hours, although 21 percent worked more, with no overtime pay.

The worker's misery did not end at the factory gates. Nearly all the workers lived in the congested tenement area, where one-third of the population resided on less than one-thirteenth of the city's land. High rents compelled tenement families to take in boarders. Five or six persons to a room was common. Immigrant wives were often responsible for doing the cooking and laundry for the lodgers, as well as for earning a wage in the mills.

Rats, filth in the halls, frequent fires, defective plumbing, inadequate toilet facilities, and rooms without windows compounded the misery of tenement life. The majority of mill workers subsisted on black bread, coffee, molasses or lard, and a cheap cut of stew meat once or twice a month. Fuel was extremely expensive. Inadequate storage facilities forced the slum dwellers to buy coal in small bags, at 40 to 80 percent over the price of coal sold by the ton. The workers in the greatest woolen center in the country could not even afford the overcoats they produced. Margaret Sanger in the winter of 1912 found that only 4 out of 119 workers' children in Lawrence wore underwear beneath their ragged garments.

Mortality and health statistics complete the agonizing tale of working and living conditions in the textile town. With other textile centers, Lawrence had one of the highest death and infant-mortality rates in the country. The unhealthy conditions in the textile factories filled the weavers' rooms with fine fibers. One-third of the spinners died before they had worked ten years. Respiratory infections killed almost 70 percent of the Lawrence workers, whose average age at death was less than forty. A medical examiner wrote in 1912 that a "considerable number" of children died within two or three years of entering the mills and that "thirty-six out of every hundred of all men and women who work in the mill die before or by the time they are 25 years of age."

Such were the conditions that drove the Lawrence textile workers to revolt—conditions, incidentally, that were at this time no worse than in other textile centers in New England and the South. The 1912 statement of the strike committee in Lawrence seems curiously understated: "We hold that as useful members of society, and as producers we have the right to lead decent and honorable lives; that we are to have homes and not shacks; that we ought to have clean food and not adulterated food at high prices; that we ought to have clothes suited to the weather."[6]

The Lawrence strike of 1912 began in January when the state put into effect its new law forbidding women and children to work more than fifty-four hours a week. Rather than cut profits, the mills responded by cutting the wages of all workers. The loss of twenty to thirty cents a week meant a great deal to families already on subsistence wages. Suddenly the daily suffering could no longer be tolerated. Within a week, twenty-three thousand textile workers had left the factories. With their families, they represented about 60 percent of the city's population; one-half of the textile workers were women and children. The strikers presented four moderate demands: a 15 percent increase in wages with a fifty-four-hour week; abolition of the bonus system; double pay for overtime; and no retribution against returning strikers.

The by-now-familiar scenario of American labor conflict continued. Lawrence mill owners, politicians, legal officials, small merchants, and religious leaders aligned themselves in opposition to worker demands. The city police, state militia, company guards, and Harvard student militia were quickly moved into place to protect the hallowed rights of property. Arrayed against these forces in Lawrence was a new labor organization, the Industrial Workers of the World. The IWW, or Wobblies, as its members were often called, represented a dramatic new departure in American labor history—the creation of an anticapitalist industrial union designed to challenge the evil effects upon the American working class of rapid industrialization.[7]

In the fifty years after Mary Vorse's birth, the physical production of American industry increased fourteen times. Such enormous growth generated a demand for labor power that could be met only by recruiting labor from overseas. Less skilled immigrants provided the sweated labor at the bottom ranks of the United States' industrial economy. By 1912 the low-paid, dangerous, heavy work in American factories outside the South had become the virtual monopoly of southern and eastern European immigrants.

Yet the American Federation of Labor, formed in 1886, adopted the attitude that the unskilled foreign born were "unorganizable." The AFL came to consist largely of skilled craftsmen, often dominated by an openly antisocialist, racist, and male-supremacist philosophy that all but barred the entry of the immigrant, unskilled, black, or woman worker into its ranks on equitable terms. The AFL concentrated on organizing the minority of skilled workers, whose numbers shrank proportionately each year as machinery and modern technology transformed the industrial labor force. Thus the AFL organizational policy had two negative results. One was that large numbers of American industrial workers remained unorganized until the CIO was formed in the 1930s. The other was that by chiefly serving the minority of skilled craftsmen, the AFL showed little interest in organizing each industry as a whole. Yet, without the solidarity of industrial unionism, the separate AFL craft unions within each industry or firm could easily be defeated during strikes by the unified power of the great corporations.

An indigenous labor organization committed to industrial unionism had developed in response to the AFL's failures. In 1905, leaders of the Western Federation of Miners and a collection of miscellaneous labor radicals assembled in Chicago to form the Industrial Workers of the World. The IWW sought the destruction of capitalism, scorned politics, and counted on the nonviolent general strike to make the revolution and to form the workers' republic. It forsook the rampant racism, nativism, and sexism of the AFL and became the most open, militant labor organization in American history. The Wobblies were known as the singing workers. Long after the IWW was smashed, its songs were still heard wherever protestors gathered, in the 1930s, the 1960s, and even the 1980s. The prime years of the IWW were between 1912 and 1917. Its later history was written in blood and ended in tragedy.

In practice, the IWW, no less than the AFL, concerned itself with immediate bread and butter gains. "The final aim . . . is revolution," said a Wobbly leader, "but for the present let's see if we can get a bed to sleep in, water enough to take a bath in and decent food to eat."[8] Despite its radical argot, the IWW rarely practiced sabotage or initiated violence.

Three of the Wobblies' most colorful and effective organizers, Joe Ettor, William "Big Bill" Haywood, and Elizabeth Gurley Flynn, arrived in Lawrence to direct the fight. By March 1912, the IWW had enrolled more than ten thousand members in its Local 20. Most of the new union members had been in the United States less than three years. To the dominant classes in Lawrence, it seemed for a time that the IWW might really activate the revolutionary potential of the poor.

Even those commentators most hostile to unionism admitted that the Lawrence strikers exhibited a fighting solidarity not seen before in American labor battles. The marvel of the Lawrence strike was that the IWW organized the "unorganizable," blending many ethnic groups and rivalries into one smoothly functioning, high-spirited unit. The gray masses flowing passively in and out the mill gates had suddenly become singing, vibrant, and unafraid. The sight of as many as twenty thousand disciplined workers walking in endless file through the mill district in the famous moving picket line, and of daily parades of three thousand to ten thousand people singing radical and Wobbly songs, tremendously alarmed the respectable elements and earned Lawrence its epic status in American labor history.

The brutality of Lawrence mill owners and city officials was so blatant, and so widely reported in an increasingly sympathetic press, that employer arrogance became an all-important factor leading to the textile workers' victory. Publicity brought large monetary contributions for strike relief into Lawrence from trade unions, socialists, and ethnic groups across the country. Despite the beatings and bayoneting practiced by the police and militia, the workers remained remarkably nonviolent through the long nine weeks of the strike, even when two strikers were killed and hundreds arrested and jailed. A clumsy plot to plant dynamite and blame it on the IWW failed when it became clear to many Americans that the plan was instigated by a Lawrence businessman and the president of the

American Woolen Company himself. The state's arrest in February of IWW leaders Joe Ettor and Arturo Giovannitti, for a murder of which they were obviously innocent, was equally inept. The arrests fueled worker resistance. Before a jury found Ettor and Giovannitti innocent more than eight months later, the case had become an international labor cause.

Still, the combined forces backing the owners were far superior to the power of the united textile workers. The strike could have easily been lost if the removal of the strikers' children from the city had not elicited such callous repression from the Lawrence authorities. Early in February the strikers, aided by Margaret Sanger, who would later win fame as a leader of the birth control movement, sent 245 of their children to friends and relatives in New York City and Vermont for safekeeping during the strike. The exodus of the pale, ragged children of Lawrence aroused public resentment against the starvation wages paid to the textile workers.

While the antilabor Hearst newspapers charged the strikers with inhuman neglect of their families, the mill ownership made plans to prevent further departures of the children from Lawrence. On February 22, seven youngsters were arrested when their parents attempted to send them from the city. Two days later the Lawrence police arrested fifteen children and eight adults as they attempted to board the train for Philadelphia. The officers took the mothers to jail and put the children in the city poor farm. The public exploded in fury. The liberal papers resounded with indignation. Beating and imprisoning strikers was acceptable, but police prevention of lawful travel exceeded even the conservatives' limits. Petitions streaming into Washington led to congressional and Bureau of Labor investigations. Reporters, middle-class reformers, social workers, magazine writers, Senators, and upper-class women, including even the wife of President William Taft, traveled to Lawrence to see for themselves how workers lived.

Mary Vorse was among those who were curious about what lay behind the seizure of children. After reading the account in the morning newspaper, she persuaded *Harper's Weekly* to send her to Lawrence. The article she wrote would lose the magazine advertising business from the American Woolen Company.

Vorse traveled to Lawrence with Joe O'Brien, a free-lance reporter whom she had met in New York in the winter of 1911. O'Brien was thirty-seven, an open-hearted, red-headed Irishman from a small farm in Virginia. He had left home when he was fourteen and gone to work in Boston as a cub reporter a few years later. There he was known for his propensity to steal city vehicles for fun and abandon them in the Boston train station.[9]

O'Brien—the hard-drinking, high-spirited socialist and suffragist—won Vorse's love with his blarney and joie de vive. "This is dawntime in my soul," his note to her read. "The dawn and the singing in my soul and my melted listening heart all belong to you. . . . I pray to the god inside of me . . . to make me work very hard and always be kind, so that my Mary will put her folding-up rose-leaf of a hand in mine and go with me to the edge of life and find contentment and singing things." She responded: "Dear, in this little piece of time you have made yourself more a part of my life than anyone else ever has. And you come into an inner piece of my spirit that I have kept closed always."[10] Warmed by new love, they were light-minded and gay as they boarded the midnight train for Lawrence.

The street lamps were still on when they arrived in the city. They walked through streets empty of people. Both were stunned by the menacing presence of hundreds of armed soldiers who stood guard at the mills and patrolled the crossings. For the first time Vorse saw troops called out against American strikers. "We got breakfast, not talking much, for our familiar New England town had become strange and sinister," she wrote.[11]

At strike headquarters, Vorse met the IWW leaders. She listened to the one-eyed giant, Bill Haywood, talk to reporters and respond to the problems of the strikers. Vorse had her first glimpse of Elizabeth Gurley Flynn, who was to become a close friend. "She stood there, young, with her Irish blue eyes, her face magnolia white and her cloud of black hair, the picture of a youthful revolutionary girl leader." Joe told Mary of his first meeting with Flynn six years before. He had been sent by his newspaper to cover the court hearing of Flynn, then fifteen years old. She and her father had been arrested for talking socialism on Broadway. The judge asked Flynn if she thought she could win converts in that way. Flynn replied, "Indeed I do." The judge sighed sadly. "Dismissed," he said. Flynn had been arrested five more times since then in the IWW's free-speech fights in Washington, Montana, and Pennsylvania. Now in her early twenties, and an immensely skillful speaker, she came to help organize the workers in Lawrence, bringing her mother and her baby with her. Vorse heard Flynn address the workers: "She stirred them, lifted them up in her appeal for solidarity. . . . It was as though a spurt of flame had gone through the audience. . . . Something beautiful and strong had swept through the people and welded them together, singing."[12]

The mass meeting over, Vorse and O'Brien shared coffee with Haywood, Flynn, and Carlo Tresca, Flynn's anarchist lover. (Tresca, the historian David Montgomery commented, was the "one man who actually incarnated the conservative's fantasy of the agitator who could start an uprising with a speech.")[13] An aged New England farmer approached them, accompanied by a young Jewish worker. The old man had come over a hundred miles, he said, to read the Declaration of Independence to the workers, so that they could understand their rights of free speech and free assembly. Haywood gently advised him that if the workers gathered to hear him read, they would probably all be arrested. The farmer decided to take the chance. Off he went, tenderly guided by the scrawny Jewish youth.

Drama crowded upon drama. Haywood told Vorse how on the day the children and their mothers were arrested in the railroad station, the police mauled a group of women pickets. Two Italian pickets had assumed they were safe from violence because they were pregnant. Both miscarried as a result of the police attack. A similar event occurred a few days later.[14]

Women at Lawrence not only led the picket lines, they ran the soup kitchens, organized relief, voted in all strike decisions, and were elected to the Strike Committee. The Wobblies held special meetings for women and encouraged rank-and-file women leaders. As Elizabeth Gurley Flynn said: "The IWW has been accused of putting women in the front. The truth is, the IWW does not keep [women] in the back, and they go to the front." Women strikers in Lawrence formed large parades, linking their arms together, jeering and hooting at police, militia, and management officials, creating a vast disturbance, and helping each other to escape when arrests were being made. Streets were often patrolled by groups of girls who attacked strikebreakers with red pepper, rocks, and clubs. The IWW understood that the support of women was a key to winning the strike, for almost half the Lawrence strikers were women and the men were dependent on the encouragement of their wives at home. Indeed, only about two-thirds of the female activists during the strike were textile workers; the others included housewives, shop clerks, a teacher, and a midwife.[15]

That first afternoon in Lawrence, Vorse visited the workers' slums. In the dreadful-smelling, sunless flats she met families who lived six to a room, supported by the labor of their children. On the walls near the mills, she saw samples of the recruitment posters that were spread throughout Europe by American mill owners. The posters showed well-clad workers with full lunch baskets standing in front of comfortable homes. She wrote that the leading Irish priest in Lawrence had "hated workers' children being sent away into socialist homes, so he instigated Colonel Sweetser, the commanding officer of the militia, to stop them as they were leaving." Wherever Vorse and O'Brien went, they were followed by several Italian workers who were intent upon protecting them from the militiamen. Joe O'Brien's instinct for direct action led him to suggest retaliation against the violence. "My boy," Haywood said to O'Brien, "the most violent thing a striker can do is to put his hands in his pockets and keep them there." [16]

The unity created among people in struggle against vast forces, their commitment and courage, her realization of the human cost of profit making—all these affected Vorse profoundly. In 1904 in Venice, she had been awed by the spiritual quality of a mass of united workers. Again, in Lawrence, the most remarkable aspect of the strike seemed to her to be the sense of community born among the strikers. Men and women who had never known each other, had never directed large groups, now all at once were maintaining relief depots, organizing mass demonstrations, picnics, and concerts, and living, singing, and marching in solidarity. The spirit of unity lifted them from isolation and poverty into a larger purpose, the individual temporarily forgotten for the common good.

A peculiar fusion also occurred among the outside observers. Lincoln Steffens, Fremont Older, William Allen White, and Vida Scudder were only a few of the reporters and writers who formed lifelong friendships as a result of the strike. Like Vorse and O'Brien they were moved by the almost religious spirit of the Lawrence workers. As the writer Ray Stannard Baker remembered: "I shall not soon forget the curious lift, the strange sudden fire, of the mingled nationalities at the strike meetings . . . and not only at the meetings did they sing, but at the soup houses and in the streets. I saw a group of women strikers, who were peeling potatoes at a relief station suddenly break into the swing of the The Internationale. . . . It is not short of amazing, the power of a great idea." [17]

Of all the strike sympathizers in Lawrence, Vorse found most interesting a woman doctor who had moved her practice to Lawrence at the beginning of the strike. The doctor came when she learned that the tuberculosis rate among children who worked in the mills was shockingly higher than that among other Massachusetts children of the same age. The doctor was lonely in Lawrence. The townspeople of her own class spurned her because she sided with the workers.

The meeting with the doctor led Vorse to do a series of interviews with the leading men of the town, all the ministers, and several prominent local women. It seemed to Vorse that these "decent people, who were like those I had lived with all my life, were indifferent only because they were ignorant of the conditions under which the Lawrence workers lived," much as Vorse had been ignorant. "If they knew the cost in lives, if they knew that one child in five died before it was five years old, if they knew the overcrowding," Vorse reasoned, "they must know at last what the people were striking about . . . against death and privation." [18]

Armed with this information, Vorse approached the town notables. Not one of them was responsive. They believed that the workers were misguided but dangerous aliens who preferred to live as they did in order to save money. Twenty years later, when Mary Vorse had lost her naiveté, nice women in Kentucky would tell her identical things about the miners in Bloody Harlan County.

The publicity engendered by the strike embarrassed Massachusetts industrialists. The governor of Massachusetts notified mill owners that he would soon withdraw the militia. Fearing that further public exposure might threaten the notoriously high woolen tariff, the owners capitulated in mid-March. Although the workers' advance in Lawrence was only temporary, it was an important victory. Within a few months of the settlement, 245,000 textile workers in New England received wage increases as an indirect result of the Lawrence fight. As soon as the mill owners granted the wage increase, however, they passed along the cost to the consumers in higher prices for woolen and cotton goods.

The experience at Lawrence did not inspire Vorse to become a revolutionary or labor leader. She was too critical to believe in a perfect society and too comfortable to accept the life of a union organizer. Most important, her choices were severely restricted by the need to care for and support two small children. But she could do one thing. She could try to make others as angry as she was.

The new career of labor reporter was born at Lawrence, when, as never before, American readers had been provided generally accurate and comprehensive coverage of strike events in mainstream journals and the large dailies. Strike leaders at once realized the vital contribution of sympathetic publicity to maintaining worker resistance and gaining liberal support. Not until the consolidation of the CIO victories, over two decades later, did the labor wars end, and with them the demand for labor journalism. Today, its survivors are channeled almost exclusively into the pages of the union newspapers and the small radical press. But for thirty years after Lawrence, the byline of Mary Heaton Vorse would represent the work of one of the earliest and most important of the new labor reporters. "I wanted to see wages go up and the babies' death rate go down," she wrote. "There must be thousands like myself who were not indifferent, but only ignorant. I went away from Lawrence with a resolve that I would write about these things always." [19]

Mary Vorse wrote this twenty-three years later in her autobiography, A *Footnote to Folly*. She made Lawrence into a powerful self-drama, the sudden turning point of her life, the moment that forever determined her future devotion to labor journalism and radical politics. But in fact Mary did not experience such a drastic conversion. Like most people, she moved more slowly into a new path, pulled along as much by a changing society and the influence of others, as by her own accumulated experiences.

Nevertheless, the heroic scenes of Lawrence did confirm and strengthen her growing class awareness. Returning home from Lawrence, she and Joe O'Brien together decided they could best contribute to the labor movement by telling the worker's story. "We knew now where we belonged," she said, "on the side of the workers and not with the comfortable people among whom we were born. . . . Some synthesis had taken place between my life and that of the workers, some peculiar change which would never again permit me to look with indifference on the fact that riches for the few were made by the misery of the many." [20]

They knew, too, that they wanted to work together. In April, they were married, both the children "coming down with measles to celebrate." [21]

Chapter Five

Banner of Revolt

From about 1912 until the First World War, New York City's Greenwich Village was the heart of intellectual, artistic, and radical life in the United States. Descriptions of the Village in its heyday—whether written by nostalgic participants, distant scholars, or disapproving conservatives—throb with superlatives. Words seem too limited to express the mood of that brief explosion of challenge and exuberance before the war. Yet so impelling is the task, that, with sneers or with cheers, many commentators have tried.

Alfred Kazin dubbed it the "first great literary society in America since Concord," a "center of contagion" where there "leaped a young generation so dashingly alive, so conscious of the great tasks that lay ahead, that it was ever afterwards to think that it had been a youth movement." For Henry May, Greenwich Village was the "beginning of a major change in American civilization," for Van Wyck Brooks, a "new insurgent spirit" revolutionizing American painting, literature, drama, and dance. Floyd Dell called it a "moral health resort." An aging Irish painter in New York, reflecting on the scene, thought he heard "the fiddles . . . tuning . . . all over America." But, as George "Jig" Cram Cook reminded his friends, "an American Renaissance of the twentieth century is not the task of ninety million people but of one hundred. . . . It is for us or no one to prove that the finest culture is a possibility of democracy."[1]

For others, the Village exuded sophomoric idealism—utopian thinking which could only stall in a personal and political dead end. Daniel Aaron cited the wit who agreed that the Village crew behaved like overgrown college students, with Bill Haywood as their football hero, the *Masses* as their college paper, and John Reed as their cheerleader.[2] Some, from either the heights of sophisticated ennui, or the prim environs of Marxism, have bemoaned the "lyrical left" as frivolous romantics. But all commentators agree on several points. The prewar Village represented youth in riotous rebellion and the arts in transition to modernity. An unstable fusion of culture and radical politics, the Village proclaimed hostility to business and religion—and a shocking new sexual freedom.

As the respected elder–warrior of the pre-1912 Village, Mary Vorse served as a model for the younger men and women enlisting in the ongoing revolt. The early Village dwellers, Floyd Dell recalled, "such as John Sloan and Art Young, Mary Heaton Vorse, Inez Haynes Gillmore [Irwin], Susan Glaspell, Theodore Dreiser . . . already had positions of importance in the realm of art and letters. . . . They had most of the familiar middle class virtues, and in addition some of their own; they were an obviously superior lot of people."[3]

Five organized groups gave birth to the prewar Village spirit—the Heterodoxy Club, the staff of the *Masses*, the Liberal Club, the Provincetown Players, and those who met at Mabel Dodge's Fifth Avenue salon. Mabel Dodge instantly recognized Vorse as a rival force attracting the Village notables; their relationship was cool from the beginning. Dodge thought Vorse "small and domestic." Vorse thought Dodge "a woman of shallow curiosities about the things in which I was most interested" and "a rich woman amusing herself in meeting celebrities of different kinds"—a kind of liberal version of Vorse's mother.[4] Thus, Vorse was only an infrequent, and often miffed, visitor at the Dodge evenings.

However, because she was one of the first editors of the *Masses*, Vorse's Village status was secure. She helped to found the Heterodoxy Club in 1912, and she and O'Brien were charter members of the Liberal Club, organized in 1913. Two years later, the Provincetown Players began on Vorse's fish wharf. In part due to her influence, Provincetown had already become, by 1913, a kind of summer resort for the New York intelligentsia.

Though lacking Mabel Dodge's flair or financial resources, Vorse was the core around whom many of the young intellectuals gathered. The source of her gentle attraction was that she combined in one person a nurturing listener, a successful writer who encouraged budding talents, a sparkling wit, and a companion in revelry that belied her thirty-eight years. Vorse could hold her own as a drinker and a talker into the wee hours. She shimmered with a radicalism so sweetly sincere in its optimism and anger that it entranced the wayward young. Lincoln Steffens and Hutchins Hapgood were also early citizen warriors. But Vorse's traits inspired in a way that Steffens's stiff perfection, or Hapgood's heated navel gazing, could not.

In the close confines of the Village, O'Brien and Vorse could find, at almost any hour, on MacDougal Street, or at one of the bars or hotels, a group of like-minded people. "Within a block of my house," John Reed said, "was all the adventure in the world; within a mile was every foreign country." Villagers knew one another, saw one another daily, and enjoyed the intimacy of a rural community without the moral restriction and intellectual rigidity of the small towns from which so many of them had escaped. "There is village intimacy, village curiosity, village gossip," Dell wrote. Susan Glaspell relished "the flavor of those days when one could turn down Greenwich Avenue to the office of the *Masses* . . . after an encounter with some fanatic at the Liberal Club, or (better luck) tea with Henrietta Rodman, on to the Working Girl's Home (it's a saloon, not a charitable organization) [it was Vorse who named it] or, if the check had come, to the [Hotel] Brevoort." In this atmosphere, it was easy to organize a picket line, a birth control demonstration, or a suffrage march.[5]

Like the 1960s rebels, the Villagers knew that one of the best ways to show their difference was in dress and home decor. So they painted their apartments in shades of orange and black and wore the Village uniform —bobbed hair, brown socks, and loose flowing gowns or tunics for the women, long hair and soft-collared, bloused shirts for the men. They stayed up all night to discuss poetry or politics, often with wine-soaked fervor. It was not until the 1930s that the moral and political structure of the late nineteenth century collapsed completely in the face of drilling armies and economic disaster. But it was Vorse and her friends in the Greenwich Village of 1912–1917 who tore the first great pieces from America's Victorian armor.

Although artistic revolt, radical politics, and the need to escape from Philistine America accurately characterized the Village leadership, the prime element attracting many to the Village was considerably more mundane. Above all else, the Village allowed a new sexual freedom to those who lived there. Just as in the youth revolt of the 1960s, sexual experimentation was as vital a component of intellectual and social release as was a new political consciousness. Focusing too narrowly upon high culture or political activity, most later commentators have tended to underemphasize this truth, even though the Villagers themselves were quite clear in their assessment of the central excitement in their lives. Much of polite scholarship has also obscured the fact that it was the woman feminist resident of the Village who pioneered and led this sexual rebellion. Rolling in her wake was her thrilled, but also startled and somewhat uncertain, male companion.

Although her male counterparts gamely supported the new feminist, the men understandably had a difficult time of it, inasmuch as they were forsaking their time-honored property rights to the female body. Still, the sexually radical woman paid the heaviest price. She risked the slanderous epithets branding those women who broke Victorian limits. Because her transgression was considered more shocking than that of the male, her commitment to sexual freedom was more consequential. Recognizing the risk, she also knew that sexual, political, and intellectual freedom had always been associated with each other in the public mind—and she believed herself to be the intellectual cream of her generation.

Of course it was urban life itself, as well as feminism and women's movement into the public sphere and paid employment, that dissolved the nineteenth-century barriers known to separate middle-class women and men. Village night life, with its restaurants, cabarets, clubs, and casual street life, prompted an easy familiarity with the opposite sex. "Sex itself was not the main object we [Villagers] thought," wrote Joseph Freeman. "You could have that in Brooklyn, Chicago, Bronxville or Davenport. But in the provinces you could not talk to your lovers." This communicative freedom allowed Villagers to envision a new male–female friendship, with or without sex, which could be emotionally and intellectually stimulating. Randolph Bourne described the unique "Human Sex" born in the Village. This "was simply a generic name," he said, "for those whose masculine brutalities and egotisms and feminine pettiness and stupidities have been purged away so that there is left stuff for a genuine comradeship and healthy frank regard and understanding." This was a far cry indeed from the Victorian sexual order.[6]

The supreme seriousness with which Village rebels treated their breach of sexual tradition seems strange to jaded moderns. Their fascination with the subject and their excessive delight as the advance guard have the overtones of a smug youngster who has just robbed the cookie jar. One has only to read the memoirs of some of the leading Villagers to catch the sense of self-absorbed, childlike pleasure they found in breaking sexual bounds. Their concentration on genital activity—their own and everyone else's—bordered on obsession and sometimes threatened to define the limits of their world. In the summer of 1914, for example, when the Western world was dissolving into war, Max Eastman, the admired Village spokesman, was holed up in an apartment in Provincetown. Here he sought "the nature of his being" and endlessly agonized over his sexual life, its origins, objects, quality, direction, and spiritual content. Yet we must acknowledge the repressive childhoods from which the Villagers had fled. Henry May cautions us that "if they sounded a little shrill and self-conscious when they talked about joy and freedom, we should remember that it took more courage, in the teens, to advocate free love than it took to preach social revolution."[7]

Four ideas shaped the sexual ideology of Greenwich Village at this time. One was a commitment to "free love." In Village parlance this did not mean sexual promiscuity, or anything approaching it. It meant the right of women to adopt the male behavior of "varietism." But this premarital sexual pleasure for women had to be informed by political intent if it was to meet the Village standard. When the coequal woman bedded down with her partner, Joseph Freeman wrote, "let her . . . be an enemy of the established tyrannical order, a socialist, anarchist or communist. Let her love . . . out of an uncorrupted heart defying the oppressive mechanics of contemporary society." Hutchins Hapgood admired the schoolteachers in the Village who during the daytime taught high school youth to respect the flag and honor the government, but at night slept with Bill Haywood. "Many of our brave young women are adapting themselves in this way of life," he said, "and thus doing their share toward a final disintegration of the community."[8]

The other two components of sexual freedom were of concern primarily to the woman. Her commitment to economic independence was the best assurance that she was not pledging her body, as well as her soul, to her male friend. The women Village leaders also shared a dedication to working and organizing as women, for women's causes. Most of them were active, at one time or another and to varying degrees, in the suffrage, birth control, and women's peace movement. For them, sexual freedom was symbolic of both personal achievement and a new sense of female unity. "All woman movements and organizations taken together form a part of feminism," said Marie Jenney Howe, a founder of the Heterodoxy Club. "[Feminism means] woman's struggle for freedom. Its political phase is woman's will to vote. Its economic phase is woman's effort to pay her own way. Its social phase is woman's revaluation of outgrown customs and standards. . . . Feminism means more than a changed world. It means a changed psychology, the creation of a new consciousness in women."[9]

Women also took the lead in creating the hotbed of political and artistic radicalism in the Village. Henrietta Rodman, the radical feminist school-teacher who founded the Liberal Club, has often been recognized as the most vital force in the formation of the Village spirit, although, as we shall see, her most important institutional contribution to the creation of Greenwich Village generally has gone unnoticed. Mabel Dodge's deepest interest was sex, but Emma Goldman, Margaret Sanger, and countless other Village women were far more active in the practice of free love than was Dodge. Edna St. Vincent Millay, a latecomer to the Village, has become the symbol of the feminist who burned her candle at both ends. But the roll call of subversive females is most notable in that nursery of modern feminism—the Heterodoxy Club.

Most historians of American Bohemia agree that when Henrietta Rodman brought the Liberal Club to 132 MacDougal Street in 1913, the Greenwich Village era could be said to have begun. But in fact the Village community had assumed organizational form almost a year earlier, when Rodman and Marie Jenney Howe, along with about twenty other women, including Vorse, formed the Heterodoxy Club. The group was for unorthodox women only, for women "who did things and did them openly," as Mabel Dodge put it. "We're sick of being specialized to sex," Marie Jenney Howe said. "We intend simply to be ourselves, not just our little female selves, but our whole, big, human selves." This unique luncheon club was a meeting place for activist women of widely differing political views who shared a loyalty to women's rights and personal fulfillment. It promised its members complete toleration of ideas and freedom of expression: "The Tribe of Heterodites is known as a tabooless group. There is the strongest taboo on taboo. Heterodites say that taboo is injurious to free development of the mind and spirit." [10]

Equally important, the club assured its members that all conversations there were to remain strictly off the record. Club members, most of them famous leaders in their fields, took vast pleasure in the opportunity offered them at Heterodoxy to express their ideas openly without fear of later retribution or misrepresentation by the press. With complete confidence in their privacy, Heterodites debated the burning issues of the day. They also listened to "background talks" given by the members about their childhood, intellectual development, and experience as women. In many ways Heterodoxy functioned like the feminist consciousness-raising groups of the 1960s, enabling the women to know one another on intimate terms and to discover their mutual rage—a sympathetic female support group nowhere else available to its members.

Amazingly, in light of the strong personalities and conflicting philosophies involved, the ban on public discussion of the club meetings was faithfully adhered to through the years. Thus, for a time, knowledge of Heterodoxy was all but lost to modern feminists. Even today, historians know very little about the actual meetings. But the centrality of the club to the emotional life of its members is evidenced in their memoirs. Elizabeth Gurley Flynn's comment is typical: "I had worked almost exclusively with men up to this time. . . . It was good for my education and a broadening influence for me to come to know all these splendid 'Heterodoxy' members and to share in their enthusiasms. It made me conscious of women and their many accomplishments. My mother, who had great pride in women, was very pleased by my association with them." Vorse's papers show that from 1912 through the late 1930s, whenever she was in New York, she adjusted her schedule in order to attend Heterodoxy meetings. Yet, in observance of her pledge of silence, and with the loyalty shown by almost every Heterodoxy member, she left no evidence of her experience there.[11]

The membership included radicals, anarchists, socialists, and reformers —suffragists, professionals, social workers, writers, artists, and housewives —all of them among the most unruly women of their time. By 1920 the membership had grown to sixty, but it never exceeded seventy-five before the club's disbandment in the early 1940s. Most of the members were in their late twenties to early forties. Nearly all of them were economically independent; few were well off. Among them were several famous lesbian couples. In Heterodoxy, sexual preference posed no barrier to sisterhood. The anniversary dates of lesbian couples were recognized and the women couples received emotional support from other Heterodoxy members when one of the partners became ill or died. But the majority of the members were heterosexual, with about half having been married at some time in their lives. Their marital patterns were as unorthodox as their lives. Between 1900 and 1920, Heterodoxy members showed a divorce rate of 33 percent.[12]

Heterodoxy meetings brought together the largest group of intellectually exciting American women ever gathered in one room. Behold the astounding collection of the eastern seaboard female intelligentsia. And imagine the clash of nimble minds. Among the writers, beside Vorse, were Rheta Childe Dorr, Zona Gale, Charlotte Perkins Gilman, Susan Glaspell, Bessie Beatty, Fannie Hurst, Inez Haynes Irwin, Edna Kenton, Helen Hull, Nina Wilcox Putnam, Anne O'Hagan Shinn, and Ida Wylie. Professional women included the stockbroker Kathleen de Vere Taylor, the anthropologist Elsie Clews Parsons, the psychologists Leta Hollingworth, Grace Potter, and Beatrice Hinkle. Among artists and actresses were Helen Westley, Beatrice Forbes, Robertson Hale, Ida Rauh, Margaret Wycherly, Fola La Follette, and Lou Rogers. Radicals and reformers included Rose

Strunsky, Rose Pastor Stokes, Elizabeth Gurley Flynn, Sara Josephine Baker. Some of the suffrage leaders were Vida Sutton, Alice Duer Miller, Inez Milholland, Paula Jakobi, Crystal Eastman, Doris Stevens, Mary Ware Dennett, Alison Turnbull Hopkins, Vira Whitehouse.

With such a feast, Heterodoxy members went to great lengths to attend the biweekly luncheons. For most, it offered their first communal experience of women loving and supporting one another—"one of the emotional treasures of life which all women desire, many of them fear, some of them seek, and a few of them find," their Heterodoxy Album stated.[13]

Josephine Baker, head of the Bureau of Child Hygiene in New York City, was one of the few members who broke the "off the record" rule. She tells in her autobiography of how Amy Lowell, lesbian and Brahmin, was asked to read her poems to Heterodoxy. Member after member requested selections from Lowell, which were so emotionally received that the socialist leader Rose Pastor Stokes actually collapsed in sobs.

Lowell couldn't go on. "I'm through," she said, glowering. "They told me I was to be speaking to a group of intellectual, realistic, tough-minded leaders in the woman's world. Instead I find a group that wants nothing but my more sentimental things. Good afternoon!" Lowell poked her cigar into her mouth and left the meeting. This memorable occasion, Baker must have felt, was too good to keep to herself. The memoirs of other Heterodites present few details of the club meetings, but many speak of Howe constantly banging her gavel as she attempted to bring order to the uproarious proceedings.[14]

Nearly all the charter members of Heterodoxy had met as suffrage workers. Marie Jenney Howe proclaimed her deviance when she trained as a minister in the 1890s. When she moved to New York in 1910, she became active in the suffrage movement and the National Consumers' League, a group of middle-class women who sought to improve conditions for working women. In 1910 she became chair of the Twenty-fifth Assembly District division of the New York City Woman Suffrage Party. It became known as the "Fighting Twenty-fifth" under her leadership. Here she met women like Vorse, Crystal Eastman, and Henrietta Rodman.

Many Heterodites left the mainstream suffrage organization in the war years and joined the more militant National Woman's Party. Several club members were among the first suffragists arrested for picketing the White House. Four received jail sentences; several were force fed while in prison. Later, members of Heterodoxy helped to form the leadership of the Woman's Peace Party and the international women's peace movement. Radicalism "was in the air," Vorse recalled years later: "It was the time of

Hull House. It was the time of social change. It was a natural thing. It was a time when great quantities of our people joined with the Socialist Party. . . . Rose Strunsky, a Heterodoxy member, had a lot of dynamite in her room that she'd cached for someone. The owner of the house would come in and say 'I smell something stuffy in here!' Being social minded—you didn't have to search at all, as you might today, because it was in the air. It was natural." [15]

The first group effort of Heterodoxy, soon after the formation of the club, was to sponsor a series of public forums in which suffragists were given five minutes to answer a trite objection to female suffrage. The staccato speeches of these articulate women proved to be a brilliant publicity tactic. Heterodoxy members went on to address wider feminist issues at the famous mass gatherings at Cooper Union in 1914. Here club members spoke on topics like "What Feminism Means to Me" and "Breaking into the Human Race."

The coming of war to Europe in 1914 shook the club. Rheta Childe Dorr and Charlotte Perkins Gilman resigned in protest over the opposition to war expressed at Heterodoxy meetings by members like Rose Pastor Stokes and Elizabeth Gurley Flynn. Stokes was later sentenced to ten years under the Espionage Act. Her sole crime was writing to a Kansas newspaper: "I am for the people, while the Government is for the profiteers." Flynn was also arrested under the Espionage Act during the 1917 roundup of labor organizers.

The war issue polarized and shattered the male-led left groups like the Socialist Party. But at Heterodoxy, there was no corresponding fracture, for the women were bound by more encompassing ties than politics alone. Mabel Dodge told how Fola La Follette, daughter of the progressive Wisconsin Senator Robert La Follette, was persecuted during the war for her father's "pro-German" attitudes. Fola rarely attended public events, Dodge said, but came to Heterodoxy luncheons: "That was a safe refuge. Everyone was glad to see her, no one there paid any attention to war hysterias, Fola was Fola, as she had always been. She would come in looking somewhat pale and pinched, but after an hour in that warm fellowship her face flushed and her muscles relaxed. It must have been a comfort to come there." [16]

During the war, members of Heterodoxy were harassed and kept under surveillance by the Bureau of Investigation, the forerunner of the FBI, because the club contained so many radicals and pacifists. Josephine Baker remembered how Heterodoxy had to shift its meeting place every week to keep from being watched. "It was just like an E. Phillips Oppenheim novel," Baker wrote. "All except the characters, that is. My colleagues in treason were not sloe-eyed countesses, with small pearl-handled revolvers in their pocketbooks, but people like Crystal Eastman, Fannie Hurst, Rose Pastor Stokes, Inez Haynes Irwin, Fola La Follette, and Mabel Dodge Luhan." [17]

The members of Heterodoxy moved far beyond the fight for the vote and envisioned the women's movement as a complete social revolution. Marie Jenney Howe wrote in 1914: "The feminist does not find all of life in a love affair. . . . She is able to be happy though unmarried. She does not adjust her life according to the masculine standard. . . . She thinks for herself. . . . Feminism is woman's part of the struggle toward humanism. After feminism—humanism." Heterodite Edna Kenton laid it on the line: "Feminism is sex-war; who doubts it. . . . For women are thinking at last not on man's terms, but in their own, and thought in a slave class is always dynamic." [18]

A disapproving Hutchins Hapgood was one of those who guessed that Heterodoxy members were "shunted on the sliding path" from the suffrage movement into the "passionate excesses" of feminism. In Heterodoxy's no man's land, Hapgood reported, the "vital lie" was developed "that men had consciously oppressed women since the beginning of time, enslaved and exploited them." His suspicion was justified. "What a Unity this group of free-willed, self-willed women has become," Heterodoxy members wrote in 1920. "We have been scarcely aware of what has been happening to us in this little order, seemingly so loosely held together, so casual, so free." A decade later, when Ella Winter spoke at Heterodoxy, she remembered: "I felt a camaraderie among these women ('girls' they called themselves), an understanding almost like a secret that could be shared because men weren't around." [19]

Many of the Heterodites were socialists, but these knew that feminists would face a bitter separate struggle even within a socialist state. The contacts at Heterodoxy refined and challenged the political ideas of the members. And all the Heterodites threatened the older stereotype of the spinster reformer. The new women of the Village were apt to combine professional training with sexual freedom, or activism with radical goals. Their socialist beliefs gave them a class analysis of root economic ills. Their feminism gave them a value system for socialist culture as a whole.

A few months after the formation of Heterodoxy, Henrietta Rodman organized the Liberal Club in Greenwich Village. Although H. L. Mencken described it as the home "of all the tin pot revolutionaries and advanced sophomoric thinkers in New York," its members called it "A Meeting Place for Those Interested in New Ideas." Rodman also brought with her to the Liberal Club the band of independent Heterodites. This faction comprised fourteen of the twenty-three women members of the Liberal Club. Rodman "was especially in touch with the university crowd and the social settlement crowd and the Socialist crowd," Floyd Dell wrote, "and it was these . . . who mixing with the literary and artistic crowds in the Liberal Club, gave the Village a new character entirely. . . . Ideas now began to explode there, and soon were heard all the way across the continent." [20]

The coed Liberal Club encouraged debate, poetry reading, drama production, and socializing. "Of novelists and story writers the Club boasted a round dozen or more. One of the most popular was Mary Heaton Vorse," Lawrence Langer remembered. The walls of the Liberal Club also featured the latest in modern art. An old electric piano allowed dancing in a close embrace—the modern style. Langer recalled that holding tightly to one another was not only sexually invigorating but also a political statement: "As you clutched your feminine partner and led her through the crowded dance floor at the Club, you felt you were doing something for the progress of humanity, as well as for yourself and, in some cases, for her." [21]

If the Liberal Club was the coed social center of the Village, the *Masses* was its intellectual organ. Founded in 1911, the magazine was first cooperatively owned by Vorse, Louis Untermeyer, Ellis O. Jones, Inez Haynes Irwin, and Horatio Winslow. The artists on the staff were John Sloan, Art Young, Maurice Becker, Charles Winter, and Alice Beach. The first issues published fiction by European authors and American socialists and muckrakers. A *Masses* cover of 1912 featured Vorse's story "The Day of a Man." Her tale portrayed a poor and unemployed worker, driven to drink by despair, but refusing work offered him by a patronizing Christian do-gooder. The magazine provided artists and writers, who received no pay, a place to publish the work that the mainstream media would not accept, but by the summer of 1912 the magazine was bankrupt.

The original group decided to reorganize. They chose Max Eastman as editor in August 1912, primarily because Art Young had told them that it was Eastman who had organized the Men's League for Women Suffrage. Vorse signed the now-celebrated note to Eastman: "You are elected editor of *The Masses*. No pay." With Eastman's appearance, the magazine assumed its legendary status in American cultural history. Eastman, a recent pupil of John Dewey at Columbia University, was enthralled by his first meeting with the staff. "The talk was radical," he recalled. "It was free-thought talk and not just socialism. There was a sense of universal revolt and regeneration, of the just-before-dawn of a new day in American art and literature and living-of-life as well as in politics. I never more warmly enjoyed liking people and being liked by them." Eastman recognized Vorse as "the popular story writer" and found her "pale and fragile. . . . Although abounding in energy [she] had a permanently weary look." [22]

The resurrected *Masses* became the rebel-Bible of its nearly sixteen thousand readers, many of them in small towns across the nation. It attacked capitalism and gentility, spoke for feminism, birth control, and artistic realism. The journal instructed its supporters to join the class struggle. It pulled no punches. A revolution, Eastman wrote, "is a sweeping change accomplished through the conquest of power by a subjected class." [23]

The *Masses* offended patriotic, religious, business, and aesthetic conventions. Its combination of high gaiety and revolutionary fervor was expressed best in its political cartoons. These portrayed the capitalist press as a brothel, or showed Christ lecturing on the rights of labor, or pictured an emaciated working girl kissing the fat, greasy hand of a priest, or a bloated industrialist trampling on the bodies of the poor. Within two years, the magazine had been banned from university bookstores, expelled from subway stations, excluded from Canadian mails, and swept from public libraries.

The devotion of the *Masses* to feminism was deep and consistent. In the first issue after Eastman's arrival on the staff, Vorse published an attack on the Goddess of Domesticity. Her target was the "sisterhood of amalgamated wives"—the women whose allegiance to Womanhood made them so uninteresting, intolerant, and sexless that their husbands fled from them. Traditional marriage, Vorse taught (and she must have been thinking of her experience with Bert), made women into domestic drudges, parlor objects, or barriers to social change. By contrast, the advanced Village Woman was free to seek unlimited goals. [24] The *Masses'* comments on the economic cause of prostitution, the need for birth control, and the value of liberated women made it very different from the orthodox socialist publications of the time, which showed little interest in such matters.

The monthly editorial meetings, at which contributions were criticized and accepted or rejected, were stormy events. The lively gatherings attracted close friends of the staff like Clarence Darrow, Bill Haywood, or Carl Sandberg. Few journals can claim such scrutiny. In the later years of the magazine's existence, before it was closed down by federal authorities in 1917, these meetings were most often held at Vorse's house. Here the two factions, the writers and the artists, divided over questions of content and format. The artists pressed aesthetic considerations; the writers were for more militant political agitation. First the cartoons were submitted to the group as a whole and then noisily voted on, often with rude comments and howls of derision. Then would come the turn of the writers.

"Nothing more horrible can be imagined than having one's pieces torn to bits by the artists at a Masses meeting," Vorse said. Nevertheless,

> there was no greater reward than having them stop their groans and catcalls and give close attention; then laughter if the piece was funny, finally applause. This was the way that the decisions were come by in the first years. The meetings were large and tumultuous. There would arise from the clamor and strife of those meetings something vigorous and creative of which we were all a part. The flame was present here too, as well as in Lawrence.[25]

In the summer of 1912, Vorse and O'Brien left the Village for their first shared experience of Provincetown. They remained there for eight months in an idyllic interlude. The house Vorse loved assumed a different atmosphere, free now of marital and financial tensions. Her tendency to closet her emotions had been strengthened during the unhappy last years with Bert and her time as sole breadwinner. It seemed to Vorse that Joe O'Brien's presence opened her spirit in a way she had never before known. Her descriptions of him are cast in metaphors of clear light, opening spaces, and fresh air. In the few years they were together, Vorse formed her lifelong habit to "try and see events through his intelligence, which so quickly pierced sham and subterfuge" in an assessment of reality. Far more than anyone she had known well, Vorse said, O'Brien "wanted light and truth and looked at the world with a long view."

In that summer the children were eleven and five. O'Brien was an eager new stepfather. Vorse felt vast relief at sharing the burdens of child care. Best of all, O'Brien genuinely supported her writing efforts and need to achieve.

He had a real flair for domesticity. Unlike Vorse, he found housekeeping both easy and enjoyable. He at once began renovation—knocking down walls, adding a workshop and study. Soon they had a children's playroom, window boxes, and a garden and chickens. She marveled at the unconscious ease with which he brought shine to the house, "the book he put in place or the picture he straightened or the garment he picked up . . . as if he weren't really thinking about it at all." All her life as a mother, Vorse had felt pressed, resentful, and inadequate. In imitation of her childhood experience (but without the ample funds that had been available to her own mother), Vorse entrusted the daily care of her children to a procession of nurses and maids as much as possible. She thus sought to duplicate her mother's ordered domesticity, while also trying to find time to write and to earn her family's living. The struggle to perform both roles had been unsuccessful in many respects. Automatically, Joe O'Brien straightened her life as he straightened her house. "Order followed him around like a dog. . . . The house was rich in children," she wrote. Living was full, precious, and symmetrical.[26]

In the summer of 1913, Vorse and her household, Neith Boyce and her husband, Hutchins Hapgood, along with Susan Glaspell and Jig Cook, formed the nucleus that would bring the town its renown as a suburb for the Villagers and as the birthplace of the Provincetown Players. That season Vorse's house was busy with the comings and goings of friends, most of them writers filled with discussion of plots and characters, all of them bubbling with talk of socialism and the workers' struggle. Wilbur Daniel Steele roomed at Vorse's house again and wrote his stories, always sure that every word he produced would be his last, his gloom alternating with periods of raucous gaiety. Joe was writing a book. Mary ground out her money-making "lollypops"—short stories for the women's magazines. Joining the three in Mary's kitchen for frequent blueberry-pie orgies was young Sinclair Lewis, who was writing his first novel.

Just as she had encouraged Steele, Vorse inspired the writing of the lanky outcast, "Red" Lewis. He later credited her with giving him the recipe for writing that he passed on in lectures and articles to young hopefuls: "Place your unpaid bills before you, then apply the seat of your pants to the seat of the chair—and write." The support and practical advice of someone with Vorse's literary sophistication could never be repaid, Lewis wrote, "except in lasting affection." The gawky, graceless Lewis was nine years her junior. Over the years he often appeared at her door in New York or Provincetown with the simple statement that he wanted to be with her. It was Vorse, Lewis said, who "taught me the three Rs—Realism, Roughness and Right-Thinking."[27]

In February 1913, Joe and Mary left Provincetown for Europe. Vorse had an assignment from the *Woman's Home Companion* to do a series on the Montessori method of education being developed in Italy. After a brief vacation in Morocco, the trip was climaxed by her reporting of the international women's suffrage convention in Budapest.

The sudden explosion of American interest in Maria Montessori's work reached a peak in 1913 and 1914. First developed in schools for deprived children of the poor, the Montessori method claimed to teach three-, four-, and five-year-olds disciplined behavior, as well as how to read and write, in as little as six weeks. The fundamental principle was the release of the spontaneous interests of the child. Child development was thus purported to proceed primarily from the liberation of the child's capacities, rather than through interaction with nurturing adults or through the more rigid control traditionally practiced in the classroom. The new pedagogy looked to many progressive-minded Americans like an easy route to fundamental reform. It seemed possible to use the method for Americanizing the large numbers of immigrants arriving from Europe, alleviating social inequalities of class, and bringing everyone to middle-class respectability —instantly and at little cost. Vorse was converted to the method and given every facility for observation of the experimental schools. Her series of articles in the *Woman's Home Companion* did much to popularize the new education among American mothers.

As Vorse described the Montessori method to American women, she stressed that strict controls stifled children's natural, harmonious development. Some American critics of Montessori were already beginning to point out that self-control could not be learned through self-indulgence. But Vorse voiced little understanding of the possible misapplication of Montessori's teachings. Indeed, Vorse's description of Montessori's work came close to resembling Floyd Dell's facetious account of the new education. "Why, my dear," Dell wrote, "it's simply a lot of things. And you put the baby down among the things—and you never have to bother about it again." [28] Vorse's Montessori articles reflected her guilty hope that her own children actually had little need of discipline or of her constant presence and attention to parenting.

Actually, O'Brien was a far wiser and more patient disciplinarian than Vorse. To her great relief, he assumed much of the responsibility for her children's nurturance. He published a series of stories on his experience as a Montessori father. O'Brien described a household in which the busy mother retreats from her riotous children in order to work, while he, the only remaining adult guide, is left to maintain family order through the application of old-fashioned methods. "Look out," the fictional Heaton Vorse warns his younger sister, "you may have a Montessori mother, but you've got a mighty sore father!" The son adds, "My mother has an angel face, her little brain is full of grace. My mother's never cross with me. She only hollers 'Let me be!'" [29]

Vorse and O'Brien left the Montessori school for Budapest where Vorse was to report the International Woman Suffrage Alliance meeting. The seventh of its kind, the meeting drew delegates from twenty-six countries and an audience of three thousand. The year 1913 marked the height of militance in the English suffrage movement. The Pankhurst-led suffragists had moved from public demonstration, window breaking, and hunger strikes, to being arrested for arson. In June a radical suffragist had thrown herself under the king's horse at Ascot, dying in protest against the government's failure to provide votes for women. Vorse delighted in the Pankhurst movement's turn to lawbreaking. She publicly attacked the propriety of the American suffrage movement and privately hoped that the English militants would not win suffrage too soon, for they were doing so much to destroy the demon of respectability that kept American women in thrall. "Respectability is really what is the matter with marriage," she wrote Arthur Bullard. "The moment we have learned to keep respectability from our homes, we will have happy ones. I am trying for nothing so much in my own personal life, as how not to be respectable when married. Up to now I have succeeded quite well." [30]

Thus, when Vorse arrived at the Budapest convention, she was mildly contemptuous of the relatively conservative nature of its American leaders, women like Jane Addams, Carrie Catt, and Anna Shaw. Yet she also came to the meeting with curiosity, eager to meet these personalities. She did not anticipate that she would be "stirred and thrilled to the depths."

Vorse was unexpectedly moved by her first experience of a large congregation of women, of all classes and ages, who had gathered to proclaim female solidarity and worth. "It seemed as if I had been present at something at once deeply touching and deeply thrilling," she wrote, "as though I had watched a young and hopeful army getting ready to march on to victories of peace such as no other army had dreamed of attempting; as though I had watched, too, one of the most impressive things in the world —the loosing of long pent up and hitherto unused forces." As at Venice and Lawrence, her carefully controlled self vibrated to masses in motion.

Vorse suddenly felt passionate oneness with women who joined to defy male power. The Fisher-Bastion, where the women met, was set high on a hill between the Gothic spire of the Church of St. Mathias and the ministry buildings. Vorse was impressed by the symbolism of Church and State, magnificently set side by side—that Church and that State that had at all times denied women equality, on the grounds that women were unable to defend the ramparts of the nation–tribe against the attacks of other males.

Yet no woman at the meeting who fought for the franchise, Vorse felt, could ever be reproached for not understanding politics: "There was no shifty trick or turn with which she will be unfamiliar, since all have been used against her." Observing the assembly, and remembering that it had been merely ten years ago that she had first traveled without father or husband, Vorse marveled that it was only in the past few years "that women had been able to move freely up and down the earth in such large numbers."[31]

Like many women since, Vorse was struck by the unique emotional tone of an assembly composed of women. Gone was the ego posturing, the barely veiled aggression, the pompous, dissembling rhetoric common to male gatherings. Throughout the women's meeting Vorse found "present a certain quality of informality; there was seriousness, but no solemnity, and there was much wit and humor. Perhaps the entrance of women into public life will put an end to the quivering voice, the chest thumping . . . and the other oratorical tricks that have so long made the public utterances of the average man so difficult to listen to," she wrote. The meeting at Budapest propelled Vorse into radical feminist thought. It seemed to her that it was against the "worst of all tyrannies"—the oppression of women by men—"that the highest forces and the deepest feeling of this Congress of women was directed." Vorse's realization of the courage and beauty of women was consistent with her awakened anger at the hierarchy of male controls. Previously, she had frequently written with distaste of the tradition-bound woman who unthinkingly opposed industrial justice and progressive reform. As a deviant woman from the Village, Vorse had never considered solidarity with all women; rather she had often celebrated her distance from the majority of them, especially those of her own class.

But in her coverage of the Budapest meeting, one can clearly sense the emotional shock that accompanied her acceptance of the spirit of sisterhood. Her descriptions of the women delegates are tender and respectful. She was inspired by two "wonderfully touching" elements. One, the group of gallant old suffrage leaders, each accompanied by the ghosts of their former companions, "women now dead who fought when no victory was in sight . . . women who for years unflinchingly faced . . . ridicule and misunderstanding." The other affecting element was the group of Hungarian peasant women, their heads covered with handkerchiefs. They had been willing to walk over 100 miles to attend the meeting. Their shrewd faces reflected "the sacrifices that had been made by no one can tell how many other women." The "white aspiring flame" of women united was ignited at the congress, she wrote.[32] It sprang out in the meeting's protest against unwanted motherhood, against the existence of class differences between women, against the persecution of prostitutes.

Vorse was indelibly stamped by her impression of the women's meeting of 1913. She would meet again with a women's convention within a year and a half, this time to protest war. For some years to come, Vorse would even cherish the hope that women across the world might combine to stop the ancient slaughter between males. After 1913, she would discuss the average female's submission to cultural mores with more sympathy and understanding. Permanently kindled too was her mistrust of the male structuring of intellectual and political values. Perhaps the most immediate consequence of her feminist vision, however, would be her attention to the part played by women in the industrial conflicts she would report in the years to come.

Chapter Six

Women's Peace, Men's War

The three years Mary Vorse spent with Joe O'Brien were perhaps the happiest of her life as a mother. Her career prospered, enabling her to hire a maid and stenographer. This brought relief from child care during the infancy of her third child as well as more solitary time for writing. O'Brien took an eager delight in her two older children, providing much of the attention and daily supervision they required. She also gained from him a new respect for political activism and a suspicion of intellectuals who limited their revolt to sexual or cultural matters. Soon after their marriage, she had her first experience as an activist when she helped to organize the 1914 unemployment protest movement in New York.

Vorse's presence at the 1915 international women's peace conference and her later tour of the European war zones strengthened the radical feminism she had embraced at the women's meeting in Budapest. Upon her return home, she found herself completely alienated from her old circle of friends. Ironically, it was then she assumed her central role in the creation of the Provincetown Players. Although she recognized the group's importance to cultural history, and forever after took pride in having been a part of its formation, Vorse regarded the birth of the Provincetown Players as nothing more than an interesting footnote to her major achievements. The scenes of war had matured her social consciousness. She would never again feel so comfortable amid the pleasurable play of the literati.

When Vorse and O'Brien returned from Europe, Vorse established a Montessori school in Provincetown and enjoyed days of fine sailing and prolific writing. By August she knew she was pregnant. She and O'Brien did not know that this summer of 1913 was to be their last quiet time together.

It was now that the group of artists and writers merged to form the celebrated Provincetown colony of the prewar period. Vorse and O'Brien were closest to two other literary couples—Neith Boyce and "Hutch" Hapgood, and Susan Glaspell and George "Jig" Cram Cook. For some summers, this little group was together almost exclusively. The three couples habitually spent part of the day writing and the rest of the time with their families in the open air—swimming, sailing, picnicking on the dunes.

Vorse's best friend was Neith Boyce, who was two years her senior. Boyce had fled the Midwest for the Village, where she worked as a reporter before marrying the writer Hutchins Hapgood. Boyce insisted that "retreat [from her marriage] must be easy." Nevertheless, she became absorbed in mothering her four children, born within seven years, while suffering in silence the forays of a husband seeking extramarital amusement. By 1913, by "writing a little every day," Boyce had published three novels. Her fiction, like Vorse's, centered on the dilemma of the modern woman.

Hapgood, ever in passionate pursuit of self, was driven wild by his wife's reserve. He longed with infantile fervor to absorb her very soul. She evaded his every intrusion. In 1914, Hapgood wrote an entire book about his unrealized attempt to penetrate her core, his forlorn need to be needed. He sent this manuscript to Vorse for comment. Her response addressed the hidden pain that Boyce had endured over Hapgood's sexual excursions. Yet Vorse was not openly critical of his infidelities. She too longed to believe that, painful as the transition might be for the pioneers of sexual freedom, the joyful end result would be, as Hapgood once put it, "the working-out of the situation into a more conscious companionship, greater self-knowledge, and a broader understanding of the relations between the sexes." Yet Vorse had her own memories of Bert. She reminded Hapgood that his extramarital affairs had been sad little loves that led nowhere. Perhaps Vorse could afford such philosophical distancing, because, as she told Boyce, Joe O'Brien was "fiercely monogamistic, both in theory and in practice." For Mary and Joe at least, still caught up in the exploration of their first years together, marital misery was the problem only of their friends.[1]

Hapgood was much like Vorse in his ability to organize a ring of admirers. He had first realized this talent as recruiter for Mabel Dodge's salon. Vorse's new friend, Jig Cook, would serve a similar function as the evangelical spirit behind the formation of the Provincetown Players in 1915. Cook also was a writer, but his work was rarely published. As Floyd

Dell noted, Cook's stories, "so magnificent when he talked about them, were not magnificent when he wrote them." Like Hapgood, Cook was a romantic and mystic, less efficient at making a living.

When Susan Glaspell married Cook and moved to Provincetown, she too made her escape from middle America. After graduation from college, she worked for the first newspaper in Iowa to employ women as reporters. By 1913, Glaspell had published two novels and a collection of short stories. She would be best known for her plays, one of which would receive a Pulitzer Prize in 1931. Glaspell, Hapgood said, was "truly sentimental," whereas Vorse was "falsely" so. Although Glaspell raised two stepchildren, she was disappointed that a heart lesion prevented her from having children of her own. As a feminist, she wanted women's options to be enlarged, yet believed that motherhood was woman's most fundamental and essential experience in life.[2]

Despite the immense differences in their mind sets and interests, Vorse for years considered Boyce and Glaspell to be her closest friends. They could share their love of good conversation, their interest in their children's activities, their passion for writing, their disdain for polite tradition, and their concern with the modern woman's discontent. Yet their personal reserve and mutual need for emotional distance need not be threatened by their interaction. Each woman, too, shared the experience of an impetuous, volatile, bigger-than-life husband—Jig Cook, of the black hat, flowing cape, and inspired visions; Hutch Hapgood, with his lyrical self-explorations and tortured confessions; Joe O'Brien, the greathearted and politically aroused Irishman. O'Brien and Vorse often chided the other two couples for their lack of political activism. For Hapgood and Cook, radical expression centered about the ideal of perfect freedom in sexual love.

Vorse and her friends were evolving a concept of "companionate marriage" to replace the older Victorian pattern of "separate spheres." But the newer ideal of modern love could be as entrapping to women as the old. Most Village men, like Cook and Hapgood, wanted intellectual and emotional intimacy with their wife–lover. At the same time they expected their women to subordinate themselves to male needs. As Floyd Dell admitted in 1919, "I wanted to be married to a girl who would not put her career before children—or even before me, hideously reactionary as the thought would have seemed a few years ago." Max Eastman expressed the contradiction plaguing the New Men in the Village better than he knew when he described his first wife, Ida Rauh, as his "friend and slender-bodied mother." In their later years, Eastman and Dell, Hapgood and Cook, enjoyed just that—maternal love from mother–wives—much like the care Bert had elicited from Mary. The new societal norm of companionate marriage would allow intimacy and lust between men and women, so long as both bed partners remained safely separated into essentially unequal spheres.[3]

Among these six rebel sophisticates, the question of sensual freedom danced in and out of their thoughts and conversations, enlivening their social gatherings, creating fantasies of endless youth, blunting the knowledge that though their bodies were bursting firm and healthy, they would be long bound through long lives to marriages that were now new, that the opening of one door inevitably meant the closing of another, and, in actuality, hearing in their separate lives and mutual relations the muted tones of initial discord. Yet they were still young, and their children cherished, and the beaches white and very beautiful. And so they attempted to combine a bohemian pattern of thought with the contradictory daily demands, traditional and limiting, of caring for one's children and making one's living through the production of salable prose.

They remained aloof from the younger radicals who were summering in Provincetown in force by 1914. Hapgood claimed the original Provincetown group "kept on working most of the time, held to family life without the prejudice of it, dined quietly but not too soberly together, and only occasionally were a part of such extreme outbreaks as the nude-bathing parties at night" on the beach.[4] As Hapgood reported, Vorse, as early as the summer of 1913, was drinking more than convention allowed:

> Sometimes I would have a cask at my house, sometimes Jig at his . . . [or Mary Vorse would have] a choice brand of Scotch. We would float together in the evening in a most amiable way . . . sometimes at Jig and Susan's [house], sometimes at Mary's, sometimes at ours. We gathered early, and would break up by midnight, having drunk just enough . . . to loosen our tongues and free our imaginations. But Mary's tongue didn't ever need to be loosened; drinking or not she went on like a perpetual brook, about her children, her work, the fishermen and their families, and how I . . . had led her into the evil habits of imbibing.[5]

Vorse drifted into greater indulgence. She drank quickly to get its effect, and then, when the alcohol was consumed, sent someone out for more. Some neighbors still recall the frequent sight of Joe O'Brien drifting home from the railroad station, with his tie and his big smile equally awry. Perhaps the memory of the native Cape dwellers was colored somewhat by their fascinated disapproval of the big-city writing crew. Yet, unmistakably, heavy drinking had become a general pastime at Vorse's house.[6]

In the fall of 1913, Vorse and O'Brien left Provincetown to spend the winter in New York. They took a furnished house on East 11th Street. The small pink brick house seemed an ideal place for Vorse's third child to be born. In February little Joel arrived, "a fine baby with red hair and blue eyes." Not long after, Vorse went to a workers' meeting in Paterson, where Carlo Tresca told her, "Maria, you are far too young a mother to be going over ferries to make speeches."[7]

The entries in her datebook stopped abruptly after February 26, 1914, when Susan Glaspell and Max Eastman came to dinner. "Life went too swiftly after that to make notes of engagements," Vorse recalled. That was because before the winter was over, Vorse's house was placed under surveillance by plainclothes men from the New York Police Department. She sometimes saw them peering in at her through the basement windows. Her little pink house had become the center for the unemployment protest movement in New York City.

During the abnormally cold depression winter of 1913–14, millions of Americans were out of work. In New York, Frank Tannenbaum, then a twenty-one-year-old anarchist, later a distinguished scholar at Columbia University, led a novel form of protest by the unemployed. He directed thousands of unemployed men to various churches, where they demanded food and shelter for the night, in a nonviolent dramatization of their plight. After a visit from the jobless army, some churches offered food, shelter, or money. But on the night of March 4, a Catholic church rector sent for the police. Tannenbaum was arrested, along with 188 others, and charged with inciting to riot; he was sentenced to one year at Blackwell's Island. The historian Paul Avrich described how the tempo of unemployment agitation increased after Tannenbaum's arrest. "Over the next three months, open air demonstrations, among the greatest ever held in New York, took place . . . at which thousands of jobless men and women applauded the speeches of avowed anarchists, denouncing capitalism and government. Night after night, marches, occupations and rallies were staged . . . to protest the iniquities of the existing order."[8]

Throughout March and April, Vorse's house functioned as a staging center for the IWW-led wing of the unemployment protest. O'Brien was elected head of legal defense. Vorse found places for the protesters to sleep. Day after day, at a hectic pace, she directed groups who visited churches and settlements to persuade their heads to allow three or four hundred men to sleep there overnight. Her house was always filled, with committee meetings going on simultaneously in every bedroom. Vorse remembered that she once answered the telephone seventeen times during a single nursing of her new baby. Meanwhile, she was trying to write. With O'Brien busy with political work, she was now the sole support of her household of seven, including the two maids.[9]

In early April, the fight of the unemployed became a battle for civil liberty as the New York police force, angered by so much overtime work, became more repressive. Often led by mounted detachments, the police viciously broke up protest meetings. Lincoln Steffens was sickened by the police violence. "I've seen such things for 20 years now," he wrote, "but I can't get used to it. It lifts my stomach every time I see a policeman take his night stick in both his hands and bring it down with all his might on a human being's skull."[10] Vorse's house filled with young men with scalp wounds, broken noses, and discolored faces, all telling their grim stories.

What had begun for her at Lawrence was now hammered into shape by police clubs, as her friends came in with their heads laid open, or disappeared into jail on trumped-up charges. She had realized at Lawrence the conditions in which workers lived. Now she was face to face with the knowledge of how churches, police, and courts cooperated to suppress radical dissent, while most major newspapers distorted the facts of the struggle.

Vorse and O'Brien were forced from active participation in the protest movements when they both became ill in the late spring. Vorse was merely exhausted. Even with the help of her maids, the job of combining the roles of nursing mother, organizer, and breadwinner completely drained her energy. O'Brien, however, was seriously ill. Although neither of them yet knew it, he had stomach cancer.

In the early summer they returned to Provincetown. By late June, O'Brien was hospitalized in Boston. Vorse and the baby stayed in Boston for a few weeks, so they could be near him. O'Brien decided to delay an operation until the fall. Vorse returned to Provincetown alone and spent most of the summer there caring for the children and household and continuing to write. With O'Brien so ill, the weight of earning their living pressed upon her even more than usual.

The worries of that summer gave rise to an intense emotional reaction. The once sparkling Provincetown parties of the Village intelligentsia turned into unbalanced drunken affairs, thick with interpersonal tensions. When in August the World War crashed down on the Provincetown group, many of the would-be revolutionaries were absorbed in masturbatory "self-psychoanalysis," fascinated with their personal pain from which

Dr. Freud's "science" promised relief. Fatuous self-reflection, high-blown radical rhetoric, sex, and drink marked the summer. Sensitive, unstable, feeling defeated by conservative reaction—the group's despair at world eruption brought on one last climactic binge, during which two suicides and one murder were attempted.

It began on the day following the final declaration of war in Europe. Hapgood, Joe O'Carroll, Fred Boyd, Hippolyte Havel, and Bayard Boyesen were slowly proceeding through a case of whiskey at Hapgood's house. All bemoaned the impotence of ideas and even blamed themselves for allowing the war to begin. Their self-importance aggravated by drink, they determined to move from guilt to propose an immediate conference of the intellects in Provincetown. Inspired, the five men first sent an invitational telegram to Vorse's house: "You are the only woman who with perfect male sympathy might be here."[11] They also called in Max Eastman and Jig Cook's mother to help prepare a resolution that would make clear to the workers of every belligerent nation why they must not kill each other for the sake of the imperialistic rich. An enunciation of Socialist Purity would surely halt the madness in Europe.

Though impelled by whiskey, the wrangling conferees could not agree on the proper wording for their statement. Vorse and Mrs. Cook floated toward home. The well-bred poet Boyesen, who had already begun his descent into alcoholism and melancholy, sat observant and aloof. Anarchist Hippolyte Havel was violently depressed. He and Polly Halladay had moved their restaurant from the Village to Provincetown that summer. Havel was more immediately concerned with Halladay's suspected sexual infidelities than with the question of war.

At this point, the young Irishman Joe O'Carroll, who had been beaten by the New York police in the unemployment demonstrations and was still recovering after a month in the hospital, escaped through the bedroom window. O'Carroll emerged naked on the Provincetown beach before a crowd of alarmed local residents. Intent on a watery death, O'Carroll was wrestled into unconsciousness by Hapgood and Boyesen, while the landlady stood by protesting the behavior of the cognoscenti. Max Eastman meanwhile broke up a struggle between two dogs who had been attracted by the commotion.

Just as quiet returned and the philosophic mood reactivated, Polly Halladay appeared dripping on the veranda. She announced that her own suicidal desires had been temporarily lessened by the coldness of the sea. Halladay was persuaded to go back to her restaurant and, like O'Carroll, to seek sleep. Returning to the conference of the intellects, Havel suddenly became bent on homicide. Hapgood followed him to Halladay's bedroom and remained to oversee the noisy resolution of their lovers' debate.

Hapgood and Boyesen, much subdued, were sipping coffee at dawn when Vorse came in, greatly disturbed. She reported that Fred Boyd, after attempting to cable their resolution to John Reed and the heads of state of Germany, England, Russia, France, and Austria, had showed up at her house, brandishing a revolver. Although Vorse had not made it home during the night, she had returned to find the children and the cook in hysterics. This was after Boyd had organized one of the nude parties held on the beach that evening. The reckless night ended, Boyd and Havel quickly departed Provincetown the next day—in order to quiet the aroused citizenry. Thus did the Villagers greet the coming of war in Provincetown.

If one can set a time that marks the end of that strain of innocence which intertwined with the exuberant chorus welling up from prewar Greenwich Village, then that morning of August 6, 1914, may be as good a date as any. When the European explosion came, it caused apolitical cultural radicals, parlor-bound revolutionaries, and bloodied activists alike to concede defeat of the ideal of workers' international solidarity. In less than two years three million men would be killed on the western front alone. Hapgood claimed that many Villagers would not recover their faith until the Russian revolution came to bring spiritual meaning again.[12]

For O'Brien and Vorse, however, O'Brien's worrisome illness was the most compelling concern. He returned from the Boston hospital to Provincetown in the fall of 1914, seemingly much recovered. Soon after, Vorse was offered a chance to attend the women's international peace congress at The Hague and to report the war in Europe for *Good Housekeeping* and *McClure's*. O'Brien strongly encouraged her to go. True to his socialist and feminist ideals, he insisted that she must report the peace conference, while he remained home to care for the children.

Shortly after the war began in Europe, twelve hundred women in mourning dress marched down Fifth Avenue in New York City to protest the slaughter abroad. The Woman's Peace Party marked the beginning of a new peace movement that was a drastic departure in style, ideology, and leadership from the prewar peace organizations. Earlier peace groups, all male directed, had focused on legalistic devices like international arbitration and the world court to stop war. The new female-led groups looked to economic and political democratization as the means to end conflict between warring males. The new women's peace movement ranged from the Woman's Peace Party, organized by a diverse collection of suffragists and various women's clubs in January 1915, to the much more radical

Woman's Peace Party of New York City and the American Union Against Militarism, both sparked by the socialist and Heterodite Crystal Eastman.[13]

When the International Woman Suffrage Alliance's biennial meeting, scheduled to take place in Berlin in 1915, was canceled because of the war, an international women's committee issued a call for a women's peace congress to meet in neutral Holland. Jane Addams, then the most respected and influential woman in America, was invited to preside over the meeting at Amsterdam. The women's peace conference would show that women, unlike the socialists in the warring nations, could maintain international solidarity in rejection of state-based madness.

Vorse was appointed as a delegate to the congress by the New York Woman Suffrage Party of New York City. Representing 151,000 women of greater New York, she sailed in April for the peace congress in Holland with forty-one other American delegates. They were a distinguished group of women, including Grace Abbott, Fannie Fern Andrews, Sophonisba P. Breckenridge, Leonora O'Reilly, Alice Hamilton, Jane Addams, and Emily Balch, the last two later to win the Nobel Peace Prize. Twelve of the delegates had advanced degrees. Several were the wives of wealthy or prominent men. Most were suffrage leaders, social workers, educators, or writers. Included were three socialists and two leaders of women's trade unions.

Abusive protest accompanied their departure. Their most vociferous critic was ex-President Theodore Roosevelt, seemingly almost crazed by his lust for war. TR judged their cause "silly and base" and called the women physical cowards who sought peace "without regard to righteousness." The American women were almost the only passengers aboard the Dutch liner *Noordam*. They sailed through mine-strewn waters, flying a blue and white homemade banner with the single word "Peace."[14]

Feeling isolated as a Villager among this collection of serious reformers, Vorse was nevertheless impressed by their heterogeneity. Along with some of the most influential and forward looking American women, she told O'Brien, she also found "cranks, women with nostrums for ending war, and women who had come for the ride, New Thought cranks with Christian Science smiles and blue ribbons in their hair, hard working Hull House women, little half-baked enthusiasts, elderly war horses of peace, riding furious hobbies."

On the way, the women met three times daily for conferences and lectures. Vorse wrote O'Brien: "Today a little Miss Wales, small, dark and slender, a thin little flame of emotion surrounding her, read a pamphlet on Armistice Without War. It is so simple and so naive that it is as though a wee child ran into one of the cabinets of Europe and with a word showed the way out of all difficulty. Such things haven't happened in real life since Jeanne d'Arc." [15]

Despite Vorse's note of sarcasm, however, Julia Grace Wales's proposal was both simple and wise. Endorsed by the Wisconsin legislature in 1915 and recommended for the consideration of Congress, the plan was an unprecedented call for continuous mediation, prior to any armistice agreement between the belligerent countries, by an international committee of experts who would sit so long as the war lasted. The proposed mediation committee was to study the issues and to continue to revise plans or to offer new ones until peace was achieved.

Vorse was mildly repelled by the intellectual hospitality of Jane Addams, who listened to the most impractical suggestions with courteous attention. The American delegation as a whole, Vorse felt, was composed of women "full of inhibitions, not of a radical habit of thought, unaccustomed for the most part to self-expression, women who had walked decorously all their days hedged in by the 'thou shall nots' of middle-class life." Yet she found their meeting all the more remarkable on that account. The women were bound by their courage to face ridicule and by their belief that the follies of male governments could be overcome by the sane, unifying diplomacy of women.

If Vorse was impatient with most of her co-delegate's nonradical perspectives, she had also learned to respect the energy and determination of mainstream suffrage leaders. Since 1911, Vorse had been active in the suffrage campaign. By 1915 the New York suffrage crusade, led by middle-class and society women, was the storm center of the national movement. Suffrage work in New York rose to a height between 1915 and 1917 that in number of participants and level of activity was never equaled in any other area of the country.

Determined to out-Tammany Tammany, Carrie Catt had organized New York's suffrage workers along political lines, dividing the state into twelve campaign districts and over two thousand election districts, each with a devoted woman director. A systematic suffrage effort of speeches, parades, and mass demonstrations operated with military precision. The male political hierarchy was astounded by the efficiency of the well-groomed women who mobilized to pass the state suffrage amendment, a goal finally achieved in 1917.

Vorse had headed one of the five subcommittees of the Press and Publicity Council of the Empire State Campaign Committee. The council members produced prosuffrage literature, newspaper copy, and advertising, while also serving as speakers and agitators. "It was our pride," Vorse said, that "we never refused a request to speak, even if it came in the middle of the night from a location far upstate."[16] In the New York campaign, Vorse learned to admire the tenacity and intelligence of the rich women who, she said, mingled with "free and democratic spirit with us poor wage-slaves of the slums." Vorse knew that wealthy Vira Whitehouse, chair of the Press and Publicity Council, could crack a whip better than any radical male labor leader Vorse had ever met.

While en route to the peace meeting in Europe, Vorse helped the American delegation prepare a series of resolutions to be offered at the congress. She volunteered to form a committee with Sophonisba Breckenridge, professor of social economy at the University of Chicago, and Leonora O'Reilly, one of the two women trade unionists in the American delegation. The three devised a resolution that stated:

> Inasmuch as the investment by capitalists of one country in the resources of another and the claim arising therefrom are a fertile source of international complications, this International Congress of Women urges the widest possible acceptance of the principle that such investments shall be made at the risk of the investor, without claim to the official protection of his government.

A controversy arose immediately as to the advisability of naming capitalists as the offending sector. Some members of the delegation wished "citizens" to be substituted for "capitalists." After a debate, the more polite "citizens" was accepted by a majority vote. But the condemnation of "capitalists" was returned to the final official resolution passed at the congress, a sign, perhaps, of the less conservative influence of the European delegates to The Hague.

The class issue surfaced several more times on the trip across the Atlantic. When Emmeline Pethick-Lawrence from England addressed the group on the subject of working girls and slum children, Emily Balch of the American delegation thought Pethick-Lawrence's words reeked with "the unconscious patronage" of the English elite. Hoping to soothe trade unionist Leonora O'Reilly's feelings, Balch "tried to counteract a little" with her story of how a striking shirtwaist worker had found most Wellesley graduates to be pampered innocents. "I think Miss O'Reilly enjoyed my effort to turn the tables," Balch noted in her shipboard diary. On another occasion, Vorse and the few radical women aboard organized an evening lecture series. O'Reilly spoke on the labor question, and Marion Cothren, a socialist lawyer and the only Heterodite beside Vorse on the ship, spoke on the breakdown of socialist internationalism.[17]

Held up for four days in the English Channel by the British, the American women's peace delegation arrived at The Hague on April 28, barely in time for the first evening session. The congress drew more than two thousand visitors and 1,136 delegates, with a thousand of these from the Netherlands. European and American press reactions to this meeting of women from warring and neutral countries, united, for the first time in the history of the world, to protest war, ranged from sarcastic derision to accusations of treason.

On her first morning at The Hague, Vorse was puzzled by the dominant rhythm of the gathering. As an experienced reporter, she struggled to sense the preoccupation of the audience. She had anticipated a more animated spirit in a group of women "whose very presence there was a revolutionary act and who were enacting one resolution after another of a revolutionary nature—resolutions, which, if they could have been carried out, would have reorganized the planet." Only after a time did she gauge the emotional mood as one of contained grief. The spirit was familiar to her. She had met it first in Provincetown. There she had observed the same "granite calm" of women during a storm when their men were at sea. "As they grow old, the faces of such women take on a sort of iron repose," she remembered, "terrible to look at when you know its reason. It was this resisting quiet that held the women at the Hague."

From the platform the women told their personal stories. They spoke of men who had left singing and who had returned wounded or dead. They spoke of infants without homes or parents, of mothers trying to feed their children on boiled grass. One woman, obsessed with the memory, repeated over and over the story of the swamps she owned. There, German and Russian soldiers had first fought each other, and then slowly drowned together. In Poland, Bavaria, Belgium, they spoke of vast suffering.

Vorse's deepest sympathies lay with the small group of radical women. Their spirit was expressed in a resolution, never voted on, but put forward by some Austrian women. It read:

> We openly declare that women refuse to do the work men cannot do because they are busy murdering other men—that women refuse to repair the damages brought about by men when they wantonly burn and destroy houses and property—that we refuse . . . our help to mitigate poverty and misery caused by the war.

Where are the women, another militant group asked, "who will lie down on the roads so that men, horses and cannon must pass over you to reach the battle fields"?[18]

The majority of women delegates paid little heed to these voices. Like Addams, they sought to stop the war, not by militant action, but through the force of public opinion, rational argument and the enfranchisement of women. Indeed, it seems unlikely that Mary—because of natural temperament or because of her responsibility as wage earner and mother—would have risked immediate action to oppose war. Her support of the radicals was more ideal than real, a fantasized vision of the brave decisiveness she longed to muster.

The congress drafted a series of resolutions that set the conditions for a just peace. Further resolutions called for general disarmament, nationalization of arms manufacture, free trade, freedom of the seas, investment made only at the risk of the capitalist, education of children toward the ideal of permanent peace, and the participation of women in the future peace settlement. When Jane Addams later presented these propositions to President Wilson, he called them the "best formulation which up till then has been put out by anybody." Many of these were later to be embodied in his Fourteen Points.

In its most hotly debated decision, the congress of women voted to send peace delegations to urge Wales's plan for continuous mediation without armistice upon the neutral and belligerent countries. The delegation to the war capitals was headed by Addams. A second delegation of four women was chosen to visit the neutral Scandinavian countries and Russia. These journeys made by a handful of women seeking peace were ridiculed by the international press. In the end the women's proposal for continuous mediation by a conference of neutrals came to nothing.[19]

From the perspective of some seventy years later, it seems apparent that the women meeting at The Hague in 1915 had a limited understanding of the possibilities of ending war. Their faith in a universal elevated morality of women has not been borne out by the coming of female suffrage or by the entire history of nationalism. The women of 1915 failed to examine another difficult question: They did not consider how absolute opposition to violence would serve to cement the status quo, and thus to perpetuate the injustice imposed by state-uniformed soldiers on oppressed peoples in many parts of the world.

Still, in retrospect, the women's plan for mediation was both sensible and humane. Like enfants terribles, they dared to speak the truth that others would not admit. They understood that economic greed, male socialization, and the ancient struggle for power between elite males create the conditions that lead to war. Perhaps the most important offering of the congress of women was its symbolic inspiration. Their statement of female horror at the barbarism of warring males, their protest at the violation of women that accompanies war, their heart-rending concern for the life of their children, their understanding of the most essential and compelling needs of humanity—these were their enduring contributions to feminism as a historical movement, and to world peace as the necessity of the nuclear future.

For Vorse, the climax of the meeting at The Hague came near the end. The delegates rose and stood silent for a few minutes, thinking on the dead of Europe and on Europe's suffering women. She wrote:

> I do not know how long we stood there in that terrible quiet. I stood looking into their stricken faces. Tears streamed down the faces of the women. An iron-faced old man opposite me held his head up, while tears slid unchecked down his face. Behind me I could hear the stifled sobs of Wilma Glucklich, for whose family in Hungary I had not dared to ask. An awful, silent, hopeless, frozen grief swept over this audience which, throughout the Congress, had been so contained. . . . When . . . we sat down at last, it rushed over me; these stricken women *were not the women who had suffered most.* They were neutral, for the most part; and those who came from the warring countries, were not, and could never be, the most deeply affected.[20]

Vorse recognized that in the belligerent countries it was the poor women, not these middle-class delegates, who would pay the heaviest tolls of hunger and want and irreparable loss. In the hall there "was only a faint shadow of the grief and despair of the women of Europe," she wrote. The meeting of these more privileged women was only a gesture, she knew, a "final protest, as brave as it was futile."

Perhaps it was her identification with the poor women of Europe, who were not present at the congress, that caused Mary to position herself as she did in the official photograph of the American delegation to The Hague. In the picture, she stands alone, several feet apart from the group, in the top tier, the only woman whose face is turned away from the camera.

While in Holland Vorse talked with refugees and interned soldiers from the war zones. The beauty of springtime in the Netherlands provided a poignant contrast to the victims of violence. By way of distraction, a kindly Dutchwoman took a group of women on a tour to the tulip and hyacinth beds of Haarlem. As the band of women walked past the blossoms, a Belgian woman at Vorse's side told her in a flat voice of how she had watched all her sons and her husband being executed in the village square.

Curious to know what the women in Germany were saying about the war, Vorse decided to travel to Switzerland via Frankfort.[21] With little difficulty she passed over the border into Germany. In contrast to anxious Holland, Germany seemed prosperous and gay. In Dusseldorf she changed cars and watched a troop train slide through the station. The soldiers carried flowers in their gunstocks. They were laughing and drinking from bottles, happy young men en route to the places where they would be shot. The people in the station cheered and waved back.

She was for the first time in a nation at war. The herd instinct was in operation. As she moved farther into Germany, troop trains became common: more boys with nosegays and picnic food, singing as they went to be killed. She had a sense of unreality, as though everyone around her were hypnotized, marching in lockstep to a wailing rhythm.

Vorse drove down from the little border station of Leopoldshohe in a clattering omnibus. She was a conspicuous figure, a well-dressed woman traveling alone, among a crowd of peasant women. The peasants were complaining to the German soldiers that their sons had lain hours on the battlefield with no care. The soldiers shrugged. "That's war," they said.

At the border, a mustached German officer searched her bags and announced that she could not pass. Vorse was taken back to Leopoldshohe under armed guard. She was sent from there by train to Locher where she was questioned again by a group of frontier officers. The inquisition went on for hours. Again and again, they asked her the date of her birthday, as though there were something dark and fatal about that day. Incredulous and frightened, she realized that she was suspected of being an important international spy. Gradually the questioning became less intense. The officers began to see her as a harmless crank, a strange woman from the peace conference who believed in female suffrage and galloped about Europe on foolish, fruitless business. The atmosphere changed; her questioners became polite. She was carried by motorcar to Stettin, where her baggage was examined once again. From there she was sent to Basel, exuberant to be safe in Switzerland at last.

Vorse was driven now to report the effect of war on the ordinary people of Europe, and especially on women and children. She deliberately ignored the great diplomatic and military events of the time. Fresh from the peace congress, she concentrated on her understanding of women as both victims and rescuers in wartime. She believed that women instinctively hated war. She had a theory that birth was woman's most intense moment—and that war was man's, that governments in which women held their rightful power would find other means short of war to resolve disputes. She wanted to tell the story of European women to those women in America who would understand and who would listen.

Moving on from Switzerland to Paris, Vorse felt more comfortable. She fancied that the French were less maddened by war than the Germans. She now noticed scenes that comforted her: "It was somehow reassuring to see a very young soldier crying as he took leave of his family who cried, too." But in the hotel foyer, her illusions died. She heard a young French boy talking of how he had killed Germans, crawling at night on his belly to shoot. The old male servants in the hotel listened to the youngster, avidly sharing his blood-drenched adventure.

At a little distance stood two women in black. The women looked at the boy with pity. Vorse felt an instant bond with them. For the women there was no pleasure or thrill in the tale of death. "There is that which makes man his own enemy and even woman's," Vorse wrote in her diary then. "Man takes passionate joy in risking his own life while he takes the lives of others. When women's understanding of this becomes conscious, it is called feminism."

During the next few days she drove around the city through the familiar streets she had known as an art student. There were a million refugees living outside the war areas. Thousands were housed in Paris. At a refugee center, Vorse saw children too small to tell their names. Many had been picked up by the soldiers in the trenches. Nearby, other orphaned children, most of them weeping, were lined up in long rows, on their way to schools.

If the scenes in Paris were terrible, those in the northern countryside of France were worse. The people lived in patched shelters. Graves with new crosses were scattered in the fields and along the roads. Except for bands of wounded soldiers, there were few young men. So topsy-turvy were all values that Vorse found nothing strange in the words of a woman who told her, "Fortunately, my husband is a hunchback [and could not go to war]."

In the spring of 1915, the staging for murder on a grand scale was pervasive. On the western front, the trench system was fixed, a continuous row of parallel excavations running four hundred miles from Switzerland to the English Channel. The front contained a total of twenty-five thousand miles of trenches, enough to circle the earth. You could smell the front lines—the stench of dead horses and dead men—miles before you reached them. Month after month, the sacrificial blood flow continued, as men, like dream walkers, advanced and retreated, dying by the tens of thousands to gain, or lose, a few hundred yards of earth. Sometimes British troops demonstrated the gallant sport of war by kicking a football toward the enemy lines while attacking. Few at home seemed to judge this an obscene act. Casualties rose to incomprehensible levels: in France, from 850,000 in 1914, to over 2,500,000 in 1915; in England, an average of 150,000 a month during 1915; in Germany, over 100,000 in a single battle of 1914. And the butchery of 1916 would be worse. Before the national savagery called the Great War had run its four-year course, over 9,000,000 combatants were dead.

Near the destroyed village of Sermaize-les-Bains, Vorse spent the night in an improvised bed atop a billiard table. Far off she could hear the guns near Verdun. She talked with a schoolmistress who was teaching eighty children and acting as mayor of the village. The woman pointed to an immense pile of unanswered correspondence. Two thousand French soldiers had died in the battlefield across the road. The teacher was attempting to answer the inquiries from their families.

Vorse walked through the heaps of rubble where the village had once stood. She mulled over the cataclysm produced by men, contrasting the work of the schoolteacher with that for which the males of Europe had been preparing. "Never had I a story with so many conflicting threads and it is going to hurt so to write," she told O'Brien in her letter home. The sum of Vorse's experience in the past weeks overwhelmed her ability to absorb it all. She had visited barracks where wounded families lived, met women searching for children, parents, and husbands, seen hundreds of lost infants whose mothers would never find them. She was bone tired and desperately lonely. "But there was more in this awful homesickness than a desire to be at home with Joe and the children," she wrote. "It was a longing like thirst to be back in a world that no longer existed, a world in which there could be no war."

When she returned to Paris, Vorse went to see Madame Etienne, her former concierge. Vorse asked her about her three sons. The concierge told her in a hard and steady voice: "They are all dead, all! All three died within six weeks. Since then I have read no papers. There is no victory for me. There can be no victory for those whose sons are dead." From the street outside the door came the sound of singing. They watched silently as cabs, draped with Italian flags, and filled with singing soldiers, clattered by. Mme Etienne stretched out her arm and cried, "So long as men love war like that, there will be war, and when they hate it as we hate it, there will be no more war!" It seemed to Vorse that the old woman had spoken a profound piece of wisdom.

Twenty years later, thinking of that moment, Vorse wrote:

> I do not believe these things any more. When the drums beat most women go to war with their men—and upper and middle class women who do war work get from war man's excitement minus the danger. While I have been writing this, there has been a parade of sailors, and marines past the house. The most martial and warlike part, by far, was the local women's auxiliary with their scarlet capes and their banging drums.

And yet, and yet—"I recall that peace conference where for the first time middle-class women of warring nations defied public opinion, and wonder what would happen if there were a peace movement as resolute and fanatical as that for suffrage."[22]

When Vorse returned home after six weeks abroad, O'Brien met her at the boat and they went at once to Provincetown. When she saw the long little town, untouched by war, she burst into tears. She found that something strange had happened to her. She felt isolated from everyone except O'Brien, unable to communicate what she had seen: "An explosion more far-reaching than that of Lawrence. A reevaluation of all life." It was the difference "between knowing academically that war exists and the emotional realization of it, as different as knowing that death exists and seeing one's own dead before one." Her little clan at Provincetown was oblivious to the war that Vorse was sure would soon engulf them. Not only was she emotionally estranged from her old friends, she could not sell any of the articles she had written on her trip through the war zones. In the summer of 1915 editors did not want to buy such disagreeable stories.

She was relieved to see that O'Brien seemed fully recovered. Drinking, writing, perspiring profusely, arguing and shouting about the war, the IWW, and all matters of social justice, he worked like a carpenter, building four bedrooms on to the house. O'Brien's last summer was a good one.

Mabel Dodge was again in Provincetown. Having lost John Reed as a lover, Dodge had given up the pursuit of social causes and returned to aesthetic preoccupation. Her new salon on the Cape featured her most recent lover, the painter Maurice Sterne. Dodge, who had never liked Vorse, pushed to assume the central position in the Provincetown circle. Hapgood became concerned that "Mary, in Mabel's eyes, occupied the position of an enemy, and I saw that Mary's friends were becoming alienated from her without knowing just why. Mary was a special outcast and she was becoming quite a witch in the eyes of Mabel's group. Mary, of course, was not permanently injured, largely because her vitality is such that she cannot be destroyed, except through the cumulative power of extended living; but it looked as if she might have been unreasonably separated for a time from her own group."[23]

But Mary wanted only to be left alone with Joe. "I am cut off as by a high wall," she wrote, "from wants and needs . . . and in the silence which I strive to make around me break children and friends with desires, complaints and turmoil." She shrank from the people around her "who had theories about keeping out of war and who wanted their lives to go on undisturbed."

In one of her better short stories of that season, Mary Vorse expressed her new distaste for artistic aesthetes: "They went so fast and they made so much noise as they went that they had no chance to meet life. Their lives were stale and flat, and they masked this staleness from themselves by their restlessness. . . . Life and more life they wanted, things moving faster and faster. It was as if they had tacitly agreed that there must be no empty moment in their lives and no instance of silence—especially no silence." She and her friends had always amused one another before; they had a "certain harmony and mutual forbearance." But now "there was in the atmosphere something uncomfortable, as though there were depths within them which some unseen thing had disturbed."[24]

The intangible barrier between Vorse and the original Provincetown group reflected the crisis of American progressivism itself. The declaration of war in Europe changed everything. It fractured the prewar alliance among the three groups of rebels represented in Provincetown. One element, the older reformists like Boyce and Hapgood, Glaspell and Cook, felt accused of only playing at social protest, of falling back to defend what they perceived as the vital middle ground. These middle-aged Provincetowners were losing the allegiance of the second group, the younger revolutionaries and anarchists symbolized by John Reed. The third subgroup, the art-for-art's sakers centered around Mabel Dodge, was denounced as frivolous by the romantic reformers and the party of youth alike. In the throes of demoralization and division created by war, and by the coming revolution in Russia, all would choose their different paths—some to cooperation with the Wilson administration, others to artistic retreat. A few would find their way to revolutionary commitment.

In quick anticipation of a mood that would become general, Vorse sensed the coming split, and wavered uncertainly outside the confines of every faction, isolated and alienated from the whole. She fell back temporarily on the comfort of family life with O'Brien. She rejoiced anew in his grasp on reality.

Suspicion and bitterness tainted the old group of Provincetown intimates in the summer of 1915. Paradoxically, it was then that they found a way to hold their fragmenting pieces together. From the midst of what Hapgood called "the poison of Provincetown" there emerged that extraordinary creation—the little theater that would become the Provincetown Players.

It began one evening when Vorse and O'Brien, Boyce and Hapgood, Glaspell and Cook, and Wilbur Daniel Steele and his new bride were sitting around a driftwood fire on the beach. Cook was vehemently blasting the commercial, bourgeois theater. Even the new little theater in the Village had refused to risk the production of *Suppressed Desires*, a play he and Glaspell had written that satirized the Freudian gospel. Boyce mentioned that she had written a play called *Constancy* that spoofed the love affair of John Reed and Mabel Dodge. Boyce and the others had been mightily amused the year before at the thought of Dodge and Reed creeping away each night for lovemaking in Dodge's silken tent pitched on the beach. The group around the fire giggled at the memory of this sunset rendezvous. They suddenly decided: Why not put on these plays themselves, for fun?[25]

The Provincetown Players were born in the Hapgood house on Commercial Street, on July 15, 1915, at 10 PM. They used the veranda with the ocean front as backdrop for the first play. The audience then reversed its seats and turned toward the opposite side of the room for the second play, seen through a broad open door.

A few days later, in response to the demand from Provincetown visitors, they decided to present the plays again. Cook convinced Vorse to donate her wharf with its unused fishhouse for the theater. The group assessed each person five dollars for alterations. Boats, nets, and oars were cleared from the wharf. In her trunk Vorse found a stage curtain she had used as a child for theater productions in Amherst. The audience brought chairs from home, while lamps were held as illumination. "I sat in the audience on the hard bench, watching the performance, hardly believing what we had done." Vorse wrote:

The theater was full of enthusiastic people—a creative audience. In spite of its raining in torrents, everyone had come down the dark wharf lighted here and there by a lantern. People had leaned their umbrellas against one of the big timbers which supported the roof. I noticed an umbrella stirred, then slowly slid down an enormous knothole to the sand thirty feet below. With the stealth of eels, other umbrellas went down the knothole to join their fellows under the wharf. The dark interior, the laughing audience, the little stage with its spirited performances, and the absconding umbrellas are all part of the memory of the first night of the Provincetown Players.[26]

Amateurs all, they acted the plays themselves and found it marvelous fun. A second bill was also produced. It included Wilbur Daniel Steele's *Contemporaries*, a drama of the Tannenbaum-led unemployment protest, and Cook's *Change Your Style*, a light satire on academic versus modern art. "No group ever had less sense of having a mission than did the Provincetown Players," Vorse said. Their success was an explosion that "comes only in times when a creative breath is blowing through all society." Except for Jig Cook's drive and passion, the Provincetown Players might have ended there, without them knowing who they were. But this rebirth was to occur the next summer.

O'Brien acted in the first play. He helped clear out the wharf fishhouse for the second bill. Then the illness came to him again.

Boyce accompanied Vorse to New York where Joe O'Brien was taken to the hospital. Vorse stayed with Frances Perkins. In late October, Boyce wrote Hapgood, "Joe died this morning. Mary is very quiet and calm, but exhausted. . . . He was with only a nurse at the end although Mary was lying down in the next room. No one expected the end so suddenly."[27]

For the *Masses*, Susan Glaspell wrote a eulogy:

Joe

It's strange without you, I do not like it.
I want to see you coming down the street in the gay woolly
    stockings and that bright-green sweater.
I want you to open the door of my house and brightly call
    "Hello!" We used to rage about the way you kept us waiting—
Honest now, were you ever on time anywhere?
But I'd wait—oh, I can't say how long I wouldn't wait if there was
    any chance of your finally swinging along and charming away
    my exasperation.

That was a mean advantage—
Letting us wait and then spoiling our grievance with a smile.
I want to sit over a drink with you and talk about the IWW and
    the dammed magazines and the Germans; I want to argue with
    you about building bookshelves and planting bulbs.
I want awfully to tell you about a joke I heard yesterday.
And now that you are gone, I want intensely to find you.
What were you, Joe? I don't think any of us really know.
Many are talking about your gaiety; none of them loved it more
    than I did.
But I want to know about those reservations; I want to know the
    you that brooded and lived alone.
You saw things straight; nobody put it over very hard on you.
The thing in you that thought was like a knife blade,
Muddling and messing made you sick.
Your scorn put the crimp in a lot of twaddle that goes on among
    our kind of folks—
How I'd love to hear you cuss some of them out again!
Graceful levity—fiery dissatisfactions.
Debonair and passionate.
Much I do not know and never shall, but this I know:
I feel the sway of beauty when I think of you.
A fresh breeze; a shining point;
Pure warmth; pure hardness.
Much given and something withheld;
A jest—a caress—an outrageous little song. A gift. A halt in
    speech—a keen grave look of understanding.
Undependable and yet deeply there.
Vivid and unforgettable.
Is that at all you? Would you laugh if you saw this?
Well, laugh, but I say again,
Unforgettable.
Strong, clear violet; the flash of steel;
The life of the party—a tree way off by itself.
Oh, What's the use? I can't.
I only know my throat's all tight with the longing to have you
    open the door of my house and brightly call "Hello!" [28]

For the second time in five years, Vorse was a widowed mother. Grief immobilized her for weeks. She did not stir from bed. As was still the custom of that day, a kindly physician eased her hurt with morphine. "We all see Mary constantly," Hapgood wrote Boyce. "She seems very weak and very soft and lovely. Under veronal and morphine all the time."[29]

Vorse would remember the grace of that dark paradise.

Part Three: 1916-1919

Since the war, even the men at home had turned to me the faces of strangers. They thought negligible what women thought important. The things we asked of one another as we talked about the war held no interest for them. The sense of men's strangeness has bred a fear in me. . . . [Women's] deepest experience is giving life and [men's] intensest moment is when they are called on by war to go out and destroy the lives for which we have risked our own.

—MHV, 1917

Chapter Seven

Down the Road Again

Throughout the winter of 1916, Vorse hardly left her house. All three children had whooping cough. Little Joel was seriously ill with pneumonia. She had an entire household to support. Again she was unable to write. She tried to create humorous stories of children and marriage. None of them sold. Her savings dwindled as rapidly as the rejections accumulated.

Once, after a long day at her desk, attempting to revise a story, Vorse stumbled downstairs, sank into a chair, and idly picked up a pair of socks to darn. The children's nurse smiled brightly, "Oh, that's *good*, Mrs. Vorse," she said. "Don't you feel better now that you have done some *real* work?" [1]

Vorse's only break from worry over family and finances was work with the suffrage movement. After ten months of campaign efforts by thousands of New York suffragists, the voters had refused, in November 1915, to support a state suffrage amendment. The women reorganized two days after the election at a mass meeting in Cooper Union where $100,000 was pledged toward the 1916 campaign. Vorse persuaded Vira Whitehouse, the chair of the suffrage Press and Publicity Council, that the council should disseminate materials that would engage the emotions of its readers. The publicity women planned a novel, published by Henry Holt in 1917, in which the heroine battled for suffrage against the wishes of her politician husband. The book was a collective production of fourteen authors, among them Vorse, Fannie Hurst, Dorothy Canfield, Kathleen Norris, William Allen White, and Mary Austin. All royalty fees were donated to the suffrage campaign. [2]

In late 1915, at a meeting of the suffrage publicity committee at Vorse's New York apartment, word came that Margaret Sanger was to be tried for distributing material on birth control. If found guilty under the Comstock Law, which banned birth control information as "lewd, lascivious, filthy and indecent," Sanger could be given a sentence of forty-five years. To escape this fate, Sanger had fled to Europe in 1914 before her trial. Now she was back, determined to face the charges and to bring her case enough publicity to inspire others to take up the cause. "The issue," Sanger said, "is to raise . . . birth control out of the gutter of obscenity and into the light of human understanding."

Vorse asked those at the meeting who were interested in working on Sanger's behalf to stay and discuss what could be done. A core of women, including Heterodites Alice Duer Miller and Anne O'Hagan Shinn, formed the "women's emergency committee" to elicit support for Sanger from well-known persons with political and financial power. For her part, Vorse won a promise of help from Amos Pinchot, Paul Wilson, Frances Perkins, and Lincoln Steffens. From this beginning arose the Committee of One Hundred, a group of reformers and feminists whose aid to Sanger was crucial in obtaining support from the media at home and abroad. The successful publicity drive that Vorse and the others initiated led New York State to drop the indictment against Sanger in February 1916.[3]

It was late in the spring before little Joel was well enough for the family to leave New York and return to Provincetown for the summer. The fishing village was crowded that season, for the war brought to the Cape the writers, artists, and sculptors who otherwise would have preferred to be in Europe. Mabel Dodge was there, and John Reed, accompanied by his new love, Louise Bryant. Floyd Dell, Ida Rauh, Max Eastman, and the poet Harry Kemp also arrived early. "It was a great summer," according to Susan Glaspell. "We swam from the wharf as well as rehearsed there; we would lie on the beach and talk about plays—everyone writing, or acting, or producing. Life was all of a piece, work not separated from play, and we did together what none of us could have done alone."[4]

After the dismal winter in New York, Vorse returned to open her house filled with memories. Joe O'Brien's presence lingered everywhere—a few clothes, his books, the carefully constructed rooms and stairs and garden plots. She felt resentful and lonely. "I had an intense reaction of willfulness," she wrote. "I did not care what I did and I wanted to believe that what I did was harmless." She began to drink more than ever and to spend a great deal of time reveling with the younger Village crowd and the camp followers of art that flocked to Provincetown that summer.

She indulged in a round of music, dance, and talk, all suffused through the dulling haze of too much alcohol and too little sleep. Such diversion also helped to avoid the knowledge that she was not writing and that her bank account was dangerously low. She took lovers, often, and with little thought. After O'Brien's death, "I was only ten months without a man," she remembered.[5]

In June, Vorse joined Neith Boyce and Susan Glaspell and the others to plan the new season of plays. John Reed matched Jig Cook in his ardor to bring about renaissance of the theater. Together they pulled the Cape colony along with them to prepare the playhouse on Vorse's wharf. As the opening of the second bill of the Wharf Theater drew near, the group began to worry that it had no more plays to offer. Glaspell met the old anarchist Terry Carlin on Commercial Street and asked him if he had any plays to read them. He had none, but remarked that a morose young man who had just arrived from New York had a whole trunk full of plays. The name of Carlin's roommate was, of course, Eugene O'Neill, and the rest is theater history. At nine that evening, O'Neill showed up on Glaspell's front porch with the script of *Bound East for Cardiff*. Those listening to the reading sat transfixed. Vorse recalled: "No one of us who heard that play reading will ever forget it, nor the reading of *Trifles* by Susan Glaspell, which took place at my house. Listening to the plays and giving them the instant recognition they deserved was a company of young people whom destiny had touched."[6] When that first reading of *Bound East* was over, Jig Cook sprang to his feet. "Now we know what we are for!" he roared. *Bound East* went at once into rehearsal. Carlin and O'Neill moved from Truro to Provincetown, opposite Reed's cottage, to be near the center of excitement. On July 1, Hapgood wrote to Mabel Dodge: "The play fever is on. Jig and Susan, Neith and Mary [Heaton Vorse] O'Brien, Reed, [Frederick] Burt, and O'Neill are the enthusiastic inner circle."[7]

In early July, a somber letter from IWW leader Bill Haywood curtailed Vorse's Provincetown romp. Would she come at once, he asked, to report the Mesabi Range strike then occurring in Minnesota? Haywood had learned at Lawrence how essential publicity of strike conditions could be to the success of workers, especially for the raising of strike funds.

But it was not until Vorse received a letter from Elizabeth Gurley Flynn, written just a week before the first *Bound East* performance, that she decided to leave the children for the first time since O'Brien's death and to travel to the range. Flynn wrote:

So far we seem to have failed to get any worth-while publicity. Carlo [Tresca], Joe Schmidt and nine others, are in jail here in Duluth since July 3rd, charged with first degree murder. It is terribly serious. . . . Mary dear, there never was a time when we needed our writer friends to get busy, more than right now, if . . . our best men are to be saved from the penitentiary. . . . Carlo and the boys . . . are charged with murder, on the theory that their speeches incited to violence. It is like the Ettor-Giovannitti case [at Lawrence] except that in this state, accessories are . . . liable to life imprisonment. . . . Of course relief is becoming a pressing problem, and we hope the East will realize this and help financially.[8]

The letter was made more poignant by Vorse's knowledge that Flynn was in love with Carlo Tresca. Flynn and Tresca had been special friends of O'Brien's. They had visited Vorse and O'Brien on the Cape and had sent worried inquiries about O'Brien's health during his illness. It was Vorse's concern for her friends that drove her to the Mesabi as much as any desire to resume the role of an active reporter. She also sensed that days of casual sex, steady play, and too much drinking were corroding her life, as well as her work. Later, when addiction became a serious problem for her, she remembered that the trip to the Mesabi provided a temporary rescue from the corrosive palliatives of drink and drugs.[9]

Leaving the children in the care of their grandmother Vorse, she left Provincetown in early August. En route to Minnesota via New York, she received assignments from the *Outlook, Harper's Magazine,* the New York *Globe,* and the *Masses.* Marion Cothren, the Heterodite who had accompanied Vorse to The Hague in 1915 and who was now a reporter for *Survey,* went with her. On the way to the Mesabi, Vorse as usual carefully prepared her background research on the conditions of labor on the range.

Until 1890 the Mesabi Range, a fifty-mile strip of low hills lying some seventy miles northwest of Duluth, was an unsettled area of swamps and forests. In that year, the Merritt brothers discovered that underneath the thin layer of clay and sand lay miles of red earth composed of 60 percent soft iron ore. The Mesabi was soon a bustling frontier. By 1902, most of the mines on the range were owned by the country's first billion-dollar company, the mighty U.S. Steel Corporation. Hopeful European immigrants came to the dusty red land of the Mesabi, enticed there by company propaganda promising them high wages and an easy life. The range held a conglomerate of peoples consistent with the most cosmopolitan cities in the nation. There were thirty-five identifiable large minorities on the range, with scattered numbers of ten other nationalities.

A spontaneous outburst of fury over lowered wages brought the walkout at St. James Mine in Aurora, Minnesota, on June 3, 1916. Four hundred men, with no labor organization to back them, voted to strike. A procession of miners, accompanied by their wives rolling baby carriages, walked the seventy-five miles of mountain roads along the range, urging others to join them. By the end of June, two-thirds of the range miners—ten thousand out of fifteen thousand men—were out. The Mesabi strike then spread to the Vermillion Range to the south, bringing out thousands more.[10]

A procession of several thousand strikers and their families was now in movement over the range. Private guards employed by the mine owners broke up a parade in Hibbing and assaulted the marchers. On June 22 at Virginia, when the guards' attack was resisted, shooting began, and a Croatian miner was killed. No arrest was made for the murder. The funeral parade, four days later, was three thousand strong. At the grave, Carlo Tresca led the mourners in the taking of an oath to retaliate "an eye for an eye" if there were further attacks on the strikers. When Governor John A. Burnquist heard this, he instructed the local sheriff to go the limit in controlling the "riot."

The mine owners hired over two thousand private police, generally thugs collected from the streets of Duluth and St. Paul, to patrol the streets of the range towns. Since war conditions restricted immigration, the employers found it difficult to import large numbers of strikebreakers. Instead, the steel companies' private army prevented picketing, harassed strikers, and arrested workers on trumped-up charges. Often drunk and brutally aggressive, the private guards "established a veritable reign of terror," the historian Melvyn Dubofsky noted.[11]

The miners called on the IWW for help. The Wobblies sent the largest number of their top talent ever assigned to one strike. A central strike committee was organized into language groups on the model of Lawrence, and a financial and publicity organization was established.

In early July the mine owners' gunmen grew bolder. They entered the home of a striker on the pretense of investigating an illegal still. In the general melee that followed, a deputy mine guard was killed, as was an unlucky bystander on the street outside the miner's house. All the miners in the house were arrested, along with a miner's wife who carried her seven-month-old baby to jail with her. That night, miles away in the town of Virginia, the chief IWW organizers, including Carlo Tresca, were arrested and sent to Duluth, charged with murder as "accessories." To deplete local strike leadership further, federal officials began deportation proceedings on the range.

The miners replaced their jailed leaders with new men, but these too were swiftly arrested and shipped to Duluth, usually on charges of violating local ordinances against holding parades or demonstrations. Homes of strikers were entered without warrants; the occupants were hurried to jail and given sentences for picketing. Attorneys scurried from one range town to another in an attempt to free the jailed miners. Within a few weeks some of the IWW leaders were released, but leadership had been weakened at a critical time.

Giving up the fight as hopeless, many strikers left to find work in the harvest fields. For a few weeks, their wives and children took over the job of picketing. At first the deputies held back from attacking the families of the miners. By early August they were beating women and children to the ground. The Duluth *Tribune* accused the strikers' wives of risking their children's lives by taking them onto a picket line.

It was at this juncture that Vorse and Marion Cothren arrived in Duluth. Vorse, at age forty-two, had never before ventured into the center of her own land. This was not uncommon at the time for those of Vorse's class and New England background, whose attention tended to center on the cultural and intellectual life of Europe and New York City. Vorse was stunned by the vast provisions of coal, lumber, grain, and ore that lay near Lake Superior. A city child of the Northeast, she was accustomed to thinking of coal and ore in buckets, while here it lay piled by the acre, sprawling past unobstructed horizons.

Elizabeth Gurley Flynn met Vorse's train in Virginia. Flynn had been on the range several weeks, sleeping in crowded workers' homes and boarding houses. As the dreaded outside agitator, "the most feared woman in the whole of the corporation world," according to the Duluth *Labor World*, Flynn was not welcome at local hotels. Vorse sneaked Flynn into her hotel room, where for a while she could have quiet, space, and regular baths. The two enjoyed an interlude of excited chatter as they shared news of old friends and the details of their lives since last they met in New York.[12]

The next day, Vorse interviewed members of the strike committee. They told her of complaints from distant mining locations that strikers were refused water from wells situated on company ground. Vorse learned that workers' houses were ransacked, without warrants, by gunmen and company guards. To verify the story, Vorse drove in a bumpy Ford, accompanied by a young IWW member, to a mining location thirty miles from Virginia.

She interviewed a burly Slavic woman who was chopping wood, her legs thrown far apart, behind a row of workers' houses. This woman had scratched and kicked a company guard who had attempted to prevent her from drawing water from the well located on company property. As a result of the scuffle, the woman had suffered a miscarriage. "No cloud without a silver lining," the woman said cheerfully to Vorse as she returned to her chopping. The pleasant little circle of intellectuals and artists at Provincetown seemed distant indeed, as Vorse contemplated this world of the Mesabi in which miscarriages were perceived as blessings and people could be denied the water they drank by the hired hoodlums of their employers.

The miners Vorse spoke to had been demoralized. The constant terror, the cutoff of local credit, the attacks by local media, the outside world's lack of interest in their fight, the arrest of their leaders, the depletion of the strike fund—all fostered a sense of defeat. There were too few Wobbly organizers on the range to preserve hope among the widely dispersed strikers. Flynn had for a while raced from one end of the range to another in an old bakery truck, until the deputies began to recognize it and take potshots at it.

One small hope remained, Flynn told Vorse. Word had come from the nearby iron mines in Michigan that a sympathy strike might begin. Frank Little, a star IWW organizer who was to be lynched by a Montana mob in 1917, had been arrested in Michigan and then expelled from the state. Several other IWW members in Michigan had been beaten. Bill Haywood wrote Flynn that it would be best if she and Vorse tried to talk to the miners there, as the authorities might be hesitant to beat or arrest women, especially since Vorse represented several important newspapers and magazines. Vorse agreed to go. She still felt secure in her position as a noted author with influential friends among the intellectuals in the Northeast.

Flynn and Vorse first visited Carlo Tresca in jail in Duluth, where he was held for five and one-half months without bail. As Vorse and Flynn entered the Duluth train station en route to Michigan, they realized they were being followed by men who they assumed were detectives. Following the directions of Flynn, an old hand at shaking police, Vorse boarded her train, walked through and got off at the other end. They then took another train into the station nearest their destination, arriving at four in the morning. At the meeting of miners in Michigan they discovered that there had been no plans for a sympathy strike. Flynn presented a rousing appeal for funds. That evening they stayed with some young anarchist Italian miners who frightened Vorse by their bellicose description of how they would shoot any detective who dared to follow their women guests. Flynn was accustomed to being threatened by police; an IWW member since 1907, she had been behind bars five times. She was amused at Vorse's relief when they boarded the train to Minneapolis without incident. They were scheduled to speak in St. Paul to a middle-class women's club on the condition of women and children on the range. As a result of their appearance, Flynn secured the help of a prominent club member in releasing on nominal bail the worker's wife who had been arrested in the fracas that had led to the jailing of Carlo Tresca.

By early September Vorse realized the strike was lost. The workers did win, at enormous cost, some minor improvements in working conditions. Repression of the strike was expensive for the mine owners. With war orders rolling in and the source of cheap immigrant labor cut off by the war, the employers granted concessions. They announced a small wage increase and a minor reform of the contract system. Most of the arrested workers and organizers were released in the fall.

The publicity given to the strike by Vorse and a few others brought in a small amount of funds and helped to hasten the conclusion of a state report, which made clear that the mine guards hired by the companies were chiefly to blame for the violence. This report caused a brief protest against the tactics of the Oliver Mining Company in the state press. Even so, the open shop was maintained by the employers, and the Mesabi miners remained unorganized until the CIO drive of the 1930s.

During the weeks Vorse spent on the range, several new experiences shaped her future involvement with the labor movement. She had for the first time been an actual participant in a strike, speaking to workers from a platform, serving as a sort of co-leader with Flynn. As an identified strike leader, Vorse experienced local hostility first hand. She had not before personally faced the scowls of hotel clerks and the threats and curses of armed men. At Lawrence and in New York she had seen policemen attacking men and women. She had read how bands of brigands with guns terrorized strikers and their families in remote locations like the Mesabi Range, but she had never before witnessed it. Vorse also had a new understanding of the idealistic stamina of the organizers. Unlike herself, they would not return to respectability after a few days or a few weeks in the field.

Mesabi strengthened Vorse's interest in the lives of working-class women and their children. It was the women, not the men of the range, who most piqued her curiosity. Although Vorse still felt ill at ease in a worker's home, she sensed a rapport with the wives of the miners. Their common female interests helped to close the gap that lay between her life and that of the immigrant poor. Vorse's sensitivity as a reporter was to the story that lay behind the white curtains at the shanty windows, the boiling pot of garden beans on the rusty wood stove, the mended clothes of the children. That women could remain intent on producing beauty and comfort for their families in the bleak ugliness of a mining settlement seemed to Vorse a remarkable triumph of humanity. On the Mesabi, so far removed from Amherst dining rooms and European liners, she met women whose courage and will to overcome seemed far greater than those of anyone she had ever known.

Even after her time on the Mesabi, Vorse continued to rely on an appeal to decent citizens in all parts of the country who she believed would be as outraged as herself if they only knew the real conditions of the workers or the tactics by which mine owners broke unions. Vorse no longer sought these good citizens among the economic elite of a strike area; Lawrence had taught her the futility of that pursuit. Yet she believed that in every locale there were middle-class Americans who "exemplified the whole American spirit." She remembered the farmer in Lawrence who came to read workers their rights. She admired the three mayors on the Mesabi who urged the federal mediators to come to the range. In 1916, Vorse held that all that was necessary to increase the ranks of these progressive few was to somehow break through the lies of the press and increase public knowledge of what was actually occurring in places like the Mesabi. The more difficult question—why the major media, the courts, the local and state governments, and most of the local clergymen and merchants, so generally and consistently hampered any effort to advertise the truth—was one that Vorse did not choose to analyze in 1916.

In her article about the Mesabi strike, published in the *Outlook* in August, Vorse denied that media distortion and news blackout of the range strike were due to any systematic suspension of the facts. Rather, Vorse wrote, the failure of the public to understand the Mesabi strike was "due to the lack of communication between the worker and that thinking part of the community which forms the public opinion and which asks that labor shall receive its fair hearing in the courts and in the press." Perhaps she wrote this tortured piece of logic as a clever stratagem that allowed her article to be published in the *Outlook*. Maybe the article was written to soften the public temper. Most likely, though, she wrote it because she still believed it was true.

The difficulty of placing the facts before the public must have been apparent to her, for the *Outlook* published her article alongside a refutation of her words written by Tyler Dennett. Dennett, who had left the ministry for a writing career, presented the "employer's point of view" to *Outlook* readers. His contempt for the sentimental idea of egalitarianism would later be manifested in his fierce opposition to the New Deal when he was president of Williams College. Perhaps the editors of the *Outlook* sought to be objective by printing two sides of the story. But the printed result was hardly educational. Dennett's sketch was a mix of company-supplied falsifications and embellished statistics. The average reader must have concluded that Vorse's carefully researched report of the Mesabi strike was open to question.[13]

Once again direct experience demonstrated to Vorse how effectively the power of wealth could block the workers' fight for a union. If she still persisted in an optimistic view of the force of "decent" people's opinions, Vorse did bring another new idea home from the Mesabi. She would never again doubt that working men and women, in order to win their rights, should forcefully resist the violence directed against them, whenever it became necessary. Vorse had also learned a new physical courage. Twenty years later, that trait would bring her a head wound as she scrambled to escape a barrage of bullets from company guards.

A few weeks after her return from the Mesabi Range, Vorse moved to Bronxville, New York. She wanted Joel to have a yard of his own and country air after his long illness. Her son Heaton, now sixteen, was sent away from home for the first time. She sent him to the boarding school in Morristown, New Jersey, that John Reed had attended. That winter Vorse hired Miss Selway, a grimly proper English nanny, to care for the younger children while she attempted to write the light fiction that had heretofore supported her family. After months of no sales, she was near panic. An inheritance of $600 from her father's sister had carried her through the previous year. Now she was down to her last slim resources. Illness again plagued the house. Joel and Ellen were ill with croup. Heaton came down with pneumonia. Vorse had to spend time with him in Morristown while he was hospitalized. She brought him home to Bronxville and nursed him there.

Through all the strain, Vorse struggled to write, with increasing despondence. For the first sustained period in her life, she could not sell her fiction. Rejection after rejection came in the mail. She began stories, then stopped, doubting their worth. Unable to finish one, she slogged on to another, devising a new plot. All her small savings were gone, with the heavy expenses of the children's nurse, medical care, and the Morristown school. Suddenly one day she dashed out a light fantasy on the Bohemians of the Village. It sold for a good price. The sale restored her self-confidence.[14]

But she could not forget that time of descent. Forty-three years old, with no formal training of any kind, she had a large family to support entirely through her own efforts. Vorse was convulsed as never before by her desire to escape daily responsibilities of child care and household, in order to write. Her need to retreat into isolation, and the difficulty of doing so with a house full of noisy children, coupled with her guilt at denying them close guidance and attention from the only parent they had, drove her into a state of emotional and physical exhaustion. As a single mother, Vorse was forced into the debilitating task of being prime nurturer, as well as sole breadwinner, for her three children. Several years later, Vorse recalled in tortured self-blame that during this period of her life she had sometimes walked the streets at night to delay her return home until the children had been put to sleep by their nurse. It was now that her guilt-laden quest to write and think in lone peace began to assume the proportions of an obsession.

It became more apparent that winter that the United States would soon enter the war. Vorse had suspected that America would be drawn in ever since her trip to Europe in 1915. But she had been so overwhelmed by O'Brien's death, family concerns, anxiety over finances, and the pressure of writing that the actual entry into war came as a jolt that abruptly curtailed her preoccupation with her private life.

It was her towering need for income, rather than patriotic support for Wilson's war administration, that caused her to accept, with gratitude, a job given to her by her friend Will Irwin. As chief of the foreign department of the federal government's Committee on Public Information (CPI), America's propaganda ministry during the war, Irwin hired her to write three pamphlets on the rights of small nations in eastern Europe.[15]

During the almost two years of war, Vorse commuted between Bronxville and her apartment in Washington, D.C. Along with her work for the CPI, she also sold a few of her income-producing lollypops to the women's magazines, as well as labor articles and reports of the activities of the War Labor Board. With Heaton in Morristown, and the younger children with Miss Selway in New York, she rejoiced in her escape from daily child care. She discovered she could work much better away from home. In Washington, her spirits soared, as did her sex life.[16]

The war years saw the acceleration of some long-sought reforms in public housing, public health, and workmen's compensation. Eight more states gave women the vote, at least on some issues, and the House of Representatives passed the suffrage amendment during the war. For the first time American trade unions were recognized by the federal government as a legitimate force in the social structure. In return for a no-strike pledge from the AFL, the government during the war agreed to support the principles of collective bargaining, equal pay for equal work for women, the eight-hour day whenever possible, and the right of all workers to a living wage. This was the greatest advance that unionism had made so far. Thus, to many left liberals, the coming of war seemed to forecast a new economic and political order.[17]

Vorse's much discussed article on wartime conditions in Bridgeport, Connecticut, published in *Harper's* in early 1919, reflected this hopeful illusion. She described "two Bridgeports," one a poor and squalid city shaped by "the old feudal system of industry," the other the new Bridgeport vitalized by the federal action of the War Labor Board, the Recreation Commission, and the Housing Commission. "The world is ever more and more clearly dividing itself between those who have the ideals of autocracy and privilege and those who have the ideals of democracy; between those who place the emphasis on a civilization run for profit and those who place it on a civilization run for people," she wrote. It was in places like Bridgeport, Vorse predicted, "that the complacencies of the old order are going to be ground into dust."[18]

Acting on this hope in March 1918, she submitted a plan to Arthur Bullard, presumably seeing him as a conduit to George Creel, chief of the Committee on Public Information. Vorse's idea, one she had "thought out in detail," was to use the existing propaganda channels of the CPI to teach the American people "contemporary industrial history." She argued that the federal government was then in the hands of liberals—"men who perceive the coming change and who hate the wastefulness of the old ways of conducting life." Yet the public remained uneducated, unaware of the inequalities between labor and capital, prey to the lies of reactionary employers. By contrast, Vorse wrote Bullard, the liberals in Washington realized that the war could not be won without industrial peace, and that industrial peace could not be achieved without industrial justice. Vorse then believed government officials had only to publicize the facts.

The facts would speak for themselves. An informed public opinion would ensure the creation of an economic democracy. It was all so simple.

The solution was indeed relatively simple for reformers who analyzed the operation of the American economy from a classless perspective. In early 1918, Vorse thought in terms of privileged and nonprivileged categories, not in the stark orderings of European Marxism. She then held, with A Clubber Walter Weyl, that "progress will come from the efforts, not of a single class, but of the general community."[19] The aftermath of war would teach her wrenching lessons.

Events were to forge for Vorse a new political consciousness. During the war, it became more and more apparent to her that the American government, in response to widespread public dissent, was using the cloak of patriotism in an effort to extinguish the organized left in the United States.

The popular myth still persists that domestic opposition to the First World War was negligible after Congress, with fifty-six dissenting votes, declared war in April 1917. Yet the radical movement in the United States, as represented by the IWW and the Socialist Party, gained strength upon the declaration of war. The IWW added thirty thousand members in the five months after the United States entered the conflict. When the Socialists called for resistance to conscription and to war-fund efforts, the socialist vote rose significantly in the municipal elections of 1917. In addition, opposition to the draft was widespread, strong, and consistent among American peace groups and segments of the urban population. George Creel of the CPI summed up the problem of the war leadership when he described domestic hostility to war as a "very active irritation that borders on disloyalty."

Two months after the United States entered the war, the Espionage Act became law. It levied a maximum penalty of ten thousand dollars and imprisonment for twenty years on anyone who interfered with the operation of the military or opposed the draft. Needing broader legislation to silence opposition and to curb radical labor, the war government passed the Sedition Act in 1918. This bill, vaguely worded, even prohibited disloyal language. It was clear that left protest of nearly every kind was now to be punished.

Draft resistance and antiwar protest were suppressed by private groups and government at all levels. Hundreds of Americans were given jail sentences for the exercise of free speech. Walter Heynacher's case was typical. Heynacher argued with a young friend in South Dakota about enlistment and expressed his opinion that "the war was for the big boys in Wall

Street." For this, he was sentenced to five years in prison. An Oklahoma minister who spoke against the draft act was given a twenty-year sentence. Walter Matthey of Iowa was sentenced to a year for merely attending an anticonscription meeting and applauding the speaker. An Ohio farmer said that the murder of innocent civilians by German soldiers was not worse than what American soldiers had done to the Filipinos; he was sentenced to twenty-one months in prison.

Many socialist and radical newspapers and journals were suspended by order of the Postmaster General's office during 1917. By the end of the war the government's withdrawal of mailing privileges had all but destroyed the radical press in the United States. Forty-five of the seventy-five newspapers repressed were socialist. The Post Office banned one *Masses* issue from the mails and then took away its second-class privileges on the ground that since the magazine had "skipped" a mailing, it was no longer a periodical. Some of the *Masses* editors, including Max Eastman, Floyd Dell, Art Young, and John Reed, were acquitted of conspiracy to obstruct enlistment and recruitment after two trials in 1918. Crystal and Max Eastman's new magazine, the *Liberator*, was more cautious in its challenge to federal power.

From the beginning of U.S. participation in World War I, the IWW became a main target of government officials and business-led vigilantes. Nearly one-half the prosecutions under the Espionage and Sedition acts took place in the thirteen federal judicial districts where the IWW was most active. Deportations, arrests, and even unpunished murders of IWW organizers were common events during the war. In September 1917, the Department of Justice agents raided IWW offices in fifty cities simultaneously, most often without warrants. Papers were illegally seized, furniture and property destroyed. The federal trial and conviction of the IWW's top leadership completed its destruction as a viable labor organization.

While the IWW trials were getting underway, Department of Justice agents arrested IWW defense committee members at many points in the country, destroyed their records, and seized their treasury. The Post Office prohibited the mailing of most defense literature or appeals for defense funds. In August 1918, 101 IWW members were convicted in Chicago and given long sentences. Vorse's friend Bill Haywood was sentenced to twenty years and fined $20,000. At least two of the Chicago defendants were not even affiliated with the Wobblies. Most of the remainder were convicted not for individual acts of lawlessness, but simply because they belonged to the IWW. Another mass trial of IWW leaders took place in Sacramento, California. By the end of the war, the once-feared Wobblies had all but passed into the realm of fable and song, a considerable memorial to the fragility of wartime civil liberties in the United States.[20]

By the fall of 1918, Vorse had seen many of her most admired friends suffer arrest, trial, or jail. Again, direct experience, not abstract theory, determined her political stance. She had read too many press attacks on the IWW and too few denunciations of the employers who sent professional gunmen against union organizers. Shortly before the Armistice, her faith in prewar and prowar liberalism disappeared. It seemed to her now that if one were rich enough, one could break many written laws in the United States with impunity. But "there is an unwritten law that you break at your peril," she wrote later. "It is: Do not attack the profit system. . . . When a new idea assaults the power of established authority, authority always screams out that morality has been affronted. . . . It is because the I. W. W. believed that the workers should control industry that wartime hysteria was used to put the leaders in jail for twenty years."

Such heresy as this quickened the surveillance of Vorse by the Bureau of Investigation, later to become the FBI.[21] The tireless red hunters would monitor Vorse's activities for at least another thirty-six years.

During 1918, Vorse was three times telegraphed by the Red Cross to do publicity work in Europe. *McCall's* and *Harper's* also gave her overseas assignments. She decided to leave the two younger children with Miss Selway for three months. She welcomed the chance to report the war in Europe and to enjoy a break from family responsibilities, with the increased time for writing that solitude allowed. Vorse sailed from New York on the day after the Armistice. Unknown to her, her lonely and distraught seventeen-year-old son, Heaton, unexpectedly released from the Morristown school for a post-Armistice holiday, searched for her all day on the waterfront in an attempt to bid her goodbye.[22]

She sailed on the last convoyed trip to Europe. It was a curious trip made under conditions of wartime secrecy, blackout, and camouflage, as though a submarine that had not yet received its orders might pop out of the sea at any moment. It was a memorable voyage, her passage enlivened by several hearty encounters with a red-haired army officer.

Chapter Eight

Footnote to Folly

Traveling through Europe in 1919, Vorse witnessed a class upheaval such as the Western world had not known since the liberal surge of 1848. The war and the Russian revolution shook the old societies to their depths. Millions of common people dreamed of far-reaching reform or even revolution; conservatives feared every labor revolt as a Bolshevik plot and quickly moved to slow the process of change. On her trip Vorse also saw the devastation of war through the eyes of the women, who were busily planting, rebuilding, cleaning up the mess. Before long, it was clear to her that with the blood barely dry on Europe's face, the male players everywhere were setting up for business as usual, trying to square things to the old disastrous measurements in anticipation of the next violent encounter.

That disheartening knowledge was tempered by the exhilaration of her six-month journey. She rejoiced in the opportunity to work and travel, to write with ease, free of immediate responsibility for her younger children, now twelve and five. Her tour of postwar Europe began a period of four years during which she would live with them for only a few months each summer. She would remember the separation as an immensely satisfying and exciting interlude, one made painful in memory because it was followed by a terrible period of isolation and guilty remorse over her failure as a mother.

Vorse found the streets of London filled with troops from throughout the empire. It seemed that parties were going on in every hotel room and pub in the city. It was a brief, magical moment—the advent of hope and peace, the "last war" ended.

In those first enchanted days after the war, many women in Britain believed that the gains made during wartime would enable the female to create a better society. After decades of struggle for a wider suffrage, the Act of 1918 granted women the vote at age thirty, adding six million women to the register. And as the western front sucked in larger and larger numbers of soldiers, British women replaced men in all sorts of traditionally male occupations; the male trade unions even opened their doors a bit to women. The number of unionized women in England rose by 160 percent during the war years.

For a time, Vorse shared some of the illusions of November 1918. She dreamed that the postwar ferment among working women was the "real feminist movement" that would bring British women out of the isolation of their kitchens to reorganize national priorities. "I have often wondered what would happen if women would act as violently and thunder as imperiously on the doors of government in a campaign against infant mortality and child labor as they did to get suffrage," Vorse wrote then. "If the women protested against war and the traffic in munitions with the furious concentration with which they demanded their enfranchisement, what would happen? . . . It has always seemed strange that they should get worked up enough to overthrow all the old conventions, go singing to jail, undergo the torture of a hunger strike for the franchise—for what? Why, unless they had a further imperative objective—the protection of all children, for instance, or an equal passion for peace?" [1]

The first big campaign of the British Labour Party was on. As elsewhere, the Russian revolution had brought a shift to the left. Large demonstrations were held to protest the Allied military intervention against the Bolsheviks. Deserting the war coalition of Lloyd George, the Labour Party sought to increase its influence in Parliament in the general election slated for mid-December. Labour's bold design included a demand for free trade, a just peace, the nationalization of key industries, the full restoration of civil liberties, comprehensive unemployment and health benefits, and new capital, inheritance, and surplus-profit taxes. American progressives hailed Labour's platform as a blueprint for a Wilsonian new world. In the first euphoric days after the Armistice, some American leftists, including Vorse, even hoped that the movement toward a farmer–labor alliance in the United States might produce an American Labor Party.

But not all were so optimistic. The illusions of prowar American liberals and progressives had begun to dissolve as early as 1917. Many had recoiled from the excesses of CPI propaganda and the vigilante and federal persecution of American dissidents and pacifists. Watching some of their heroes and heroines go to jail was a sobering experience for many American liberals. Jane Addams and Randolph Bourne were among the first of many to recognize Wilson's "great crusade" as a colossal sham. By the fall of 1918, diehard prowar progressives like John Dewey were brooding uneasily. The *Nation* and the *New Republic* assumed a more critical stance. For many American liberals, Versailles would be the last stop on their ride to a new realism.

The peacemakers in Paris convened in January 1919. They met to establish a new territorial status quo, to agree on safeguards against future aggression by the defeated enemies, and to place the peace of Europe on more lasting foundations. The majority of them sought to achieve these grand objectives while attempting to maximize the impulses of nationalism, greed, and revenge.

Their deliberations took place at the opening of a revolutionary era of soaring class protest. The Russian revolution had not been a single cataclysmic storm, which rent the land, but then passed on. The revolution was rather like a chain reaction, where blasts of energy ignited others in their turn. The upheaval in Russia and the threat of further revolution that hung over Europe in 1919 left their prominent mark at Versailles. As Thorstein Veblen noted, if the Allied desire to contain Marxist ideology was "not written into the text of the [Paris] Treaty [it] may rather be said to be the parchment upon which that text was written."[2]

As Vorse traveled in England, reporting the Labour campaign, she heard jocular allusions to the American labor leader Samuel Gompers, the head of the AFL. "He is a favorite joke in England," she wrote in *Harper's*, "and they are unanimous about him, from the Ministry of Labor, where you may be asked, 'I say, but *is* Gompers the best you can do in America by way of a leader?' to a revolutionary girl organizer from the Clyde who rudely termed him 'that old fossil.'" British labor had progressed far past the AFL, which under Gompers still fought for the right to exist and for better working conditions. In Britain, workers were thinking of socialism and disarmament, Vorse wrote, "for you will find more workers there than a few who do not believe that this war was fought for Democracy, but that the game of chance we call Commerce resulted in a gambling brawl called War."[3]

Vorse went down to the Black Country, so-called for the perpetual smoke that covered it. A well-known union organizer, Mary MacArthur, was the Labour candidate for Stourbridge, one of sixteen women running for Parliament in 1918. Vorse joined MacArthur's campaign with enthusiasm, addressing envelopes and spending part of election day in a committee room in Oldsbury. Although the Labour Party won enough seats in the election to emerge as the official opposition, most of its leaders were ousted and virtually all of its candidates who called for a nonvindictive peace were defeated. Victory in war strengthened the national forces of reaction and order; the progressive forces on both sides of the Atlantic experienced a series of defeats as the 1920s began.

Traveling with a contingent of Red Cross nurses, social workers, and entertainers from the YMCA, Vorse arrived in Paris five days before Christmas. Where London had been gay, Paris was ecstatic. Strangers embraced one another in the bars and restaurants. Yankee soldiers, recognizing her as an American, approached to ask questions or to introduce themselves. President Wilson, just back from his triumphal passage through Italy, was in Paris for the peace conference.

Vorse was invited to board the special train of the president of France, which took Wilson and General Pershing to dine with the Rainbow Division on Christmas Day. The unheated cars were icy cold throughout the trip. Lining the route from the train station stood mile after mile of silent American soldiers. They presented arms, a soft rain falling on their tin hats. She was unexpectedly moved by the sight of the serene faces of hundreds of young men who wouldn't have to be killed.

On the way to Chaumont, they stopped for President Wilson to address his troops. A wet snow was falling on the muddy open field, which held a small bandstand. The soldiers turned rapt faces toward Wilson, who seemed transfigured by the grandeur of the moment. No one could know that he was then at the peak of his power. He said the words his audience wanted to hear. He spoke of the "fruits of victory" and the "establishment of peace upon the permanent foundations of peace and justice." The troops cheered. It was a rarified moment. He believed what he said. The soldiers believed him. Vorse, charged with emotion, longed to believe, against all odds.

They drove on to the mess hall at Chaumont. Vorse, two other journalists, and three women in the president's party were the only women present. But the hall was filled with men she knew, writers and artists from Provincetown, Amherst professors, New York newspaper and professional men, "and all of us," she wrote, "were pumped full of hope by the fine phrases of the President whose grave profession of faith about a new world and justice was to mean exactly nothing."[4]

On December 28, she began a surreal trip through the war zone. Past Château-Thierry and the Argonne forest, through Reims, on to Verdun—the destruction was so complete as to seem unreal. She could think only of a vast and lamentable and damaged stage set. She saw empty roads running through orchards that seemed to have been cut down by a giant scythe, despoiled towns where only chimneys still stood, munitions dumps, fleets of stranded camions, yards of dilapidated canvas camouflage flapping in the moist winter wind. Rusted barbed wire lay in the fields. Scattered bands of French soldiers piled mounds of unexploded shells along the roadside. She came upon a detail of American troops still hunting for corpses six weeks after the Armistice.

Vorse passed an American cemetery where thousands of small white crosses stood as far as she could see, with names and numbers on them. There were many other cemeteries, each filled with the bodies of Germans, English, French, Italians. Meanwhile, the American officers she met along the way told her tales of sacrifice, a river forded here, an impenetrable point taken there. It was New Year's Day. She listened to the officers recite the familiar mythology that glorified the horrors of war, but said nothing.

Vorse had a military pass and Red Cross travel orders to write an article on American troops in occupied countries. She encountered endless red tape in getting transportation to Germany. With the business of killing over, hundreds of travelers swarmed into the train station. Conductors had to push people off the cars. When she finally did board a train, a pudgy American lieutenant refused to budge from her seat. Joining others in the corridor, she sat down on her bags, with the snow sifting in on her through the broken window. She dozed sitting up, as those around her chatted, drank, and kept her awake with singing. No one really complained of the physical discomfort, for the war was over and many of the passengers were going home.

She was intensely aware of the excitement of her passage, at this spot on earth, at this moment, of being able to observe and talk with the famous and the simple folk alike, all playing their roles in the momentous postwar drama with an unknown ending of unimagined consequence. Male journalists of similar achievements—riding on this train toward Germany, fingers monitoring the pulse of these times—might have shared some of

Vorse's emotions. But there was more to her happiness. She was a woman, freed by her own hand from historic bonds—there was great pride in that —propelled by courage into risk and adventure not attempted by many of her sex. Measuring herself against male reporters, she knew herself successful. She realized the extra curiosity and energy required to approach the core of action, in search of the stories she wanted most to tell. She thought of Joe O'Brien, and felt sure of the approval he would have given. She thought of her mother, too, defiantly. She reminded herself that her children were safe at home. She could relish the weeks free of family care, could delight in the wonder of day after day that belonged only to her and that could be shaped according to her own desires and no one else's claims. She had never felt such a quiet sense of power and happiness.[5]

Her sense of self seemed at once remarkable and tenuous, because, as a woman, it was less assured as one's due reward for talent and gumption. "I marvel at my *luck* at being offered these grand assignments," she would emphasize again and again in her letters to Miss Selway, the children's nurse. She was half plumped with pride, half filled with fear that fate might suddenly snatch away her "luck" and with it her consciousness of excellence and joy.

In the lovely Rhineland countryside, almost untouched by the war, she met the American publisher S. S. McClure. They were whisked in plush army cars on a tour through twenty towns. From Germany, she received an assignment to Rome to do a series of articles on Red Cross activities in postwar Europe.[6]

For several weeks she rarely removed her coat or gloves, working or sleeping. By rail, car, and barge she traveled free on a military pass through the cities of northern Italy. On the plains beyond the Piave, she saw the same war wreckage as in France. At the Red Cross headquarters, the people traded ducks, fish, and vegetables for extra milk or some other household necessities. Life was reduced to essentials, the finding of warmth, shelter, and food. Everywhere she saw the women of Italy furiously cleaning, building, or planting, fighting to restore some normality to the lives of their families.[7]

Vorse's agreement with the Red Cross included an assignment to study postwar labor conditions in Italy. In the fifteen years since she had marched with the workers in the general strike at Venice, the Italian labor movement had become a giant. Powerful worker cooperatives of production and consumption prospered. Socialism, with a strong anarcho-syndicalist component, flourished in the northern industrial cities. By 1920, the

Socialist Party would become the largest and best organized in Italy, and it and the Chambers of Labor would control local governments in twenty-six out of sixty-nine provinces. "All the objective reasons for social change were present," Vorse wrote. There was a war-swept land, a weak government, which had maneuvered its people into war, and a large body of militant workers, disillusioned, angry, and organized. The attempt at massive factory and land seizures by the workers and peasants was soon to follow.

Vorse traveled to Bologna to report on the convention of sugar-beet workers and a demonstration there for the liberation of political prisoners. In the town square, where thousands of peasants and workers gathered for the speeches, old trade-union banners fluttered next to new red flags. Vorse became separated from her friends in the crowd and found herself next to an old peasant woman. For the sake of hearing her speak, Vorse asked her what the meeting was about:

> "Signora," she said, "the meetings of working people are always about one thing. They are about the Three Fears." I asked her what they were. She looked at me from her deep eyes.
>
> "The fear of unemployment, the fear of sickness, the fear of old age. That is what we are always having meetings about. How to get rid of them."

Standing in the square so far from home, Vorse again felt the electric thrill of people banded together for a moment, united by a great idea. It seemed to her that the old peasant woman represented tens of millions of people. This host seemed newly aware that poverty and war were not, after all, inevitable conditions of human experience, but were rather predicaments maintained to protect the privileges of the nameable, the guilty, the powerful few. "How to get rid of them?"[8]

In February, Vorse left Italy to report the Internationalist Socialist Conference in Bern, Switzerland. It was the first gathering of the socialists of the Second International since the war. Delegates from twenty-six countries met in the hope of influencing the peace conference at Paris to secure a good—a Wilsonian—peace, and to unite the cause of labor in the postwar world. But the Bern meeting failed to revive the Second International or to exert pressure on the peacemakers. Instead, it became a platform for nationalist rivalries and socialist disunity. The 1919 Bern conference, like the Lenin-inspired rival formation of the Communist Third International, which formed in Moscow a month later, illustrated the impassable doctrinal gulf that separated the right, center, and left wings of the socialist movement in 1919. This gap could no longer be bridged by the prewar expedients of rhetoric and compromise. The war and the consolidation of the Russian revolution ended the development of global socialist unity. But these events merely accelerated the dissolution of a movement that had never agreed on theoretical foundations.[9]

As Vorse walked along Bern's snowy streets to the Volkhaus where the conference would be held, she thought of the last time she had seen the city after the Women's International Peace Conference of 1915. Then Angelika Balabanoff, the passionate revolutionary, overcome with misery because the Italians were entering the war, had seen her off at the station. And Fritz Platten, the Swiss socialist leader, had advised Vorse, when she asked who in the French trade unions would oppose the war, to get in touch with a man named Trotsky of whom, in 1915, Vorse had never heard. Now Trotsky's name was known to every head of state. Balabanoff was in Russia defending the revolution. Platten, still in Switzerland, hotly opposed the Bern meeting of socialists as a traitorous gathering of agents of capitalist governments.

Vorse discovered that the dissonance of Versailles was reproduced in Bern in miniature. Remembering the women's peace meeting four years before, she contrasted the eloquent speeches she had heard then with the "incredible adventures in vanity" at Bern, "where men with nothing to say afflicted the audience unchecked for hours." With the other journalists, she sat at the long press tables, reading the papers, chatting with her friends, writing her copy, and moaning at the lengthy boredom of the speeches. Meanwhile, the delegates wrangled. "It was the antithesis of Lawrence. Absent completely was the creative flame, the group illuminator," she wrote.[10]

It was downstairs in the Volkhaus restaurant and in the informal gathering in the hotels that the real meeting of socialists took place. Here she got the echoes of the revolutions in Germany and Austria and Hungary and spoke with the men and women who stirred the protest then convulsing Europe.

The polarization of postwar socialism was vividly brought home to her in a two-hour conversation between Fritz Platten and George Lansbury, in which she served as translator. Platten represented the extreme left; he argued that socialists should not participate in the parliaments of the bourgeois states. Lansbury represented the extreme right, speaking for the British version of gentle, evolutionary replacement of capitalism. As she sat translating the feverish rhetoric of one Great Man to the other, she realized that, for them, she was nearly invisible, as a female intellect or as a female facilitator. She marveled that neither man was sensitive enough to recognize the scornful alienation she felt toward both of them. She judged Platten's uncompromising militance infantile and disastrous, and Lansbury's sweet optimism shortsighted and self-defeating.

Immediately after her return from Bern to Italy, Vorse was offered an opportunity to join the Balkan Commission of the Red Cross to report relief activity in the area of Serbia, which would become Yugoslavia. In all the murderous havoc created by the war, there was no place, not even Russia, where the results were more tragic than in Serbia, where the war began. By 1915, the country was overrun by invading armies. The Serbian soldiers, accompanied by thousands of civilians, retreated to the seas over the snow-covered mountains of Montenegro and Albania. Of the 250,000 Serbian soldiers in retreat, fewer than half survived the march. Many Serbians fled their homes at that time.

Not only were Serbia's transportation and communications systems, buildings, hospitals, food animals, and crops destroyed, but one out of every five Serbians died during the war from starvation, disease, exposure, or battle. In early 1919, 150,000 Serbian children were in desperate need of food. Clothing was so scarce that newborn babies were wrapped in paper. There were over 71,000 abandoned or orphaned children. Vorse learned that the attempt to alleviate suffering on such a scale drove the Red Cross officials in Italy to bitter wrangling. They debated what should be loaded on the first relief ships to Serbia—food, clothing, or medical supplies. Each item was needed as badly as the other. If some were clothed or fed, they died of their wounds or typhus. If medical care was provided, they lay naked or starved.

She longed to report the Balkan relief effort, but the time that she had expected to stay in Europe was over. During the four months she had been abroad, Miss Selway had become increasingly impatient at Vorse's several postponements of her return. The responsibility drawing Vorse back was compelling, but stronger yet was her desire to continue her work in Europe.

Vorse returned a note of fait accompli to Miss Selway. It was flavored with a smattering of the guilt allotted to womankind, a bit of artifice, and a great dash of self-direction:

Rome—Italy
March 14, 1919

Dearest Miss Selway,

This morning the Balkan Commission sent you a cable asking if you would mind if I stayed away a month longer. They have offered me a most wonderful job. I am to go to North Serbia, Greece, Bosnia-Herzegovina and Albania and write articles. It will give me an experience such as you may imagine and also an opportunity to do some good. . . . The only regret I have is to stay away from my children a month longer. This last week I was not very well, and I thought I should have died for lonesomeness for you all. . . . One opportunity after another of the most wonderful kind comes to anyone who can write and who is over here now. . . . You will think that I am never at all coming home, but that is not so, as this is positively the last delay which I will make, no matter if I am offered the starry crown of Persia, although, as far as I can see, I could keep on traveling for years with my expenses paid. . . .
With dearest love to my darlings and kisses, ever,

Mary Vorse

P.S. Honest to God, when this work is finished I am coming home. Nothing but work like this would make me now extend my stay. The work, which besides being an unparalleled opportunity, also comes in the nature of a real duty. If you could see the work of the Red Cross as I have seen it in the devastated countries and see how actual life and hope comes back to the people when they have received food and clothes again for the first time in years you would understand how I feel I ought to do this if it is a possible thing for you to remain another month.[11]

Vorse made a bargain with the Red Cross officials. In return for her work, they promised to find her transportation home when she returned to Paris. She obtained vaccinations and a new Red Cross uniform and boarded the train for Serbia.

Vorse was detained in Trieste, awaiting transportation to Belgrade. There she had a chance to admire the efficiency of the American Relief Administration, which was headquartered in the hotel. The ARA was one of the organizations under the direction of Herbert Hoover, who in 1919 launched the most massive relief program in history. As director of relief in

Europe, Hoover coordinated and delivered over a billion dollars of goods to twenty-two countries in Europe in the nine months after the Armistice. The need for help was great. In the great territory of southern and eastern Europe, a population of 200 million people was on the verge of starvation, without adequate clothing or medical care. In this area, torn by national and political hatreds, the delivery of relief goods required herculean effort and determination. Hoover's staff of volunteers was required to perform countless minor miracles each day.

The ARA was renowned for its effective operation, a result of Hoover's policy of strict accounting, tight administration, and allotment of authority to subordinates who in turn were subject to his indisputable one-man control. The Red Cross, Vorse wrote, was a lumbering organization, "floundering on its amorphous way, smartly or amateurishly, according to the initiative and ability of its commanding officers." Hoover's ARA, however, "worked with the swiftness and economy of a well-oiled machine." [12]

But Vorse realized that the ARA had political as well as humanitarian goals. Hoover used his power of life and death during the Russian civil war to aid the counterrevolutionary White armies attacking the Bolsheviks. Hoover at first provisioned only the civilian population behind the White forces. By July 1919, he had expanded his aid to feed the White military personnel as well.

The ARA also withheld food from the new Bolshevik government in Hungary, which had come to power two weeks before Vorse's arrival in Trieste. The victory in March 1919 of the Communist government of Bela Kun in Hungary had thrown the peace conference into near panic. All around her Vorse saw evidence of Allied plans to overthrow the Hungarian Bolsheviks. She met British officers assigned to patrol the Danube and learned that Serbian divisions and French colonial troops were being concentrated near the Hungarian border. Meanwhile, the Red Cross prepared hospital boats to care for those to be wounded in the anticipated Allied attack on Communist Hungary.

At last Vorse reached Semlin by train and after a long wait was ferried to Belgrade. The city had been devastated by constant bombardment. Finding a room required hours of effort. When she found one, it was miles from the Red Cross headquarters or any restaurant. The streetcars had not run in years. Picking her way through the uprooted cobblestones in the streets, she jumped aside to let oxcarts and droves of hogs pass. Soldiers swarmed everywhere in colorful uniforms from a dozen countries. There was almost no civilian who was not dressed in rags.

Vorse found hundreds of peasants in line outside the Red Cross clinic.

Some of them had traveled in ox carts for days to receive medical care. The overworked American nurses in the Red Cross hospital were furious at the Serbian soldiers who had been assigned to them as orderlies. The Serbian soldiers refused to do any task normally performed by women. "It was the women whose work kept Serbia going," Vorse wrote. Here, as in the rest of Europe, she saw it was the women who were cleaning, planting, weaving, rebuilding.[13]

In Belgrade, Vorse befriended young Drew Pearson, then with the American Friends Service Committee, and the Red Cross typists Holly and Sylvia Beach. Sylvia Beach was soon to open the famed Parisian bookshop Shakespeare and Co., haunt of James Joyce, Ezra Pound, Gertrude Stein, and other expatriates. Colonel Herbert Robinson, the Red Cross office manager in Belgrade, suspected Vorse was a corrupting influence on the young Americans. "That Vorse woman scandalized Belgrade not only by smoking—which was not done by women in those days—but by chain-smoking in public," Robinson remembered years later. "She actually ate with a fork in one hand and a cigarette in the other! She would leave Hostess House in the evening to address [revolutionary] meetings, taking the Beach girls and Drew Pearson with her."[14]

Vorse was given a choice by the Red Cross officials of going west to Herzegovina on an expedition to bring food, or of going south from Belgrade, through Macedonia, to visit the medical missions at Salonika and Monastir. Her choice to go south was a fateful decision. She later learned that the Red Cross officer who headed the expedition to the west got typhus and died.

The railroad between Belgrade and southern Serbia was destroyed. The road was cut and the bridges dynamited. Vorse traveled south over perilous side roads in a camion driven by a Serbian who had learned to speak German in a prison camp. The roads were almost empty. It was Easter Monday. Every now and then they passed a soldier, to whom they offered a ride, picking up a traveler here, dropping him off there.

At Raska, the children who came running out to meet them had the sores of malnutrition on their faces. In this bleak town Vorse and the collection of hitchhiking soldiers found a room and a restaurant. A soldier shared his bottle of Chianti. To her astonishment, she heard the familiar words "socialism," "capitalism," "bolshevism" flashing out at her from the spirited Slavic conversation. In this remote spot, she met the same discontent born from war and its consequences that was stirring in every country in Europe in early 1919.

At Mitrovika, "a lost and vicious little hole," her driver left her. She awaited the train to Salonika. No train was ready; none was expected. Looking for bread for her journey, Vorse walked through the rain to the market. Veiled Turkish women drew back and turned to stare at her. At a distance, a boy of twelve or thirteen stood watching her. He was dressed in rags. Drawn by his speculative gaze, she went to him. Offering him bread, she asked if he were hungry. He shook his head, and slogged off through the ankle-deep mud.

Back at the train station she sat waiting on her duffel bag. The air smelled of wet clothes and garlic. Gradually the station-agent's room filled with damp groups of soldiers and peasants, all waiting patiently. The ragged boy she had seen in the market stood on the platform. He began to cry. Vorse reported the boy's story for her *Harper's* readers.[15]

> The soldiers gathered around him, kind in their curiosity. "Why do you cry?" . . . they asked. He cried on disconsolately, without answering.
>
> Then his story dripped out slowly, like rain falling. He raised his head and looked at the soldiers and talked without emphasis, with the manner of recounting the inevitable. There was no protest and no hope in his voice.
>
> "He is an orphan, He has no one—he has no one at all," they reported. . . .
>
> The boy stood looking out over the railway. . . . His face was brown and sharpened with hunger. . . . He seemed so lost and forlorn that a chill crept over us. . . .
>
> I went up to him with a soldier in horizon blue who spoke French with me. . . .
>
> Please ask his name," I said. . . .
>
> At the soldier's question, the boy turned to me.
>
> "Milorad Bachinin," he told me.

When the train arrived, the passengers entered a boxcar. They sat on the floor, pulling their blankets, coats, or rugs about them. Drawn together by their cold encampment, they opened their packages and shared their supper. Milorad ate hungrily, perched on a bale of goods, smiling at Vorse across the others' heads. A woman beside her wondered aloud what would become of the boy. One of the soldiers said he could use the boy's help at his little store in Mladnova. When Vorse promised to find Red Cross transportation for the boy and the soldier, Milorad gravely agreed to go.

The train drew into the Uskub station. The soldier assured her that he would find the boy when it was time for him to leave. The next day Vorse looked for Milorad at the station, for she had promised to buy him some new clothes. She searched for him all day along the main streets and in the market. It was the next morning before she found him:

> His flight to me was like a leaping, happy animal. . . . He looked up at me and love streamed from his eyes, and the radiance of it transfigured him. He was so happy that he walked along in a sort of quiet ecstasy. He was so happy that it hurt me to look at him. . . . I record this as the high moment, higher even than when we got his clothes at the Red Cross store-room, walking proudly ahead of the crowd waiting for distribution.

When Vorse entered the train station the next day before dawn, her heart expected to find Milorad there. He ran to her, smiling, yet tense with anxiety.

> He clasped my hand and put it to his cheek with that lovely gesture of his. . . .
>
> We were strangers, and we did not speak each other's language, but the spiritual bond of mother and son was ours. Not a very good mother—not watchful enough, not patient enough; Milorad a boy on whom adversity had put its cramped hand, with no high courage, nor with the promise of much high endeavor—but to him the love of my heart flowed out, and in my heart were the things Milorad had found in none of the compassionate women of his own land. I loved him not for his goodness, but for his need of me, and because I must. Now there came to him slowly the bitter knowledge, that I, his mother, was leaving him to loneliness and misery. His pain welled over in tears, his sobs racked him and left him gasping. I have never seen a child feel such grief as that which bankrupted Milorad of hope. He had not believed I could go. He came to me and pleaded with me, his words rushing out in the torrent of his tears.
>
> I did not need to know what he said; he was emptying his heart. He threw the treasure of his love before me, and his belief and his pain. People came up to comfort him. . . .
>
> The train moved. I could no longer see his face for my own tears. . . .
>
> But when I look out over the implacable silence that divides us, I wonder if it would not have been better if we had not met.

Predictably, Vorse did not record any realization that she found it easier to write about others' children than to care for her own. Her story of Milorad was more than a powerful message to her readers about the obscenity of war. It was also an anxious attempt to assuage her guilt about the two children who Miss Selway insisted had been abandoned in Provincetown.

Mary Heaton Vorse (MHV) at eighteen, in 1892. *(Courtesy of Heaton Vorse)*

MHV, c. 1900. *(Wayne State University, Archives of Labor and Urban Affairs [WSU, ALUA])*

Albert Vorse, c. 1900. *(Courtesy of Heaton Vorse)*

MHV with her
daughter Ellen,
c. 1909. *(Courtesy
of Heaton Vorse)*

Hutchins Hapgood, William ("Big Bill") Haywood, and Joe O'Brien in front of MHV's house
in Provincetown, c. 1913. *(Courtesy of Heaton
Vorse)*

MHV, c. 1914. *(WSU ALUA)*

Joe O'Brien, c. 1914. *(Courtesy of Joel O'Brien)*

MHV and Joe O'Brien, after their marriage, c. 1914. *(Courtesy of Heaton Vorse)*

MHV's and O'Brien's son Joel on Robert Minor's shoulders, Provincetown, c. 1920. (*Courtesy of Heaton Vorse*)

MHV with her daughter Ellen in 1922, when MHV was addicted to morphine. (*Courtesy of Heaton Vorse*)

MHV, c. 1930. *(WSU ALUA)*

Strikers and their families marching together in Lawrence, Massachusetts, textile strike, 1912. *(WSU ALUA)*

Police attacking striking textile workers in Passaic, New Jersey, 1926. *(WSU ALUA)*

A national guardsman struggling with two women textile workers during a strike in Gastonia, North Carolina, April 1929. *(WSU ALUA)*

Members of the Women's Emergency Brigade during the Flint, Michigan, sit-down strike against General Motors, February 1937. (WSU ALUA)

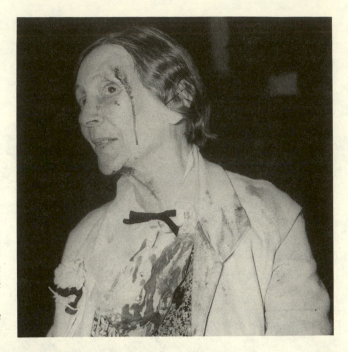

MHV bleeding
from a head wound
suffered during the
"Little Steel" strike
at Youngstown,
Ohio, 1937. *(Wide
World Photo)*

MHV addressing strikers during the "Little Steel Wars" in Youngstown,
1937. *(WSU ALUA)*

MHV as war correspondent in World War II, c. 1945. *(WSU ALUA)*

MHV—at eighty-eight—receiving the Social Justice Award of the United Auto Workers in 1962. With her, Upton Sinclair, Eleanor Roosevelt, and Walter Reuther. *(WSU ALUA)*

Chapter Nine

The Left Fork

When Vorse returned to Paris she discovered that the transportation to the United States promised her by the Red Cross was not available. She was forced to remain in Europe through May and most of June, awaiting space on a ship. Those few weeks were central to her life, for it was then she fell deeply in love.

Vorse met Robert Minor through an old friend from the Village, the reporter Griffin Barry. (Barry, who would later attain some fame as the actual father of the two children born to Bertrand Russell's wife, had also introduced Vorse to Joe O'Brien.) Twenty-three-year-old John Dos Passos, recently released from the U.S. Army medical corps to attend classes at the Sorbonne, was another member of Barry's circle of friends in Paris in early 1919. Dos Passos remembered meeting Vorse and Robert Minor then.

"Paris was the capital of the world that spring of the Peace Conference," Dos Passos wrote. "It looked as if every man and woman in the United States who could read and write had wrangled an overseas job." Dos Passos recalled Robert Minor as "a big opinionated Texan, whose charcoal cartoons we had all admired in the *Masses*. Bob Minor was just on the edge of becoming an active revolutionist. He dropped tantalizing hints about the hazards of the Russian revolution and the German underground and Jack Reed's adventures. He was already a little too deaf to listen to anyone else's notions. With Minor came Mary Heaton Vorse with her charming look of a withered Irish rose." [1]

Dos Passos wrote this memory of Paris decades later. His postscript was shaded by the compassion he felt for Vorse's tailspin of the 1920s, a descent for which Dos Passos always blamed Minor. Dos Passos was not the only one, however, to find Mary Vorse and Bob Minor an incongruous pair— Vorse, at forty-five, the well-bred New England lady, and Minor, ten years younger, the frenetic Western zealot.

Like Dos Passos, many who knew Bob Minor have been most impressed by his dogmatic opinions, his inability to recognize or balance contradictions. Orrich Johns remembered Minor's "tremendous definiteness" and "implacable rejections." Joseph Freeman, who admired Minor, spoke of his "gleam of fanaticism" and the "pontifical finality" of his words. Steve Nelson thought Minor "bombastic . . . not seen as much of a thinker." Waldo Frank captured the essence of Minor's personality when he described a conversation he once had with Minor over the validity of Marxism as an absolute science:

> Robert Minor was a cartoonist of genius who gave up his art to become a Party functionary. He was a man with a mission, convinced that his faith in Marx was objective and precise as mathematics. I recall an argument with him on the beach of Truro on Cape Cod. We were talking about the "certain" Marxist future; and I cried: "But the imponderables, Bob! The imponderables. . . ." His smile was somewhat a sneer: "There are no imponderables," he said.[2]

Bob Minor was six feet, two inches, with extraordinarily bushy eyebrows, a long cocky stride, and a booming voice. The rebellious son of a Texas lawyer, he began work as a reporter and cartoonist at the St. Louis *Post-Dispatch* in 1905. There he was schooled in radicalism by Leo Caplan, his socialist physician who treated him for growing deafness. Minor joined the Socialist Party in 1908. By age twenty-seven, he was reputedly the country's highest-paid political cartoonist.

He was offered a larger salary in 1911 from Ralph Pulitzer's New York *Evening World*. As an inducement to Minor to accept the job, Pulitzer gave him a salary advance to study art for a year in Paris. Minor spent more time talking to French workers than he did in art classes. In France, Minor became an anarchist. He worked at the *Evening World* until the paper changed its policy and moved to support the war. With the intransigence that was his major trait, Minor refused to draw prowar cartoons. He contributed his biting art to Emma Goldman's anarchist monthly, *Mother Earth*, and to the New York socialist daily, the *Call*. In August 1915, he joined the staff of the *Masses*. Pulitzer promptly fired him.

In 1916 Minor moved to San Francisco to head the defense effort to free

Tom Mooney. Mooney—charged with planting a bomb that killed ten bystanders at a military preparedness parade in San Francisco—was convicted by a conspiracy involving the San Francisco district attorney, who bribed witnesses and created false evidence in order to convict Mooney. Imprisoned for twenty-three years, Mooney was pardoned in 1939 by California's first twentieth-century Democratic governor. By that time, tens of thousands of Americans had joined the worldwide campaign to release Tom Mooney. Theodore Draper concluded that Minor, "who organized the first Mooney defense committee and wrote the first pro-Mooney pamphlet," did "more than any other single man" to save Mooney. Minor would later write: "The last underpinnings of respect for the 'democratic' social organization were knocked out of me by the Mooney case." In this experience, Minor was not alone. As Draper observed, Mooney's plight was "a crisis of conscience" for a whole generation of American radicals.[3]

Minor traveled to Russia in March 1918, determined to judge the revolution for himself. In early 1919 he spent three months in Germany, where he witnessed, and apparently participated in, the failed Spartacist uprising of the extreme left against the moderate socialist government. Minor reached Paris at about the same time that Vorse arrived there from Serbia. They became lovers almost at once after meeting.

Vorse's attraction to Robert Minor sprang from a complex set of emotions. She seemed to feel most comfortable with a decisive male companion. Perhaps less certain males only served to remind her of her father's passivity before her mother's will. The presence of a powerfully self-directed male also served to counter her own impulse toward action, which she had been taught to contain, as well as to strengthen her own courage to face conflict, which she had been trained to avoid. Strong men seemed to alleviate her deepest anxieties about self, allowing her more power without fear of its impact, while providing her with a sort of surrogate ego to confront the world bravely.

Minor's concentration of purpose and absorption in work delighted her. She found in him a commitment to ideas and effort as intense as her own —a welcome contrast to her memory of Bert Vorse's defeatism in the face of struggle. Minor's vitality, physical and mental, was memorable. For Vorse, he was "more alive and sensitive to life than anyone in the world."[4] His obstinacy of belief could also emerge as scorn for tradition. Like Joe O'Brien, Minor pierced the world with a keen radical analysis. At times he could sweep away the mystification shrouding events with a few phrases. Vorse saw in him someone as concentrated as herself. She felt she had never before "met anyone . . . who seemed as unafraid of life as I."

Most important, Minor never chided her for inattention to her family. For Minor, there was no higher responsibility than to labor against injustice. He encouraged her effort to escape the restrictions imposed on her by tradition and by children. He would let her go. "The only way I can have a sweetheart or a husband," she wrote him, "is to let go. . . . Someone to go out into the world and bring back new things. Someone who will like *me* to go out into the world and bring back new things." She once grumbled at one of his letters to her, which seemed to address her as a mother. Domesticity as identification repelled her. "Did you write that letter to me or to the mother of Joel?" she scolded him. "I have a house and children and I can paint screens and cook and darn stockings; but I can also swim and sail a boat and my spirit goes streaming out to the dangerous places. . . . I am not Home or Peace or a Mate!" she warned him.

And after five years, Vorse's body was fired again, no small thing for a woman of her sensuality. She felt young and strong and free—rocketed to the "wide horizons of a wind blowing clouds across the sky that I always feel when I have been with you." Exhilaration was rebirth: "At a moment in my life," she wrote to Minor, "I said to life 'No more—I have had all of you. No more. My body is young but I am old—peace—quiet—Let me be.' Since then life and love in a thundering torrent have overwhelmed me. I found I didn't know love and that growth was in the future."[5]

While Vorse and Minor awaited a berth home to the United States and relished the dual pleasures of new love and springtime in Paris, she was offered an impelling assignment. The officials of the American Relief Administration asked her to go on a mission to Central Europe, in exchange for their assurance of speedy transportation home upon her return to Paris. She was told that ARA director Herbert Hoover wanted her to publish in American popular women's magazines the story of how the lifting of the Allied food blockade affected women and children in Austria.

On June 3, Vorse left Minor in Paris and departed for Vienna on a Polish military train. She was accompanied by a friend from New York, the socialist newspaper editor Abraham Cahan. Thus, solely because of fortuitous circumstances and timing, Vorse became embroiled in the political intrigue of the moment, which centered around the denial of American food relief to the new Communist government in Hungary.[6]

In company with Cahan, she arrived in Vienna on the morning of June 5. The streets were crowded with men and women in light clothing, the cafes and boulevards gay with tricolored flowers. But after a while, the flowers seemed to her more like the decor for a funeral than a sign of spring.

The working class of Vienna was still suffering from famine, eight months after the end of the war. The Allied blockade was only partially lifted. Vorse sat at lunch in a restaurant off the Ringstrasse. She cut an unsavory piece of fat from her ham. A middle-aged woman, selling field flowers, approached. Looking fearfully over her shoulder at the waiter, the woman asked Vorse if she could have the discarded strip of fat. At Vorse's nod, the woman "snatched at it with a gesture of horrid and eloquent eagerness" and shoved it into her mouth.

Vorse visited the model tenements of Vienna, especially built for the large families of the workers. Many of the inhabitants were now widows. "Everywhere swarmed the children: pale children, children with blotched and scarred faces, children with skinny, crooked legs," Vorse reported. The women told her the stories of their slow starvation, of the long nights they waited in line, wrapped in bedclothes to keep warm, to obtain bread for their children. In doorways, little boys and girls stood staring at her. Most of them had tubercular lumps under their eyes, or showed signs of skin disease or rickets. Children who looked to be nine or ten years old told her they were actually in their teens.

The upper class of Vienna, and the people of the middle class with salaries or savings, could afford black-market food. It was the poor and their children who were most affected by the Allied blockade. The armies were fed; the national leaders were inconvenienced; the women and children of the wage earners of Central Europe paid for the blockade with suffering and their lives. In Germany, where the blockade was still in force, eight hundred people a month died of malnutrition. The Viennese workmen on the street who saw her American Red Cross uniform shouted at her: "Why don't they take the men out and shoot them instead of starving our children to death?"[7]

When the ARA began the importation of food into Austria, Vorse witnessed the public feeding of fourteen hundred children at the palace of the Hapsburgs. Austrian women with brisk, competent movements fed the children soup, cocoa, and bread. The hunger of the youngsters here was but a dim mirror of the hunger of children in the industrial areas of Eastern Europe and Russia. The barbarism of war, and her knowledge that the families of the poor bore the brunt while the workers cleaned up its mess afterward, again overwhelmed her.

In Vienna, Vorse met with Captain T. T. C. Gregory, ARA director of Central Europe. She was probably unaware that six months before, Gregory had been appointed as one of the covert American political intelligence officers operating in Central and Eastern Europe. Gregory, like the Allied chiefs then meeting in Paris, had been thrown into panic in late March 1919, when a Bolshevik government under Bela Kun took power in Hungary. With Lenin victorious in Russia, the Spartacist uprising in Germany, the flare of Bolshevik organization throughout Europe, left-led strikes in England, France, Italy, and the Ruhr, the fear of communism greatly accelerated at the peace conference. Lloyd George told the Council of Four: "The whole of Europe is filled with the spirit of revolution. . . . The whole existing order in its political, social, and economic aspects is questioned by the masses . . . from one end of Europe to the other." Moreover, the red governments in Russia and Hungary stressed that their own survival depended on the extension of social revolution throughout Europe. Although the Allied chiefs in Paris held diverse opinions on how to counteract Communist successes, they were at one in their perception that bolshevism was an immediate threat to international capitalism.[8]

The proclamation of the Soviet government in Hungary was quickly followed by withdrawal of all Entente missions from Budapest. With official diplomatic relations cut, ARA chief Herbert Hoover and President Woodrow Wilson were dependent on a few Americans for direct knowledge of the situation in Hungary—chiefly ARA officials and the American professor A. C. Coolidge, head of a mission sent to Vienna to study and recommend new boundary lines in Central Europe. In late March, President Wilson had directed Hoover to send him daily reports on events in Hungary. Captain Gregory necessarily became Hoover's main source of information.

Desperate for detailed knowledge of developments in Hungary, Captain Gregory urged Vorse to go to Budapest. He wanted her to carry a message to Count Mihály Károlyi, the former prime minister who had capitulated to Kun. Gregory felt that as a woman journalist she would not be suspected as a courier. She might be allowed to interview Károlyi and to observe freely the operation of the Kun government. Vorse needed no persuasion to accept such a journalistic plum.[9]

Before her departure, Gregory briefed her on recent developments in Paris. Gregory gave her a copy of the five-page letter he had written to Hoover on June 4 in which Gregory argued for direct Allied military intervention to overthrow Kun. At Versailles, the French general Foch also urged the peacemakers in Paris to advance their armies through Hungary to attack the real source of Communist contagion in Russia. Hoover and Wilson initially rejected a military solution. They still hoped that Kun could be brought down through internal pressure. They were reluctant to begin what amounted to a new war, and opted instead for the use of American economic force against Kun. In mid-May, however, Kun had won a spectacular military victory over the Czechs and held his own against the rapacious advance of the Rumanian army bent on swallowing large chunks of Hungarian territory. By June 9, Professor Coolidge and ARA chief Herbert Hoover would join Captain Gregory in his hard-line stance in favor of Allied military intervention in Hungary.[10]

On June 8, Vorse sped in an American car over the empty, flat roads to Budapest. Abraham Cahan went with her. The duo was a most unlikely crisis team on a mission for American politicians. "When we got to the frontier and [Cahan] actually saw the Red guards, the hammer and sickle upon their caps," Vorse recalled, "he got out to embrace them. Mr. Cahan, an old Socialist, was in a state bordering on ecstasy. He was like a spiritualist who, having had to go on faith all his life, finally sees a materialization and can hardly believe his eyes for joy." How ironic, Vorse wrote sixteen years later, remembering that day, that Cahan became one of communism's bitterest enemies.[11]

The city of Budapest was silent, its streets nearly empty, its gray shutters closed. The new Communist society announced itself on the walls of Budapest in red flags and gigantic posters. The revolutionary placards were everywhere, in enormous quantities, most in color with red dominant—figures swinging sledges against chains, pictures of Red Guards rushing to aid their comrades, posters linking prostitution to alcoholism, and both to capitalism. Over the Austro-Hungarian Bank hung a scarlet banner: "Property of the Proletariat of Hungary." The atmosphere was unreal. The Communist government had established, overnight, through government fiat, the people's state in feudal Hungary.

The Bela Kun regime inherited the results of four hundred years of aristocratic and clerical brutality toward the peasants and workers of Hungary. In 1917 Hungary had been ruled by feudal lords as though it were the Middle Ages. One-half of the rich land was held by a few nobles; one-third of the people were illiterate; one-fifth suffered from tuberculosis induced by malnutrition; only one-twentieth of the males were allowed the vote. The outbreak of war in 1914 had been welcomed with the usual delirium by the military and politicians, while the clergy blessed the guns and beseeched God to kill the enemy. Austro-Hungarian war losses were horrendous. Two-thirds of the monarchy's soldiers were killed, wounded, or imprisoned. The war pushed the masses past endurance and focused their infinite hatreds on the old regime. The spread of socialist ideals, massive strikes, and the disintegration of the German armies had brought the bloodless October Revolution of 1918, which dismissed the monarchy and installed Count Károlyi as prime minister.

The Károlyi union of bourgeoisie and assorted malcontents preached revolution while stumbling toward mild reforms. Károlyi's failure to carry out land reform was fatal. His center coalition was already near collapse when, on March 20, 1919, the representative of the Entente in Budapest issued an ultimatum to Hungary that abrogated the Armistice agreement by slicing some 100 more miles off its territory as a gift for the Rumanians. The Entente's purpose in setting these new lines was to secure the rear guard of the Rumanian army in the hope that the Rumanians could be used against the Bolsheviks in Russia. Betrayed by the Entente, Károlyi resigned and handed over power to the Social Democrats. But the popularity of the Hungarian Communists had grown day by day, even though their leader Bela Kun was in jail. The Social Democrat leaders rushed to Kun's cell to negotiate. Thus did state power virtually fall into Kun's lap. Released from jail, he immediately declared a workers' republic, sweeping land reform without compensation, separation of church and state, universal suffrage, the organization of a Red Army, and alliance with the Russian Bolsheviks.

In Budapest, Vorse found Count Károlyi in seclusion at his villa, protected by Red Guards. He asked her to forcefully impress upon Hoover and Wilson his belief that some form of socialism would prevail in central Europe. He argued that the shortage of food and goods due to war and blockade, as well as the huge indemnities to be imposed on the Central Powers, would necessitate the cooperative endeavor of a socialist economy, rather than the expensive competition of a capitalist one. He was "absolutely convinced," he told Vorse, that despite what American business and political leaders might prefer, "capitalism is henceforth 'impossible' in Central Europe. It is doomed." [12]

Later, Vorse and Cahan set out on a fantastic Marxist sightseeing tour in a society turned upside down in three months. In retrospect, Kun's short-lived revolution-via-proclamation seems like opera buffa, so rapidly was the old world abolished and the new instituted. The output of government directives was phenomenal. Alcoholic beverages, prostitution, and horse races were outlawed. Artists, writers, and composers were placed on the state payroll. Dozens of tubercular children in the city were shipped to fresh air and nutritious food in the country. All material glorifying war was erased from the school curriculum. Suffrage was granted to all but capitalists, idlers, priests, criminals, and the insane. Women's equality in work and at home was proclaimed. Medical care was socialized. All the workers' cherished goals were legalized: the abolition of piecework; the forty-eight-hour week; higher salaries; accident, health, and maternity insurance; and full employment. All industries, mines, transportation, stores, banks, and hotels became state property. Even death ensured equality; rich and poor, all were to be buried in identical graves.

Vorse observed the darker side of Communist rule. Rigid state censorship of the press, the publishing houses, and the schools was established. The vast state bureaucracy so suddenly born was corrupt and inefficient, mostly because so many of its officials were the same people who had served the old regime. Speculation and the hoarding of food and goods contributed to bitter relations between urban and rural populations. The botched land-reform program and overall monetary chaos lost Kun the support of peasants and trade-union leaders. The effect of decades of economic exploitation, religious oppression, and enforced ignorance could not be cured in a few months by government decree, particularly in a country fighting a defensive war on its borders.[13]

Six weeks after Vorse left Budapest, Kun's government collapsed. With Allied encouragement, the Rumanians resumed their attack on Hungary. On June 26, at Hoover's urging, the Council at Paris issued an ultimatum: If a non-Communist government was established in Hungary, the Allies would lift the blockade and begin shipment of food and goods to the Hungarian people. On August 1, Kun fled into exile. Captain Gregory in Vienna sent the first trainload of food through to Hungary the next day. Gregory would later claim that he and Hoover, by their machinations, had toppled Kun's government.[14]

After a brief Hapsburg revival under Archduke Joseph, the bloody Admiral Miklós Horthy regime assumed power in Hungary. Anti-Semitic pogroms of Christian Terror convulsed the land. The dictatorship of Horthy and his associates lasted for the next twenty years. Thousands were killed, tortured, and imprisoned and the old feudal tyranny was let loose again. Allied policy makers could relax. Communist Hungary was but a memory.

On her return to Vienna, Vorse was greeted by the hotel manager who cheerfully announced that tomorrow her room might be nationalized. "Revolution tomorrow," he explained. Vorse went to investigate. She spent the day going about the city by foot and on streetcars. Everywhere people told her, "Tomorrow is the Revolution." Most seemed resigned. Things were so bad they might as well try a new government, they said.

Inspired by Kun's victory in Hungary, the Austrian Communists planned to end their uneasy alliance with the Social Democrats. The Communists planned a putsch, hopeful that the Volkswehr, or People's Army, would refuse to fire on Communist workers. Vorse arranged to go to the Revolution the next morning with a young ARA man. So odd was the atmosphere of the time that the bizarre appointment seemed perfectly natural.

Her young friend failed to show, so she went alone. During the night, the government had arrested 115 Communists. Several thousand protesters demanded the release of their leaders. Vorse took a cab and cut through town to the university where she intercepted the marchers. A row of spectators watched, and a crowd of little boys ran along the edge of the demonstration. She got up on an iron table to see better.

The marchers broke through a line of soldiers thrown across the street. Suddenly the machine guns spit. She watched as a score of men were hit, threw up their hands, and dropped. For the first time she saw workers shot down before her eyes. A policeman forced her off the table and ordered her to her hotel. She walked a few blocks, then doubled back to the university which had become an impromptu hospital. She spent the day walking about the city. By nightfall, Vorse saw hundreds of soldiers who were wearing red flowers like the ones the demonstrators had worn in their buttonholes. The flowers indicated that the soldiers supported the workers. But finally enough troops stood with the government to defeat the putsch.[15]

The next evening, Vorse left Vienna for Paris. She carried with her copies of the correspondence that Captain Gregory had impulsively shown her. The documents contained Gregory's and Professor Coolidge's advice to Hoover to support Allied military intervention to overthrow Kun. But Vorse had somehow obtained from Gregory's office knowledge of a much more interesting document—Hoover's June 9 dispatch to Wilson in which Hoover also had urged immediate military intervention against Kun by the French troops then stationed in Yugoslavia. Wilson's reply to Hoover on June 10 had counseled caution, but Hoover's June 9 dispatch exposed as false the ARA chief's hard-won reputation for moderation.

An ARA official in Vienna in some way discovered Vorse's scoop, and wired Gregory, who was then in Trieste: "Mrs. Vorse has returned your letters to Hoover which you gave her but obtained copies of them without my knowledge and is leaving tonight for Paris with them. Stop. She will arrive Paris Thursday morning and sails for America Saturday."[16] Apparently there was no attempt by the ARA in Paris to confiscate the copies Vorse held, possibly because of bureaucratic snarl. More likely,

Gregory was reluctant to admit his own ineptitude to his chief in Paris. Vorse arrived in Paris on June 19 and made her report to Hoover. She sailed for New York on schedule two days later, carrying the incriminating documents with her.

She returned home with great ambivalence. On the one hand, she knew she must return to her children since Miss Selway could no longer be persuaded to stay in Provincetown to care for them. Yet Vorse could not bear to leave France, for when she returned to Paris from Vienna, she learned that while she was in Hungary Robert Minor had disappeared from his Paris apartment, mysteriously abducted by the French police. He was being held by American military authorities in solitary confinement at Coblenz, guarded day and night by a soldier with a fixed bayonet. Minor was accused of spreading Bolshevik propaganda among American troops in Germany with intent "to create unrest, dissatisfaction, defection, revolt and mutiny." He was charged with treason and faced a death sentence. Her first day afloat she wrote him: "My life, my heart has been torn before, but never as it is now on going and leaving you. There is every reason to go, but my reason shrinks back, ashamed before the light of my heart. . . . I went swept out by the epic tide of small things and work to do, a story to write. . . . I did not know before how much I loved you." [17]

When she reached New York, she read that he was to be tried by a high-powered military court composed of five generals and two colonels. Meanwhile, labor circles in England, France, and Italy had launched a campaign to save Minor, the man who had championed Tom Mooney. Lincoln Steffens claimed to have played the major role in the effort to win Minor's release. Steffens approached Colonel Edward House, President Wilson's close friend, in Paris. He convinced House that if a well-known radical like Bob Minor were executed, the resultant chaos would jeopardize Steffens's and House's plan to win a general amnesty for all the political prisoners being held in the United States. House asked Banbridge Colby, soon to become secretary of state, to urge the army to free Minor. Minor was released without explanation on July 8.

In early July, the New York *Times* got wind of political influence in the Minor case. It began a countercampaign to ensure Minor's conviction. The *Times* kept up its front-page and editorial crusade against Minor through the fall of 1919. The Senate Judiciary Committee held a special investigation to inquire into the proceedings of the Minor arrest. Two right-wing senators charged the Wilson administration with harboring Bolsheviks in high places. Upon his return home, Minor went on a national speaking tour to denounce American military intervention against the Soviet Union. He traveled most of the way under the surveillance of Department of Justice agents. His report on conditions in Russia drew large crowds in cities across the nation, according to the federal informers.[18]

Minor's narrow escape from persecution and the aid extended him by high political officials made him seem to Vorse more heroic than ever. To cement the physical and emotional tie she felt to him came the added pleasure and reflected glory of involvement with a radical figure of some international standing.

During their first year together, Vorse and Minor shared a common politics. His experience in revolutionary Russia convinced him that highly centralized government was not the best road to socialism. When he presented a critical analysis of his interview with Lenin in the New York *World*, Max Eastman denounced Minor for holding to old-fashioned utopian dreams and for printing his anti-Bolshevik comments in a capitalist newspaper. In the summer of 1919 Vorse also was one of the few American reporters who had seen a Bolshevik-style government in operation. She agreed that Bolshevik leaders favored an oppressive state bureaucracy. Her strongly critical view of Kun's censorship cost her the intellectual approval of Max Eastman and Floyd Dell, who were then arguing that tyranny was an unfortunate but necessary component of revolutionary change.[19]

Yet Vorse's political judgment fell far short of the hatred of communism felt by many American liberals in this period. She was most concerned with her own government's denial of food and medicine to diseased and starving peoples, a savagery it defended as realistic and democratic in aim. How uninformed and utopian her single-minded focus on famished children would have seemed to the great Allied leaders, faced as they were with massive political dilemmas, the solution to which would theoretically determine the movement of vast armies, the wealth or poverty, the freedom or oppression, of millions of people. How uninformed and utopian her single-minded opposition to state dictatorship would have appeared to the great Marxist rulers and thinkers, faced as they were with immensely powerful reactionary enemies, the destruction of whom would theoretically determine the liberation of all the peoples of the world from centuries of grinding exploitation.

Vorse's social thought, in 1919 as for the rest of her life, had carried her into the no man's land of political philosophy cordoned off and marked "effeminate," "visionary," "unrealistic." These ideas, together with the few who voiced them, were regarded as peripheral to world events. They were not so much denounced, for that would accord them a sort of power, as they were simply dismissed by the ruling powers and intellects of the time.

Vorse did not move any further left during her three-year affair with Bob Minor. Yet because American society was moving to the right so fast, federal surveillance of her activities increased. In June 1919, Vorse returned to a country gripped by conservative reaction. For over ten years trade unionism and radical politics were suppressed, all amid continuing and increasing maldistribution of wealth—only to end in 1929 in what Edmund Wilson called "the sudden unexpected collapse of that stupid gigantic fraud."[20] American radicals were to spend their energies during the 1920s fighting a defensive holding action.

By 1920, the IWW had been effectively eliminated and the Socialist Party severely damaged by the joint impact of governmental and vigilante action. Beginning with the Armistice, there came one and one-half more years of reprisals against the left in the United States. This period left the stain on American history called the Red Scare.

Often historians have explained the Red Scare through reference to the residue of wartime discords, the fear of bolshevism abroad, or postwar dislocations such as the inflation of 1919. In naming these valid factors, many historians have failed to emphasize that the Red Scare was not irrationally based. Rather the Red Scare was the response of government and business elites to the tremendous upsurge of American radicalism within and without the labor movement in 1919. The Red Scare destroyed this developing threat to the status quo. When the destruction was nearly complete, the Red Scare ended.

In June 1919, just as Vorse returned from Paris, the left–socialist groups in the United States split over whether an American Communist party should be formed at once or in September. The extreme factionalism that marks the early history of American communism was off to a fine start. Signs of radical influence were apparent far beyond the formation of Communist parties in 1919. Support for fundamental reform was widespread among American intellectuals, clergymen, and progressives. Demands for the enactment of minimum-wage laws and for social insurance against unemployment and old age sounded like red propaganda to many members of the American elite in 1919. To business leaders, the most ominous sign of unrest was the increasing radicalism within the organized labor movement. The tremendous number of strikes occurring in 1919 was a monumental threat to the old political and economic bosses. More than fifteen years would pass before the trade-union movement again demonstrated such militancy. One of every five workers in America was on strike in 1919.

While Vorse was in Europe, several other events fueled the Red Scare, which would peak in early 1920. In February 1919, sixty thousand workers held on for four days in the Seattle general strike; one thousand federal troops and three thousand police moved into the city. In April, thirty-six packages of unknown origin filled with explosives were mailed to prominent public officials and nationally known antiradicals. On May 1, riots erupted in ten large cities from coast to coast, the result of assaults by police and hoodlums on labor sympathizers celebrating the workers' holiday. In June, another set of eight bombs was placed outside the homes of public officials and businessmen; one exploded at the home of Attorney General A. Mitchell Palmer. In July, the federal General Intelligence Division was established, led by twenty-four-year-old J. Edgar Hoover. For six decades to follow, Hoover would successfully connect demands by Americans for social justice to agitation by the reds.

Among the antidemocratic activists, the Lusk Committee of the New York State Legislature can still claim the worst record. In a series of raids it confiscated twenty tons of "radical" material. Since only six of the almost one thousand persons arrested in these raids were subsequently prosecuted, the gravest damage done by the rampaging Lusk Committee was caused by its indiscriminate use of smear tactics. In its full report, it branded as seditious the words of Jane Addams, Roger Baldwin, Lillian Wald, and a host of other American liberals and reformers. The Lusk Committee was the first of several governmental investigative groups to name Mary Heaton Vorse as a threat to the American Way. She was singled out for her treasonous support of Margaret Sanger's birth control activities back in 1916.[21]

When Vorse returned from Europe, *Harper's* asked her for articles about Bela Kun's government and the Vienna putsch. Before she could finish the work, Kun's government had fallen and the putsch was no longer news. In Paris, Vorse had met Thomas Wells, the editor of *Harper's*. Wells had complained to her that the war was never portrayed in its undistilled horror in American magazines. Now, in New York, Wells had changed his mind. Vorse was infuriated by his advice to her: "You were brought up in a rose garden and then lived by the sea. Why don't you write about rose gardens? Why don't you write about the sea?"[22]

Vorse planned to publish her inside knowledge of the machinations against Kun by Herbert Hoover and ARA officials in Europe. She thus hoped to bring pressure on the Wilson administration to lift the food blockade against Soviet children. Hoover had repeatedly stated that the ARA was ready to feed the Soviet Union as soon as there was a stable government there. Vorse meant to contrast the ARA's policy toward Hungary —where it was then feeding the children during the reign of the highly unstable government of the restored archduke—with its policy toward the Soviet Union. Despite her government's high-minded pronouncements, American policy was simply "not to permit aid to children in a communist government," Vorse believed.

In August 1919, the *Dial* agreed to publish the documents she had smuggled from Captain Gregory's office in Vienna. The editor wrote Vorse that these materials would "get the situation before the public" and "leave no doubts as to the policy of the Administration and the Supreme Council." But Vorse's knowledge of Herbert Hoover's political use of food was never printed. Before she could gather the background information she felt she needed for the article, a fire at her mother-in-law's house in Virginia destroyed all Gregory's letters and the other documents she had stored there.[23]

Devastated by the loss of one of her greatest journalistic scoops, Vorse unsuccessfully attempted to get more information from Captain Gregory and Herbert L. Gutterson, the New York official of the ARA European Children's Relief. Gutterson stalled his reply to her, pretending that he did not understand what material she needed, while assuring her that he was "in no way attempting to criticize your excellent efforts to inform the public." To Captain Gregory, Gutterson meanwhile wrote: "We have had to put the soft pedal on this lady" in view of Vorse's arrogant belief that "she is privileged . . . to publish articles . . . on ARA without any OK of our New York office."[24]

In September 1919, Vorse returned her older son, Heaton, to school. She left her younger children with Joe O'Brien's sister in Virginia. Vorse was on the track of what she felt to be one of the biggest labor stories yet. With an assignment from the *Outlook*, she headed to Pittsburgh to report the beginning of what would come to be known as the Great Steel Strike of 1919. She planned to finish her steel report in two or three weeks and then return with the children to New York for the winter. Instead, she began a long period of labor work. It would be three years before she and her children would live together again.

Part Four: 1919-1928

I always say you are like a moon. You wane to a mere hairline or crescent under trouble or sorrow and wax whole and full and bright when your needs are satisfied. May this happen again soon.

—Neith Boyce to MHV, 1924

I have heard my own flesh frying, have seen seven cold moons wheel over a desert which grew thorns, one for every star in heaven. I have scratched over bubbling black rocks under a sky of burning blue which strikes dead.

—MHV, 1925

Chapter Ten

Union Activist

The next eighteen months marked Vorse's most intense personal involvement in union work. She emerged from the 1919 steel strike and the 1920 Amalgamated lockout as the single most experienced labor publicist in the nation. Six years later she would put that hard-won knowledge to work at the 1926 Passaic, New Jersey, textile strike, where her brilliant supervision of publicity revolutionized union tactics and helped to set the pattern for the CIO battles of the 1930s. During 1919 and 1920 her work in labor publicity, and as a union organizer among shirtwaist workers in rural Pennsylvania, completed her radicalization. During the twenties, she lost any remaining faith in American liberalism as a route to fundamental change.

In 1919 the American steel industry was the marvel of the manufacturing world, producing more steel more cheaply than any competitor. Calculation of cost dominated every management decision. The greatest saving was made in the cost of labor. After the famous 1892 labor defeat at Homestead, Pennsylvania, the steelmakers eliminated unionization through well-financed blacklists and spy systems. In 1901, one-third of U.S. Steel's mills had union groups; by 1919, there was no union at all.

The industry's enormous rate of profit depended on the exploitation of the semiskilled and unskilled workers. Composed almost entirely of recent immigrants, this bottom two-thirds of the labor force existed on abysmally low wages. The accident rate of the unskilled was almost twice the average of the English-speaking workers. Local officials habitually cheated and jailed the lowest-paid workers for minor offenses, raking off a portion of the fines. Ethnic differences divided these workers from native workers and each other. Life in the Hunkyvilles of the steel district was dismal, harsh, and hopeless.

Labor stability was disrupted by the beginning of war in Europe, which slowed immigration and brought a labor shortage. Most important, the federal government, in an abrupt departure from tradition, set up a National War Labor Board that defended the right of labor to organize and put pressure on the steel companies to end the hated twelve-hour day. The unprecedented neutrality of the federal government led some AFL officials to believe that the time had come to organize the steel industry. The impetus came from Chicago, where William Z. Foster had successfully organized packing-house workers during the war. Representing the National Committee for Organizing the Iron and Steel Workers, Foster began work in the key Pittsburgh district in 1918. Meanwhile, however, the war ended and federal controls over business were relaxed. Steel management again had a free hand.[1]

During the first months of 1919 a fight for freedom of speech and freedom of assembly was waged by the steelworkers in the Pittsburgh district. Labor meetings were often forbidden by local public officials under pressure from the steel companies. "Jesus Christ himself could not speak in Duquesne for the A.F. of L.," the mayor there boasted. After 98 percent of the workers voting called for a strike, Foster and AFL President Samuel Gompers reluctantly set the date for late September. The Great Steel Strike, covering ten states and bringing out about 350,000 workers, could not be stopped. In preparation, Pennsylvania's Allegheny County sheriff forbade the meeting of three or more persons in any public outdoor place and deputized five thousand men who were chosen, paid, and armed by the steel companies. In addition, the mounted "Cossacks"—the state troopers—were spread thinly through the steel towns.[2]

Confronting this power, a small staff at the underfinanced headquarters office in Pittsburgh attempted to direct the revolt of over one-quarter of a million men. These included Foster, his wife and stepdaughter, one stenographer, a publicity agent named Edwin Newdick—and Mary. She began work as an unpaid publicist, serving as assistant to Newdick. She helped write the weekly strike bulletin, ran the mimeograph machine, handled correspondence, and visited the strike towns on various missions, sometimes on matters of relief, sometimes to speak at or to organize women's meetings. Within two days the strike consumed her completely. For the next seven weeks, her days were very structured. She arose at seven and wrote until ten. Then she reported to the strike headquarters and usually worked until eleven each night. At first, she "lived in a state of white-hot anger."[3] There seemed to be no end to the tales of violence and injustice. Later she became inured to the hourly reports of beatings, arrests, jail sentences, and fines.

Vorse seemed to be the only office worker who did not realize the strike was doomed from the start. The twenty-four AFL craft unions under the umbrella of the National Committee sabotaged their own effort. They refused to provide adequate funds or organizers and fought bitterly among themselves, split by jurisdictional disputes and ethnic hatreds. Civil liberty in western Pennsylvania simply ceased to exist for the strikers. From almost all the pulpits and newspapers of the country came hostility or silence. The strikers even lacked communication with one another. The wonder is that they held on as long as they did, through almost four months of strife.

When the strike began, the steel companies financed a media campaign that portrayed the union leadership as Soviet-inspired revolutionaries bent on destroying political democracy. That this charge was wholly without basis is a point on which all modern scholars agree. In fact, the left-wing parties at this time were urging the steelworkers not to follow AFL leadership. But in 1919, government, church, and press were almost unanimous in their denunciation of the nonexistent red menace.[4]

Charges of radicalism and violent repression of unionism by industrialists were hardly novelties in American labor history. Nor were news distortions or media blackouts of strike events anything new. But the circumstances surrounding the 1919 steel strike varied in one respect from previous labor wars. The difference was the existence of a private, reputable outside investigating body, which collected affidavits and sent investigators throughout the steel district to collect notarized evidence of illegalities and information on the workers' wages and living conditions. The report of the Interchurch World Movement, a liberal Protestant civic organization supported by forty-two denominations, exposed the sins of the steel industry in two volumes published in 1920 and 1921. The Interchurch Report was to make an important contribution to the eventual end of the twelve-hour day, and to the influential Senate investigation of the 1930s which exposed the union-busting tactics practiced by many employers.[5]

Vorse worked as an investigator with the Interchurch Commission of Inquiry, traveling widely through several states to gather facts. Her first sight of the Pennsylvania battlefield was in Butler and Braddock, where Foster sent her during the first week after she arrived in Pittsburgh. At Butler, strike organizers were arrested without warrants, robbed of their belongings, and slapped in jail without charges. In Braddock, by the end of December, 150 workers would be arrested, jailed, and fined on charges of laughing or smiling at the police or going out of their houses before daylight.

Vorse watched two of the trooper Cossacks ride abreast down the street; they were swinging their clubs. "The word went through the courts and alleys," she reported. "All the little boys ran out to stare at them. Women came out of houses and stood on doorsteps, their babies in their arms; striking steel workers came out from courtyards. . . . The Cossacks walked their horses to the end of the street; then they turned and smartly trotted their horses back. They drove the people from the street. They drove the women and children back from their stoops into the houses. . . . They looked as if they were having a good time seeing the people scurry into their homes like frightened rabbits." On an opposite corner a Polish worker stood defiantly. "I'm standing on my own stoop," he protested to the troopers. The officers cursed him, lifted their clubs, and made as if to ride into his house. The man very slowly turned and went into his home. A woman pulled at Vorse's arm and said: "Come inside missus, you'll get hurt."[6]

At this juncture, on November 12, a report on the activity of the Interchurch Commission was prepared by a corporation spy. The document gave prominent attention to Vorse.

> Mrs. Vorse . . . was a former member of the I.W.W. and took a very active part in the Range strike several years ago. . . . She has been active in a large number of the I.W.W. strikes and other radical movements, acting as a special writer for newspapers and magazines she gets away with a lot of propaganda for the I.W.W. . . . These are the worst kind of Reds to be connected with as they are to a certain extent high up in circles that are hard to reach and they can spread propaganda that hurts the work of others.[7]

This report was distributed in hundreds of thousands of copies by the steel industry as proof that the Interchurch Movement was controlled by "radical Reds." In December, ministers representing the Interchurch Commission of Inquiry met with Judge Elbert H. Gary, chairman of U.S. Steel. Gary refused to discuss any mediation plan for ending the strike; he instead grilled the nationally known clergymen for over two hours about the charges made in the document.

The Ohio Manufacturing Association published the report on December 9 and circulated it among its seven hundred members. After weeks of legal battles, in which the Interchurch Commission was forced to squander thousands of dollars of its slim resources, the Ohio Association retracted its charges. Nevertheless, the report was published in *Industry* and anonymously distributed nationwide. Even as late as the summer of 1920, the Industrial Conference Board, representing the country's largest manufacturers, circulated hundreds of copies.

In early November 1919, Vorse learned that the aged radical agitator, Mother Jones, was in Pittsburgh. Jay Brown, a union leader, warned Vorse not to be hurt if Mother Jones was rude to her, for she didn't like middle-class women. Mother Jones had not changed her style of dress in two decades—a black silk basque with a lavender vest and lace around the neck, a bonnet covering her white hair.

"Why Mary O'Brien, it's you," Mother Jones cried and kissed her.

Mother Jones had admired Joe O'Brien. "For the hundredth time I had a friend because I had been his wife," Vorse remembered.

Vorse traveled with Mother Jones on a speaking tour to Ohio. Mother Jones sat beside Vorse on the train, talking almost to herself: "Oh, it's coming. . . . There's a terrible bitter tide rolling up and welling up in this country. . . . Look at these towns; look out of the window. . . . Look at . . . the wealth . . . made by the blood of slaves."

Mother Jones could not endure the suffering of the workers' children. It was related in her mind to the indifference of rich women. She talked of "brutal women hung about with the decorations they have bought with the blood of children." This was to her a literal fact.[8]

Vorse spent two weeks traveling with Mother Jones through Pennsylvania, West Virginia, and Ohio, talking to the strikers and organizers. She visited a women's meeting in the basement of a Slovak church in Pennsylvania. There were about seventy women there, many carrying their babies. Most of them wore the frilled caps the women in steel towns used to keep the slack out of their hair. "They did not sit quiet the way the men did at meetings," Vorse wrote. "They talked back to the organizer. He sweated under their questions. They wanted to know the exact status of the strike; they wanted to know their chances of winning. They wanted to know if they got out on the picket line if it would help." The organizer talked to them in their own language, his voice tight with earnestness. "You could feel the women's will to fight. It was terrible to realize that all their sacrifices and all their courage were in vain."[9]

Day after day, Vorse strained to write stories like these about the steel-workers and their families, driving herself to find the right combination of words, the exact tone that would elicit the reader's understanding, would dissolve the fog of press lies and half-lies that obscured the progress of the strike, would express the meaning of lives strung in conflict against overwhelming power. Her stories appeared in the strike bulletin, in labor newspapers, in the *Survey, Outlook,* and the *Nation.* She made hardly a dent in the national press coverage so hostile to "Red Foster" and his gang of "revolutionaries."

Privately, Vorse and her co-worker Edwin Newdick bemoaned Foster's closed nature, his lack of communicative skills, his rigid and suspicious spirit. When Vorse visited Samuel Gompers's office in an attempt to win a statement of support from him, Newdick reported to Vorse that Foster resented her interference. "I feel very much up in the air," Newdick wrote her, "if every publicity idea which we work up ourselves is to be sat upon by Foster." Toward the end of the strike, Newdick again voiced his despair to Vorse. "I have felt that there was a tragic inadequacy in the smug advice of the [daily strike] Bulletins—of course, we were doing the best we could, but sometimes it sickened me to think of those fine strikers alert and waiting for a leader. . . . Thank you so much for your help and encouragement. I realize *poignantly* what it means. Economic determinism grant us a chance some day to retrieve this inadequate performance and apply some of the things which we've learned here." [10]

Vorse traveled twice to New York during the strike. Her liberal friends were amazed to learn that thousands of men were still out. "A reader of the Pittsburgh newspapers," the Interchurch Report stated, "must have gained the impression that the large number of men conceded to have gone out on September 22 had done so with no other intention than that of turning round and flocking back to their jobs beginning September 23." The editors in New York were not interested in stories of a living strike. With all the steel centers crippled, the strike went on as though in a vacuum.

From Pittsburgh, Vorse wrote urgent emotional appeals to liberals across the nation. To William Hard, author of the famous muckraker article of 1907, "Making Steel and Killing Men": "I beg you to write the story of this steel strike. . . . If we who call ourselves liberal . . . do not cry out when all the rights and liberties on which America is supposed to rest are cynically denied in this fashion, no one else will." To Will Irwin, her boss on the Committee on Public Information: "I wish it were possible for you to use your pen in fighting Prussianism at home." To William Allen White, a liberal editor: "I wish to goodness you would see your way clear to take a trip up here. . . . Here is a strike which is the turning point perhaps of the industrial history of America, and it is of the greatest importance that the public at large should know all they can about it. But none of the liberal writers have yet turned up here. . . . Not a word has been said about the sweeping denial of the liberties of the people."[11]

Vorse's political experience during the steel strike and later so intrigued the author John Dos Passos that he patterned several of his fictional characters on her life. He and his wife Katy were longtime friends and neighbors of Vorse's, Katy having settled in Provincetown in the early 1920s. Scholars who have discussed the work of Dos Passos have not recognized that he used Mary Vorse as the model for his portrayal of Mary French, one of the twelve leading characters in his classic trilogy *U.S.A.* Through Mary French (and later in his creation of Anne Comfort in *Chosen Country*), Dos Passos showed his grudging fascination with Mary Vorse's wholehearted devotion to labor's cause.[12]

Yet Dos Passos presented Mary French's courage and idealism, her propensity to make sacrificial personal choices, as essentially pathetic, because unrewarded. Mary French is steamrollered by powers beyond her reach and eventually betrayed by every political force, even by the left. If Mary French earns more sympathy and respect from Dos Passos than any other character in his trilogy, she is nonetheless shown to be as uncomprehending and helpless as every other radical in *U.S.A.* He wrote the story of Mary French at a time when the disastrous effect of Mary Vorse's love affair with Robert Minor was still fresh in his mind. Dos Passos used the life of Mary French to illustrate his theme of humanism destroying itself in collision with the rigidity of the egocentric left.

As portrayed in *The Big Money* in 1936, Mary French develops a social conscience through the example of her gentle father. She is inspired to redirect her life, "thinking of the work there was to be done to make the country what it ought to be, the social conditions, the slums, the shanties with filthy tottering backhouses, the miners' children in grimy coats too big for them, the overworked women stooping over stoves, the youngsters struggling for an education in nightschools, hunger and unemployment and drink, and the police and the lawyers and the judges always ready to take it out on the weak." In Pittsburgh, Mary French is fired from her job as a reporter when she writes a story sympathetic to the workers during the 1919 steel strike. Like Mary Vorse, she then becomes a publicity worker in Foster's office in Pittsburgh.

As publicist for the strikers, Mary French "had never worked so hard in her life." She sees "meetings broken up and the troopers in their darkgray uniforms, moving in a line down the unpaved alleys of company patches, beating up men and women with their clubs, kicking children out of their way, chasing old men off their front stoops." She "spent hours trying to wheedle A.P. and U.P. men into sending straight stories" out of Pittsburgh, and "smoothed out the grammar in the Englishlanguage leaflets."

The fall flies by. Her clothes fall into disrepair, her hair is uncurled, she has no money. She cannot sleep "for the memory of the things she'd seen, the jailings, the bloody heads, the wreck of some family's parlor, sofa cut open, chairs smashed, chinacloset hacked to pieces with an axe, after the troopers had been through looking for 'literature.'"

Finally, Dos Passos allows Mary French to realize that the strike is over, "that the highpaid workers weren't coming out and that the lowpaid workers were going to lose their strike." Mary French hardly knows herself when she looks "at her face in the greenspotted giltframed mirror over the washstand." Like Mary Vorse in 1920, Mary French had "a haggard, desperate look. She was beginning to look like a striker herself." With so much in the balance, the defeat of the strike has become Mary French's personal tragedy.

"Do we live in two worlds?" Mary Vorse wrote in her journal in late 1919. "Is there no means to communicate what I see to those who live outside? I am living inside a world where people are toiling only to hang on to life, and their efforts for betterment are met with suspicion and hate. But I do not mind the hate as much as the complacent indifference, or that complacence so much as the ignorance and hostility of the good who are the unknowing tools of rapacity and greed." [13]

When Mary Vorse visited Youngstown she heard the gasping sobs of a man outside the union office. A steelworker was crying because he had scabbed. He said, "I didn't mean to. They told me everyone had gone back to work." His friends stood around him, embarrassed, silent, clumsily patting his shoulder. He leaned against the wall, sobbing, his face in his arms. For Vorse, the sound of the steelworker's groans in the dark hall outside the strike office in Youngstown would always represent the doomed soul of the Great Steel Strike. [14]

In the last dreary weeks of the strike, before its official end on January 8, 1920, came the raids of the Department of Justice. In the steel towns workers were spirited away. Their families were left without support, told nothing of their men's fate. Some of the workers were deported. Most, after having been held in prison for months without charge, eventually returned home. The steel strike concluded without a single gain for the workers. Twenty workers' lives had been lost. William Foster gravitated toward the Communists and Samuel Gompers became even more vehement in his denunciation of "bolshevism." The "lean years" of labor in the 1920s had begun.

In early January 1920, the Red Scare climaxed with the Palmer raids. Virtually every Communist or left-socialist leader was either forced underground or arrested during the next few months. Attorney General A. Mitchell Palmer's rampage netted some five thousand persons in over thirty cities. Wholesale arrests were made in pool halls, homes, cafes, or wherever radicals were believed to meet. An orchestra and all the dancers were arrested at an allegedly left-wing dance. In one town in Connecticut, the persons who visited the suspected radicals in jail were also arrested. It was not until the late spring of 1920 that the illegalities of federal, state, and local agencies were stemmed by a tardy protest from some outraged judges, reporters, government officials, and prominent liberals. By this time, the disruption of the American radical movement was nearly complete, and the trade unions thoroughly cowed.[15]

After her return to New York, Vorse feared that her radical connections, or her involvement with Robert Minor, might also sweep her into the Department of Justice net. When the raids began, Minor and all of her socialist and Wobbly friends who were able to had either left the city temporarily or were staying with relatives or friends for a few days, until they could judge the nature of the terror raised against them. Vorse's class background and literary reputation were no certain proof against arrest. By late 1919, not only workers and aliens, but liberals of every type—clergy, teachers, publishers, journalists, even elected officials—were coming under suspicion from right-wing groups and government spokesmen.

Vorse may have realized that she had been under the surveillance of the Department of Justice since at least early 1919. While she was still in Europe, the Bureau of Investigation had begun an investigation of the source of an anarchist pamphlet that was first distributed in San Francisco. The trail eventually led a bureau agent named McDevitt to Hippolyte Havel in the Village. Posing as an Irish radical, McDevitt fed Havel liquor, waited until he passed out, and then stole Havel's address book. Vorse's name was one of those reported by McDevitt when he presented the bureau with his discovery of that dangerous "radical group"— the Provincetown Players. McDevitt had a special grudge against Vorse. He warned his superiors that it was she who, through a mysterious "government connection," had tipped off Havel about McDevitt's true identity and thus blown the agent's cover in the Village.[16]

During the Red Scare, J. Edgar Hoover collected a "Weekly Radical Report" from his field officers across the nation. Vorse's involvement with the organizations graded "Ultra-Radical" was periodically noted; these "subversive" groups included the steelworkers' organizing committee, the Interchurch World Movement, the Federated Press wire service, the Amalgamated Clothing Workers, and the American Civil Liberties Union. Hoover also kept confidential files in his personal office. These special files, kept separate from the bureau's, and later, the FBI's central records, sometimes contained information obtained by the government through illegal means (such as break-ins or mail robberies), or held tidbits of political intelligence that Hoover thought he might later use to ingratiate himself with powerful men and high public officials, or to influence those persons into cooperation with bureau needs.

In November 1919, Hoover's "Personal and Confidential" file held a copy of an illegally obtained letter addressed to Vorse at Pittsburgh. The letter was from Harry Weinberger, a liberal attorney in New York City. Weinberger was intent on awakening labor organizations to the way in which the federal government's deportation arrests in the fall of 1919 were designed, not to catch reds, but to break strikes. "The first manifestation of that has appeared in the steel strike," Weinberger wrote Vorse. He asked her to obtain the names of all strikers recently arrested in the Pittsburgh area, the circumstances of their arrests, a copy of the alleged charges, and a statement of where the men were being held. Special agent R. B. Spence from the bureau's Philadelphia office forwarded to his superiors a copy of this stolen letter. Spence marked it, "Refer to Mr. Hoover," with the warning: "Inasmuch as this letter came from a very confidential source out of the Department, and the original reached Mrs. [Mary Heaton Vorse] O'Brien through the usual course of the mails, it is requested that you handle this information very carefully." Hoover placed it for safekeeping in his separate "Personal and Confidential" file system.[17]

Thus in early January 1920, with so many of her friends in jail or fleeing the city, it is understandable that Vorse was afraid to stay in New York. At this time the Amalgamated Clothing Workers of America was providing transportation for some of its best people, those who felt most vulnerable to Palmer's "Reign of Terror," to areas outside the state. Making use of her union friends, Vorse hastily acquired a job as an organizer with the Amalgamated—in the safely distant coalfields of rural Pennsylvania.

After the grim struggle in steel, her work with the Amalgamated seemed to her almost a light interlude. Yet state troopers were to be called out on her account. She was to lead a strike, to be thrown out of halls, to be called a Bolshevik and a wildcat, and to have her union stolen from her by the AFL. Only to someone who had come from the scenes of the steel strike could organizing shirtmakers seem a relaxation.

————

Vorse was sent to Pottsville, Pennsylvania, eighty miles northwest of Philadelphia, where the Amalgamated was conducting a campaign in the heart of the anthracite region. She was assigned as assistant to a neophyte organizer, Ann Craton, who would become a lifelong friend and a major financial benefactor in Vorse's last years. The story of Ann Craton's political and intellectual development before 1920 is important for all it reveals about the influence of Vorse's generation of rebellious women on their younger admirers, and about the effect of tumultuous social protest on idealistic young people of this era.[18]

Ann Craton had been born to wealth in North Carolina. Her social education began with the suffrage movement. As a college student in Washington, D.C., she had marched in cap and gown with fifteen thousand women in the suffrage parade of March 1913. The women's ranks were attacked by a jeering mob of men. She saw hoodlums drag women out of line, tear their clothes and banners, and pummel them with rotten fruit, while police and soldiers stood by laughing. Linking arms, four abreast, the women stuck to their aim, pushing through the hostile throng. It was Ann Craton's baptism in politics.

After graduation from George Washington University in 1915, Craton worked briefly in a settlement house. She left social work in the autumn of 1918 when she joined a team of three hundred women field agents hired to gather statistics for the U.S. Bureau of Labor. The fieldworkers were to go to seventy-one large industrial cities and twenty-six small cities to collect facts and figures on how much it cost workers to live. Craton's teammate was a young socialist woman who stressed the evidence of class exploitation which they daily observed on their tour.

After her government job ended, Ann Craton knew New York City—with its "foreign restaurants with red tablecloths and its Greenwich Village tearooms, with dripping candles, frequented by socialists, labor leaders, the intelligentsia"—was the place for her. She took a job with a child labor committee that sought to keep children in school and out of the crowded labor market. She was too open in her criticism of the rich women who helped to finance the program. "You have such a regrettable way of putting the wrong emphasis on things," said her supervisor with patience. "Try to remember that we are living through most disturbing times and we must all keep the proper balance. Avoid turning to the left, my dear," the supervisor told her.

Craton had her red card now, not in the Socialist Party but in the left wing of the socialist movement. She could not warm up to the Communist Labor Party leaders. The comrades implied that she did not read enough party literature. Craton didn't like the theoretical approach, she told them. She thought it was silly to distribute party leaflets on the waterfront that called on the peasants and workers of New York to unite.

After social reform and leftist politics had failed her, Craton decided to try the labor movement. She chose to work with the Amalgamated Clothing Workers, which in 1914 had broken from the AFL in protest against craft unionism and the corrupt labor bureaucracy. With courage born of naïveté, she made an appointment to see Sidney Hillman, head of the Amalgamated. His receptionist kindly sandwiched her between two labor delegations who were waiting to see him. Hillman listened politely to her halting explanation about how she wanted to be an organizer. He fired questions at her: "Did she belong to a Union? Could she run a machine? What did she know of factory conditions?" She found his Russian-Jewish accent hard to follow. "Just as I expected," Hillman dismissed her. "You sentimental middle-class liberals take up my time. The labor movement has more to offer you than you do to it." If she was really sincere about wanting to work in the labor movement, he said, why not work in a nonunion factory and demonstrate her capacity by organizing her co-workers? She managed to stammer that as an English-speaking native American, she could be helpful in organizing the large number of women in the shirt industry, the majority of whom were native-born young girls. Hillman looked thoughtful for a long moment. Then he shook his head firmly. He was a busy man. "I am sorry I can't use you," he said. Crestfallen, she crept away.

The next morning's mail brought Craton a letter from the Amalgamated Clothing Workers. It was signed, "Sidney Hillman, General President." She read that she was appointed a general organizer and directed to report at once to the Shirtmakers' Union in Philadelphia.

And so it was that Ann Craton, in Pottsville, Pennsylvania, on January 10, 1920, a week after the Palmer raids, intersected with the "distinguished novelist" and "veteran labor reporter," Mary Heaton Vorse, as the Pottsville newspaper described her.[19] Craton felt "proud and protected" to be teamed with Vorse. Vorse was nearly twice Craton's age, but she liked the young woman at once. In many ways they shared a common history.

They seemed a good team, novice organizers though they were. Craton looked too small and too young to be charged with such a difficult responsibility, Vorse thought. She looked hardly older than the girls they hoped to organize.

When the clothing trades were organized a decade before, some of the shirt manufacturers had escaped union wages by moving their factories to the little mining towns of Schuylkill County in Pennsylvania. There was little other employment available to the miners' wives and daughters who were recruited for the shirt factories. The factory girls—many under fifteen years old—worked for as little as $3.50 a week. Most worked a six-day week and an eight- to nine-hour day. The sweatshop had also moved into the beautiful Schuylkill valley towns. The older women—widows or women with large families or sick husbands—did piecework at home. They were paid an average of ten cents an hour.

In the Schuylkill valley, the Amalgamated fought the AFL. Employers who feared an Amalgamated victory in their factories frequently called in AFL affiliates like the United Textile Workers or the United Garment Workers to raid the Amalgamated's organization. Employers preferred to deal with the more conservative AFL unions, which had demonstrated less obvious concern for the welfare of women workers.

Vorse went to Pottsville with Dora Lohse, the Amalgamated's ace woman organizer, and Abe Plotkin, a union official from Philadelphia. Plotkin told them how Department of Justice agents had seized union records and broken into some of the union members' houses in Philadelphia. Dora Lohse had been at a Socialist Party meeting in Brooklyn when Palmer's agents struck. They had broken down the door and searched everyone for "subversive" literature. In the confusion Lohse escaped and hid in a rear hallway. Later she climbed down the ice-coated fire escape into a courtyard where she hid behind the garbage cans for hours, until she could go to a friend's house. The Amalgamated officials had promptly shipped her off, along with Vorse, to the safety of the Pennsylvania coalfields.

Lohse announced that she was too tired to speak at the union meeting Craton had arranged that evening for the young girl workers from the silk mill. She complained that her back still hurt from sliding down the fire escape.

Vorse agreed to speak in Lohse's place. When Vorse and Craton reached the meeting hall, the door was locked from the inside. A policeman and a man wearing a red hat and carrying an ax came toward them. Mr. Stevenson, the fire chief of Pottsville, was also the president of the Pottsville Central Labor Union. He shouted: "There they are." He pointed his ax at Vorse and Craton. "There are the wildcats. Throw them out!"

The lone policeman looked at tiny Ann Craton and Vorse. "Throw out *them? Throw?*," he asked in wonder. Stevenson assumed a heroic pose to bar the door, as though he were stopping the Red Hordes.

Just then, the door opened and a disheveled Abe Plotkin was shoved violently outside. More people emerged from the room. The officers of the new silk workers' union were accompanied by two portly men smoking cigars and wearing heavy gold watch chains.

"AF of L organizers," Craton heard Vorse gasp.

Stevenson made a long speech about how Vorse and Craton were trying to lead the good working people of Pottsville into a red union. The Central Labor Union had discovered their deceit in time, he said, and had invited the only legitimate union, the United Textile Workers, to take over the silk workers' local.

Vorse and Craton were escorted away by the friendly policeman.

Later they knocked on Lohse's door. She was in bed reading. They told her of the evening's events. She stood on the bed in her long white nightgown. She threw books and pillows at them. She cursed. She flung her bedroom slippers at them.

"You didn't force your way into the hall you had paid for?" Lohse cried. "You didn't try to speak? You let the United Textile Workers steal your $300.00 Treasury, your 300 members, and your charter?"

Lohse stumbled over the bedclothes to reach Plotkin who was sitting on the edge of the bed, his face in his hands. She shook him vigorously before she pushed him onto the floor.

"The three of you stood there? Without opening your mouths? You innocents, you intellectuals, you parlor pinks! What good are you in the labor movement?" Lohse shrieked.

It was not a propitious beginning for Vorse and Ann Craton. Yet Stevenson, in his ludicrous fireman's outfit, and the genial policeman were not, after all, the hard-mouthed troopers and armed drunken thugs of the steel district. She was now in Molly MacGuire country, Vorse knew. The young girls they sought to organize were the daughters of miners with a long history of union fights behind them. The sympathy of local labor was a comforting background for her work in these small towns of eastern Pennsylvania. Despite her initial failure, Vorse felt contented—and safe.

It was not long before Craton and Vorse, inexperienced as they were, signed up the girls and called a strike. Vorse helped organize the picket lines. One morning Craton stopped one of the young scabs hurrying by and put her hand gently on the girl's shoulder. For this Craton was arrested for assault and intimidation. The Amalgamated officials in Philadelphia paid the six-hundred-dollar bail and impatiently explained to their two green organizers that the law forbade them to touch anyone.

When Vorse and Craton learned that an AFL man was coming to town, they were determined to redeem themselves from any reputation as "parlor pinks." The best tactic, they decided, was direct confrontation. They enlisted two boys to announce throughout the miners' quarters that there would be a special meeting that night, an unusual mixed meeting for women and men together.

Strange rumors circulated throughout the day and the meeting room was jammed. Vorse and Craton explained that the AFL would try to use the miners to influence their daughters, when the Amalgamated had been first in the field, had made the first effort to organize their daughters. Everyone agreed that the miners would allow Vorse and Craton to debate their case freely with the organizer from the United Garment Workers before a decision was made.

Finally the UGW man arrived, a Mr. Berkson. A mammoth overflow meeting was held in the United Mine Workers' Hall. Berkson looked nervous and very unhappy. "He says that he did not come here for a debate," the miners told Craton and Vorse. "He says he thinks he will go." The miners, however, were not about to cancel the show. Many of them had left their night shifts for the anticipated entertainment. On the floor sat the giggling Amalgamated girls. They had been allowed in by the doorkeeper. Berkson was forced forward.

It wasn't much of a speech. Berkson lauded the AFL. He claimed the Amalgamated was an IWW union. He wanted to save their innocent girls from such a red union, he said. Then Vorse and Craton spoke. No matter what they said the miners cheered them. Vorse asked sweetly if "Brother Berkson" had anything more to say. He did not. A miner rose to announce to their visitor that there was no train leaving town that night, but that there was one that left early in the morning. More cheers.[20]

It was a day that Vorse and Ann Craton called forever after "The Perfect Day." The bourgeois intellectuals lost a strike. But they made a union.

Vorse continued her work with the Amalgamated in New York City for another year, primarily as general publicist and writer for the union's newspaper, the *Advance*. Although the work paid very little, she was able to survive through the sale of a few lollypops to the women's magazines and several articles on labor and postwar Europe to the better-paying journals like *Harper's* and *Outlook*. With her two youngest children living with their Aunt Josie in Texas, her expenses were low. Vorse felt her work with the Amalgamated produced some of the best labor pieces she ever wrote during her long career as a labor journalist.

By 1920, the counteroffensive of capital was in full stride. Conservative clothing manufacturers charged the Amalgamated with bolshevization of the American clothing industry. After a bumbling attempt by several employers to bribe union officials was exposed to the public by Hillman, the Clothing Manufacturers' Association of New York made clear its determination to break the Amalgamated and to institute the open shop in New York City. On December 8, 1920, the famed New York lockout began when thousands of union members were fired; the next day Vorse began full-time work with the publicity section at the Amalgamated headquarters in New York City. The long lockout, lasting six months, was a war of attrition. The union had the task of feeding tens of thousands of union members and their families, organizing armies of pickets, and keeping up union spirit, while informing members and outsiders of the real meaning of the strike and its progress.

Heber Blankenhorn (later to marry Ann Craton) was director of union publicity. Blankenhorn, an ex-editor of the New York *Evening Sun*, had first known Vorse well in his position as investigator for the Interchurch World Movement during the steel strike. He hired Vorse, her sister Heterodite Gertrude Williams, and former A Clubber Robert Bruere to staff the publicity office for the Amalgamated during the lockout. Blankenhorn and Bruere had earlier established the Bureau of Industrial Research, one of the first efforts to generate favorable publicity for trade unionism. Their work on the Interchurch Report taught them that union survival depended on adequate labor research and reporting, then virtually nonexistent as an organized effort. In the fall of 1919, they helped to form the Federated Press, a nonprofit daily news service providing labor news and national news from a labor viewpoint.[21]

Blankenhorn convinced Sidney Hillman that the big job of publicity was not with Amalgamated members, but with "the metropolitan dailies that influenced the big employers, the reporters, the courts, the police department and city hall." Vorse was hired to do human interest news "for the labor press, the string of 200 small labor papers around the country, and 125 out-of-town papers" that subscribed to the new Federated Press Service. Hillman soon learned the value of effective publicity. Later, he added an information service, which distributed daily communiqués to union halls all over the country and to press and government officials.[22]

During the long months of the lockout, Vorse traveled the union-hall circuit, arranging meetings, investigating relief cases, organizing the speakers' bureau, interviewing the workers. Her series of articles was syndicated throughout the labor press of the country. She was "fulfilling the promise that she had made to herself eight years before," to "write about workers, and for workers." [23]

By April, the solidarity and peaceful determination of union members severely demoralized the employers. The lockout ended when the union shop and conditions that Hillman had offered six months earlier were accepted by the employers. In the dismal labor history of union defeats in the 1920s, the victory after the Amalgamated lockout is one bright spot.

Vorse was now a seasoned union activist. At Lawrence and the Mesabi, in the steel strike, in mining towns in Pennsylvania, in the New York lockout, she sharpened her political and social analysis. Her best lessons about the nature of the forces opposing the poor and unorganized were gained firsthand.

At age forty-six, she had pushed a long way past Amherst.

Chapter Eleven

Smashup

From her return home from Paris in June 1919, until her next trip abroad two years later, Vorse rarely remained in one spot as long as she did during the Amalgamated lockout. Aside from the summer she spent in Provincetown in 1920, she commuted almost biweekly between New York and Washington or Pittsburgh. During 1920 she published two books of light fiction and completed the manuscript of her well-received ninth book, *Men and Steel*, the story of the steel strike. Her literary production in this period included a string of short stories and articles. Her writing and labor work represent an astounding output of energy during the immediate postwar years.[1]

She saw her children infrequently. Heaton was away at school. Joel and Ellen lived with Joe O'Brien's sister in the Southwest. Although Vorse later claimed to regret her "neglect" of the children during this time, there is no trace of remorse in her journal. One senses that she was too busy and absorbed to think much of the two youngest children, who seemed content under the care of their aunt, Josie Harn, the childless wife of an army officer.

Vorse's movements from 1920 through 1922 are difficult to trace. The rich documentary record of her personal life that she normally maintained is missing; during these two years she apparently destroyed the material or never recorded her activities. Perhaps her frequent movement left her no time for correspondence, or to write her usual "Daily Notes" and "Yearly Summaries." It is possible, too, that she later found a record of this time —a period marked by her affair with Robert Minor and her absence from her children—as either too painful or too guilt provoking to preserve. Forty-five years later, Vorse instructed her sons upon her death to destroy her collection of Minor's letters, a request they dutifully honored.[2] It also seems likely that Vorse hid the evidence of her activity as a means of self-protection against sundry redbaiters and Department of Justice agents. Her reluctance to record her doings can be reasonably explained by this factor alone, in light of the political hysteria that then convulsed the nation.

Vorse's activities were closely monitored by labor spies, informers, and government agents. Distorted descriptions of her involvement were given in weekly and monthly reports to J. Edgar Hoover. In November 1919, the Thiel Detective Agency, an anti-union group for hire, informed the Department of Justice that Vorse—along with several anarchist, IWW, communist, and AFL leaders—had met in Chicago and formed a plan, under the leadership of John Reed, to overthrow the U.S. government and kill all high public officials. Prisoners taken in the Red Scare Palmer raids in Chicago were questioned about this supposed meeting.

In March 1920, Department of Justice agent Rodney from Chicago reported to Frank Burke, chief of the Washington office of the Bureau of Investigation, describing Vorse's trip from Chicago to New York in company with Roger Baldwin of the American Civil Liberties Union. Rodney warned his boss that Mary Vorse and Roger Baldwin were plotting to arrange a meeting at Madison Square Garden where Bill Haywood would speak.

The Department of Justice record of Rodney's report is preserved at the National Archives in coded and decoded form. Apparently, the federal agents had a great deal of fun when they devised their code. Their mortal enemy, the American Civil Liberties Union, they hopefully dubbed CHECKMATED BASSOONS. Roger Baldwin's big-mouthed socialist rhetoric, they must have felt, made him deserving of the code name FABIAN HEVMOUP. Vorse's reputation with the agents as a woman of quality was stained. She emerged as an old cow of easy sexual availability. Her code name was BISON QUIXWOO.[3]

A few months later, Vorse began her investigation of the historic Sacco and Vanzetti case. When Carlo Tresca and his group of anarchists decided to raise money for defense, Tresca and Elizabeth Gurley Flynn asked Vorse for help with publicity. Minor and Flynn produced the first Sacco and Vanzetti defense pamphlet. Vorse and Flynn traveled to the Dedham jail to see Sacco and also met with Sacco's wife in the late spring or early fall of 1920. The Sacco and Vanzetti case, Vorse reported, "is bound up with all the fight that is going on for the closed shop and the unalterable determination of the employers to smash the workers." Vorse's discussion of the interviews appeared in the New York *Call* in December and in Norman Thomas's magazine, the *World Tomorrow*, in January 1921. This and John Beffel's article in the *New Republic* on December 29, 1920, were the first published journal alerts to the significance of the case. It was also Vorse who first brought the plight of Sacco and Vanzetti to the attention of the American Civil Liberties Union. She appeared before the ACLU Executive Committee on November 22, 1920, to elicit the first funds and support from them for the defense effort. Aided by the ACLU, Felix Frankfurter, later a Supreme Court Justice, eventually took over the leadership of the Sacco and Vanzetti defense, enlisting the aid of prominent intellectuals and bringing the cause new respectability.[4]

In the two years after the war, Vorse enjoyed only one extended period of quiet. The summer of 1920 was a memorably happy one for her. She realized her hope to have Minor with her in Provincetown for a few weeks without interruption.[5] She finished *Men and Steel* that summer. Minor, as he later described it, settled down in this "out-of-the-way place" to study Bolshevik theory. To assist him in his reeducation program, he was joined for a while in Provincetown by Leo Caplan, his frail mentor from St. Louis who had won him to socialism in 1907. Minor and Caplan, who was now a supporter of Lenin, debated the nature of the new Soviet state. Minor's 1919 trip to the Soviet Union had convinced him that Lenin and Trotsky had established "a complete monopoly of news, fact and opinion" in order to silence the "more radical revolutionaries . . . behind the dark cloak of secrecy."[6]

Vorse shared Minor's opinion of Bolshevik terror. She likened Lenin's true believers to religious fanatics. She wrote Minor in 1920:

> The peculiar stern gloom of the Communist state . . . is not alone the result of blockade and war. It is part and parcel of these people who think that they and they alone have the truth, and who also think they have *all the truth there is.* . . . The Communists are the chosen people and they have all the unsufferable qualities which God's elect and anointed have always had. Leo [Caplan] resented my saying they were like the Puritans. . . .
>
> Leo is a great wizard, he explains everything. He almost explains away the things I myself have seen and the things you say you have seen.[7]

Minor's and Vorse's rejection of Bolshevik dictatorship—their views simplistically stated, and based on little evidence, for they wrote this at a time when westerners knew little of Soviet events—revealed their longtime revulsion at elite control. Yet, within a few months after his 1920 summer in Provincetown, Minor would become a fervent believer in Bolshevik theory and a pliant functionary in the service of Soviet state policy.

By January 1921, Minor's allegiance to Soviet-style communism was complete. He never turned back. Until his death in 1952, he followed every twist in the party line dictated to the American Communist leadership by the needs of Soviet foreign policy. So adept did Minor eventually become at Communist Party hopscotch that he has achieved some symbolic value as an example of the ultimate party hack for many students of American communism. One must not conclude, however, that he saw himself as an agent of a foreign power. On the contrary, he was a committed internationalist who could give himself freely to the control of the Comintern because, in theory, it was the world party, which would further economic equality for oppressed people in all countries. For Minor, the failure of the world revolution, apparent by 1920, made all the more splendid the success of the revolution in the Soviet "workers' state."

In light of Minor's domineering personality, it seems probable that his relationship with Vorse could not have continued had she firmly opposed his new political ideals. But neither could she accept them in the way he wished. He was able to accept an impatient compromise. Vorse promised to read and study the works of Lenin while Minor was away on a national speaking tour. "Minor always called me bourgeois," Vorse recalled in 1957 for the Oral History Project at Columbia University. "He never pressured me to become a Party member. I don't think he thought I was fit for it."[8] Their political differences were placed in limbo for the time being.

Political disagreement was not the only conflict that shadowed their union. Even in the blissful summer of 1920, her love for him carried barbs of ambivalence. For one thing, she found herself unable to accept his literary criticism with what he felt to be the proper grace. She discovered that his overflowing self-esteem could be wearing, his verbosity stifling, his purity of soul impregnable. In the early months of their partnership, he chided her for sending him a book of poems: "Mary, child, don't you see that writings like that in which the meaning of words is warped, twisted, ravished, aimlessly to drag on in a perfectly inane sound recurrence is not beautiful?" So much for poetry. She confided to her diary that it required of her "something full of effort" to endure his single-minded concentration on revolutionary politics, to the exclusion of most all other enjoyment in living.

In the summer of 1920, her repressed scorn for Minor's puritanical certainty was best expressed in the little game that she played with her teenage son, Heaton. Whenever Minor approached, she and Heaton were in the habit of humming—surreptitiously, to be sure—the opening strains of Richard Wagner's *The Twilight of the Gods*, a paean to the Teutonic deities who were greater than life.[9]

But the most terrible blow to Vorse's serenity during the 1920 summer in Provincetown came with the invasion of a specter from Minor's past. In mid-August, Minor received a letter from Lydia Gibson, the beautiful young radical poet whom he had first met in San Francisco four years before when he worked on the Tom Mooney defense effort. Minor had fallen in love with Gibson then, but had been spurned by her.

Gibson's first letter to Minor in Provincetown, addressed to Vorse's house, was direct. Why, she asked, had he not told her that his divorce from his first wife, Pearl Minor, was final? And why was he living with Mary Vorse? Did he love her more than he had once loved Lydia Gibson?

Minor's initial response was cool. He and Vorse had a perfect under-standing, he wrote Gibson: "She is independent and so am I. We tell each other nearly everything because we want to and we can, and not because we have to. . . . If ever it becomes otherwise we must part. But [loving] Mary and admiring her and being free, I have no intention of leaving her." Yet, he hedged, if ever his feelings should change, he would not live with Vorse if he preferred another, "for [Mary] is not the kind of person I could treat in such ignominious fashion." Within a week Gibson returned two special delivery letters and a telegram to Minor. Her lavish interest in him produced a sudden change of tone in his next letter to her. Minor promised to see her during his next lecture tour; "with unlimited joy I will see you."[10] Thus did he overcome his distaste for rhyme and elevate his lust for a young poet to an abstraction worthy of consummate union on his next trip west.

When Minor left to begin his speaking tour, Vorse awaited his return in Provincetown and New York. At first, her letters to him were warmly adoring. But as the weeks grew to months with only an infrequent letter from him, the tone of her letters grew plaintive. "A sense of loss rises about me. . . . I love you so it hurts. I had not wanted again in my life to have my heart so in the keeping of someone else." Next, Vorse voiced distrust, poorly disguised as bravado: "These long tests of endurance and patience to which you have of necessity put me place their inevitable wounds deep in my unconscious. It may take a while for my inner self not to flutter frayed on the wing of doubt. . . . There is another thing: I wrote Elizabeth [Gurley Flynn] giving her a humorous description of my state of mind.

She answered in a panic: 'Mary, any woman can love him too abjectly and too indulgently.'"

Finally the letters from Minor stopped coming. Vorse hardened herself against the hurt. "*I will not suffer*," she wrote in her diary. "A stubborn pride makes me tear pain from my heart. . . . Pain is a prison. I hate what limits or encloses me. . . . I have felt the terror again. . . . Intolerance, hate, meanness. Back of it, murder. . . . I am proud. I would not tolerate unhappiness long. Life has imprisoned me now and then but I have always found my way out." [11]

In the late spring of 1921, Vorse traveled to the Southwest to see her children. There she received an unexpected letter from Minor. He asked her to join him at the Moscow meeting of the Third Congress of the Comintern, where he was one of the American party's four delegates.

At this point, and for three more months to come, members of the capitalist press were forbidden entry into the USSR by the Soviets. In mid-June, when news of a terrible Soviet famine began to dribble into the West, correspondents from the capitalist countries began to pile up at Riga, awaiting entry into the Soviet Union. Western reporters would be required to wait until late August, when negotiations to bring food relief into the Soviet Union were concluded between Herbert Hoover's American Relief Administration and the Soviet government.

As the "wife" of Robert Minor, and as a well-known left labor journalist herself, Vorse would be welcomed into the Soviet Union in 1921, several weeks before the majority of American reporters. She was offered a unique opportunity—to be one of the first, and few, Western reporters to observe the new socialist state whose creation had shaken the political structure of the world.

"In looking back," Vorse wrote in 1935, "I am always of two minds about that sudden Russian trip. It is as though the road of my life forked off there and I left the highway on a long detour. I had come to the place where I needed to do a long book to distill what I had learned about life and while I was in the Southwest that spring I began a book called *Women's Lives*." (Vorse never finished that central interpretive work, although she took it up several times more; her ideas were instead to become the core of the feminist satire "Men," which she completed in the 1950s.) "I needed to give out, not to take in," Vorse wrote of her monumental turn toward the Soviet Union in 1921. "Already I was at the point of saturation."

She had worked "with scarcely a Sunday off" for four years, reporting the upheaval in Europe and the uprising of labor in the United States. Most of her labor work paid nothing: "Always in odds and ends of time I had to write stories and articles to earn [my and the children's] living." She had little money and she was tired. Despite her doubts, she decided to go. To be one of the first American journalists to report the famine occurring in the Soviet Union, to study the Soviet experience, to see Minor—all this overruled her certain knowledge that being with him brought as much misery as it did pleasure into her life. She left Stettin for Moscow on June 25, four days after the opening session of the Comintern. Her 1921 passport identified her as Mary Heaton Vorse Minor and listed her as thirty-nine years old, a curiously traditional subterfuge for a radical woman who was actually forty-six.[12]

Vorse joined Minor in his large room on the second floor of Moscow's Lux Hotel. The prerevolutionary building, on one of the busiest streets in the city, housed the foreign delegates to the Comintern. Everything was free to the visitors in the hotel, just as the citizens of Moscow did not pay for public services like streetcars and apartments after the revolution.[13]

"The summer of 1921 was zero hour for Russia," Vorse wrote. Although the civil war and the Allied blockade ended in late 1920, there was a staggering domestic crisis within the Soviet Union. The economy was near collapse. War communism, dictated by military necessity, had been marked by centralization of government controls over the army and the proletariat, and forcible seizure of food and livestock from the peasants, in order to feed the soldiers and workers in the cities. Soviet rule was on the verge of being swept away by a swelling wave of peasant insurrections, labor strikes, and urban revolts. The climax of the anti-Bolshevik disturbances came in March, when the sailors of the Baltic fleet at Kronstadt rose in protest, with a prime demand for a decentralized socialist government.

The Kronstadters suffered bloody defeat, but their revolt marked a fundamental change in Soviet policy. In the summer of 1921 Lenin's New Economic Policy (NEP) replaced compulsory food collections from the peasants with a 10 percent tax in kind. The government also gave the peasant the right to lease land, hire labor, and trade food in a free market. Trade unions were granted a small measure of autonomy. While the Bolshevik state retained control of heavy industry, foreign trade, transportation, and communications, it restored capitalist operation in small businesses and in consumer production. Concurrent with the economic relaxation of the NEP, centralized Bolshevik authority was fastened on the country more thoroughly than ever.

When Vorse entered the imposing premises of the former German embassy, where the Comintern met, she was mightily impressed by the historical grandeur of the moment. Intensely conscious of the "magnificent dream" here afloat, she wrote: "Here the accumulation of individual wealth is to stop. Here one of the main preoccupations of mankind is meant to cease." The packed hall was filled with long tables on either side of the aisle. Her first impression was that every expanse was draped with heavy red material. She sat down, gaping, transfixed by her first look at the distant men who had shaken the world—Lenin, Trotsky, Zinoviev.

The Third Congress, meeting from June 22 to July 12, 1921, was the largest Comintern gathering yet, attended by delegates from forty-nine countries. Its meetings were dominated by recognition that the postwar ferment in the West had ended. With world revolution indefinitely postponed, the Soviet Bolsheviks pronounced a sudden policy shift. The new slogan was "To the Masses!" The American Communists were directed by Soviet leaders to "try by all ways and means to get out of their illegalized condition into the open among the wide masses." After a brief skirmish among the American factions, the Workers' Party of America was born in late 1921, with Minor on its Central Executive Committee.[14]

Even before the Third Congress ended, stories abounded in Moscow of famine in the Volga basin. Agricultural production in the Soviet Union had plummeted because of war, civil war, and the partial crop failure of 1920. The drought of 1921 brought disaster in the great food-producing regions. By the end of July the full horror of the famine was apparent. Fifteen to twenty million persons were sure to die by winter if food was not provided. Thousands were already dead. The peasants near Samara were eating grass, acorns, and sawdust. Hundreds of thousands had left their villages to migrate to the banks of the Volga or to village railroad stations to escape the famine area.[15]

In early August, the Soviet government prepared a political propaganda train—"The October Revolution"—to travel through the famine district and bring hope to the stricken. Mikhail Kalinin, the president of the USSR, headed the mission. Vorse convinced Lunacharsky, the minister of propaganda, to allow foreign reporters to join the expedition. She had an assignment from International News Service to cover the famine for the Hearst papers. *Izvetsia* reported that the train left Moscow on August 12 "with five Americans and the same number of non-party journalists" aboard.[16] Among the American reporters, beside Vorse and Minor, was a sister Heterodite, Bessie Beatty, author of *The Red Heart of Russia*, an eyewitness account of the revolution.

In Penza, on the edge of the drought zone, Vorse first saw famine-stricken children. She visited a maternity home, where hungry mothers gave birth to already starved babies. The building was filled with constant feeble wailing. In the cribs, Vorse saw "tiny, dying skeletons, jerking their heads from side to side, even in sleep searching with their blue mouths for food." The newborn "were shriveled beyond recognition of anything human. Their parchment-like skins were drawn so tight across their faces that their noses looked like tiny beaks."

Observing the wasted children, she felt outrage "that in Europe and America statesmen still debated whether it was politically expedient to send food to Russia." In fact, the delay between July 30, when the Soviet government asked Maxim Gorky to appeal to the West for help, and August 20, when the agreement to bring food into Russia was reached between Herbert Hoover's American Relief Administration and the Soviets, was due as much to Lenin's suspicion of the motives behind Western relief as it was to the conditions of aid established by Hoover. Yet Vorse's revulsion was fair, if judged from the standpoint of humane action and not from that of the political chieftains in both the Soviet Union and the West.

She reached Samara, the heart of the drought. In some places the earth was as hard as pavement, in other places the dry dust swirled like talcum powder. All day long, boxcars, each piled with sixty men, women, and children, crawled out of the station taking the haggard human freight to provinces that had food. But most of the ash-colored crowd she saw at Samara was doomed to die. The famished lay piled on sacks and bundles along the tracks, under the cars, filling every inch of the train station and marketplace beyond. A crowd of thousands made no noise. Creatures with yellow faces, bloated stomachs, fever-bright eyes, they stood mutely or lay down to die quietly. Hundreds of orphaned children sat dazed and solemn, blue-mouthed with scurvy, hunched in hunger and pain, too apathetic and weak to cry or speak. They looked like ghosts of children, a group that had once been children, barely recognizable as children now.

Vorse returned to Moscow after a thirteen-hundred-mile trip by rail and ship. "As I recall the days spent in the famine region," she wrote in 1934, "it is the recollection of the children that still hurts the most." In Moscow, the ARA had begun to feed Soviet youngsters. By December 1, ARA relief had reached beyond the Urals and southward to Astrakhan. More than a half-million children were fed daily. At the height of its effort, the ARA sustained over ten million people. It withdrew from the Soviet Union in 1923. Ironically, the new Soviet government was stabilized partly through the effort of that devoted anti-Communist, Herbert Hoover. But when the famine ended, hostility resumed between Soviet and American officials.

The possibility of a new pattern of Soviet–American relations was again lost.[17]

Vorse remained in Moscow for five months after her return from the famine region. In the winter of 1921 each foreign newspaper was allowed only one correspondent in Moscow, ostensibly because of limited housing. Vorse was the representative of the Hearst papers and one of four American newspaperwomen in the city.[18]

News gathering was difficult in the Soviet Union, complicated by the great size and complexity of the country, the physical problems of travel, the government's regulation of the reporters' movements, the sometimes secretive and suspicious officials. Getting about the city meant walking, for autos were few, taxis rare, and buses unreliable. Vorse spent the mornings hearing translations from the daily Soviet press. In the afternoons she worked on copy or sought interviews with Soviet officials. The government's scanty approved press releases were usually distributed after midnight. Each night Vorse would write her copy, have it passed by the censors, and then walk to the telegraph office a mile away to make the 2:00 A.M. deadline for New York publication. "At that time gathering news in Russia was like mining coal with a hatpin," she remembered.

In Moscow she heard Lenin speak many times, and twice spoke with him. She once asked him what was the main problem of the Communist Party in Russia. He answered: "The main problem with the Communist Party in Russia is that it is entirely composed of human beings." Vorse also heard Trotsky address the shop stewards of Moscow. "I sat not twelve feet from him during the long afternoon," she wrote with an uncharacteristic lack of sophistication, betraying her excitement at contact with these historic giants who had altered the fate of the world.

Her friend Melnuchansky, whom she had met in 1916 at an oilworkers' strike in Bayonne, New Jersey, was now a high official in the Moscow trade unions. At his request she traveled to Kazan to speak to the workers about conditions in the United States. In Moscow, Vorse frequently saw Nadezhda Krupskaya, Lenin's wife, and came to know Clara Zetkin well. Vorse and Mikhail Borodin, who was later to direct Communist work in China, also became friends and sometimes went to the opera together.

In those early days of the new Russia, Vorse wrote, people were telling their stories wherever they went: "At that time . . . the great romances of the Revolution were told many times as people gathered together in trains, in railway stations, in steamboats." What most clearly remained in her memory was an impression of great crowds of people moving over the land, crowds so large the individual dwindled, and the sense of an "immense stir among the people. . . . Wherever you went people were . . . talking, discussing. Old people learning to read. Young people feeling responsible for building a new world. No one had anything. There was want, there was famine, but a new life flowed warmly through the innumerable conventions and meetings down to the small gatherings in private rooms where discussions seemed so exciting. It was hard even to go to bed," she wrote.[19]

Emma Goldman and Alexander Berkman were in Moscow that winter, both having been expelled from the United States during the Red Scare. They saw the tightening Bolshevik dictatorship as a betrayal of their hope for a socialist republic in Russia and were soon to leave the Soviet Union and live in exile for the rest of their lives. Minor was angered by their concern for the imprisoned anarchists in Moscow. According to Goldman, Minor told Berkman: "You people make me sick, you . . . forget this is a revolutionary period. What do these thirteen [jailed anarchists] matter, or thirteen hundred even, in view of the greatest revolution the world has ever seen?" Goldman considered Minor's view "an outrage of revolutionary ethics. Individual life is important and should not be cheapened and degraded into mere automation. That is my main quarrel with the Communist state."

In her autobiography, Goldman blamed Vorse for not coming to visit her in Moscow: "Mary Heaton Vorse, an intimate in my New York circle, was a kind soul and a charming companion. Her political views came to her by proxy. She had been an I.W.W. when vivid Joe O'Brien was her husband, and no doubt she must be a Communist now that she was with Minor. Reason enough why Mary should not have allowed her superficial political leanings to obscure the friendship [with me] that she had formerly so often proclaimed." Their friendship abruptly ended when Goldman warned Vorse to stop her "irresponsible talk" about an American anarchist then in Moscow; Goldman feared Vorse's indiscretion might send him to jail.

Goldman's critique of Vorse's politics by proxy cut deep. In 1935, when Vorse published her own autobiography, she returned Goldman's jab. In Moscow, Vorse wrote, "there were individuals as far apart as Isadora Duncan and Emma Goldman and Alexander Berkman, bitter and disillusioned, exemplifying Lenin's analysis of anarchists who, he claimed, would by their philosophy of necessity find themselves fighting the revolution with the bourgeoisie."[20]

There remain only fragments of evidence to indicate the nature of

Vorse's relationship with Minor during her trip to the USSR. "I had perfect goodness with him in the beginning, but that was shot to pieces in Russia," she said in 1923. Her diary notation of 1921 noted with scorn how Minor "listened so unquestionedly" to the pronouncements of the Bolshevik leaders. Just before she left the Soviet Union, Minor made clear his expectation that she would join his support of Bolshevik policies. He also ordered her to change her literary style. The time had come, he said, for her to "write indecently." Their evident conflict was softened by her still eager desire to please, to enmesh her needs in his. In the Soviet Union they were married, perhaps at her insistence, but whatever the exact nature of the ceremony, it was not recognized as legal in the United States. In 1921, she wrote, she was certain "she was the mate of the most interesting man in America." Surely this belief could lead to the conclusion that she was thus the most interesting of all women.[21]

After six months in the USSR, she sailed for home in early 1922 with the "impression of having left a society being born for one that was dying." Her sudden shift from the austere political intensity of the Soviet Union to the world of the bourgeoisie was shocking. The contrast enabled her to see the bustling people aboard her ship from an entirely new perspective. Their lives seemed to center about material accumulation or the pursuit of "fun." Their morality seemed shaped by a religious dogma that primarily concerned itself with restrictions on sexual behavior. The suspension of norms during the passage led to debauchery by a wayward few, while the rest worried over the iniquity of the deviant. Here were paraded all the barbarities and hypocrisies of the capitalist world assembled in the iron confines of a ship, she wrote. The experience was absorbing enough for her to publish a book about it in 1928, entitled *Second Cabin*.[22]

When Vorse returned to New York, she joined the amnesty campaign to free American political prisoners. These were persons sentenced under the Espionage Act, not for criminal acts, but solely for their expression of political dissent in either speech or writing. When liberal and radical Americans united against this injustice in late 1921, the amnesty campaign gained political strength and fairly widespread support. President Warren Harding and Attorney General Harry Daugherty agreed to release their main prisoner, the socialist leader Eugene Debs, as a way to cool the growing demand for amnesty. Their policy paid off when the AFL thereupon ended its amnesty drive. But 113 political prisoners were still in jail in 1922. Some of the prisoners were pacifists, but most had been sentenced for their real or suspected activity as labor organizers while associated with the IWW. As the historian William Preston has explained, "the amnesty of political prisoners depended on strikes, unrest and domestic radicalism rather than on the justice of the convictions or the adequacy of the punishment. The war was over, but the class war went on."[23]

Vorse worked for amnesty under the direction of Kate Richards O'Hare, the "first lady" of American socialism. In 1917 O'Hare had been sentenced to five years in prison under the Espionage Act for uttering "seditious" words at a political rally. Released in May 1920, she organized the "Children's Crusade" as a publicity tactic for the amnesty movement.

Composed of thirty-five mothers, wives, and children of the political prisoners, the Children's Crusade for Amnesty left St. Louis in April 1922. The prisoners' families headed for Washington where they hoped to present their petition for amnesty to President Harding. They were greeted at Terre Haute, Indiana, by Debs himself and treated to a bounteous reception and dinner. But at Indianapolis, where the American Legion opposed their entry, the city officials refused to let the children march or distribute handbills. Jane Addams met the group in Chicago and arranged a meeting where university professors and society women donated money to the cause. At Dayton, Cincinnati, and Toledo, the crusaders were greeted, fed, and housed by organizations ranging from conservative women's clubs to Communist and anarchist groups. In Cleveland, a mass meeting was arranged; clergymen, businessmen, and trade unionists spoke to two thousand people demanding release of political prisoners.

But when this brilliantly conceived and publicized procession ended in Washington, the cheering stopped. Policemen barred the way into the White House. President Harding refused to see the petitioners. He was engaged in receiving Lord and Lady Astor that day, after which he was scheduled to play golf.[24]

Vorse helped Elizabeth Gurley Flynn make the arrangements to greet the group in New York, where they were received at the Fifth Avenue home of the wealthy liberal Mrs. Willard Straight. The travel-worn women and children paraded from Grand Central Station up Madison Avenue, accompanied by reporters, photographers, and members of the New York bomb squad. At the Amalgamated Food Workers' headquarters, the group was fed. The waiters brought a gift for the children—a small bank in the shape of the Statue of Liberty.

In the *Nation*, Vorse told the story of some of the women. Mrs. George Bryant had saved enough money to travel to the prison to visit her husband. "Nickel by nickel, and dime by dime, with sacrifices that soft people

like us do not know about, she saved the price of a ticket to Leavenworth—
one hundred dollars," Vorse wrote. "The bank where she kept the money
failed. She has not seen her husband." Vorse wrote of Mrs. William Hicks,
the wife of a Quaker preacher who had been convicted for a letter he
wrote to a friend in England that foretold the war and decried the effects of
capitalism on American workers. A month after he went to jail, his baby
was born. "That made four babies under seven," Vorse wrote. "Mrs. Hicks
had to be cared for by the county. The judge took her next older baby, and
when in the courtroom she wept and begged for it, he told her she could
not have it because she was a county charge and the wife of a convict. So
you see, Mrs. Hicks knows a good deal about the benefits of a democracy."

The mother of the prisoner Clyde Hough stayed in Vorse's New York
apartment overnight. Mrs. Hough had two sons whom she had advised to
follow their conscience. One son enlisted and went to France. Clyde, who
belonged to an IWW woodworkers' union, refused to register for the draft
and went to jail. On the day he was released, he was arrested by federal
agents for conspiracy under the Espionage Act, even though he had been
in prison when the act was passed. He was sentenced to another five years.
"I stood it all right for a long time," Mrs. Hough told Vorse, "but then
I got sick and took to thinking about Clyde in the night and I could not
stand it and I took to crying. I cried and cried and could not stop crying
for two days, thinking of my Clyde. It was too much. One boy in France
and the other in jail."

The day in New York was over. Vorse stood with the little group of crusaders waiting in Pennsylvania Station for the next train. Curious people
crowded around. "It's an interesting sight," Vorse wrote, "brimming over
with human interest. A wonderful spectacle for a fine, free country."

It had been ten years since Vorse met the train carrying the workers'
children from Lawrence. Now she ended the decade meeting the children
of the prisoners—again the children coming to New York to seek help
and publicity from the urban liberals and intellectuals. But America had
changed since 1912. The reform period was over. "The world broke in
two in 1922 or thereabouts," as Willa Cather summed up the reaction of
many to postwar America.[25]

During the amnesty campaign of 1922, Vorse and Minor shared an
apartment in New York. He was working at the *Liberator* office, alongside
his old love, Lydia Gibson, who had come east to join the journal's staff
that spring. Vorse was uneasy about his daily contact with Gibson, but
Minor assured her that he had no time for any interest less pressing than
politics. Unknown to Vorse, her telephone was tapped by the Department

of Justice; the federal transcript of the conversations indicates that from morning to night, Minor seemed to be in a political meeting or in transit to one, or at least this was what he claimed to be doing.[26] Through this period, he was immersed in the struggle within the American Communist movement against those who wished to retain the Communist underground organization despite the Comintern's instructions to disband it.

In April, Vorse realized she was pregnant. She was forty-seven years old, posing to Minor as forty.

In the early summer, she and her children moved to the resort town of Highlands, New Jersey, across the bay from New York City. She planned to stay in Highlands through the summer, to be near Minor and to escape the heat of the city.

She walked daily to the beach from her apartment in Highlands, down the high wooden staircase that led from the top of the high bluff to the beach below. In mid-July, when she was four months pregnant, she stumbled and fell down the long flight of steps. She immediately miscarried. A local female physician treated her with morphine, to provide momentary relief for her physical and emotional distress.

Vorse was still confined to bed when less than a week after her fall, Robert Minor and Lydia Gibson suddenly appeared at Highlands. Standing before her bed, they gave her the unwelcome news. They were in love with each other, Minor told Vorse. He and Gibson were going to be married. After this brief announcement, Minor and Gibson abruptly left. Vorse's twenty-one-year-old son, Heaton, cared for her in Highlands until she was well enough to return to Provincetown in September.[27]

Despair was total. For she was about to suffer another tragedy more devastating than the loss of her child or the rejection from Minor. As a result of her medical treatment after the miscarriage, she became addicted to morphine.

Although some medical authorities warned against the free use of morphine as early as the 1870s, many doctors continued liberal use of the drug, especially to their already addicted patients. Complicating matters was the knowledge that morphine was easily available in dozens of patent medicines before 1914. The doctor's desire to relieve pain, and inadequate medical education, were the major causes of medically induced addiction. A report released by the Bureau of Internal Revenue after World War I estimated that the major cause of addiction was still the use of physicians' prescriptions.

Morphine addiction is rapid, usually occurring within ten to fourteen days of use. Unlike many drugs, morphine does not create a feeling of abnormality. One does not experience an altered state of consciousness, such as hallucinations or changed sensitivity to sight or sound. Rather, one feels normal, except for an unusually pleasant sense of freedom from pain and worry and a quickened flow of ideas.

The withdrawal from morphine, however, quickly leads to a feeling of abnormality, accompanied by intense anxiety, depression, and physical distress. Thus the function of morphine for the addict finally becomes not to induce euphoria, but to avoid the extreme discomfort of withdrawal. Withdrawal symptoms occur about forty-eight hours after the drug is stopped. Intense depression is followed by hot and cold flashes, chills, extreme nervousness, short jerky breath, and excessive nasal secretions. Painful abdominal cramps, a sense of suffocation, and violent spasms of diarrhea and vomiting occur. The horrors of morphine withdrawal drive the addict to maintain addiction, and larger doses are required to maintain a sense of normality. Within a few months, addicts require the drug approximately every four hours to prevent discomfort. The only known cures for morphine addiction are abstinence or gradual reduction of dosage; both demand the dreaded passage through withdrawal. Willpower seems ineffectual, as the addict bitterly learns from relapse after relapse. Addiction leads to a fundamental alteration of personality for the addict trapped in secretiveness and loss of self-direction.

In the 1920s, the distress of the addict was compounded by the popularization of new personality theories that sought the origins of drug addiction in personality defects. Whereas drug addiction had once been perceived as a tragic vice, or perhaps the result of heredity, it came to be seen as the hideous crime of a degenerate mind. Social rejection further turned the addict inward, to take refuge in self-pity, self-blame, or grandiose dreams of eventual freedom and accomplishment.[28]

Vorse's diary of the early 1920s is filled with the addict's typical sense of regret, despair at unfinished work, and an overriding miasma of loss and failure. Her personal relationships receded in importance. Separation from society and loss of self-esteem sapped her energy and thought.

In *The Big Money*, published in 1936, John Dos Passos described this time in Vorse's life: "She didn't seem to have any will left." Mary French, the character in *The Big Money* who is modeled on Mary Vorse, leaves the defeated steel strikers of 1919 and travels to New York to work as a publicist and organizer for a ladies' garment worker union, just as Mary Vorse left Pittsburgh to serve the Amalgamated Clothing Workers. In New

York, Mary French meets Don Stevens, who, like his counterpart, Robert Minor, is a self-centered, single-minded Communist. Mary French is betrayed by her selfless idealism. She is least unhappy when she is running small errands for Stevens, or providing small domestic comforts to him, all of which he never seems to notice. When Stevens abruptly leaves on a mysterious mission abroad, he never writes. She waits patiently, doing union work and fixing up the apartment for his return. When she learns he is landing, she scurries to the dock to greet him. He is evasive and cool. A few days later, she learns he has married a young redhead he met during his trip. Mary French, wrote Dos Passos, her spirit shattered, retreats into drink and drugs, "seeing faces, hearing voices" through a "blank, hateful haze." If Dos Passos meant Mary Vorse (as Mary French) to serve as a radical heroine, he portrays her without glamor or toughness, quirkishly devoted to ideals, asking no questions, and making no struggle against her fate. He presents a fundamentally nineteenth-century Victorian view of women, wherein the standard historical pitfall for women's illicit love is pregnancy and sordid defeat.[29]

In Provincetown, Mary Vorse was taken under the care of a local physician. "Mary was absolutely flat broke and very, very ill," the doctor's widow recalled. "For months, my husband used to visit her every day, sometimes several times a day. It was often necessary for him to take food to her house for her children." Apparently Vorse's doctor was attempting to restore her to health by a gradual lessening of the morphine dosage that she required.[30]

During the next year, Vorse suffered a great weight loss. Her eyes sunk into deep holes. A photograph taken in 1922 shows her with her wan and confused looking teenage daughter seated at her feet. Vorse appears untidy and bewildered. Her great, sad eyes dominate her face, with its peculiar pallor and shallowness of expression. "She was a skeleton," a neighbor said, remembering Vorse in that time. "She looked so terrible." After a long pause, her friend said softly, "We were all so sure that she was going to die."[31]

Chapter Twelve

The Long Eclipse

"I am imprisoned," Vorse wrote in 1923. "I hold myself by free casting around to find a way out—the detail of the house is horrible and I crawl through as if expecting blows. I have the children about me and I function as mother, yet life is intolerable to me. It offers me less at this moment than in all my life." Contrary goals brought her pain beyond measure. She continued to work, but without her usual ease in writing the fiction that had always supported her family. Self-isolated by illness and dejection, she allowed herself only surface female friendships. And Vorse permanently forsook love of all men, haunted by longing for Minor, whom she also hated. Her greatest trial would be her relation to her children. When she finally got beyond debilitating self-sacrifice, she had learned little more than the necessity to leave them.

Through most of the 1920s, Vorse was obsessed with one thought. She had failed her children. With the labor, radical, and feminist movements quieted, she returned home to be a mother. Her massive guilt centered around the behavior problems of her sixteen-year-old daughter, Ellen. For seven agonizing years, Vorse concentrated on serving the demands of her daughter: to make it up to Ellen, to save Ellen, to shape Ellen. Vorse decided that her work must be put aside. She must pay whatever price necessary to compensate for the years spent away from her children. She excused her absence as unavoidable. This was a disingenuous explanation, at best, which ignored her desire for freedom from child care in order to write and travel.[1]

Whatever the source of the clash between mother and daughter, Vorse was unable either to accept or control Ellen's behavior. Harboring their mutual suspicion, rage, and hurt, they fought on and on—about Ellen's curfew, boyfriends, dress, household chores, and general failure to conform to Vorse's expectations, about Vorse's "desertion" of her children, insensitivity, and domineering manner. Between bouts, Ellen was either sullen or hysterical, always depressed and accusing, while Vorse was placating, "cheerful," and "rational." A repeating pattern of conflict emerged. Vorse, already physically ill, scrambled to find the odd hours of work she needed as a writer to produce the family income. Resentful of Ellen's heedless calls for immediate service and attention, Vorse covered her anger with a facade of endless kindness and patience. When the inevitable explosion of feeling occurred, Vorse first attacked, then retreated into remorse and pacification, usually giving in to Ellen's demands, whereupon the whole circle of pain began again.

Vorse's painful memories of her mother's denial and distance shaped her response to Ellen's often self-centered demands. As a youngster Vorse had been taught to hide her most powerful negative feelings, especially toward her mother. She had learned that resistance to maternal will was sure to bring either isolation or rejection. "I imagined children to be rather as I remember myself," Vorse wrote in her diary in 1925, "gay companions to their parents. Spiritually self-supporting. Making few demands. Contributing, not taking away." Unlike her mother, Vorse was unwilling either to ignore or to overrule her daughter's perceived needs. On the one hand, Vorse expected polite subordination from Ellen. At the same time, she could not bear to deny her daughter anything. "If one does not place one's children first," Vorse moaned, "they come down on you worse than jealous lovers. Their love turns to fury." [2]

From the birth of her first child, Vorse had felt unfairly limited when she devoted her full energy to the daily routine of child care. As they grew older, she entrusted their care to educators and relatives. She shared the experience of most fathers. She loved her children dearly, placed them at the center of her concern and affection, while largely turning over their daily care to someone else. And like many males of her class, she wanted, and believed she deserved, a strictly personal route to excitement and fulfillment. She found this in work, in travel, and in immediate connection to the great social issues and world events of her lifetime. In some sense, her position as breadwinner for a large family, forced on her by tragic circumstance, also served as a lucky exit from societal demands. Her evident need to earn a living offered a neat answer to the expectation that she center her life on home and children. For Vorse, being enmeshed in domesticity, to the exclusion of writing and an active public life, meant only frustration and boredom.

Yet Vorse, like so many women before her, was unable to elicit the external or internal support needed to legitimize a duality of womanhood balanced between the two joys of work and children. Stranded in the unfriendly social climate of the 1920s, tortured by her fear that she had failed to nurture her brood, vastly disturbed by Ellen's maladjustment, Vorse could see only one way out. She would lay herself before her children "like a field to be plowed." She would become "a stationary washtub instead of a kite." She steeled herself to play the role of Supermom—abjectly self-sacrificial, continually nurturing and noncritical. She spoke to this strange self through her diary, giving the alien firm instructions: "If your instinct had been of utter faith none of this would have happened. If it had happened it wouldn't have touched you. For you would have been in agreement with it. It is only by utter goodness that you can conquer this situation." She would do her writing at "odd moments. Do it now and then. Hide it. . . . I will arrange my work so [the children] will be barely conscious of it."[3]

Virginia Woolf and Tillie Olsen have written of the mighty, centuries-long struggle of women authors to surpass, negate the "silences" imposed on them as women, as mother–writers. "Where the claims of creation cannot be primary, the results are atrophy; unfinished work; minor effort and accomplishments; silences," Olsen reminds us. In motherhood, as it has been structured through time, the need to write cannot be first.

> Not because the capacities to create no longer exist, or the need . . . but . . . the need cannot be first. It can have at best only part self, part time. . . . Motherhood means being instantly interruptible, responsible, responsive. Children need one *now*. . . . The very fact that these are needs of love, not duty, that one feels them as one's self; *that there is no one else to be responsible for these needs*, gives them primacy. It is distraction, not meditation, that becomes habitual; interruption, not continuity; spasmodic, not constant, toil. Work interrupted, deferred, postponed makes blockage—at best, lesser accomplishment. Unused capacities atrophy, cease to be.[4]

Vorse suffered another diminishment. As Virginia Woolf has noted, women writers, women's lives, women's experience, are by definition minor, to be judged inferior in significance, as in literature. How many thousands of women writers like Vorse constricted their intellect to sell their work, to deny the authenticity of self, to identify with masculine experience, to repeat, in forgettable fiction for frivolous women's magazines, male-made stereotypes of women's needs and thoughts? Women writers are forever moved to crowd "into that smugly isolated inner space of art which they have often described as the 'living centre,' a space which always looks disturbingly like the kitchen," the literary scholar Elaine Showalter has remarked.[5] Or, in Vorse's writing, the bedroom, permissible by the 1920s. In that decade Vorse also met another kind of silence—the quieting of feminism itself and its natural ally, the forces on the left. Overborne, she broke down, gave in, gave up. To women of her own generation, she may have seemed exceptional, like an escapee from female circumstance. Perhaps she was, in some ways, but mainly by chance, and just barely.

Through most of that long decade, Vorse lost contact with her women friends. She even came to doubt the long-term advantage of her feminism. Perhaps it would have been better to have lived like Neith Boyce, Vorse thought, devoted above all to her children. "What did I get out of it?" Vorse asked. "What good does it do to poke one's nose into Salonika or Serbia? Why travel on boats going down the Volga? . . . When it was all over and the processions had done and the guns silenced . . . I was a curious answer to feminism." At age forty-eight, Vorse had lost not only her health, but also the man she loved—and she had lost him to a younger, more traditional woman.[6]

After Minor's exit with Lydia Gibson, Vorse would not meet him again for seven years. From her home in Provincetown, she wrote him tender love letters punctuated by fierce stabs of hatred. To deal with the pain, she opted for the "perfect goodness" of self-immolation. In 1923, she wrote in her diary: "I am your lover, who cares for you without hope of love, without a knowledge that you and I shall again even speak to each other face to face. Since I ask nothing, I have everything. My love flows out to you tirelessly and endlessly."[7] Skewed by contradiction, Vorse also brooded about the other side of her relationship to Minor—the memory of her terrible anger toward his fanatical "drive for perfection" and her "longing like thirst" to be free of his domination. After her affair with Robert Minor, Vorse never took a lover again. She liked others to believe that she still pined for Minor, and could find no other to match him. This was a puzzling claim to most of Vorse's friends, and especially to her women friends, who recognized his egocentrism. Perhaps she abandoned the love of men because she could not risk another disappointment— after Bert's infidelity, after Joe's death, after Bob's rejection. Or perhaps, nearing fifty, she simply decided that her sexual life was over—another puzzling notion, in light of her previous highflying sensuality.

The strange riddle of her professed love for Minor, coupled with her evident disdain for both his personality and his politics, is best explained as the stoical defense of a mature woman who had accepted her own deviance, and who had come to see that difference as both permanent and desirable. One way to master men was to repudiate them. If Minor's rejection precipitated her own, perhaps her response was in large part a pretext; if she had not found one reason to stand alone, she would have created another. That Robert Minor was an insensitive sexist and egotist, all accounts agree. For her purpose, then, it was not an accident that she chose a man like him to "love." Hutchins Hapgood sensed this possibility when he told her that, because of Minor, she had "shut herself off in a *triumphant* sort of way."[8] To a woman of her time, with Vorse's strength, intelligence, and ambition, it was a victory to break free from the usual male's restrictive presumptions about the role and nature of women. Yet so long as she maintained the fiction that she yearned for her lost love, Vorse need not admit, even to herself, the implications of her escape into freedom.

Vorse's diary notations of the twenties betray her new direction. "Now it seems to me that I have had a greater share of popularity than most women," she wrote in her diary in 1923, "and that I have worked out a very complete experience of sex and now is the time to put that definitely to one side—a gesture of complete total relinquishment. If, with returning health, I find that I have no familiar instinct for adventure or experiences with men, or that I could say no to this instinct with consistency, that would be a *much more realized life*."[9]

Through 1923 and 1924, however, Vorse's addiction to morphine bound her life like a shroud. Isolated in her shame, she struggled against the demon need. Denial of reality was her defense. Secrecy was her cover. She assumed the pose of curious observer of her own downward spiral, professing intense interest in her "state of nerves."

Vorse's solemn struggle with morphine was complicated by her increased use of alcohol. She again attempted to believe in the rapture of release unknown to the forever cautious. "Women are the sober race," Vorse wrote in *Cosmopolitan*,

> because drink is the enemy of domesticity, even as religion, love and art are all domesticity's enemies. Do you dare to be drunk? Unless you have been drunk in one way or another you do not know yourself, you have not dared to look down the abyss of your soul or gaze upward awe-struck into the path of the northern light. . . .

> The doors of love and beauty and religion have remained closed to you.

But in fact she drank to bring peace and sleep. "It was like chloroform in childbirth," she wrote in her diary. "The unbearable anguish was taken from me. . . . I *must* learn to take anguish without an anesthetic," she added.[10]

Even during the turmoil of the war years and after, Vorse continued to produce the short fiction that supported her family. The successful plot formulas she had developed earlier maintained their appeal to her wide, chiefly female, audience, although by 1917, changing standards enabled her to write more openly than before of sexual encounters and unhappy unions. Increasingly, however, a string of lollypops of lesser quality— many of them little more than recitals of current romantic myths—began to creep onto her long list of published work. Her constant movement and politically involved, hectic life style from 1917 to 1922 taught her to dash out these quickly written, easily sold pieces of fiction designed to match the prosaic taste of the more conservative middle-class mass audience of the twenties.

Four times between 1918 and 1923, she was awarded one of the top spots in Edward J. O'Brien's popular annual series, *The Best Short Stories*. From 1914 to 1926, even when she did not receive the highest ratings, Vorse's work was prominently featured in O'Brien's "Role of Honor" listing. In 1919 and 1921, her work achieved "runner-up" status in the O'Henry Memorial Award short story contest. In 1922 and 1926 she won an O'Henry annual prize. Some of these attention-winning stories reflected her familiar themes. But most of these pieces focused less on gender role conflict than on the central romance of the two protagonists, and usually ended with the socially compliant pair locked in the standard embrace.

Despite the notice given her fiction, Vorse's faith in her literary ability was shaken in 1924 as never before. Indecision was followed by literary experimentation, and finally by accommodation with financial reality. It all began when she took Norman Matson as a boarder into her Provincetown home. Matson was almost twenty years younger than Vorse, a gruff poet and newspaperman with heavy-lidded eyes and a perpetually bored expression. He was writing his first novel and was soon to court and marry Susan Glaspell, who had returned to Provincetown from Greece after the death of her husband, Jig Cook. In her needy state, Vorse was particularly vulnerable to Matson's harsh opinion of her work.

In a remarkable article entitled "Why I Have Failed as a Mother," published in *Cosmopolitan* in 1924, Vorse described her encounter with him.[11]

"You have failed in the two main objects for which you've lived. You have failed in bringing up your children. You've failed in your work," Matson told her.

Vorse was stunned. "What's the matter with my children? They love me, don't they?" she challenged.

"You've no discipline. You can't even keep them out of your room when you're working. Do you suppose there is a man who would stand for that? You're blind if you can't see they hate your work," Matson said.

Crushed, Vorse could not deny the truth of his accusation. She had realized fully Ellen's resentment at not having a "regular" mother. Matson believed that Vorse and her children were victims of circumstance, since Vorse was the sole support of the family and could not be the mother she otherwise might have been. But Vorse knew her "failure" as a mother was more willful than Matson imagined. If she had originally begun to work only to earn money so Bert could have more time to write, she soon became more ambitious. She learned to do good work for its own sake, and for hers. From that time, she knew, she would not have stopped writing, even if she could have. Moreover, she had found plausible reasons for leaving home in order to work.

"The truth was I lusted for new experiences and new forms of work," Vorse wrote in *Cosmopolitan*, thinking of her trip to Europe in 1919 and of the years-long break from family care that it began. "Instead of merely being absent behind closed doors, I was really away. And I liked being away. The relentless details which all women must meet if they would see their homes run well slipped from me like a burden. . . . I know I needed to go away as much as I knew my children needed me home. . . . I found peace in constant traveling which I hadn't known in my quiet house, because at home there was the never ending conflict between my two jobs. I had been faithful to my house and its demands so many years. Don't housewives deserve a sabbatical year? I assume that all women with imagination, however much they care for their families . . . crave the experience as much as men." After the long absence from her family she had become as indignant at an interruption in her work, now that she knew what it meant to be uninterrupted, "as a man would be if his work were held in light esteem." When combining love and work, must women always experience a "double failure"? Vorse asked.

Despite her conscious resentment of the wider privileges and freedom of men, she felt less fury at the power of male arrogance than she did guilt at not meeting her own ideal of womanhood. If Vorse could not demand more from her children, it was chiefly because she had failed to behave as "good" mothers "naturally" would. Most especially, she blamed herself for her failure even to *want* to place their needs before her own. Finding it impossible to perform well all the roles she played, she had simply tried harder, given more, worked more, and tortured herself for wanting more, so much more, than motherhood alone. She turned her anger inward, still the daughter of her Victorian mother, despite all their apparent differences. Vorse would eventually emerge from the impasse, perhaps influenced more by a changing society than by her inner growth. It would be thirty more years, however, before she reached the angry understanding that she and her children were equally the victims of male-made definitions of the natural order.

Her interaction with Matson in the mid-twenties led her to alter her writing style. From 1924 to 1927, she attempted to sell realistic fiction to the general interest and women's magazines. Experimentation brought quick knowledge, borne on a stream of rejection letters, which carried warning phrases: "must modify behavior of girl"; "no premarital sex or female sexuality"; "opinions would enrage our readers"; "the heroine must never undermine the hero." As the fall of 1927 approached, her financial situation grew desperate. Of the seven stories she produced that year, only two had sold. The women's magazines did not want to buy descriptions of the darker realities of women's lives—of repressed dreams, towering rage, marital unhappiness, parental stress. "The time has come when I want to experiment [in writing] and live on very little," she wrote in her diary one sleepless night, "but instead I have [to support] this large and adult family which requires that I give my attention to stories for which I do not care." [12]

Nevertheless, beginning in 1929, Vorse would establish a new priority in her work, one that satisfied her sense of self-worth, while still serving, though just barely, her basic monetary needs. She would concentrate on labor journalism and investigative reporting, stopping to whirl out the familiar love stories only when she literally ran out of money. Over time and with growing lack of interest in the work, Vorse's skill at writing light fiction declined. By the 1940s, she found she could sell precious few lollypops. But she never regretted her decision to center her work on free-lance journalism. She would find and maintain a solid self-respect, although her income would dwindle steadily from 1930 on.

It was in November 1924, during a three-day visit to New York, that Vorse reached bottom. The details of her descent are not explained by the available evidence. Her New York episode, which she felt had publicly disgraced her, as well as completely exposed her pretense at normality, ended in what she called "my tragic gesture of suicide."[13]

Apparently it was the public embarrassment that shook her free of every rationalization. Leaving Ellen in an apartment in New York, she retreated in December to join ten-year-old Joel at her sister-in-law's home in western Texas. Vorse was determined to stay there, under Josie's care, until she had broken her dependence on both morphine and alcohol. It was a simple leap of faith, born of desperation and some grand reserve of courage.

Through the first five weeks in Texas, Vorse rarely left her bedroom. She did not describe the physical agony of withdrawal. But as her body healed she wrote in her diary of the quiet days, the home bright with Indian patterns on woven rugs. She passed one day after another shut in her room. Josie brought coffee to her bedside, breakfast at eight. All day Josie was in the room next to hers, the door open between them. "I felt her lovely presence like a benediction," Vorse remembered. "She never seemed to tire. Unfailing affection and bounty for me and for Joel streamed from her." In committed union, Josie and Mary together fought —and won.

The four months Mary spent with Josie formed an exquisite balanced rhythm of days. She gained seventeen pounds. "Getting well is so lovely," she wrote. "I feel so light and happy." The spacious days gave her time to take stock. She felt certain again of her writing style. "I am maturing something under the cover of the long silence. . . . Something of significance is happening. . . . I am gathering strength to tell the truth. [Heretofore I have written] only the surface of the things I know best." Time brought a reevaluation of her relationship with Minor. "I was so stupid . . . I forgot . . . that quick agreement with him against all reason was the only way to get along with him. Someway I wished myself to become exhilarated in someone else's service and yet remain myself. . . . When I think of him I feel only a swift impression of black honey. Too heavy for me with all the rest of my life to live."

Victory over morphine restored pride. "Nothing ever stopped me, not anguish, nor the ever present desire for death. I have survived. . . . When I consider the handicap, the tremendous difficulties, I am proud. I have a knowledge and a certainty that a nature which can weather such storms will surmount anything it is told to." In April 1925, Vorse left Joel in Texas and returned to Provincetown. "Oh, lord, keep me from messing up my life again," she wrote in her diary before she left Texas.[14]

======

When Vorse returned to the Cape she worked on a "serious" new book and a set of more realistically based short stories. Intending a brief visit to New York to visit her agent and editors, Vorse left for the city in late January 1926, unaware that she would not return to Provincetown for six months.

Reaffirming her female ties in New York, she lunched at Heterodoxy and met almost daily with Elizabeth Gurley Flynn, about whom she was writing a biographical sketch for the *Nation*.[15] On her second weekend in New York, Vorse attended a party where many of her old friends on the left gathered. The content of the conversation was predictable, the tone familiar.

The topic of the evening was the woolen workers' strike, which had erupted two days before at Passaic, New Jersey. Long abandoned by the AFL, enraged by a 10 percent wage cut, eight thousand workers left the mills on February 3, 1926, led by Albert Weisbord, a young Communist organizer who was a graduate of Harvard Law School. The historians Selig Perlman and Philip Taft described events at Passaic as "the outstanding labor conflict of the Coolidge era," chiefly because of the strike's impact on public consciousness.[16] To contemporaries of the strike, and to Cold War enthusiasts of the 1950s, the Passaic struggle was notable because it marked the first major strike in American history in which the workers accepted Communist leadership.

Listening to her friends' discussion at the party, Vorse felt alienated and irritable. "Suddenly there is another world," she wrote later that evening. "The Anarchists. How Tired . . . The Communists. Clapping empty jaws, slavering at [Sidney] Hillman and the socialists." It seemed to her that the older radicals, people like Elizabeth Gurley Flynn and Carlo Tresca, had been pathetically outmaneuvered by the disciplined band of ardent young Communists. The new left had bypassed her old comrades, leaving them like "big fish . . . gasping high on the conventional rocks." She was again struck with the contrast between the humorless Communists and the verve and idealism of the prewar left. "Where will you find today picturesque revolutionists like Jack Reed? . . . So much for my vanished generation. It happened so quickly. It suddenly came to me that this growing old is a sad business."[17]

Yet within days Vorse would join the fray at Passaic, which more than any other labor battle of the 1920s was destined to replay all the prewar themes of romance and drama symbolized by Lawrence and John Reed. As at Lawrence, she would thrill to the sight and sound of hundreds of women, marching, singing, defying police. She found again the exploited in motion, "a slow massive upheaval of Nature, as though a continent had shifted."[18] Like the cast of a giant morality play, the thousands of actors would take their place on the Passaic stage: impoverished, courageous women; club-swinging police; venomous reactionaries; progressive politicians and local clergy; side-stepping obstructive officials; determined radical leaders; famous liberal supporters. Unlike the coalfields of the Mesabi Range or the steel mills of western Pennsylvania, the woolen mills of Passaic were close to New York City, which made it easier to get the attention of the national press and prevent official brutality from attaining ultimate power.

It is questionable whether the Passaic strike awakened the dormant class struggle in the 1920s, as Vorse claimed, but the publicity methods she developed at Passaic helped to set the pattern for the successful labor uprisings of the next decade. She organized a systematic flow of information —not just to the radical press—but to the national and world press as well. Her publicity techniques involved the production of human-interest stories that evoked sympathy for the workers and their families. Vorse's mobilization of endorsements for the strike from recognized liberal leaders, political figures, artists, and intellectuals would later serve as a model for the CIO-led conflicts of the 1930s. The wide participation of liberals in the strike at Passaic was a harbinger of what was coming. If the old economic order was slow to collapse, it was nevertheless crumbling.[19]

On February 20, 1926, Elizabeth Gurley Flynn, acting for the American Fund for Public Service, hired Vorse to serve as publicity director for the over eleven thousand Passaic strikers. Vorse directed the publication of the *Textile Strike Bulletin*, a newspaper distributed to strikers and outside sympathizers; the first issue appeared on February 25. Vorse fortuitously stepped into a power vacuum during the first weeks of the strike. Unhampered for a while, she shaped the *Bulletin* into a brilliant agitational forum.

Drawing on her experience in the suffrage movement, the steel strike, and the Amalgamated lockout, she appealed to her readers' emotions through tales of human relations. A women's column, with stories of the women strikers and workers' wives, was one of the *Bulletin*'s most popular features. Poems by the strikers' children were frequently printed. Pictures were prominent. Humor, too, was prevalent, as in the pictures of the workers' ragged children over the caption "Outside Agitators." The newspaper was written in a simple style easily read by those new to the English language. It printed announcements of classes, meetings, and demonstrations, and stirring reports of picket lines, police assaults, and outside support for the strike. As the historian of the Passaic strike, Morton Siegel, wrote: "None of the issues of the *Bulletin* ever called on the strikers to join the [Communist] Workers' Party; none of the issues contained even indirect praise for Soviet Russia; none of the issues suggested that the dictatorship of the proletariat was an inevitable necessity, and none of the issues quoted any Marxist classic or source."[20] The *Bulletin* followed a class line, to be sure, but the reality of class struggle was readily apparent to the strikers. The Passaic workers hardly needed to be told that the mill owners, many public officials, and the majority of local policemen and judges were allied against them in their battle for a union.

Vorse first saw Passaic on February 16, two days before the first clash between workers and police at the mill gates. Half an hour from New York by rail, Passaic was the national center of the woolen and worsted industry. On the east side of the city, the houses of the foreign-born workers, half of Passaic's population of sixty-three thousand, were compressed into one-sixth of the city's area. Passaic's illiteracy rate was one of the three highest in the nation and its tubercular rate twelve times higher than the national average. Death took 116 of every 1,000 Passaic infants in 1921.

Beginning in the 1890s, when American tariffs rose to restrict importation of woolens from abroad, the large German woolen mills relocated in the United States. Here they found an abundant supply of cheap labor and an escape from social welfare legislation. Passaic's population almost tripled between 1900 and 1920 as the chiefly Slavic immigrant work force found its place in the slums. Enjoying a protective duty of 73 percent in 1926, the mill owners earned great profits, especially during the boom years of World War I. The mill owners, who feasted on average returns of well over 100 percent on their invested capital, neglected to reinvest their returns in capital improvement. Poor management and merchandising, coupled with the postwar recession and the new consumer preference for nonwoolen cloths, sent the woolen industry's profits plummeting after the war. The mills responded with layoffs and increased hours. In 1925, all but one of the large Passaic mills announced a 10 percent wage cut. Unable to affort decent houses, medical care, or adequate living conditions, the Passaic textile worker felt little sympathy for the financial setback suffered by the mill owners after the war.

When Vorse arrived at the crowded strike headquarters in Passaic, "where relief workers, strikers, lawyers, reporters, delegations from unions, outside sympathizers all jostled each other," she felt the immediate exhilaration, so long absent from her life, of involvement in the service of a high cause. A sense of youthful strength pervaded her spirit as she made arrangements for a tour of worker homes. Most of the women she met in the tenements worked eight- to ten-hour shifts, five nights a week, with a fifteen-minute recess at midnight. At dawn, they returned to care for their families. "It would be impossible for any right-thinking man or woman to go into the homes of Passaic and talk to the women who work on the night shift without feeling that a personal responsibility had been laid upon him or her," Vorse told the liberal readers of the Nation. "Where there is such want and suffering, when conditions of toil are so degrading, when the places that human beings live in are so indecent it becomes the concern of the public at large to make its power felt and to see that the state of things is altered."[21]

Until the last week of February, strikers and police in Passaic and the neighboring mill towns of Garfield and Clifton got on rather well. Moral and financial support for the strikers came from some local clergy, merchants, and city politicians. But on February 25, the Passaic commissioner of public safety proclaimed that mass picketing—then a rare tactic used mostly by left-wing unions—was a form of intimidation and also like a parade and thus could not proceed without a permit. He announced he would break up any mass picket lines with a three-hundred-man reserve police force.

On March 1, with New York reporters swarming everywhere, the workers' ingenious response was effected. Two thousand strikers ambled past the police. They walked in pairs, "just passing by," they explained, thus continuing the picket line while technically obeying the police orders.

The authorities, caught off guard, watched sullenly. "Ride 'em, cowboy," the workers and their children jeered, taunting the few mounted police.

The next day, the workers—unarmed, orderly, and buoyant in spirits—again walked in line, two abreast, past the walls surrounding Botany Mill. For twenty minutes the police allowed the pairs through a break in the police line drawn across Dayton Street. Then the police suddenly closed the gap. Fifteen mounted police made sorties into the crowd. One of the iron hoofs landed on a young girl. The Passaic police chief threw three tear-gas bombs into the group of trapped strikers while firemen battered them with powerful streams of water. The crowd broke and swirled away.

The police followed, clubbing backs, heads, and shoulders of retreating strikers and bystanders as well.

On the following morning, scores of cameramen and reporters, and hundreds of college students and Villagers sympathetic to the strike, flocked to the New Jersey town where horses, tear gas, hoses, and police sticks had been turned on unarmed workers. The police again attacked, this time not only the local citizens, but the photographers and reporters too. The officers smashed cameras, clubbed reporters' notes from their hands, and singled out members of the press for unrestrained kicking and beating. The police action stirred "newspapers in New York like a hive of angry hornets," Vorse wrote. Police violence "made laughter on Olympus," she crowed.

Passaic was by now a national sensation. The liberals' indignation was white-hot. On March 4, the press arrived in Passaic in bulletproof limousines and armored cars, while an airplane, hired by a New York newspaper, circled low overhead. Famous liberals from New York City came in rows of shiny cabs. On that day the workers provided their newly solicitous allies with terrific copy and pictures. The pickets, carrying an American flag, were dressed in discarded war helmets and gas masks. They marched with a young Slavic woman wheeling a baby carriage at their head, a publicity tactic reminiscent of Mesabi. The cooler heads in the power centers prevailed; the strikers were permitted to picket en masse.

The New York newspapers never again so flamed with righteous protest: The Passaic police issued cards to representatives of the major newspapers and promised that persons displaying these cards in their hats would not be molested. Nevertheless, after the early March events, many newspapers became distinctly cool toward the New Jersey authorities and toward the mill owners in and near Passaic. The major periodicals followed the lead of the great dailies. A stupendous propaganda victory had been won for the workers—by the police. Sympathy for the strikers now came from many quarters, from free-lance investigators, ministers, lawyers, authors like Fannie Hurst and John Dos Passos, women's clubs, Rutgers college students, and trade unionists. It was clear by mid-March that prominent liberals and leftists, many of them hostile to Communist ideology, had joined in support of the Passaic fight led by a young Communist. Contributions in money and goods to the strikers probably reached over six hundred thousand dollars in all.[22]

Conservatives, in counterattack, charged that the Communists, as general advocates of violence, had deliberately engineered the police riots.

Vorse was singled out for attention in a press report of mid-April, which accused her and other "higher thought" agents of causing the Passaic policemen to lose their heads. At a meeting in Concord, Massachusetts, where a group of American Legionnaires pelted members of a youth peace group with eggs, Fred R. Marvin, editor from the New York *Commercial* first blasted the women's peace movement, then accused Vorse, "the wife of Robert Minor," of being on the Communist payroll at Passaic.[23]

Benjamin Gitlow, an ex-Communist turned informer, later claimed that Vorse was a secret member of the Communist Party at Passaic, acting directly for the party's Central Committee's Textile Committee and posing as a "fake liberal" in order to make contact with real ones. Vorse was following party instructions, Gitlow alleged, when she cleverly "held conferences with Sidney Hillman, with manufacturers, with United States Senators, with Congressmen, judges, ministers and priests" during the Passaic struggle.[24]

There is no convincing evidence to suggest that Vorse was ever a member of the Communist Party. Indeed, if she was an agent, the record shows her to have been an exceedingly unreliable one. Her writings on Passaic reflect her political understanding of the need to advance her cause by appealing to different factions in different ways. Throughout her career as a labor journalist, Vorse took little interest in theoretical revolutionary constructions. She continually sought one immediate goal—greater and greater worker control over conditions of labor. To Vorse, this goal realized *was* the ongoing revolution. If that did not square with the current Communist line, then so much the worse for theoretical purity. At Passaic, Vorse had her first good look at the American Communist movement, which in 1926 was stricken by internal disorder as its leaders fought among themselves and scrambled to conform to the shifting demands of the Soviet line. She learned that most of the party members who were part of the active leadership at Passaic were more interested in perfecting revolutionary doctrine than in running a strike. Vorse was sure that ultrarevolutionary rhetoric—largely unconnected to the daily reality of workers' lives—only obstructed the achievement of immediate, desirable, and cumulative change, only strengthened the power of the already dominant reactionaries.

On March 24, Vorse attended a meeting of the party's textile strike Central Executive Committee, then headed by Gitlow. She reported to them her recent lobbying failure with Congress. Vorse blamed the setback on the bad publicity generated by the party leaders themselves. She outlined to the CEC the specifics of her charge against them. So long as the Communists clung to sophomoric theories of "leading the workers to revolutionary efforts," rather than concentrating on building a union, she said, they subverted both their party and the workers. After weeks of dealing with the unreality of party dogma, her frustration boiled over. The party had been only a debating society, Vorse went on. Now that it was part of a real strike situation, it should emerge from the stage when it seemed to believe that a revolution could be produced by a printing press and stirring manifestos. A party capable of committing so many political errors in just one week, Vorse ended, was little more than a strange group of "adventurous anarchists."

After her dressing down of the CEC, Vorse was not again admitted to be heard before the party's high council. It must have been apparent to all factions that she was hopelessly undisciplined—untutored in the mysteries of revolutionary theory.[25]

Vorse's opinion of her allies on the right was equally grating. As publicity director at Passaic, she joined the effort to elicit help from progressive politicians in Washington. Apparently Vorse was too impatient, too demanding, in her presentation of claims. Senator La Follette had been "seriously offended" by her pressing attitude, Isabelle Kendig, the ACLU lobbyist in Washington, clucked to the ACLU director, Forrest Bailey. Bailey agreed that Vorse "was the last person in the world, I think, who ought to be entrusted with work requiring tact and pleasing approach." When Vorse returned to Washington for a second lobbying effort in May, Kendig reported that she had been able to "more or less . . . smooth over the effects of [Vorse's] descent on Congress. . . . Mrs. Vorse . . . came down feeling that if the issue were pushed a little more aggressively we would get farther. . . . By rushing in too impulsively [she has] managed to antagonize both La Follette and Senator [Burton] Wheeler, and thereby make it a little harder for [the ACLU] to deal with them."[26]

Support for the strike was eroding. The American Fund for Public Service informed Vorse on April 29 that her salary as publicity director could no longer be supported, partly because the Sacco and Vanzetti case was siphoning away left-liberal interest and funds. With the wool production season drawing to a close, the employers had no immediate need to end the strike. Mill owners increased their propaganda campaign and vowed that they would never meet with "revolutionary Reds." Still, the workers persisted, in spirited mass meetings and on singing picket lines.[27]

From a distance, Vorse sought to reinvigorate the *Bulletin*. Since others had assumed its direction, she felt it had become lifeless. "Where are the children's writings and the fine stories written by young strikers? Where is all that self expression I nursed along so carefully?" she complained to Weisbord. Vorse suspected that some dogmatic Communist was at fault for the *Bulletin*'s decline. At one time, Vorse wrote, "even the capitalist dailies and the liberal journals like the *Nation* quoted articles from the *Bulletin*. The entire labor press used it." Now, with the strike in crisis stage, Vorse felt the *Bulletin* had grown "stiff, conventional, choked with jargon, stifled with dusty words."[28]

After almost thirteen months, the Passaic strike ended with the wage cut rescinded in most mills and union recognition granted in some cases. Meanwhile, the factionalized wrangling within the increasingly isolated American communist movement reached even more fantastic levels. Weisbord was officially expelled from the party in 1930, shortly to establish yet another splinter group of leftist theorists. Only a long-range view justifies the Passaic workers' sacrifice and struggle. The short-range results must be judged meager.

During the strike Vorse had limited her income-producing writing to weekends only. Now her savings were gone. She had an assignment from the International Labor Defense to produce a pamphlet on the Passaic strike. "There is no other work quite so important as writing the strike," Vorse said. "The other fiction stories are only to give me time." She labored for three months over the twenty-two-page booklet, earning a mere fifty dollars. She was proud of her publicity work at Passaic. "Probably no better piece of agitational work has ever been done," she knew.[29]

As the strike collapsed, she and the other strike leaders were "isolated in a sudden sorrow." She consoled Elizabeth Gurley Flynn, additionally stricken at this time by the abrupt end of her long affair with Carlo Tresca. Flynn had been devastated by her discovery that her sister was pregnant with Tresca's child. Vorse made several emergency trips to New York to nurture Flynn. Vorse saw Flynn's "terrific will crushing against circumstance. I have never seen her lose calm before. . . . She in a dress of moonlight on jungle talking like a girl of her lost love. Telling over precious details. . . . Elizabeth for the first time in all the years I have know her destroyed . . . as though she were some . . . pitifully balanced creature." Like Vorse, Flynn would pay a high toll in the twenties; she would retreat into a ten-year exile from political work. To Vorse, it seemed that the prewar radicals had been "swept aside by the broom of time. . . .

We all have a grim sense of death," she wrote, "made more terrible and pointed by Elizabeth's grief."[30]

Vorse's despondence increased when her children returned to Provincetown for the summer. Her hope for a new family harmony, so hard won in Texas, was suddenly shattered. She fumed at the extra expense posed by Ellen's house guests. "What a strange sight," Vorse wrote, "me struggling to work, on stories I abominate to support a household in which I cannot live. . . . I creep home nervously for fear things are going to be unpleasant." It occurred to Vorse that there was one way to escape the parental role and thus avoid confrontation. She could simply turn over her house to her children and go elsewhere.[31]

Suddenly her spirits rose. A telegram in November announced the sale of two short stories to *Woman's Home Companion* and *Harper's* for the grand sum of two thousand dollars, enough to carry her for months. She quickly sold several more stories for a good sum.

But the year ended sadly. At a New Year's Eve party with her children and friends, she felt a discard. She was fifty-two. Norman Matson, seventeen years her junior, ignored her to flirt with Ellen. Sunk in depression, Vorse returned in her mind to the fateful year of 1922. Now it was her trip to Russia that was to blame; it had marked her decline as an author, sucked her of life. Leaving the party early, she wrote in her diary, "From now on my hair will grow thin. My teeth will come out. I shall become old and sluggish. I do not care to dance anymore. I hardly ever sail."[32]

The yearned-for rebirth after her recuperation in Texas failed to occur. Her work displeased her. Her relation to Ellen was troubled. She was middle aged. She had no male to enhance her ego.

The dancer Winifred Duncan, a Provincetown visitor and lesbian who fell in love with Vorse in 1926, pinpointed the source of Vorse's confusion better than Vorse knew. According to Duncan, Vorse held to the "sweet and early Victorian" idea that women could be divided into three groups. First there were the "women who have captured a man and are therefore happy," Duncan told Vorse. Next, there were the women "who haven't a man and therefore must be noble and unhappy." And third, there were the women who rejected male demands and therefore felt doomed to live half-lives. Duncan thought Vorse saw herself as the last type. Vorse rebuffed Duncan's pursuit of her, and seemed to settle for the belief that women without men could never find more than weak substitutes for real happiness and self-fulfillment.[33]

In early 1927, Vorse was flush with new money from her writing. She planned a tour of Europe with Ellen. Remembering the efforts of her own parents to tend her development, Vorse hoped that the experience of European culture would discipline Ellen's mind and prepare her for serious endeavors. The trip had to be delayed for three months when Vorse fell and broke her leg; they sailed for France in mid-April.

Vorse's broken leg had been set improperly. As soon as they reached Paris, she was forced to spend almost four weeks in the hospital. During her confinement, Vorse foundered in fury and grief. She felt that Ellen deserted her "in pursuit of wild pleasures, without thought of propriety or ordinary kindnesses." The tension with Ellen worsened during the "awful darkness" of the European stay. Vorse decided twenty-year-old Ellen was hopelessly selfish and grasping, "intent on getting everything and giving nothing."

At Ellen's insistence that she modernize her appearance, Vorse agreed to have her long hair cut in the new bob fashion. Afterward, as the Italian barber hovered nearby in panic, Vorse sobbed without restraint. She was near complete breakdown. "I must be very quiet. My mind must go free. I must not see many people," she scrawled in her diary. When they returned to New York in August, Vorse knew that "the trouble with Ellen has been so painful that it is now [my] neurosis. It is literally impossible for me to live with her. . . . Bruised, battered and disgusted, I am torn between being a 'good mother' and my need for work." Vorse could see no way to combine the two; one would inevitably nullify the other in her mind.[34]

For the next year and a half, Vorse retreated to near seclusion in Provincetown, sometimes traveling to New York. Ellen lived in the city, dependent on her mother for support, while attempting a career as an actress with the Theater Guild. One scrape followed another. Soon after their return from Europe, Ellen wrote she was marrying a young man who needed her because he suffered from venereal disease and was out of work. Vorse quickly moved to prevent the marriage, but Ellen just as quickly moved on to a new lover. One has a sense of Ellen, gay and lively, self-centered and abusive, steaming from one crisis to another, and of Vorse, the grim-faced mother, alternating between outraged resistance and guilty subservience, wallowing in her daughter's wake, all the while lecturing, pleading, or weeping. By the winter of 1927, Vorse had no more money. She begged a few hundred from friends to carry her through until a story sold. Running out of money offered one sure means of escaping responsibility for family support.

In the spring of 1928, Ellen reached new heights of dash. On March 25, the New York *Times* ran the story on page six. The headline read: "Fiance Marries Mary Heaton Vorse's Daughter: Cables for Her Passage Home."

Ellen had met a young free-lance writer, John Hewlitt, at his bon voyage party, had taken a dare, and stowed away on the liner *Deutschland*. The first news story erroneously reported that Ellen, discovered while at sea, had been married to the young stranger by the sea captain. "Mary Heaton Vorse, playwright and novelist, is ill and therefore could not comment," the *Times* reported. It was several days before Vorse learned that Ellen was not married after all. Young Hewlitt's father, a wealthy Georgia banker, had even agreed to pay Ellen's passage over. Ellen assured her mother in a lilting letter from France that she intended now to "find herself" and become "independent." Vorse cabled money. Ellen stayed abroad until mid-July when she sneaked out of her Paris hotel at midnight without paying the bill. Vorse paid that too.[35]

The shock of Ellen's latest escapade broke Vorse's fragile reserve. Gripped as never before with evidence of her "failure" as a mother, she suffered a complete nervous breakdown. She later wrote of that time:

> I was so tired . . . that when I woke up in the morning it seemed to me I was coming up painfully, from some smothering depth below the surface of the water. . . . I have a picture of myself in those days, sitting in a chair, trying to make myself get up from it, knowing that there was a great deal to be done. . . . I couldn't get up from the chair to walk across the room. It was as if nature revolting now kept me quiet in some waking trance, though I felt as if I were whirling around and around in space like an insect. I had never felt like a whirling insect before, and I said it in those words: then I said: "This is crazy!" tears came to my eyes, but they did not fall; I was too tired even to raise my hand to wipe them away.[36]

It was then that Vorse wrote her remarkable short story "The Hole in the Wall," later published by *Parents' Magazine*. The editor inserted a message under the title: "If you are a sentimentalist, don't read this story. But if you are willing to call a spade a spade, you won't want to miss a word of it."[37]

Vorse's story began:

> Emily Nearing and George Nearing lived in a usual-sized house on a pleasant street in a usual-sized town. They had three children, Stephen, nineteen, Annette, seventeen, and David who was only ten. One day when George got rather fed up with his family, he went off on a motor trip. He wanted Emily to come too, and she wanted to come, but of course she couldn't leave the children.

Emily is first shown as she is accosted by her children: Annette and Stephen wrangle over the household chores and David cries out for money. Emily feels she is being hunted. "People after her, telling her disagreeable things, making her decide quarrels, wanting something of her. Always and forever wanting something of her. . . . She wanted to run. There was no place to run except upstairs. She ducked into her room and shut the door." To close off thought, Emily picked up a magazine to read "one of those modern stories about the wise mother who solves all her children's difficulties."

As if by itself, her arm jerked up and she threw the magazine violently against the wall. Where it hit it left a large jagged hole. She peeked in the hole and saw strange scenes and figures moving: "By her act of violence she had torn the veil of illusion which mercifully keeps us from reality and she was looking down the hole on reality's stark face."

What she saw was her son Stephen walking toward her. "His mouth hung loosely ajar. His brow, as void of expression as an eggshell, was wrinkled. A sour, petulant frown was spread over his face." He demanded that she bring his white flannel trousers from the cleaners. Emily saw herself hopping nimbly uptown to the cleaners, then moving to the stores to buy things. She saw herself as she really was: "a grotesque figure, like a kangaroo." Emily started dealing objects out from her kangaroo pouch— "shaving soap, white trousers, more white trousers, shirts, bathing suits, drinking glasses . . . scissors, shoes, brassieres, trousers, glasses. . . . Emily dealt things faster and faster, but the faster she dealt the louder they all howled. Now she had no more to give them and she began throwing little pieces of her life to keep them quiet."

In the hole in the wall, Emily saw herself pushing the house around on its axis. She could not move the heavy house, so she tried to wind it up, but she could not find the key. She began to push the house, round and round on its axis. " 'If I don't push it around,' she thought, 'I'll have to carry it on my back.' "

Emily went down to dinner with her children. But everything had changed. *"She still saw her children through the eyes of Reality."* Only young David had not changed. He remained "a dirty, savage little animal, in whom she rejoiced. He was the only natural thing in this unnatural world of reality." After dinner, Emily went to her doctor. She felt ill and old. He gave her a charcoal pill and told her to rest. On the way back home, she noticed the faces of the friends her own age. "All of them had a worried, baffled look. *Then Emily knew that they too had looked at Reality.*

They knew what their children were like. And they were all keeping it from one another. Each woman thought she walked in misery alone."

At home, Emily looked down the hole in the wall again, drawn to it as though it were a magnet. She saw herself screaming at her screaming children. "'Get out of the house!' she cried. 'Get out of the house, Go away where I can't see you for five years.' That was what she wanted! That's what would make her well again!" Emily's story abruptly ends with her mental breakdown.

It was then, sometime in the early summer of 1928, that Vorse briefly returned to morphine. This time she managed to surface after only a few months. She sent for Josie in late July. Six weeks later, with Josie's help, Mary recovered.

More than her physical health was saved. For the first time in over six years, she was "Free, Free, Free at last!" she exulted, suddenly freed of the obsessive maternal guilt which had distorted her relation to others and to her work for so many years.[38] The nervous collapse of 1928 forced her to choose. She must remain emotionally disabled, or deal with the role conflict that had shattered her life. Her answer was only a partial one, but enough to ensure her recovery. She decided to give up the effort to remother her children, the belated attention to the reshaping of their goals and behavior. Through the twenties she had performed a constant balancing act, suspended unaware between the expectations of the community and the dreams of her own generation of achieving women. Now, with excruciating sorrow, she accepted her limitations as a mother, and opted to go on as best she could, regardless of the agony, conscious of the dreadful, never to be regained loss of what she might have created for her beloved children and for her future.

A long-repressed rage fueled her recovery. "Fury that my work should be interrupted. Fury at my own uncontrolled emotion. Fury that I should have spent these five years—doing what? Undoing what I had accomplished in the world." Vorse knew she was "truly getting well. . . . I have the first delicious feeling of health. . . . I wake up in the morning . . . to take in the sun." She wrote in her diary, "For years now I have written practically nothing of value. Because my mind was full of Ellen, and worrying over her safety and welfare. I had anger at her unkindness and brutality. Now I know that I must keep away from her." Again retreat— complete withdrawal from the field of battle—was the only solution to her problems as a mother that Vorse could find. She also knew that this "sudden transition which sloughs off the training of years and smashes the cake of custom is very painful for the family to observe." No matter. "The curious shellshock in which I lived begins now to fade." By September, she could write, "I feel as though it were the end of something more than the summer—The end of a whole phase of life."[39]

In 1928 a plum dropped. The publishing house of Horace Liveright gave her a twelve-hundred-dollar advance to write *Second Cabin*, a novel based on her voyage home from the Soviet Union in 1922. The money bought her time to begin work on the quality labor journalism she dreamed of producing.[40] Vorse made another twenty-five hundred dollars from the sale of her fish wharf that had been the birthplace of the Provincetown Players. She sold it to her dear friend Katy Smith, who would marry John Dos Passos the next year.

She felt something new waiting for her, she wrote in her diary. "Time is short . . . and I feel hurried to fulfill certain responsibilities. Above all else, I want to leave a true record of this reticent country which is my blood and bones, and which has wounded my spirit for so many years."[41]

In New York in late January, she attended Heterodoxy meetings and saw much of Sinclair Lewis, Art Young, and George Soule. She was content to be with persons "who think and who write." On February 25, she made a sudden decision. "Without having the least thought about it," she went into the office of the Communist Party's *Daily Worker* to see if Robert Minor was there. She described the visit to a friend:

> I hadn't seen him in seven years. Chance playing a great part but also I had heard he had become old and fanatical and it is awful to see people you have once cared for extremely and wonder, "How could I?" . . . We went out to dinner and began talking with the eagerness of people who have been together constantly and who have been separated. I had the most extraordinary feeling of having come home and I felt smooth like cream. . . . It was like going through death and finding the one loved not dead after all. *Now I can write anything I want to.*[42]

Later that day she remarked to her diary, "I do not wish my life to be at jeopardy to his demands." In some curious fashion, the last sore healed.

Significantly, her diary stops here, in February, and does not begin again until May. By that time she had resumed fully the adventurous life. April drew her to the southern Piedmont to report the great textile strikes of 1929.

Part Five: 1929-1941

It is what I have run after in the labor movement. Those moments of illumination when it rocks together, no longer isolated alone but beautiful in its power for good.

—MHV, 1938

Chapter Thirteen

War in the South

In the springtime the low hills of the southern Piedmont turn misty green. Swift streams cut through the red clay farmland. Along their banks in 1929 were strung dozens of cotton mills and Protestant churches. The proprietors of the two institutions formed a close alliance in the mill villages to build "civic consciousness"—a euphemism for the training of the southern textile workers to regularity, diligence, and submission to their economic superiors. As one southern mill executive put it with unconscious high humor, "We had a young fellow from an eastern seminary down here as pastor a few years ago, and the young fool went around saying that we helped pay the preachers' salaries in order to control them. That was a damn lie—and we got rid of him!"[1]

Life in this wooded country seemed far removed from the social problems of the industrial cities of the East, with their massed concentrations of wealth, technology, and the immigrant poor. Yet the Piedmont, where the nation's cotton textile industry was concentrated, became a bloody union battleground in the spring of 1929. A spontaneous uprising in eastern Tennessee spread through South Carolina and North Carolina within a few weeks. The most famous of these textile strikes occurred in Gastonia, North Carolina, a town of thirty thousand, which held the largest number of spindles in the state and in the South, and the third largest number in the nation. Before the strike was ended, the name of Gastonia had been trumpeted throughout the world as a symbol of Communist-led struggle in a brutally hostile environment.

The textile workers' revolt appeared doubly shocking since it came in a region that had been widely advertised as a refuge from unionism, high wages, and restrictions on child labor. Northern capital poured into the textile towns, drawn by the promise of a labor force composed of helots believed to be content with long hours and low pay, so happy were they to escape tenant farms and mountain cabins for steady mill wages. This well-defined underclass provided a reservoir of native white mill hands, supposedly "free from outside influence and consequent labor unrest," as a letter from a southern Chamber of Commerce boasted in 1928.

By World War I, employer–employee relations in Gastonia had grown hostile as great wealth accumulated in the pockets of absentee mill owners. Employee protest seemed hopeless, wrote Theodore Draper: "The workers were herded into isolated villages in which the companies owned their shacks, provided what schools there were, paid the teacher if any, ran the stores, extended credit, built the churches, subsidized the ministers, and administered 'law and order' through mill guards, company spies and deputy sheriffs." [2] But shock troops entered Gastonia in 1929. A tiny band of Communist organizers gave a rude challenge to racial prejudice and Protestant theology—those key supports of the southern economic elite.

In 1926, southern textile workers earned an average of $15.81 for a fifty-five-hour week, about two-thirds of what New England textile workers earned for forty-eight hours of work. The 1929 uprising of fifteen thousand textile workers in the southern states was an outraged response to the recent introduction of the stretchout—an increase in each mill hand's workload by speedup rather than by technology—and to the sharp reduction in wages that accompanied it. The mill hands who had endured six-day weeks, and ten- to twelve-hour days at wages so low that everyone in their families over fourteen was forced to work, refused to accept the new burden. One after another, they told Vorse, "We could not do it." [3]

The Piedmont textile workers were drawn from two sources, the lowland white tenant farmers and the mountain folk of the South. They were virtually all religious, nearly illiterate, and of undiluted Anglo-Saxon stock. Many of them were fiercely individualistic, easily provoked to violent defense of their honor or their meager possessions. "We cut and shoot one another at a rate not even equalled in the centers of urban civilization," a guidebook to North Carolina noted. [4]

The southern textile strikes presented several radically new situations to the northern organizers who were veterans of the immigrant strikes in the Northeast. The native white work force of the South was more prone than the foreign born to answer the violence of the authorities with equally violent resistance. Most of the workers, unrestrained by southern law, were fully armed. When the strike leader at Gastonia forbade weapons on the picket line, Vorse reported, "The mountaineers were glum. . . . Without their guns they felt emasculated, deprived of manhood."[5] Many of the men on strike in Gastonia flatly refused to enter a picket line unless they could carry weapons. Although this may have been a wise personal decision on the part of the men, who refused to function as helpless targets, this meant that women and children were usually the only strikers in Gastonia the organizers dared allow on the picket line.

The southern workers' arms were but a reaction to another difference in the southern situation—the prevalence of unrestrained and generally sanctioned community violence. Vorse was accustomed to assaults against workers from policemen and soldiers and hired hoodlums, but before Gastonia she had not experienced the terror induced by impromptu mobs led by local gentry and composed of townspeople.

The southern textile protest began in March 1929, when five thousand workers rose to protest their fifty-six-hour week and average wage of $9.20 in the mills near the remote small town of Elizabethton, Tennessee. They were led by enraged women, which did not prevent Sherwood Anderson from praising the strikers' "religion of brotherhood." The revolt was met by a crushing injunction and then an agreement from management to raise wages, an accord canceled by the owners as soon as the strikers began to drift back to work. On April 4, twenty men, some of them police and businessmen, including the local bank president, drove a northern AFL man from town at gunpoint. Another mob beat on a local unionist until his sister scared them away with rifle shots. On April 15 the Tennessee governor sent in a helpful military force, which was paid directly by management, to suppress the strike. The mill provided food, free cigarettes, and an officers' club to the troops. The mill workers retaliated by blowing up the town's main water line. When the Tennessee strike ended in May, the workers had won nothing, except a promise, quickly broken, that they could discuss their problems with the mill's new personnel director. He was the same New Jersey textile executive who had represented the employers at Passaic.[6]

The revolution was proclaimed at Gastonia on April 1, by a lone, brand-new Communist who had been in town just a few days. Thirty-three-year-old Fred Beal was a chubby, anxious, and sincere man. He began work in the textile mills of Lawrence when he was fourteen. There inspired by Bill Haywood, Beal passed through the Socialist Party and the IWW before he joined the Communists at the 1928 textile strike in New Bedford, Massachusetts. Beal was sent South as an organizer in January

1929, by the National Textile Workers Union, the Communist dual union formed in late 1928 to challenge the moribund AFL. Without funds, Beal came South on a motorcycle, arriving in torn clothing and shoes so dilapidated he felt his appearance hampered his effectiveness.

When the manager of Gastonia's Loray Mill, owned by Manville-Jenckes Company of Rhode Island, was warned by a company spy, he fired five union sympathizers. At once, eighteen hundred impoverished and resentful mill hands walked out. They did so against the advice of Beal, who realized he was not prepared to sustain a strike. The workers' demands were moderate—increased pay, union recognition, and improved housing—except for the call for a forty-hour week, then not feasible for many workers in the North and unthinkable in the South. The owners responded with a court injunction that prohibited all strike activity.

Within four days of the walkout Governor Max Gardner, a mill owner, rushed in five companies of the National Guard to prevent the overthrow of the U.S. government by the two young reds in Gastonia. Beal had been reinforced by the addition of Ellen Dawson, a twenty-eight-year-old spritelike Scotswoman with cropped black hair who had been a weaver at Passaic.

A wall of hate and hysteria was erected by the local press and mill owners. The Gastonia *Daily Gazette* warned on April 4 that the strike at the Loray Mill "was started simply for the purpose of overthrowing this Government, to destroy property and to KILL, KILL, KILL. The time is at hand for every American to do his duty." The employers' circular warned: "Our Religion, Our Morals, Our Common Decency, our Government and the very foundations of Modern Civilization, all that we are now and all that we plan for our children IS IN DANGER. Communism will destroy the efforts of Christians of 2000 years." The clincher in the local diatribe was that the reds did not believe in religion, or the sanctity of marriage, and, even worse, upheld free love.[7]

In early April, the Communists sent two more organizers into Gastonia. Amy Schechter, the thirty-seven-year-old daughter of an Oxford professor, was bent on conveying what she thought was a proletarian appearance. She rarely brushed her hair and was notoriously sloppy in appearance. Schechter was a feverish admirer of Earl Browder and represented the Communist-led Workers' International Relief. She called the New York party office every day. By the end of the evening, money was usually telegraphed in to buy beans, flour, and staples for distribution to the workers. This piecemeal existence, with occasional money left over to give the strike leaders, was bewildering and frustrating to all but Schechter who unhesitantly accepted the inconvenience in the interest of some higher meaning known only to party leaders.

The other newcomer, Vera Buch, fulfilled the most awful fears of the Gastonia establishment. She was the unmarried lover of Albert Weisbord, whom she had met in Passaic. Buch was just then recovering from an abortion, which Weisbord had insisted she undergo in the name of party commitment. At thirty-four, Buch had been a Communist for ten years. She was shy, ill at ease, and just beginning to develop her own sense of self and leadership style. In the judgment of the historians Paul and Mari Jo Buhle, Vera Buch was psychologically "dependent upon the direction of the Party on the one hand, and on her relationship to Albert Weisbord on the other. . . . To lend herself fully to either was to rob herself of the other possibility."[8]

The young Communist leaders in Gastonia were a hapless lot, isolated victims of both a hysterical community and a factionalized party. In accord with new directions from the Comintern, the American Communists believed they were then entering the "Third Period," when American workers were supposedly on the verge of revolutionary upsurge.[9] This coming gigantic class struggle, according to Stalin, would unleash imperialistic wars and colonial movements; thus American Communists were instructed to organize dual unions outside the AFL and to discredit the non-Communist left in every way possible. Some national party leaders greeted the Gastonia strike with ecstasy. Earl Browder hailed it as "the opening of a new period in the American class struggle." After all, the events at Gastonia, where a walkout had erupted that was led by only one party organizer, who had been at work for only a few weeks and operated with no money, seemed to justify the Comintern's prediction that revolution was at hand. The Third Period, it seemed, was a reality. The Gastonia strike had the additional virtue of providing relief from the internal struggles in the party, which had reached a crisis by the spring of 1929, what with the Jay Lovestone and William Foster factions in Moscow, fighting it out, through all of April and May.

But the ultrarevolutionary line of the Third Period, when joined to local southern hatred and to the wrangling in party headquarters, ultimately was to prove disastrous for the strike leaders in Gastonia. North Carolina reactionaries must have been pleased when Weisbord and other northern Communists briefly dropped in down South to announce that the workers themselves would take over the Loray Mill once the strike was won, or that the Gastonia battle would transform economic and social life in the South as drastically as the Civil War had done.

As national secretary of the National Textile Workers Union, Weisbord also insisted that the Gastonia strike leaders integrate blacks and whites into union activities. To its great credit, the American Communist Party, throughout its history, has stood for racial equality. But racial integration of the union was anathema to most southern white mill hands. It was perceived as sheer madness by the blacks themselves, who made up perhaps 5 percent of the mill labor force and were restricted to the most menial work performed outside the mill buildings. Faithful Vera Buch, following the party's directives, sought out black women workers sorting rags in a mill doorway near Bessemer City. Intent on saving their lives and those of their loved ones, the black women refused to talk, or even to look at her.

The employers were quick to advertise this red threat to southern wealth: "Would you belong to a union which opposes White Supremacy?" their handbills gloated. On April 5, the Charlotte, North Carolina, *Observer* printed a report on strike developments in Gastonia. One sentence from a speech by Beal was set in bold type: **"There must be no division between White and Colored Workers."** The Gastonia newspaper combined anti-Semitism with racism. "Albert Weisbord," it reported, "an East Side Russian Jew, knows as much about American ideals as a Hottentot." [10]

Actually, the Gastonia strike collapsed almost as soon as it began. With no relief or publicity organization worth the name in operation, most of the strikers drifted away within three weeks, some back to the hills or to work in other mills. The strike leadership, so pitifully small in number and resources, was easily stampeded. The picketing women and children were dealt gun blows, pricked with bayonets, and dumped in jail. As a non-Communist reporter sympathetically observed, the strikers' "parades were broken up every day and just as consistently the strikers would form again the following day to march, with full knowledge of what they were doing, into the clubs and rifles. I saw a woman striker knocked down and struck with a bayonet until she bled profusely. She struggled to her feet and marched on—in the parade." [11] With the whole textile industry in the South a tinderbox, ripe for ignition from organizers, erupting in spontaneous strikes in Henderson, Whare Shoals, and High Point, all near Gastonia, and in South Carolina mills, the North Carolina authorities could not honor mere legalities.

The Gastonia mob spirit triumphed on the night of April 18. Over 100 masked men destroyed the union headquarters near the mills, razing the shack and burning relief goods. A block away, the National Guard "slept" through the noise of demolition but appeared in time to arrest nine strikers and to charge them with destroying their own property. [12] Despite a small flurry of protest in the liberal press, no attempt was ever made to arrest the real culprits. It now seemed safe to withdraw the state militia. On April 20 they were replaced by sheriffs' deputies equipped from the state arsenal. Attacks on strikers by a local force organized by the Loray Mill intensified. Several workers received bad bayonet wounds or were beaten unconscious in jail. Meanwhile, the frightened, faithful, and courageous young Communists in Gastonia remained at their post, gamely directing the few recalcitrant strikers still left, who numbered approximately eighty-five families by mid-April.

A few days after the destruction of union headquarters, Fred Beal was arrested for allegedly abducting a striker's wife and carrying her to New York. In fact, the woman, who had left her husband some time before, had traveled to New York to speak on behalf of the workers. Ellen Dawson was also arrested and held on two thousand dollars bond. She was charged with violation of immigration laws. The southern authorities claimed not to know she was an American citizen. Vera Buch and Amy Schechter were arrested as they led a strikers' parade and were charged with drunkenness. Attorneys from the American Civil Liberties Union hustled about for several weeks before all these charges were dropped for want of evidence.[13]

Seven days after the mob's attack, Vorse reached Gastonia on the midnight train. Early next morning she took a taxi to the new strike headquarters in West Gastonia. She passed the demolished old one on the way. It was the symbol of "grotesque savagery" that had led her to Gastonia first on her tour of the southern textile towns. The great Loray Mill dominated the settlement, behind it the mill village, where a flock of houses, all alike, perched on brick stilts. The small strike headquarters was a dim store building, filled with silent men, lounging on the dusty counters. They seemed to Vorse to have the most worn clothing she had ever seen on workers. Many had toothless gaps, the rest tobacco-stained teeth. They eyed her with suspicious reserve. "There is an element of phantastic about the whole situation," Vorse thought as she watched them looking over copies of the *Daily Worker*. The Communist newspaper carried wild exaggerations of the success of the strike, perverting reality in its desire to please its Soviet mentors.[14]

Vorse waited for the strike leaders to appear. Vera Buch, "unresponsive as usual," according to Vorse, saw her first. Vorse remembered Buch as the silent office worker at Passaic who had always managed to place the newspaper clippings where they could not be found. In her journal, Vorse entered her bad-tempered impressions of the young organizers. She judged Buch "faultlessly fearless and totally unimaginative," a "pedantic

Communist, impossible to talk to because of her mouthing phrases," but with a deep determination that belied her colorless impression. Vorse met Fred Beal for the first time: "a nice boy, a weak boy, oppressed with the tremendous weight of the strike. He seemed to me at first touching and petulant . . . over-anxious." Vorse found disorderly and tireless Amy Schechter, with snarled hair and dirty clothes, "perpetually twitching her shoulder and winking her eye in a nervous tick," to be the most animated. Ellen Dawson, "a little wren of a girl," instantly confided to Vorse her dislike of Vera Buch.

The entire atmosphere was one of fright, disorganization, and factionalism, "the impressions of a first day which were all chiefly of deep criticism on the part of the women of the men," Vorse wrote. Fred Beal was so frightened that he slept in the nearby town of Charlotte and "left the girls in the field alone." Yet he was "depressed by the failure of the girls to acknowledge his leadership." The three women leaders, on the other hand, were resentful that Fred Beal refused to accompany them and the striking women and their children on the dangerous picket line. They were all panicky about money. All except Schechter were highly critical of the distant New York office.

Slowly Vorse began to realize the extraordinary spectacle the ardent radicals presented. Floating in the sea of homicidal fury that surrounded them, they had no funds other than the occasional dollars doled out daily by Schechter. There was no money for strike publicity, relief work, or even food for themselves. There was no auditing system, no definite plans, no outside members of the union in all of North Carolina or Tennessee, no preparation of questionnaires, no press releases, no plan to elicit liberal help. There was, Vorse marveled, "no education of the workers, no division of labor, not even a record kept of how many cars were available or any organization of motor service," and the strike leaders were governed by a relief organization in the North, part of whose leadership opposed their efforts. When Fred Beal called Robert Minor—acting secretary of the party while the other party leaders were in Moscow—and asked for money, Minor was complacent and cheerful. Minor told Beal he had no money to send. "Carry on Comrades," Minor bid him blithely.[15]

"The strike scarcely seemed a strike. It was more like a relief station," Vorse wrote in her journal.

> Owen, the negro organizer [sent by the party] remained in Gastonia for three hours and disappeared. . . . Owen went after one smell of the place. [There is] a wide gap yawning between Albert's plans

and what really is—Albert Weisbord's grandiose outline of "rolling strikes," spreading from the North paralyzed by isolation, by half-understood instructions, by lack of the elementary things such as a mimeograph, money for circulars, decent places to sleep, a little privacy. Going through the motions of strike activity but no two thinking alike, no two having confidence in each other.[16]

All the organizers desperately wanted to return North, yet they remained, encircled by furious hatred, riveted by duty and ideals.

Vorse's first reaction to their plight was annoyance and a grating stance of superiority. She felt they exaggerated the danger they were in because they were young and had always been on strikes with a base of radicals or liberals near them. "They have never been isolated. It seems very natural to me," Vorse wrote, indicating her political growth since Lawrence, "to have to take for granted that the respectable community and the forces of society, church, law, police, newspapers, will all be railing against the workers and their leaders." Vorse remembered the spirit of Mesabi as deadlier than any she found in Gastonia. And "this community seemed to bubble with violence less than did Pennsylvania, during the [1919] steel strike, where during the first two weeks, fourteen strikers were shot down."[17] So far, Vorse reasoned, there had been only mutterings in the local Gastonia papers. Even the masked mob had not mauled the workers at the destroyed headquarters. For once, Vorse's journalistic acumen failed her, as her direct experience and later events would prove.

Still acting as critic and wise guide, Vorse urged the strike leaders to organize the middle-class women in the area to provide a milk fund for the strikers' children. The organizers laughed at her naive assessment of southern culture; no middle-class women here would do that. Again, Vorse suggested that working women and their children form marches, to be publicized and to elicit liberal support. Vorse thought that Vera Buch was reluctant to do this only because Albert Weisbord had ordered that only militant demanding male workers be publicized, and Buch wanted only to please Weisbord. Buch's resentment of Vorse's snide carping was evident.

Mary Vorse was a sophisticated person, a trusted sympathizer to whom I felt I could talk more or less freely. Often she referred to "Bobby" (Robert Minor, her former husband) and I think she felt some reflected glory in that association. She had a long history of association with radical causes. An air of self-pity, an apologetic manner were part of her understated personality. She was tall, slim, with sallow skin, thin brownish hair and heavy eyelids. She had a gravelly voice.[18]

Although Vorse had not intended to stay, she remained four weeks in Gastonia, circulating among the striking workers, taking affidavits, meeting the women, reporting the scene for several New York papers and the Federated Press. Gripped by the real-life drama around her, she began work on *Strike!*, her novel about the Gastonia strike. She and Vera Buch, for whom she felt growing affection and respect, roomed together in a small boarding house, sharing their meals and observations. Before long, they had become friends.

When the police broke up a strikers' parade and arrested Buch, Vorse dispatched a scathing denunciation of Gastonian justice to the New York papers. The Gastonia *Daily Gazette* was incensed over "what Mary Heaton Vorse and other radical writers persist in describing as 'Bloody Monday.' In enforcing the law it became necessary for the police officers to use some force with blackjacks and bayonets but [after all] no one was seriously injured."[19]

Vorse was surprised that so many New York papers gave unexpected publicity to the southern textile strikes. The New York *Telegram* and New York *Times* sent special correspondents. The *World*, too, had coverage that Vorse felt was fair. She suspected that northern newspaper owners felt a decided relief that the South had labor troubles. "The New England interests undoubtedly dominate the benevolent attitude [toward the strikers] so far expressed in the capitalist press," Vorse mused in her journal. "Since all the strikes are small—rarely more than three thousand being implicated —it is hard to figure why so much favorable publicity should occur in the New York press, unless the New England interests, those which have not gone South, are delighted that the South could have so swiftly come to conflict with its one hundred percent American workers, guaranteed to give no labor troubles."[20]

As always, Vorse's primary focus was on the women. Two especially stuck in her mind. One was aged Mrs. Ada Howell. Vorse met her in her wooden shack of a home, with open knotholes in the floor and walls. The roof leaked. Howell had never been able to afford the five dollars to have the electricity turned on. She had been beaten by a drunken Gastonia policeman who attacked her with a bayonet as she returned home from shopping. She had two black eyes. "Prather hit me with his fist between the eyes," Howell told Vorse. "He hit me not once but twenty times, I reckon.

My face was swole and bruised double size and black and blue all over." In *Harper's*, Vorse wrote: "It gave one a sense of embarrassment and impotent anger to look at her. She told her story in a detached way." Ada Howell added: "He cut my dress and he cut me too. Lawyer Jimison told me I should keep that dress without washing it so I could show it, but I didn't have enough dresses to lay these clothes away." Vorse wrote: "We didn't say anything. There didn't seem to be anything to say. I suppose when comfortable people read such stories they think, 'This can't be true.' . . . We went on. Strike sightseeing is a rather awful thing. There is obscenity in the fact that old women can be beaten for no reason when they are peacefully proceeding on their business. . . . It does not seem reasonable that such things should happen here in this country, in 1929."[21]

The other woman who impressed Vorse was Ella May Wiggins, fated before the year was over to be immortalized in American labor history. She was a stocky Slavic woman, about thirty, who had born nine children in ten years. Deserted by her husband, she came to Bessemer City, near Gastonia, to work in the mill. Her oldest child stayed home to care for the rest while Wiggins worked her ten-hour shift. One day four of the children died of croup while she was at work. The other five were now being cared for by the oldest, who was eleven. A fervent supporter of the strike, Wiggins had attempted the unthinkable. She had approached a few black workers in the mills and passed union cards to them. Ella May Wiggins was also the popular bard of the Gastonian strikers, singing her mournful mountain ballads that described the workers' struggle.

On May 6, the mill owners evicted sixty-two striking families from their company-owned houses. The deputies piled the meager belongings outside and padlocked the houses. The Reading *Advocate* reported that a small girl suffering from smallpox was carried out of her home by the deputies and placed in the yard. A man watching left quickly. If he stayed, he said, he was afraid he might kill one of the policemen. Vorse interviewed a woman who with her children was sitting on a pile of clothing and goods in her miserable dirt yard. The woman was weeping, shaking her fist at the house, which had "killed her too long." When Vorse based an article for the *World* on the events she had seen—the violence toward the workers, the low wages, long hours, child labor, night work for women and children—the Gastonia *Daily Gazette* published an angry editorial saying she had gotten her facts from hearsay. "It is a strange state of mind," Vorse wrote in her strike journal, "in the community having a just pride in its accomplishments and like a doting parent being unwilling to face its faults . . . a morbid extension of civic pride."[22] The comfortable citizens of Gastonia were convinced that the workers were paid all they deserved and that outside agitators like Vorse were causing all the trouble.

Vorse was soon to see a little bayonet work for herself. She observed the usual picket line composed of women and children forming in the spring sunshine—"young girls in bright cotton dresses, toothless grandmas grasp one another firmly by the arm." Two boys about fifteen and sixteen were leading the line. From behind came cars with ununiformed men armed with guns and bayonets. The men piled out of the cars and arrested the two boys. Five men pulled the hair and twisted the arms of a woman near the front of the line, as she struggled to escape. "Neighborhood women near me began to cry. A deputy told us to move on," Vorse reported. The woman still struggling with the men was not a picket but had come to get her boy out of the line. She was arrested and thrown into a car. As they drove away, Vorse heard her screaming that she had a young baby alone at home to which she must return. The guards, many of whom were drunk, despite the early hour, jabbed at the women's skirts with their bayonets.[23]

At this juncture, Vorse left Gastonia to report the textile strikes in Elizabethton. The economist Broadus Mitchell later recalled meeting her there: "Mrs. Vorse was much respected by all who knew or knew of her, [she] took part in all that went forward, was elderly, dressed in black, an appreciated presence." Vorse slept in a rooming house where the strike leaders stayed. That night the occupants received six bomb threats. Young boys stood armed guard while they slept. Vorse and the others could not rest. "We are on edge, and we appear, each one at our doors, like people in a farce," she wrote. Around midnight, the occupants of the house gathered their chairs around a cold cast-iron wood stove, discussing the possibility of a "sellout" by the negotiating AFL strike leaders.[24]

At some point during her trip to Tennessee, Vorse became greatly alarmed by something she may have discovered, or perhaps overheard, or only sensed. On her way home to the North, Vorse went out of her way to make a special stop at Gastonia to share this new knowledge with Vera Buch. She had returned to Gastonia to warn Buch to get out of Gastonia as soon as possible. Buch remembered the scene:

> Mary Vorse had taken me aside outside the headquarters to warn me of some trouble she was sure was brewing. "Something's going to happen, Vera," she said seriously. "And perhaps soon. I've been in so many of these situations, I can smell it. I smell danger here." I told her it had always been dangerous; we had been threatened from the beginning. She insisted this was something special. . . .

Mary Vorse was gone the next morning; she had left without saying goodbye.[25]

Although she did not convince Buch to go with her, Vorse left Gastonia just in time. Within a week of her departure, Gastonia became front-page national news. On June 7, fire was exchanged on the ground where the workers expelled from the company houses had set up a tent colony near the mill. When the police chief and three deputies entered the tent colony without a warrant, four officers were wounded. Gastonia's police chief, O. F. Aderholt, was dead. Hysteria and hatred boiled over. A mob of two thousand led by a Gastonia attorney completely destroyed the workers' tent colony. Those residents who could not flee were chased down, beaten, and thrown in jail. Every northerner was arrested. Fourteen strike leaders were jailed and charged with conspiracy leading to murder. These included Fred Beal and three young women—Buch, Schechter, and nineteen-year-old Sophie Melvin.

Vorse arrived in Provincetown on the day that the Gastonia mob ran amuck. Her first days at home were totally consumed by the press of domestic chores and cleaning and supplying the house. Four days passed before she learned of the destruction of the tent colony and the arrest of the strike leaders. Her neighbor, John Dos Passos, brought her the news. "I think of my last look at the colony," Vorse wrote in her diary that night, "people living under trees, curly-haired Sophie Melvin leading a band of children with a flag and the tragedy seems unbearable." [26]

After her six weeks in the textile towns, Provincetown seemed a wondrous haven. She remained there through most of the summer, writing a series of labor articles describing her experiences in the South. Two of them brought large checks. She dashed off a lollypop, which sold to *Harper's*. With her new wealth, she bought a sailboat. She passed the days of summer sailing, hiking, sunning, and partying with the Provincetown intelligentsia. Thinking later of that interlude, Vorse remembered it as the moment "when I divorced my family." She wrote Ellen not to come home that summer. For the first time since the spring of 1922 Vorse felt healthy and whole, full of self-esteem and purpose.[27]

During the summer she exchanged letters with Fred Beal and Vera Buch, promising them her assistance. From Provincetown, Vorse successfully initiated an effort, via the ACLU, to mobilize liberal feeling within South and North Carolina. She worked with a view to getting articles in the southern papers: "such few as we can get in, and also to have a basis for appeal to the Governor. . . . Certainly everyone of us who know how Fred Beal tried to keep the workers from shooting, should do all we can," she wrote a southern liberal.[28]

In mid-August, Vorse won an assignment from the New York *Graphic* to report the trial of Beal and the others. She also agreed to serve as correspondent for the Federated Press and TASS, the Soviet wire service. Vorse and Dos Passos had asked the *New Republic* to send them to report on Gastonia, but both were thought to be too far to the left to be reliable from the journal's point of view. The liberals, Dos Passos told *New Republic* editor Edmund Wilson, "are all so neurotic about Communists!" Dos Passos wrote Vorse, "I'm going to try to make some newspaper connections. It's no use trying to fuss around with the liberal weeklies. They have damn little influence anyway."[29]

After a change of venue, because of presumed prejudice in Gaston County, the trial opened in Charlotte in late August. The Charlotte *News* greeted the event with a peculiar defense of due process: The strike leaders "believe in violence, arson, murder. They want to destroy our institutions, our traditions. They are undermining all morality, all religion. But nevertheless they must be given a fair trial, although everyone knows that they deserve to be shot at sunrise." The International Labor Defense, legal arm of the Communists, retained Tom P. Jimison of Charlotte as defense counsel. Vorse described Jimison as "tall, slender, with a delicate air of grace about him, burning eyes, a well sculptured mouth, a spiritual adventurer knowing how to use people's emotions like stops in an organ." He had left the Methodist ministry in protest against the mill owners' control of the churches. Vorse judged him a violent man, with a zest for martyrdom, who considered the accused "as very touching, a tiny band confronting a tremendous organized society, confronting the lions."[30]

Jimison was joined by Arthur Garfield Hays and John Randolph Neal, the notable attorneys associated with the famous Scopes-trial evolution controversy in Tennessee; they were all supported by the ACLU. The attorneys for the prosecution made an awesome crew. They included Clyde R. Hoey, brother-in-law of the governor, and R. G. Cherry, state commander of the American Legion. Presiding was a laconic young judge, whose words were barely audible. The presence of the largest gathering ever of the press in North Carolina, according to the *Nation*, probably had "a somewhat sobering effect on the prosecution."[31]

During the eight days of jury selection, the trial proceeded genially.

The audience in the crowded courtroom was almost entirely male. The upper gallery reserved for blacks was cleared to make way for the whites. The defendants chatted, passed notes, smiled, sometimes slept, in amiable innocence. The state dropped the demand for the death penalty for the three women, in the name of southern chivalry. To the prosecution's dismay, Judge Barnhill ruled that he would not allow any evidence to be presented concerning the defendants' political, racial, or religious beliefs. The only evidence he would consider was what happened on the night of the shooting. The Communists were forced to admit the judge's equitable rulings throughout the proceedings. The courtroom feel of gentle and unhurried justice was heightened by the constant presence of the jailer's two barefooted children, who wandered about, sometimes sitting on the judge's lap, or leaning on the knees of the prisoners or reporters. North Carolina law demanded that the names of prospective jurors be drawn at random by children too young to read or write. The whole scene heightened the northern reporters' sense of their presence in a weird and alien culture.[32]

After 408 challenges, the final jury, a young, primarily working-class group, was selected: seven working men, four tenant farmers, and a grocery clerk. Most of those examined expressed their belief in the right to shoot in self-defense.

The first day of the trial began with a prosecution stratagem borrowed from a similar scene in a movie that had recently been shown near Charlotte. As Vorse reported the event:

> Waggling through the doorway near the judge's bench came a rigid figure. It was covered with a black shroud and jerked along by the sheriff. The shroud fell dramatically and disclosed a life size mannikin of [the dead] Chief of Police Aderholt. Solicitor Carpenter ran nimbly forward and pushed back the wide policeman's hat disclosing the deathly face of the chief. There stood the ghastly figure in full police uniform, blood stained collar, blood stained coat, white death mask. The audience gasped. Was it possible that these eminent attorneys had used this cheap trick of melodrama? "We object," cried the defense. "Objections sustained," said Judge M. V. Barnhill, eyeing the figure. "We only wish to show the location of the gunshot wounds," pleaded the solicitor.
>
> A brief altercation occurred while the blood stained figure remained to tax the incredulity of the beholders.

"I said to take that out," said the Judge with finality, and the bloody mannikin of the chief waggled solemnly away amid a ripple of laughter.[33]

During the next four days of testimony, the state was unable to present any convincing evidence to connect the accused with the shooting of the sheriff. Vorse was convinced, as were most northern commentators, that Fred Beal and at least four other of the defendants were unarmed at the time of the shooting. In the terror and confusion of the moment, it was all but impossible to determine who had fired the fatal shots. Vorse concluded: "I cannot really know nor can anyone else what happened except that a lot of boys shot in self-defense."[34] With everything going its way, the defense was shattered when the judge called a mistrial on September 9, caused when one juror suddenly behaved as though he were insane, the breakdown allegedly induced by his sight of the life-size model of the dead police chief.

The mistrial decision was a serious setback for the defense. Several of the released jurors stated that the flimsy case presented by the state would have brought in a verdict of not guilty. To Soviet readers, Vorse explained that the jury's sympathy stemmed from the rigid class structure she observed in the South.

> All around Charlotte are residence sections of miles and miles of splendid private houses with garages and gardens. The standard of wealth is incredibly high, even for America. There are almost no small middle class districts. The acres of small but comfortable bungalows or small houses which one sees in most American cities are absent. There are the poor shacks inhabited by the workers and the magnificent houses of the well-to-do. Every mill or factory is surrounded by a hundred of these shacks. Each mill owns the houses of the workers, who can be evicted when the owner chooses. It is in such a community of class cleavage that the trial is taking place.[35]

The mistrial declaration set off a reign of terror. On that evening nearly 100 automobiles containing mill superintendents, businessmen, and lawyers for the prosecution, as well as local thugs, wrecked the union headquarters in Gastonia and Bessemer City, another union stronghold. The next morning the mob moved on to Charlotte, twenty miles away, where, singing hymns, they ransacked the offices of the International Labor Defense and a local hotel where Communists and sympathizers were staying.

To the tune of "Praise God from Whom All Blessings Flow" the mob kidnapped a union organizer and stripped and beat him unconscious, Vorse reported in the New York *Evening Graphic*. They then drove to defense lawyer Jimison's home, shouting "Lynch him," before they dispersed.[36]

On September 14 the Communist-led National Textile Workers Union announced a union rally to be held in South Gastonia, reasoning that to fail to do so would encourage more mob violence. That morning Vorse wrote in her diary: "How gladly I would stay at home today instead of going out to what I am sure is a trap for the union." Two thousand men mobilized to prevent the union meeting, setting up roadblocks in all directions from the town. En route to the rally, Vorse entered a car with Liston Oak, publicity director for the International Labor Defense, and his wife, Margaret Larkin, whom Vorse had earlier brought to Passaic to do publicity work. The driver was union member A. A. Grier. Within minutes, wrote Vorse, as their car "proceeded slowly between ranks of the mob, howls went up. 'Union organizers, union organizers! Stop that car.' Cars sped ahead and intercepted us and blocked our way. Guns bustled around us." Saved by the infrequent police, Vorse and her companions were pulled from the car and the men arrested. Oak was charged with carrying a concealed weapon and Grier with "reckless driving."[37]

Vorse's apprehension by the police was fortuitous, for it was just then that Ella May Wiggins, in a nearby open truck carrying twenty-two union members, was shot and killed by a member of the mob who fired point blank into the group of workers. "The last time I saw her," Vorse wrote, "she said to me, 'I belong to the union because of my children. I haven't been able to do anything for them. I never sent a child to school. How could I buy shoes or books? Even if I could, I couldn't let the oldest go. She has to take care of the smaller ones while I am at work. But when they grow up they won't have to work twelve hours a day for nine dollars a week.' She looked at me with extraordinary earnestness and said, 'They would have to kill me to make me leave the union.'" Ella May Wiggins had not been singled out by chance. Her well-known songs and her effort to organize the black workers made her a prime target for North Carolina justice.[38]

Vorse remained in Gastonia three more weeks, a period "of almost unbroken mob terror," reporting the daily outrages she observed, her dispatches seared with fury and near disbelief. The trial was reopened on September 30, but she did not stay to see it.[39] On October 2, she rushed to Marion, North Carolina, where she would record the latest horror in the South.

Since early July, AFL organizers had been busy in Marion. The anti-communism of the AFL's United Textile Workers was no barrier against official terror. Vorse arrived the day after the massacre of six textile strikers, all shot in the back, by the Marion police force and mill deputies. Sinclair Lewis described the event:

> When Sheriff Adkins threw tear gas at the strikers, Old Man Jonas, the striker nearest to Adkins, attacked him with a stick. Adkins was broad, fat, strong, about forty years old. . . . Beside Jonas was the . . . constable Broad Robbins, aged perhaps fifty. . . . And Old Man Jonas was sixty-eight, and so lame with rheumatism that he had to walk with a cane—the cane with which he struck the sheriff.
>
> One would have thought that these two proud and powerful guardians of law and order would have been able to control Old Man Jonas without killing him. Indeed they made a good start. Adkins wrestled with him, and Broad clouted him in the back of the head. Jonas fell to his hands and knees. He was in that position when he was shot. . . .
>
> After the riot, Jonas, fatally wounded, was taken to the hospital with handcuffs on, was placed on the operating-table, with hand-cuffs still on, and straightway he died on that table . . . with his handcuffs on.[40]

The deputies' fire killed five other workers and wounded twenty-five. The president of the Marion Manufacturing Company, interviewed by a correspondent about the massacre, said of the police: "If ever I organize an army, they can have jobs with me. There was three tons of lead used in the world war to kill every man. Here we used less than five pounds and four are dead and 20 wounded. Damn good, I say."[41] Later, six unionists were convicted of rioting and the sheriff and deputies were acquitted in their trial for murder. The Marion strike would be completely crushed by December.

Drawn from her experience of three months in the South, from her memories of the tears rolling down the faces of women in grimed paths, the excitement of the young, the piles of belongings in the rain on red dirt, the laughing oneness of fight, the hatred for the respectable, the black faces so silent and still—Vorse wrote her story of Marion. Surfeit, exhaustion, hope, and hopelessness, she caught it all in her description in the *New Republic*. It all came together somehow, sharply honed words, stacatto sentences, the beauty of truth and feeling. Even the most comfortable, the most cynical, the most removed reader could not help but pause, for just a moment, to be moved, just an inch, to feeling, and perhaps to understanding.

Lights shine in the mill village of East Marion. . . .

With a party of strikers, I went "visitin' the dead." A striker drives us. We plunge in darkness down a sheer hill. We are at the Brysons'. The room is full of quiet visitors and watchers. People come in quietly and go out. Little is said. There are women sitting with their heads in their hands near the fire. The visitors pass quietly before the coffin. They are talking in low tones in another room. This is no ordinary funeral. This is murder—mass murder in cold blood of many people. . . .

"It's a sorry day," says someone. "We haven't seen the end of this," comes the answer. There are no threats of vengeance. There is an ominous quiet. . . .

We wind dark corners and scale rutted perpendicular hills. Before the Vickers, the road is so steep we must block the wheels. There is a pile of home-made wreaths of dahlias on the porch. Inside in one room lies murdered Sam Vickers. They call him Old Man Vickers. He was only fifty-six. Men come and men go before him . . . and recall how he ran four miles to join the union.

From the other room, the "warm room," comes the keening of Mrs. Vickers, terrible and monotonous. . . .

There are no tears at the Jonas's. There in the "warm room," people are asleep. Three young girls and a child in one bed. George Jonas' daughters, worn out with grief. The visitors murmur: "They beat him after he was shot and handcuffed. He was handcuffed when he came to the operating table. . . ."

Hall's next. Hall was twenty-three. . . . His record in the strike was that except for one night, during nine weeks of the strike, he picketed every night for twelve hours. He had had a twelve hour day's work always, so he worked twelve hours for the union.

"He was running away, and the deputies chased him shooting," murmur the visitors. . . .

The day of the funeral . . . the gray caskets of the four murdered union men stand end on end in a long line. They are heaped with fall flowers. . . . People who haven't gardens made paper-flower wreaths. . . .

The open coffins stand before the "speakin' stand," where for

nine weeks the strikers came every day to hear the speakin'. . . .
There are union flags. There is no American flag. . . .

Behind the flower-heaped coffins, a line of fifty relatives and friends sit in chairs. Up the shaded hillside are a thousand people more. . . . A thin fine note of weeping comes from the mourning women, a high keening of grief. They have been quiet for a long time. . . .

It was more of a demonstration than a funeral. . . .

The services were over. The hymn singing had finished. The entire company of a thousand people filed slowly, slowly, one by one, before the dead. Every man and woman, every child, looked into the faces of the four murdered fellow-workers. . . .

People went slowly away in little groups.

"We haven't seen the end of this," men said gravely to one another.[42]

The red holes in the ground were filled. Mounds of red earth were heaped over the dead. The mourners walked silently away. Like them, Vorse could not help her striving, although she, too, knew that something precious had ended without happiness or a sense of wholeness.

Chapter Fourteen

Holding the Line

During the early Depression years, Vorse's precarious monetary condition was balanced by joyous release from her isolation of the twenties. She returned to the pattern of constant travel and reporting she had begun after Joe O'Brien's death. She also turned again to other females for emotional support. Vorse had found little in common with most women of her own generation, so few of whom shared her radical politics or overarching ambition. But beginning in her mid-fifties, she became close to several admiring younger women as deviant as herself. During these same years, although she still worried over her children's welfare, her daughter's marriage brought a measure of financial relief. The publication of her tenth book also lifted her spirits.

In the early thirties, Vorse returned South to cover stories in Alabama, and in Kentucky, where she was expelled from the state by nightriders. Accompanied by her new radical women friends, she also reported the revolt of farmers and the unemployed. In all these labor stories, as at Passaic and Gastonia, she had an opportunity to study Communist activists at close hand. First privately in 1929, and then publicly in 1933, Vorse decisively rejected Soviet-style communism and the American leadership of its followers.

Even in this, her stand, as always, was at odds with mainstream liberalism. Vorse differentiated between the high priests of the party and the rank-and-file members who in the early thirties often led the battle of the poor against reactionary forces. She discovered that most of the labor activists working with the party knew or cared little about the scuffling for personal power or the doctrinal debates that were so dear to party officers in New York. Her labor experience of the past twenty years had convinced her that militant left protest was necessary in order to move the country's political center to address urgent social problems, and she knew that in the early Depression years Communist organizers were among the most courageous and committed workers in the field. Vorse decided to continue her association with party organizers she admired, while distinguishing between their struggle and the pronouncements of party leaders. She would hold to her wider vision, even through the perilous 1950s, despite its negative effect on her reputation and popularity.

From North Carolina, Vorse headed directly to the art colonies of New Mexico, there to finish a novel based on her experience in Gastonia. Both Mary Austin in Santa Fe and Mabel Dodge in Taos had offered her a room where she could work. Vorse longed for a quiet and inexpensive haven. During the three months she spent in the Southwest, her writing went easily. She polished off a few lollypops to pay her way. "The days are round and full like eggs," she wrote in her diary. "I have a lovely feeling of coming back to the small niche in the world I made for myself, and from which I was absent for a while. . . . I have a feeling of delight in getting back to my own quiet place. The solidity of daily work."

By the mid-twenties, a colony of American writers and artists also flourished in Mexico City. John Dos Passos had told Vorse about his happy weeks spent in Mexico in 1926. Mexico especially appealed to Vorse as a writing retreat because life there was cheap as well as redemptive. She began Spanish lessons while in Santa Fe and used the proceeds from her recent sales of lollypops to pay off the loans accumulated during the bleak period from 1922 to 1929.

Just before she headed south, Vorse received a telegram from her daughter. Ellen announced her pending marriage, neglected to tell her mother the name of her husband-to-be, and requested funds. Vorse sent fifty dollars for a dress and a wedding present. Now she had eighty dollars left, enough to last her four weeks, she judged. After a brief visit with Josie and Joel in Texas, Vorse arrived in Mexico City in mid-February.[1]

She took a room with a Mexican family whose bathroom was placed off limits to protect the privacy of a turtle dove nesting on the floor behind the toilet. "I have suddenly run into a dazzling happiness," Vorse crowed, "just like that of my student days in Paris." As was her custom, she wrote each morning while lying in bed. She spent the afternoons and evenings with members of the radical coterie assembled about the American writer Carleton Beals. Sometimes she walked across town to watch the artist

Diego Rivera at work.[2] But Vorse's closest companion in Mexico City was Dorothy Day, who would some years later win fame as the founder of the Catholic Worker movement, an event greatly influenced by Vorse's effect on Day. The two women had first met in the Village in 1917. During their time together in Mexico, they formed a deep friendship that would join their disparate lives for over thirty years.

Twenty-three years younger than Vorse, Day had been radicalized in 1916 when she heard Elizabeth Gurley Flynn speak at a fund-raising rally in support of the Mesabi miners. Soon after, Day joined the staff of the *Masses*. Arrested as a suffrage picket at the White House, she went on a ten-day hunger strike until released from jail. When she fell in love with a grumpy, unemployed actor and became pregnant, he insisted on abortion. Creeping home after the illegal operation, she discovered he had left town. In 1919, still smitten, she pursued him to Chicago. There, while visiting a sick woman friend at a Wobbly boarding house, Day was swept up by a Department of Justice raid and arrested and jailed on a false charge of prostitution. This experience drove her farther left.

Precisely like Vorse, Day endured a desperately unhappy winter of 1922–23. Ironically, Day had then worked as secretary to Robert Minor in Chicago, where he and Lydia Gibson had moved after Minor left Vorse in the summer of 1922. Day had found his melodramatic style amusing: "When I took dictation from Bob, he kept telling his friends that he was being followed. Pacing up and down the room, glancing out of the window he would say, 'at this moment of writing there is a man standing in the doorway across the street who had been shadowing me for the past week.' This was repeated in each letter."

Vorse served the admiring younger woman as a political model of purpose and zest. "Like a warrior scenting battles," Day wrote of Vorse, "she dashes off for the fray. . . . But her movements are never dashing. Rather, she quietly appears where labor trouble is, and gets to work. For months she wanders around from strike headquarters to picket line, to jails, to courts, to the homes of strikers. And then she spends further months (with her feet higher than her head, as though it helped her to think) immobile for hours, dictating pamphlets, stories, articles and novels about the trouble." In Mexico, Day's secretarial assistance helped Vorse to write the last chapters of *Strike!*[3]

When Vorse returned to Provincetown she found her house full of young people. All the children came home that summer, including the new addition to the family, Ellen's pianist husband Marvin Waldman. At first, Vorse welcomed her return to the routine of children and life in the resort setting. She settled into a familiar pattern of writing, play, and housework. "It has been a good year," she mused. "A year lived selfishly."[4]

The literary and artistic colony at Provincetown assumed a new shape that summer as a younger generation came to join those who had founded the Provincetown Players fifteen years earlier. Edmund Wilson and his new bride moved into Eugene O'Neill's old house. Katy and John Dos Passos were in nearby Truro. Of the old Provincetown crew, there were Susan Glaspell and Norman Matson, Hazel Hawthorne, and the poet Harry Kemp. Unlike earlier times, when the Provincetown summer colony had centered its activity around family and small children, the adult gatherings of the 1930s were more hard-drinking affairs, but with the conversation still directed toward literary or political analysis. As before, the group usually worked until mid-afternoon, then joined in shifting combinations to swim, sun, or hike the dunes, before their evening frolics. Vorse knew her social skills were a bit rusty after her travail of the twenties. "I have not nearly enough relations in my life. No one near to me. No one. I talk to dozens—But no intimacies. No loves." A few months later, she added: "It is a sad fact I do not like men as much as I did. . . . I have no weather eye out for men who would naturally like me . . . the shutting on life of one of the doors."[5]

By summer's end, Vorse's hope for a new family harmony dissolved. She and twenty-three-year-old Ellen quarreled bitterly about Ellen's neglect of daily chores and about the noisy crowd of young visitors who disturbed Vorse as she tried to write. That summer, Vorse developed a constant pain in her side. Despite the doctor's reassurance, she worried that she might be dying of some obscure malady. To escape Ellen's "pullings and howlings . . . her scenes and excitements," Vorse asked her sixteen-year-old son Joel to row her out every morning to a friend's boat in the harbor where she could work in isolation. Finally, she relapsed into hysteria. "Suddenly, I go to pieces," she wrote in her journal. "I cry and cry. I can no longer carry the burden. I cannot go alone as I have in the past doing everything and only unkindness for a reward. I feel my own inadequacy as a mother. . . . I feel as if I were sinking and calling for help to people who answer, 'Don't make such a horrible noise.'" The support of the children was a financial burden as well, during this first Depression year. Vorse borrowed money to pay the previous year's interest on the mortgage. She fantasized that next season she would rent her house and "go to some quiet place where I can work. . . . Here, in Provincetown, maybe."[6]

In the early fall of 1930, Horace Liveright published *Strike!* Following the chronology of actual events in Gastonia, Vorse described working and living conditions, the discomfort of the few southern liberals, the host of labor spies, the wavering morale of the strikers, the shootings, the deaths, the trials, the vigilante mobs. *Strike!* is marked by its theme of women's courage and strength, a point that escaped the notice of reviewers. The young strike organizer, Irma Rankin, who represents Vera Buch, and Mamie Lewis, the name given to Ella May Wiggins, are the fearless characters about whom the action revolves. Rankin knows that "the women [workers] are pluckier than the men." Rankin and a male reporter wrangle over this. He finds Rankin's unwillingness to subordinate herself to the male strike leader unsettling. In *Strike!*, Vorse described the real scene in Gastonia, where Vera Buch and the other female organizers derided Fred Beal's lack of organization and resisted his demand that he be given direction of a strike in which it was women who "manned" the dangerous picket lines.[7]

The story is told from the perspective of two eastern journalists, Rogers and Hoskins. Both men represent Vorse in various stages of her life. Like Vorse at Lawrence in 1912, Rogers came to report his first strike believing that the only reason the "good" people of the community opposed the strikers was that they lacked understanding of the facts. Hoskins, however, is a cynical veteran of the labor movement. He chides Rogers: "There's no use being shocked about a thing that always happens. Whenever the workers make their initial revolt the instinctive action of the comfortable people is to put down the rebellion with violence—any violence, all violence." Like Vorse, Hoskins "made a good living as a special writer for popular magazines, and would have been well off if he could have left the labor movement alone." But "let a strike come along, and there he'd be," always experiencing "the worker's willingness to fight as more exciting than anything else in the world."

Her decision to reveal the growth of her philosophy through two male characters is significant. As a female labor journalist in a male profession, she realized that speaking through a male reporter would legitimize her views in a way that a woman character could not. Vorse had always deprecated her work as a popular fiction writer—a domain judged appropriate for women authors—and yet made her living from it. In her role as labor journalist—her deepest interest—she felt forced to pose as a man. Sex-role conflict followed her even into the symbol making central to the writer's work.

The novel received wide attention. Mike Gold praised it in the *New Masses* as a glorious example of "proletarian realism." Liveright issued the book with a detachable paper band, which proclaimed Gold's belief that "it was a burning and imperishable epic." This worried Sinclair Lewis who voiced his fear in the *Nation* that an endorsement by the Communist Gold might prejudice readers against the book. Carl Haessler wrote Vorse that Lewis was "praising you as the very best of all the writers on the textile strikes in the South." The *New Republic* and the *New Yorker* reviewers were strongly positive; the *Saturday Review of Literature* and the *New York Times Book Review* gave mixed, but sympathetic, support. The book sold well, despite its bewildering number of characters and unwieldy presentation of the southern mill-hand's dialect. Vorse was pleased to learn it would be published in German, Russian, and Japanese for distribution abroad.[8]

Strike! appeared in the ultrarevolutionary Third Period (1928–1935) of American Communist history, when Stalin was erasing his opposition in the Soviet Union. In Russia, cooperation with farmers and traders came to an end; the corollary was that Communist parties abroad must conform by opposing an alliance with democratic socialists. The new turn to the left included an attempt by the American Communist movement to appeal to intellectuals and writers, a group they had previously scorned for its resistance to party discipline and tendency toward independent thinking.

The party attempted a ham-handed authority over literature and social comment during the thirties. Overblown, intemperate attacks on liberals and independent radicals appeared in party-influenced publications, as Communist leaders denounced intellectuals unwilling to adhere to the party line. Yet many American thinkers were moving left during this time of unprecedented economic collapse and consequent misery. The party's authoritarianism and slavish admiration of the Soviet Union repelled many intellectuals, but at the same time, serious writers were attracted by the party's willingness to fight for the deprived. As one rank-and-file Communist activist explained years later: "The Communists seemed like the only group doing anything about everything" in 1930 and 1931. With nowhere else to go, dozens of American writers joined party-affiliated groups, supported party actions, and even participated in the debate over the appropriate content and structure of "proletarian culture."[9]

As author of a book that sympathetically portrayed the workers' struggle in Gastonia, Vorse was pursued by Communists eager to build a coalition with non-Communist writers. Jack Stachel, the party's organizational secretary, and Mike Gold and Joseph Freeman, editors of the *New Masses*, frequently "plagued" her, Vorse wrote, to attend party-led meetings and to write for party publications. Vorse resisted these efforts. Through long contact with the Communist left, she was more aware than most of the petty quarrels and infighting then convulsing the party elite, as Earl Browder slowly gained a lead over William Foster in competition for the top position. She agreed with Elizabeth Gurley Flynn, another old-timer on the left, who wrote Vorse in 1930: "The movement is a mess, torn by factionalism and scandal, and led by self-seekers, with one or two exceptions. I am glad to be out of it all." The American Communist Party, Vorse wrote in her journal, was headed by functionaries with "closed minds, so certain, so dull . . . miserable, pathetic, static. They *bore me, bore me, bore me.*" [10]

More important, Vorse shunned the party because she had become deeply critical of the evolution of socialism in the Soviet Union. She knew that the GPU, the Russian political police, was in place, increasingly at Stalin's disposal, and ready for large-scale repression of dissent. The first "show trials" had begun. Stalin had also gained control of the trade-union apparatus. But the Soviet betrayal of her socialist ideals that most horrified her was the state's attack on the Russian peasantry, which led to at least ten million deaths between 1928 and 1933 during the collectivization of agriculture and the famine that followed. The realization of this catastrophic barbarism marked a turning point in her political development. Vorse was now certain that Bolshevik-style socialism had become but another form of despotism; she was unforgiving of the American Communist leaders who supported and defended a red dictatorship. "I find myself in a bourgeois frame of mind about the kulaks," she wrote in her diary in early 1931. "[The peasants] for the fault of having a wrong psychology have been killed or sent to forced labor. The moment you get any large group living in virtual slavery (and for ideological reasons) the world should say, 'Why bathe humanity in blood if we still have to keep enslaved a considerable number of people so that the new civilization can march?' . . . *Who cares which class rules so long as the sum of injustice remains the same?*" Later that year she added: "I am a communist because I don't see anything else to be. But I am a communist who hates Communists and Communism." [11]

Vorse did continue her friendship with Communist-affiliated but independent activist–intellectuals like Adelaide and Charles Walker. In mid-September 1931, Vorse was invited by them to accompany Theodore Dreiser and a group of other writers on a trip to Kentucky. Dreiser's group intended to publicize the denial of civil liberties in Harlan County, where a battle raged between union miners and coal operators. Vorse agreed to go. She did so more reluctantly than Dos Passos, who had not experienced southern hostility first hand. But on September 17, at a Provincetown party with Dos Passos, Vorse made a sudden decision to travel to England instead.

"The British Empire has cracked right before one's eyes," she chortled just before she left.[12] The British economic crisis had toppled the Labour government and had led twelve thousand men of the British fleet in harbor at Invergordon to mutiny in protest against pay reductions, which had fallen in undue proportion on the lowest ranks of seamen. No Anglophile, Vorse felt righteous glee at the threat to British imperialism. The unthinkable, a British naval mutiny, combined with the possibility of the unbelievable, the felling of British bankers, was too good a story for Vorse to miss. With assignments from the Federated Press and *Harper's*, she sailed a few days later.

By the time Vorse landed in Scotland, pay cuts had been reduced and the immediate crisis resolved. The wider national crisis was not solved. After the demise of the second Labour government in 1931, the extremes of class inequality persisted, with almost three million unemployed. Two-thirds of British families received one-third of the aggregate income. The old set of old boys ruled in Britain, unimaginative, cautious, eminently respectable.

After seven weeks, Vorse left with the conviction that the Labour Party leaders were no better than the Tories and even more pretentious. Socialism could not be built "almost behind the backs of the ruling class," she wrote. "Personally, I belong to those who believe you can't sneak up on a nation with a program of socialism. Anything like real socialism will mean expropriation for the working classes." For Vorse, her 1931 trip to Britain would always be symbolized on one side "by the brave rhetoric of the Labor Party Conference and [on the other by] the sight of the King and Queen in their glass and gold coach—bowing to the cheering people on their way to open the new Tory Parliament." Two crowds, equally bamboozled.[13]

Wanting to report events in Germany "before the deluge," Vorse spent two weeks in Berlin before returning home. In the Reichstag election of September 1930, the Nazis had become the second largest political party. The German Communists, on orders from the Comintern, refused to align themselves with the Social Democrats against Hitler. The Communists believed the Nazi regime would be a temporary phenomenon, which would pave the way to their own seizure of power. Paramilitarism and political violence soared. By the end of 1932 several hundred Germans had died and thousands had been injured in clashes between political parties.

In Berlin, Vorse spent most of her time with Louis Lochner, then the chief of the Berlin Bureau of the Associated Press, earlier, a founder of and, like Vorse, reporter for American labor's Federated Press. Vorse and Lochner attended a Nazi–Communist student debate. She wrote, "I, who have seen plenty of crowds on the edge of trouble, have never sat through so prickly an evening." After four chill hours of talk, the opposing factions in the hall began to scuffle. "Then a gentleman in the gallery dropped a chair from two stories up—just quietly dropped it," she wrote. The police came instantly. Vorse went away, sober and breathless. No one knows what will happen, she reported, but "cataclysm is at hand . . . the end of an epoch. The next act will be starker. It will be steel instead of rococo marble," she warned the readers of the *New Yorker*.[14]

Shortly after her return to Provincetown, Vorse received a telegram from Adelaide and Charles Walker:

> Kentucky miners face crisis distribution of food account armed thugs. We are sending trucks of flour and vegetables into Harlan to test fundamental rights to feed strikers. Asking well known persons including [Charles] Beard and Sherwood Anderson to go in on truck. Will you go too. Probably starting Tuesday Wednesday night next week. Want you very much and sure expenses can be raised.[15]

During Vorse's absence in Europe, Theodore Dreiser had led his writers' committee, which included Dos Passos and the Walkers, into Kentucky to publicize the terror unleashed against striking miners. A Kentucky jury promptly indicted each member of Dreiser's group for criminal syndicalism, an extraditable offense carrying a possible sentence of twenty-one years in prison. When the same jury indicted Dreiser for adultery, he assured the press that he was impotent and thus innocent. The sex scandal attracted more national attention than the exposure of conditions in the Harlan coalfields might have otherwise received. As a result of the publicity, a group of charity organizations in Kentucky initiated relief efforts, which saved some miners and their families from death by malnutrition and disease.[16]

The tale of "Bloody Harlan County" during the Depression is today an American epic of labor struggle, memorialized by one of the most enduring of protest songs, "Which Side Are You On?" For several years the violent class war that raged in Harlan and Bell counties forced all the inhabitants to choose a side. In 1932, Harlan miners, who composed two-thirds of the county's population, existed in feudal-like peonage, their lives bound by the lords who owned the coalfields. Sixty-one percent of the county's population lived in unincorporated company towns, governed by the mine superintendent and policed by deputy sheriffs paid by the coal company. Union organizers or sympathizers were immediately evicted and fired. A recent scholarly study of Harlan's history in the 1930s concludes: "Harlan's coal firms were not just running a business in Harlan County: they were running the county. . . . The few small farmers were about the only truly free people in the county."[17]

Cut off from political action by fraudulent election practices, the miners fought back through the institution of unionism. When a 10 percent wage cut was announced in February 1931, the local miners decided they might as well die fighting as die of starvation. Looting of grocery stores by hungry miners began. In May, at the famous Battle of Evarts, where one thousand shots were exchanged in the course of about thirty minutes, several deputies and miners were killed. The appearance of the National Guard halted picketing, while mass arrests eliminated union leadership. The United Mine Workers called it quits after its last public meeting was dispersed by deputies throwing tear-gas canisters into the orderly crowd of assembled workers. Given the choice of starving, leaving the county, or going back to work, all but about a thousand angry miners had reentered the mines at reduced wages by the summer of 1931.

At this point the Communists' newly formed dual union, the National Miners Union (NMU), entered Harlan to organize the embittered minority of workers who had refused to relinquish their unionism or sign yellow-dog contracts. But the Communist union struggle in Harlan was doomed from the start. Lacking organizers and relief money, and recruiting unemployed workers who could exert no economic pressure on the operators, the Communists were in fact leading what was more a political demonstration than a strike.

Vorse "mulled and stewed" for several days as she pondered her reply to the Walkers' telegram asking her to join the second group of writers to be sent into Bloody Harlan, this time to bring food to the blacklisted miners and to test again the state of civil liberties. Vorse was frankly afraid. Five months earlier she had decided not to join Dreiser's group, partly because she feared its members would be jailed, or worse. After her experience in Marion and Gastonia, Vorse fully understood the nature of southern justice. Moreover, she suspected that the Communists would deliberately use the writers' committee to provoke a violent confrontation in the hope of further radicalizing the workers. She did not want to be caught in any resultant maelstrom of terror. Dos Passos came to her Provincetown home three nights in a row to help her reach a decision. He was cautious, but supportive of her need to help the hungry people of Harlan. Finally, her political commitment, as well as her journalistic curiosity, won. Before she left Provincetown for New York, she wrote in her diary: "There is all this talk about appealing to the nation. One good story syndicated with the Hearst papers will do more to crack things open. The people can't visualize [the hunger]. The miners are starving. The children are starving. I do not want to go very much yet I suppose I will go." [18]

Vorse traveled to Harlan as a representative for the Federated Press. She knew the fate of the last two Federated Press reporters to enter Harlan. In mid-August, twenty-one-year-old Boris Israel had been removed from a courtroom by three sheriffs who threatened his life and shot him in the leg as he escaped. The Federated Press next sent Jessie O'Connor, who remembers that when she arrived, she was handed a note from "100% Americans and we don't mean maybe." The note told her "that the other redneck reporter got what was coming to him, so don't let the sun go down on you here." O'Connor wisely fled Kentucky at once. Her husband, Harvey O'Connor, telegraphed Forrest Bailey, of the American Civil Liberties Union: "Considering going to Harlan tonight. Have you anyone there?" Bailey replied: "We have nobody in Harlan. Farewell. Forward last messages." Even critical journalists of the nonradical variety were forbidden entry to Harlan. In late July, before the Federated Press reporters had appeared, a Virginia editor had been ambushed and shot in the ankle. [19]

In New York, Vorse conferred with Edmund Wilson, who had also consented to join the writers' committee bringing food to Harlan. She and Wilson won a pledge from the Walkers that no inflammatory Communist rhetoric would be publicly expressed by anyone who might travel with the writers. On February 6 she wrote in her diary: "I get a very bad impression of the outfit. The men going . . . are all soft. They are hairsplitters. . . . The same old radical ebb and flow & wailing around. I feel I'm a fool to go. That I'm going to get into a meaningless mess. Time taking. Nerve racking."

The next day, Vorse left for Knoxville, where the writers would assemble. She met Wilson in New York's Pennsylvania Station. He found her "dispirited," worried about being spotted and followed by coal company detectives. "It's different [in Harlan] from up here," Vorse warned him again. "Those people—are likely to mob you!" She refused to join the rest of the group until the train was ready to pull out of the station. On board, she found Charles Walker very excited. Wilson remembered that Walker's "mouth opened, and a program from the *Daily Worker* fell out, making Mary and me very uneasy." Walker urged the group to insist on the right to free assembly and free speech when they reached the coal-fields. Immensely scornful of Walker's optimistic judgment as to what might await the group in Kentucky, Vorse withdrew on the train into silent contemplation of the *New Yorker* and *Redbook* while Wilson and Walker discussed the ideas of Marx and Henry George.[20]

In a dingy room in Knoxville's Farragut Hotel, watched by detectives outside the door, the assembled party held a tense discussion under a bald electric light bulb hanging on a cord from the ceiling. The best-known writers in the group, beside Vorse and Wilson, were the *New Republic* editor Malcolm Cowley, the broadcaster and journalist Quincy Howe, and the novelist Waldo Frank. Cowley wrote that, except for Vorse, "a novelist with radical sympathies who had been reporting strikes for thirty years, . . . [the rest of us] had no experience in labor disputes. Waldo Frank had written more books than the rest of us, and we made him our chairman." John Henry Hammond, the young radical who was heir to a Vanderbilt fortune, Benjamin Lieder, the Paramount newsreel cameraman who five years later was to be killed while flying a plane for the Spanish Loyalists, Harold Hickerson, a New York playwright, and Allan Taub, a Communist attorney, who had recently been expelled from the coalfields in return for his pledge never to return, also joined the group. Another member, Liston Oak, whom Vorse had last seen in Gastonia, when they both had been arrested just moments before Ella May Wiggins was killed, looked gaunt and nervous. Wilson noticed that Oak's hands were shaking, probably be-cause Oak, like Vorse, knew what they faced. The two other women on the committee were Elsa Reed Mitchell, a retired physician from California, and Polly Boyden, whose militant pronouncements annoyed Vorse. Years later, Adelaide Walker remembered of the group: "Wilson was apoliti-cal; taking him was a mistake. Cowley was overboard for the Communist Party, and Polly Boyden was wildly CP."[21]

Drawing on her experience of labor conflict, Vorse told the members of the group to leave behind every piece of literature they might have with them. She warned that their luggage and persons were sure to be searched, and any radical or suspicious literature could endanger them all. The rest of the committee chuckled at her fears. Twenty-one years later, she still felt angry when she recalled how her cautionary instructions were "met

with the patronizing assurances that men give to an hysterical woman."
She was unable to convince them to leave their papers behind. Vorse felt
as if she "possessed some dark truth that she could not communicate to
the others. They were innocent, babbling about holding meetings and
visiting mining camps. They had not seen a Southern mob in a killing
mood." Her first encounter with the committee members increased her
rising sense of doom.

Early the next morning, the party drove in private cars to La Follette,
Tennessee, where they ate some spongy hotdogs at the local soda fountain.
Vorse had great difficulty in persuading young Hammond not to play the
jukebox. A crowd of silent men watched them. Vorse's group then learned
that Harry Simms, the nineteen-year-old Jewish NMU organizer from
Massachusetts who had left Pineville that morning to meet the caravan,
had been attacked. Simms was walking near the railroad tracks when two
sheriffs riding a handcar shot him in the stomach and left him to bleed to
death. Most of the committee members expressed shock and indignation at
the news of Simms. They were still so innocent, Vorse thought, still so sure
that no one would dare harm such a distinguished crowd as themselves.
"This is no class struggle," Vorse told Wilson. "This is class war."[22]

Wishing she had never come, Vorse wrote, "I had a gritty feeling that I
alone among all . . . [of us] knew we were heading for trouble. . . . When
Southerners make a threat, they mean it." The little entourage moved up
the mountain, the food trucks lumbering behind. The young Kentuckian
driving her car was armed. He whistled in amazement when he was told
that none of the men in Vorse's party carried guns.

After a time they came to a crossroads where a crowd of about thirty
silent men with rifles and shotguns stood. She and Wilson took a short
stroll while the rest of the committee bought lunch. To lessen their anxiety,
they talked of other things. As Wilson remembered it: "Mary and I walked
up and down—Mary's troubles with her children—Ellen had come down
with her husband and intimated that she wished Mary were dead so that
they could have the house, Mary had intimated a little less crudely that
she wished Ellen were dead—we discussed marriage, husbands and wives
who both did things and competed with one another.—Liston Oak [joined
us]. What does this remind you of, Mary? (He meant Gastonia.)" Finally
the trucks came and they went on. They learned then that one of the
trucks carrying clothing had been stopped and overturned.[23]

At the Pineville city limits, another silent armed force of deputies
watched them pass. The town square looked like it was under siege.
Cowley remarked he hadn't seen so many guns since France in 1917. On

top of Town Hall Vorse saw a nest of machine guns. Conspicuously armed men were everywhere. The nervous banter between committee members faltered to a halt.

The group scampered up the steps into the office of the only Pineville attorney who would plead for the miners. He told them he would try to find a vacant lot in which they could hold a meeting. Vorse's attention fixed on the office wall calendar with a big picture of a grinning, barely clad brunette with a black bob and black silk stockings. The attorney warned the members of Vorse's group to move away from the windows. "They've got their machine guns trained on it," he said. Some of the male writers, with bravado, looked out the window. They had the right to do so, they said. Smiling sadly, the lawyer shrugged, "You've got the right, but you want to understand whatever these people want to do, they'll do it anyway." Vorse thought her little band of crusaders seemed absurd. She reflected that they would be grotesque but for the death of Harry Simms. Murder had been committed because of them. Death made them authentic. Only the danger of their mission gave them a burnish of heroism.

The writers were escorted to the gloomy lobby of the old-fashioned hotel. There Waldo Frank spoke to a crowd of hostile men about matters of free speech and free assembly. A coal operator walked up to Cowley and said, "I admire your nerve in coming here where you don't know anything about conditions or the feeling of the people. If you don't watch out, you'll find out how ugly we can be." Nodding toward Vorse who was scribbling notes, the coal operator added: "and I don't care if your stenographer takes that down." Frank warned the assembled citizens in the hotel lobby that his group would publish "from New York to California" what they saw. "As far as I'm concerned," the mayor replied, "I think the citizens should run ye out of town." The ritual of insolent courtesy was cracking on both sides. At this point, the confrontation degenerated into a defense of manhood, when Wilson, Frank, and Cowley all insisted that they *had* registered for the draft during the war. Vorse's alienation from her comrades reached a new height.[24]

At last, they were allowed to drive outside the city limits where the food was to be distributed from the trucks. Vorse stayed in the car with a local woman while the food was handed out. It was getting dark. Later she learned that the last two hundred pounds of salt pork were stolen at gunpoint by one of the sheriff's men. A young miner who tried to make a speech was chased away by a deputy waving two drawn guns.

Back at their hotel, the assembled committee met in the empty lobby, sitting on dark red, thronelike chairs. They first pulled down the shades on the street side. Much to the surprise of everyone but Vorse, they found their luggage had been searched. Gathering evidence for a charge of criminal syndicalism, the deputies had found a pair of Frank's shoes wrapped in an old copy of the *Daily Worker*.

Within an hour, men came to their rooms and arrested all of them. Elsa Mitchell, Wilson wrote, "looked a little taken aback for the first time —her hat on a little bit crooked." Followed by a crowd of about seventy-five men, they were marched three blocks to the courthouse, taken to a crowded basement court, and charged with disorderly conduct. A deputy sheriff accidentally dropped his gun. It clattered across the bare courtroom floor, creating a deep silence. A local white townswoman in the courtroom audience complained loudly because a window had been opened in her face by the black observers standing in the alley outside the building. The county attorney asked the judge to drop the charges and he quickly agreed. Back now once more across the square to the hotel, Taub, uneasy when he saw a crowd of men outside, asked for protection. His appeal was ignored.

A Kentucky newspaperwoman who had been in the courtroom grabbed Vorse outside the hotel and made her sit down in one of the chairs on the narrow hotel veranda. The reporter was "much excited and all quivery." She told Vorse that the male invaders were to be taken for a ride, but that since Kentucky men were gentlemen, Vorse and the other two women in the party would be allowed to escape in taxis. Vorse refused to leave her group.

Two by two, the writers were placed in cars waiting in a long line outside the hotel. Each car carried three deputies, heavily armed. Vorse and Dr. Mitchell were taken out through the front door, the men out the back. The thirteen cars gunned their motors, moved slowly, then rapidly, down the highway out of town. After about thirty miles, the motorcade stopped at the Cumberland Gap, a paved semicircle where three states meet. Here the committee members were told to stand in front of the headlights while their luggage and purses were searched again, this time for any film.

In the light, Vorse saw Waldo Frank and Allan Taub, the two Jewish members of the committee. The back of Frank's head and Taub's face were covered with blood. They had been removed from their car and beaten with car jacks or pistol butts. The next day the Pineville newspaper reported that Frank and Taub had quarreled, fought, and injured each other. The driver of Vorse's car, before he drove off, told her through the car window, "Never come across that border again, sister, or worse will happen."

The writers' group stumbled about a mile down the dark road to the town of Cumberland Gap, where the operator of the small hotel had been told to expect them. Vastly excited, babbling and angry, now that the fear was gone, the writers felt a new and brave solidarity. Some even talked of returning to Kentucky. Vorse, feeling immensely relieved and terribly fatigued, was in bad temper. Such an idea was foolish beyond measure, she told them. They were lucky to be alive, she said angrily. Chastened, the committee hired cars and drove to Knoxville.

Although the NMU strike was dead, the efforts of the two writers' committees generated considerable publicity and prepared the way for the United Mine Workers' return to Harlan. With the aid of the New Deal government, the miners were organized successfully between 1937 and 1939. In time, Vorse knew her decision to go to Kentucky was right and profitable. As Theodore Draper observed, it was the Communists and their front groups who won the initial publicity that helped to end the rule of the gun thugs: "In a few months, the Communists made up for years of neglect. Thanks largely to them, Harlan County became a byword for industrial oppression." [25]

Only two days after Vorse returned from Kentucky to New York, she accidentally encountered Robert Minor on the street. They greeted each other like warm friends. She walked with him to the Communist Party office. Her visit with Minor gave her "a feeling of going from a world of light into an obscure cellar," she wrote that night in her diary. "There was such a divorcement from reality [in her talk with the party officials], such an inability to communicate with them, that one felt as though they stood back to back with the coal operators. Each looking different ways but close together with closed minds. I went away feeling very sad. I met . . . [William] Foster coming out. Foster, having more than ever the innocent blank look of an Irish Roman Catholic." [26] Her ambivalence about her work with the Communists remained unsettled. But whatever the nature of the romantic obsession that had once held her to Robert Minor, it had clearly dissolved.

In the summer of 1932, Vorse's work was rewarded by an invitation to spend the summer as a guest at Yaddo, an artists' and writers' colony on a large estate two miles east of Saratoga Springs, New York. A working retreat for writers, composers, and painters, Yaddo offered free room and board to its residents, who usually numbered about twenty, and assured them privacy in a beautiful wooded setting. Elizabeth Ames, the autocratic director, enforced Yaddo's few rules with an iron will. No resident could visit with another between breakfast and 4:00 P.M.—after then, only by invitation. Everyone was expected to attend the evening meal in the turreted dining room of the fifty-five-room Victorian mansion. Director Ames was apt to send a reproving note to those of her charges who began love affairs while at Yaddo. She also disapproved of their frequent evening trips to the sleazy night spots on Saratoga's Congress Avenue.

During Vorse's six-week stay at Yaddo she made notes for her autobiography and wrote several money-making lollypops. Working without interruption—temporarily free of financial worry—brought ecstatic release. She spent many days alone, strolling through the blue spruce woods and marble-statued rose gardens, or sitting quietly on the banks of one of Yaddo's four small lakes. During this healing time, she turned inward and sometimes felt guilty that she was not more social. As her son Heaton perceptively remarked in 1984, "Yaddo was the complete enclosure she had always dreamed about." [27]

At Yaddo she was closest to the writers Josephine Herbst and George Milburn. The three of them, Vorse said, were "on the rowdy side" in comparison with the other residents. The writer John Cheever told his daughter "about the fun they used to have at Yaddo when he was young, and about the night he and Jo Herbst got drunk and dragged Mary Heaton Vorse down the guest staircase in one of Katrina Trask's ornamental troikas with Mary shouting 'Hooves of Fire!' " The Yaddo group that summer included Max Lerner and Sidney Hook. "A good crowd," Vorse wrote. "These people are more serious . . . maybe more solemn is better, than my group of [Edmund] Wilson, [Theodore] Dreiser, Charles [Walker], Waldo [Frank] and Dos Passos. My crowd is finer," she decided.

Vorse and Josephine Herbst became instant, and as it turned out, life-long, friends when they met at Yaddo. But Herbst, passionately consumed in her first love affair with a woman, the artist Marion Greenwood, could think of little else during that summer of 1932. Vorse—a generation older than Herbst, and two generations removed from Greenwood—was drawn into the erotic drama played by her new friends. For some ten years now, she had forgone sexual pleasure. She apparently maintained that choice at Yaddo, despite the steamy atmosphere of the retreat, so suspended outside time and group norms, so tolerant of experiment and difference. Jo Herbst remembered the Yaddo magic of "the summer before the presidential election that we believed might decide the temporal fate of us all. . . . The setting was positively high theater of the Victorian order. . . . [We were] like citizens who have escaped from a bombardment to the safety of an underground cellar."[28]

While at Yaddo, Vorse resolved to seek a quiet haven in which to write, if only she could find the necessary funds. Vorse assumed that it was she, and not her children, who should leave the Provincetown house. Looking through her diary notes from 1928 to 1931, Vorse learned that they revolved "around the same themes with punctual monotony. The pattern of my life is a revolt against the children's disturbances." She added: "As I look back on my life, what gleams out is that I am never quite good enough. Never quite ample enough. The long uneven fight from which I have distilled certain convictions. It is impossible for a woman to be breadwinner and mother both. There are women of immense and enormous vitality who have managed homes and careers, but I do not know any who have managed well. . . . Most writing women who have done both have able husbands to help them. It is a heartbreaking business. The house will not be run well. The children will not be adequately mothered." Vorse added: "When I think of Lydia [Gibson, wife of Robert Minor] it is having a man to whom it was possible to dedicate all of herself —and no children."[29]

Vorse could not escape her self-laid trap. Temperamentally unable to confront directly the cause of her discontent, much less solve it, she hid the extent of her angry feelings toward her children, exploded into tears and shrieks when the pressure grew too strong, and then quickly retreated into another guilty round of motherly service to their needs. So dependent was she on their affection, so cut off from other intimate adult relationships, that she could not risk even momentary rejection. Her self-immolation and definition of herself as a "failed mother" assured her continued connection to love, even though she railed against its dictates. She could not live happily with them, yet, in truth, she did not want them ever to leave her.

By the fall of 1932, Vorse had a larger problem. As the national economy crumbled, her money finally disappeared altogether. Somehow she brought the family through from one month to another, surviving on fifty-dollar loans from Edmund Wilson, Waldo Frank, or Neith Boyce, and selling a lollypop now and then. That year Vorse returned to her piece "Women's Lives," which she had begun in 1915, returned to in 1921, and dropped after her trip to Russia in 1922. She had read a great deal of Virginia Woolf at Yaddo. Vorse envisioned "Women's Lives" as "about what men don't know and women don't write about. I have the feeling this should come only when I've made a success!" she added. She set the manuscript of "Women's Lives" aside once again, without explanation.

In early September 1932, Vorse won an assignment from *Harper's* to report the launching in Iowa of one of the most militant agrarian protests in American history—the Farmers' Holiday Movement. Two years after the Wall Street crash, hundreds of thousands of small farmers faced foreclosure and forced sale of their holdings. Suddenly, in August, over fifteen hundred striking farmers had assembled to guard all the roads into Sioux City, Iowa, virtually halting all milk and livestock delivery into the city. The uprising spread into South Dakota and Nebraska, as deputies confronted farmers armed with clubs and rocks.

Vorse traveled to the Midwest with her new friend Jo Herbst, who came to report the farmers' revolt for *Scribner's*, and with John Herrmann, Herbst's husband. Vorse and Herbst visited the picketing farmers on the road north of Sioux City, squatting on pieces of wood around the bonfire near the blockaded road. The pickets carried sticks as weapons. In her *Harper's* article Vorse strongly supported the Communist call for immediate action to stop foreclosure. The farmers had discovered at once, she said, how their militant resistance had brought "more notice from press and legislature than all their desperate years of peaceful organization." By December, when her article was published, redbaiting of the farmers' movement had already begun. But the farmers saw their enemies as foreclosures and bankruptcies, not the capitalist system itself, Vorse told her readers.[30]

A few months after her return from the Midwest, Vorse reported a new Communist-sparked protest movement. In the depression winter of 1929–30, in city after city, the Communists had led the unemployed in hunger marches and in protests against evictions. The demonstrators demanded adequate relief and urged passage of unemployment-insurance legislation. Large demonstrations of the unemployed caused serious clashes between police and demonstrators in several major cities. National publicity of police attacks against the unemployed broke "through the generally optimistic, cheerful tone of a press which had talked of little but quick recovery and happy days," the historian Daniel Leab wrote.[31] For a few months the Unemployed Council movement mushroomed, at a time when millions of Americans lacked work.

The Communists called for a National Hunger March that was to start from various points in the country and converge on Washington, D.C. on December 4, 1932. Vorse joined Dorothy Day to report the demonstration. Vorse represented the Federated Press and Day *Commonweal*, the liberal Catholic weekly. When they arrived in D.C., they took a dollar-a-night room in a tourist home on Massachusetts Avenue and, as Day reported, ate at lunch wagons.[32]

The capital city prepared for the unemployed demonstration as though for war. Ten thousand nearby federal troops, all leaves canceled, stood ready to meet the "national emergency" proclaimed by the D.C. press. Seventeen-hundred police and Capitol guards patrolled the streets, power plants, bridges, and water plants. City firemen were called in to augment the police force, all issued vomit gas, tear gas, guns, and gasmasks. Salesmen peddled riot insurance to alarmed residents. All this was created by the approach of some twenty-five hundred unarmed marchers, one-third of them women.

The Washington *Post* reported the assemblage of police power in breathless headlines. On December 2 the front page featured a letter sent to President Herbert Hoover and the D.C. commissioners, and signed by Vorse, Sherwood Anderson, Theodore Dreiser, Malcolm Cowley, Waldo Frank, Robert Morse Lovett, and Edmund Wilson. The letter predicted countrywide waves of protest if the marchers were barred or mistreated. The writers expressed their hope that "Washington authorities have learned something of the state of mind of large masses of our population since last summer." Earlier in 1932 the Veterans' Bonus March had been routed from D.C. with unnecessary violence by soldiers, resulting in several casualties and widespread public indignation.

On December 4, the unemployment marchers were ushered into the city under heavy guard. In what the Washington *Post* described as a "master police stroke" they were hemmed into a small area on New York Avenue, blocked at both ends by police ranks five deep. Three army planes circled over the heads of the crowd. No sanitary facilities were provided them. Communist leaders circulated through the group, urging discipline and peaceful order.[33]

Observing the scene, Vorse pondered the many demonstrations she had seen—some ending violently, some peacefully. "Demonstrations are designed to make those in power feel as uncomfortable as possible," she wrote.

> They are designed to make the well-to-do think furiously. For instance, the girls in white with their provocative banners marching in front of the White House concentrated people's attention on the fact that women in this country lacked the vote. It made the police seem ridiculous to march off quiet women to jail. . . . It is a strong

state which understands the purpose of a demonstration and is not seized with terror when a people come to present its wrongs to its rulers; it is a weak and uncertain state which meets a demonstration with police violence. . . . In this country we seem to feel convinced that every time people march . . . they are about to break out into revolution.[34]

Young Dorothy Day listened to Vorse's analysis of the purpose and power of worker unity. Day's sympathy lay with the marching dispossessed. "Is Christianity so old that it has become stale, and is Communism the brave new torch that is setting the world afire?" she asked. How wrong it was that "when Catholics begin to realize their brotherhood and betake themselves to the poor and to all races, then it is that they are accused of being Communists." Tremendously moved, Day slipped away from Vorse to visit the national shrine at the Catholic University, there to pray "with tears and with anguish, that some way would open up for me to use what talents I possessed for my fellow workers, for the poor." Newly inspired, Day established a newspaper a few months later. She distributed for a penny apiece the first copies of the *Catholic Worker*, the Catholic response to the Communist *Daily Worker*. Thus the American Catholic Worker movement was launched, destined to be confirmed, albeit only temporarily, during the stirring days of the Second Vatican Council, and to bring Dorothy Day national renown.[35]

Except for a few summer months spent at home in Provincetown, Vorse had been in almost constant motion—traveling, writing, reporting—for the past three years. She was able to find the money to keep her youngest son, Joel, in school in the Southwest. The hard times of the Depression years brought the two oldest children back to the Provincetown house. Heaton, whose venture as a restaurant owner had failed, returned with his new wife in 1931. Ellen came back with her second husband the next year.

Six weeks after her return from the December 1932 unemployment march in Washington, Vorse again entered the Deep South, this time to report the Scottsboro Boys' second trial in Alabama. Two years earlier a fight had broken out between two groups of young male hobos riding a freight train between Chattanooga and Memphis. Several white boys were pushed from the slowly moving cars by the group of black adolescents. The ousted white youths complained to a stationmaster. A few miles down the line, the train was stopped by a white force of armed locals who took nine black boys off the cars and to the nearest jail in Scottsboro, Alabama. The oldest of the Scottsboro Boys, as they were forever known, was twenty. Two were thirteen. Two miserably poor white girls, Victoria Price and Ruby Bates—part-time prostitutes—were also taken off the train. The terrified black boys learned the next day that the girls claimed that they had been raped aboard the train by the jailed black youngsters. Neither of the two physicians who examined the girls immediately after the alleged attack found any evidence of motile semen or any other physical sign to support the girls' rape story. But within fifteen days, with no reliable evidence presented by the prosecution, one thirteen-year-old black boy was sentenced to life imprisonment and the rest to death. The first national protest at this legal farce came from the Communist Party and its front groups who organized a militant campaign that brought thousands of dollars and petitions in support of the Scottsboro Boys from all over the world. In November 1932, the Supreme Court of the United States reversed the lower-court verdict on the grounds of inadequate counsel.[36]

At the second trial Vorse was one of two women present in the crammed courtroom made stifling by the constant cigarette smoking of both audience and players. In the *New Republic* Vorse unwound the core of the case in "How Scottsboro Happened." She described the thousands of white women like Price who were born into the impoverished existence of working-class life in the southern mill towns. There virtue was rewarded with demeaning work and constant insecurity. Only the "nigger" beneath could support Price's shaky status, could confirm her hope for better things. So it was, Vorse wrote, that when Victoria Price opened "her hard mouth . . . all the rest of the trial" became "a legal dance, a posturing . . . a huge game, a gigantic keeping up of appearances" to maintain the vital lie of the honor paid to southern white women.[37]

In mid-April 1933, Vorse significantly shifted her public political stance. Accepting assignments to report events in Europe for the *New Republic* and *McCall's*, she also represented the newly established journal *Common Sense*, founded in late 1932 by young Alfred Bingham, the radical son of a conservative senator. Vorse remained as one of the contributing editors of *Common Sense* from 1933 to 1935, serving alongside other prominent insurgents like Selden Rodman, John Dewey, John Dos Passos, George Soule, and Stuart Chase. Despite their real political differences, all these united in their rejection of Soviet-style communism, and urged instead the value of a democratic socialist society. Vorse's decision to ally herself with *Common Sense* marked a public statement toward which she had long been building. In 1933, *Common Sense* served as a center for anti-Stalinist independent radicalism in the United States.[38]

Three months before Vorse reached Berlin, Hitler had been appointed chancellor. He moved at once to crush dissent. An emergency decree banned all public meetings and anti-Nazi publications. The Prussian civil service was purged and nazified. Storm troopers roared through the streets, rounding up victims. By early March, 100,000 enemies of the regime had been arrested. Many hundreds disappeared or were killed. So quickly did Germany become a police state that by May 1, the German trade unionists who took part in the traditional Labor Day parade marched under the sign of the swastika.

The four weeks she spent in Berlin coincided with this peak of nazification, giving her a uniquely well placed seat from which to view Hitler's final assumption of power and to study the base of Nazi support. In addition to her facility in German, Vorse was blessed as an investigative journalist for another reason. Exploiting her connection to several wealthy German families who were distant relatives or long-ago friends of her parents, she found herself being squired about by S.S. leaders eager to give her guided tours of the new Germany. Vorse even won an invitation to attend one of Joseph Goebbels's tea parties; this scoop elicited the massive envy of several experienced American reporters in Berlin. She was also making good use of her contacts with the European left, all the time sharing and piecing together with American and European reporters the hidden story behind the German "revolution." Rapid movement left her physically exhausted and intellectually overwhelmed. It seemed to her that she had never faced before such a difficult job of analysis and writing: "I don't think another country ever voted itself out of voting. . . . I have so many impressions that my head bulges, my head bursts."

Shortly after her arrival in Berlin, Vorse decided that support for the Nazis came from a middle-class youth movement, as well as from a large segment of the German proletariat. Her interpretation ran directly counter to the Communist claim that fascism was a capitalist plot to maintain the power of big business in Germany. Vorse's judgment of the nature of Nazi support generally agreed with that of Alfred Bingham and *Common Sense*. Unlike Bingham, however, Vorse saw as early as 1933 that Hitler's rise to power would lead to war.

In the spring of 1933, Hitler issued orders that barred Jews from most employment and proclaimed a national boycott of Jewish shops. Vorse at once recognized that "the foundation stone . . . of the Nazis is that of Race and Blood." Eager to tell the story, she claimed to be the first gentile to visit the Jewish Help Verein in Berlin. Hundreds of Jews from all over Germany came here to get help in leaving the country. Vorse tried to comfort a young Jewish woman who was leaving for Denmark. The woman could not stop weeping, for she was forced to leave her children behind until she could earn enough money to send for them. "The Nazi usually is as surprised by the concern and indignation expressed abroad over the persecution of the Jews as one might be at having a neighbor bring in the S.P.C.A. because one was fumigating vermin," Vorse wrote. Americans should understand this, she mused in her diary later that evening, for "we employ only in a much more thorough way the same method against the Negro." At this point, she did not anticipate the wholesale slaughter of Jews that was to follow her stay in Germany. Her day spent at the Help Verein led her to recall in her diary a conversation she had heard in Gastonia while she was waiting for a streetcar. She remembered: "A nice looking boy drawled to another without animus, as one might talk of opposum hunting":

> "Did yer ever hurt a niggah?"
> "No, I never hurt a niggah."
> "I'd kinda like to hurt a niggah."
> "Yeah, I'd like to hurt a niggah." [39]

In May 1933, book burning began in Germany. Not only the works of Marxist and modern authors, but also those of some German writers, were tossed into the flames. Just before she left Germany, Vorse observed her first book burning as she stood in the square of Kaiser Franz Joseph. There was none of the pageantry and speech making that usually accompanied this Nazi ritual. The silent passersby looked uninterested; only a few paused to watch. Young boys in Nazi youth-group uniforms stood in a long line near huge trucks filled with literature and unenthusiastically passed the books from hand to hand into the flames. The teenager at the end of the line called off the authors' names in a bored tone as he threw the books on the fire. Vorse heard the names of John Dos Passos, Ernest Hemingway, Sinclair Lewis. For Vorse, the drama of the scene lay in the swirling book leaves, caught by the spring wind, pushed by the draft of heat up from the flames. The pages danced by the hundreds in wide circles high above the square, pirouetting against the night sky, rolling and dipping above the buildings. "Bright as fire they mounted upwards, farther and farther they soared high above the blaze." She fancied that the surviving pages held the distant promise that "they could be torn and banished but never destroyed." Recounting the scene in the *New Republic*, Vorse recalled a photograph she had been shown of an "old Jew with a beautiful, benevolent face" being dragged through the streets in a small cart by a German crowd. The old man had sat "calm and unmoved, filled with a sweet dignity as triumphant as that of the high-soaring, invulnerable book pages which fire could not burn."[40]

Vorse made a sudden decision to visit the USSR before her return home. The generous royalties from the Soviet publication of *Strike!* had created a stock of rubles reserved by the Soviet government for her use, in effect making her the guest of the state during her stay. The three weeks Vorse spent in Moscow were full with planned activities. Soviet authorities, in carefully arranged tours, showed the best they had to foreigners in the early thirties. By flattering foreign authors, who often were not accustomed to such recognition in their own countries, the Soviets indirectly promoted the regime, just as providing guests with superior accommodations netted returns. Vorse was whisked by earnest Intourist girl guides to visit model factories, schoolrooms, department stores, people's courts, and the Park of Rest and Culture. She marveled at the number of steamboats, factories, and streets named after John Reed.

Vorse saw that impressive industrial progress was being achieved in the USSR. Her critical attitude toward Soviet censorship and restriction of movement was tempered by her knowledge of the heavy-handed repression of labor organizers and activist radicals in many communities in the United States. In the report of her Soviet visit published in *McCall's*, which brought her a hefty nine-hundred dollars, she emphasized the contradictions of Soviet society, which made her feel "alternately attracted and repelled."[41]

Vorse learned most about the way Soviet socialism worked during the evenings she spent with the ex-newspaperman Spencer Williams, director of the American–Russian Chamber of Commerce, and especially from her frequent meetings with the American journalists assigned to Moscow —William Chamberlin and Eugene Lyons. Both men had gone to the USSR as ardent supporters of the regime. By the summer of 1933 they had become disenchanted, angry cynics. They confirmed all she had heard about forced labor camps and Soviet attempts to hide from newsmen the effects of the Russian famine of 1932–33. Foreign journalists would lose their visas, they assured her, if they filed reports critical of the Soviet government. The newsmen attempted to win her an interview with Stalin, never obtained. Vorse planned to ask Stalin why the Communist Party allowed classes to exist with cultural and material privileges higher than those of the workers. When leaving the Soviet Union, she entered a cryptic note in her journal: "I came here to learn the truth, and I have learned it."[42]

Chapter Fifteen

Washington Whirl

Ten days after Vorse returned to Provincetown in September 1933, she left home—broken in spirit, determined to stay away for an indefinitely long period. She rented an apartment in Washington, D.C., where she would live for most of the next three years. "I have had enough. I have blown up. . . . I smash under," she wailed. The climactic confrontation with her children occurred when she returned to find the house in disorder. Ellen was now married to the artist Jack Beauchamp, a moody alcoholic. It seemed to Vorse that her house was filled with "people on a perpetual holiday for which I am paying." As always, she blamed herself. "It has now been established. I am a bad mother. What should I have done different? When? What moment? I guess I could not grieve more if they were dead. Despair," she wrote in her diary.[1]

"Mary Heaton Vorse has returned from a long stay in Russia and (like the rest of us) looks 100 years old," Heterodoxy founder Marie Jenney Howe wrote to Fola La Follette in late 1933. Edmund Wilson, who saw Vorse when she passed through New York, recalled:

> [Mary] got back and found . . . the children had had the garage repaired and had moved out under a tree and left there an old trunk of Mary's which contained . . . Mary's wedding shoes, an old garment with just a spare hole to put your head through that Joe O'Brien . . . had given her and an old velvet thing called "the ahssless," because she had sat the bottom out of it writing, worthless but she was attached to it. Mary was so furious that she burst into

tears. . . . Her troubles with her children kept getting mixed in with her reports on international affairs.[2]

Flight from her Provincetown home was the only answer she could devise. She had been moving toward this break for over five years. "I am suffering from homesickness—for my house—for them. I want to go home. Then I remember I can't go home," she wrote.[3] She could not counteract the weight of guilt, for she believed that her "neglect" alone was responsible for her children's "troubles." But surely her noble pose as wounded mother does not fully explain her decision to leave home. One cannot avoid the suspicion that much of her pain over Ellen's behavior was created to justify Vorse's escape to the solitude she craved in order to live and write as she pleased. For many years, she had sought a sufficient reason to escape from maternal pressures. Finally, in 1933, she had accumulated —had manufactured—enough grievances to allow her that option.

━━

Vorse lived quietly in Washington with her younger son, Joel, who was completing high school. Her older son Heaton and his new wife Sue, of whom Mary was especially fond, moved to Washington in 1934, when Sue found a secretarial postion with one of the new government agencies. Many of Vorse's friends were working in or passing through Washington in the early years of the New Deal. She often saw Robert Bruere, Jessie and Harvey O'Connor, Ann Craton and Heber Blankenhorn, Matthew Josephson, Fleeta Springer Coe, Edmund Wilson, and Charles and Adelaide Walker.

Vorse found the progressive bustle of Washington exhilarating. The mood was experimental; the movement frenetic. To heighten the drama, a conservative defense against New Deal change was already building. No one knew, Vorse told *McCall's* readers, how to mobilize a nation, make the machine go without scrapping it, put millions of people back to work. "They only know that from the White House comes the sound of laughter and the feeling of unswerving belief that the New Deal truly means recovery."

The capital teemed with hearings and public meetings, which she reported for the Federated Press and the *New Republic*. The mighty had fallen and Vorse rejoiced in the knowledge. The idea of the National Recovery Administration—the organization of economic life under government direction, with union recognition thrown in—would have been enough to send a Wobbly to jail in 1919. But in the morass of the Depression, business and political leaders were willing to try almost anything that might promise recovery. At a consumer hearing to discuss the unwieldy new NRA codes, she saw row upon row of dark-suited men with somber, strained expressions. "There sat Pa," she chortled. "For the face of big and little businesses is overwhelmingly middle-aged. Pinkly gleaming bald pates punctuated lavishly the rows of silver heads. Business . . . was a worried face. Written across it was unmistakingly the track and disaster of four desperate depression years. . . . Suddenly they had been asked . . . to submit to profit fixing and to give up price fixing and hardest blow of all, to allow labor to organize. . . . Poor Pa! Poor old dog! Is he going to learn the new tricks?"[4]

Vorse was most alert to the contribution of women to the Washington whirl. To her surprise, one old friend from the prewar Village, Frances Perkins, "snubbed" her in Washington. At first disappointed and hurt, Vorse soon reached the gracious conclusion that Secretary of Labor Perkins needed to stay clear of radical associations while serving as the first woman Cabinet member.[5]

The thirties offered a new public role to many women like Perkins who achieved prominence in New Deal government. The network of women's leaders in Washington included Perkins, Eleanor Roosevelt, Women's Bureau chief Mary Anderson, Congresswoman Mary T. Norton, Mary W. Dewson of the Democratic National Committee, and government officials like Josephine Roach, Hilda Worthington Smith, and Sue Shelton White. Vorse often visited the offices of these women, but with the exception of Hilda Smith, her relationship to them was not particularly close, even though they were of Vorse's generation, born in the 1870s and 1880s —"the generation after the great pioneers," as Molly Dewson described the group. Most of the New Deal women leaders consciously shied away from identification as "feminists" while they struggled for social reform. Perhaps, like Perkins, the network of powerful women in Washington found Vorse too far to the left to fit into its personal political strategies. Despite her position on the sidelines, however, Vorse mightily admired these women, who she felt were the most "potent" voices for compassion in Washington.[6]

Although Vorse was generally content during her years in Washington, she was also aware that at age sixty she was no longer part of the vital center of national progressive action. This recognition, and the new sense of aging that accompanied it, influenced her decision to begin work on her autobiography. She had fallen behind on her mortgage payments, but was living comfortably enough, although with little money for extras, through the sale of a few lollypops and articles for *McCall's*, and a much smaller income from her journalism. In May 1934, a fifteen-hundred-dollar advance from Farrar, Rinehart Publishers allowed her to work full time on *Footnote to Folly*. Significantly, she ended the story of her life in the smashup year of 1922. For Vorse, the most exciting and momentous period of her life had ended twelve years before, all the rest a drift downward from the pinnacle. She could not know then that in the thirties her reputation as a labor journalist would peak, or that she had three decades more of writing and work before her.

In late 1935, her autobiography elicited a series of highly positive reviews from both left and mainstream journals. *Time* noted that "few men or women have a better right than she to consider her reminiscences of an active life a footnote to the history of her time. . . . Her crusade never faltered." *Forum* concluded that Vorse had "lived twice as hard and twice as intensely as the average person." The *Nation* called *Footnote to Folly* "one of the most powerful documents against war in our time," while the *Saturday Review of Literature* praised it as "one of the most notable pieces of autobiographical writing by an American woman." John Chamberlin recommended in the New York *Times* that it be "read along with Lincoln Steffens' 'Autobiography,' Frederic C. Howe's 'Confessions of a Reformer,' Floyd Dell's 'Homecoming,' and Brand Whitlock's 'Forty Years of It' and the other great documents of liberal America." Many reviewers commented that if there were one disappointment with the book, it was the lack of detail about Vorse's personal life.[7]

In Washington Vorse was for a while part of a network fated to receive wide attention in 1948 for its connection to the Alger Hiss case. Her "Daily Summaries" written during the winter of 1933 and early spring of 1934 show that she met frequently with persons associated with what would come to be called the Ware group: Hal Ware (son of the Communist leader "Mother Bloor"), his wife, Jessica Smith, Jerome Frank, Nathaniel Weyl, Josephine Herbst, and John Herrmann. Except for Herbst and Frank, all were Communists interested in farm policy and associated with the left-liberal faction within the Agricultural Adjustment Administration. Vorse came naturally enough to this group. She had long been interested in the plight of the southern tenant farmer. She had worked with Jessica Smith on Russian relief in the early twenties. She had traveled with Jo Herbst in 1932 to report the farm strike in Iowa. There they had encountered Hal Ware, who was then organizing farmers in the Midwest. In 1934,

Hal Ware invited Herbst's husband, John Herrmann, to come to work in Washington whereupon Vorse and Herbst renewed their friendship.

Whittaker Chambers, Nathaniel Weyl, and others later testified that the Ware group was a cell of the American Communist Party. According to Chambers, who claimed to have joined the group after his arrival in Washington in the summer of 1934, it was an "underground" organization that concentrated on recruiting Washington bureaucrats and discussing Marxist theory and practice—a kind of study or support group that considered strategy and pooled ideas. Its later prominence rested entirely on Chambers's testimony that Alger Hiss was a member of the Ware circle. In August 1935, Hal Ware was killed in an automobile accident and the group disintegrated. Vorse apparently had broken her connection with it at least a year earlier, about the same time that Nathaniel Weyl claimed to have withdrawn from the meetings.

The acceptance of Vorse into the Ware circle, despite her public alignment with anti-Stalinists as a contributing editor of *Common Sense*, is another indication of the fluid political alliance between liberals and radicals in the early thirties, before the Cold War freighted such associations with ominous implications and personal danger. At any rate, it is doubtful that, as women, Mary Vorse, Jo Herbst, and Jessica Smith would have been tightly included in the deliberations of the "top level, a group of seven or so men," as Chambers described the leaders of the network. Despite the Communist rhetoric of sexual equality, the party was very much a male-dominated outfit in the 1930s.

Still, especially in consideration of her close friendship with Jo Herbst, then and later, it seems likely that Vorse would have known that Hal Ware and John Herrmann were involved in a half-secret, half-open—mostly melodramatic—courier operation between Washington and the New York Communist Party office. Herbst's biographer Elinor Langer reported that Herbst regarded this transmission "as a lot of self-important revolutionary hocus-pocus and she was irritated by it in the extreme. . . . For the Communists to function underground when they could function perfectly well above ground she believed was a mistake." Vorse left no evidence of her opinion of the Ware group or its activity. Nor did she preserve her side of the 1940s and 1950s correspondence regarding the Alger Hiss case and its impact on Jo Herbst and John Herrmann.[8]

———

Vorse's less radical friends in the labor movement were as exultant as the Ware group over the scenes of New Deal Washington. The 1932 election of Franklin Delano Roosevelt began a new era in American labor history. In the next four years a major power shift in American society occurred. In the winter of 1933, more workers experienced greater destitution than ever known before in the United States. The misery of depression discredited business supremacy and motivated a significant portion of the labor force to fight a savage class war. Backed by a progressive federal government and encouraged by militant union leaders, workers won concessions from employers for which they had been fighting for decades. When millions of American workers demonstrated their determination to win union recognition, by violence if necessary, an upsurge of union organization transformed the balance of political and economic power in the United States. Despite employer opposition, the United Mine Workers, the Amalgamated Clothing Workers, and the International Ladies' Garment Workers Union, led respectively by John L. Lewis, Sidney Hillman, and David Dubinsky, rebuilt themselves into important forces.

By 1933 a confrontation between the AFL and the labor coalition led by Lewis was already building over the question of craft unionism versus industrial organization. Because of the growth of great corporate structures and the lessened proportion of skilled workmen, the AFL's craft unionism had become obsolete in many industries. Yet the AFL leaders —representing the labor aristocracy of skilled, white males—refused to give up their traditional jurisdictions and petty fiefdoms. The AFL leadership showed little interest in organizing semiskilled, unskilled, black, or women workers.

In the spring, summer, and fall of 1934, American labor exploded. Four major strikes and over eighteen hundred smaller ones involved almost one and one-half million workers. Many of the labor protests were led by radicals. The vast majority of American workers did not want to overthrow the government or establish socialism. They simply wanted to choose a union, win living wages and decent working conditions, break the arrogance of the owners, and claim a measure of dignity and security for themselves. They followed radical leadership because it so often seemed the only hardworking group willing to lead their fight without compromise. Business leaders and much of the nation's press attempted to counter labor militance by the old technique of manufacturing a red scare. But the timeworn tactic did not distract labor from its goal.

The thunder of mass revolt shook the nation in 1934. In Ohio, A. J. Muste's American Workers' Party organized the unemployed to join the mass picketing of strikers against Auto-Lite. At "The Battle of Toledo," workers fought police and the National Guard, attacked jails, defied tear gas and rifle fire, cheered their union leaders in courtrooms, hurled bricks, bolts, and hinges, threatened a general strike, and at last won union recognition and restoration of wage reductions. In Minneapolis, a bastion of the open shop, almost a third of the county population consisted of the unemployed and their families. Led by socialists and Trotskyists, the city's truck drivers shut down the city market. In May, July, and August, tens of thousands of massed workers, armed with clubs, supported by local farmers, fought pitched battles against bullets, tear gas, police, and the National Guard in the city streets. In the end, the teamsters smashed the open shop in Minneapolis and were guaranteed that union representatives elected by the majority would bargain for all. On the West Coast, the radical Harry Bridges led a strike of longshoremen that closed down most coastal ports and won union recognition and reform of the hated "shape-up" system. This stunning labor victory came after strikers fought police and guardsmen with rocks and bolts in the face of gunfire and tear gas, after a dramatic funeral parade where more than thirty thousand mourners silently marched behind the bodies of two workers killed in the labor war, and after a four-day general strike. In Philadelphia, in 1934, cab drivers burned taxicabs; in New York, cab drivers refused to drive. Communists led strikes of the miserably exploited farm workers, from California to New Jersey. In Des Moines the electrical workers cut off the switches. Across the nation, cooks, reporters, typists, clerks, copper miners, skilled and unskilled, marched, fought, and picketed, often joining in renditions of the "Internationale" or old Wobbly songs.

The Republicans were routed in the elections of 1934. "Boys—this is our hour," Harry Hopkins said. "We've got to get everything we want— a works program, social security, wages and hours, everything—now or never." In New York City, Clifford Odets's play *Waiting for Lefty* drew large crowds. The script ended with the audience rising to shout: "STRIKE! STRIKE! STRIKE!" Vorse saw *Waiting for Lefty* two nights in a row, returning the second evening with Josephine Herbst. With thousands of other progressives, they rejoiced at the new power of labor. "The impetus given labor under N.R.A. . . . would all have been in vain without the million marching feet," Vorse wrote, "labor in a thousand unions and factories demanding organization and going into the conflict with new techniques, with new spontaneous inventions, with a brilliant suppleness of combat hitherto unimagined." The spiraling-up hope of 1934 brought Vorse a letter from a dear friend from whom she had heard nothing for years. "Dear Mary . . . Are we revoluting or not?" wrote Elizabeth Gurley Flynn.[9]

But the largest strike of 1934 was to end in a bitter labor defeat. Called by the AFL affiliate the United Textile Workers, the national cotton-textile strike brought out almost half a million strikers from Alabama to Maine. Employers responded in the customary manner—armed guards, spies, eviction of strikers' families from company houses, attacks on union leaders, jailing of organizers, and pressure on state authorities to send in the National Guard. Reporting from the strike areas in New England, Vorse also blamed the UTW loss on FDR's board of inquiry, which issued its findings against union recognition and suggested that wages, hours, and working conditions receive attention from future government "studies."[10]

Back in Washington in early 1935, the left-liberal faction within the Agricultural Adjustment Administration was purged, including some members of the Ware circle. The showdown came over the issue of the rights of southern tenant farmers who had been dispossessed of their shacks and brutally oppressed by southern officials and landowners. When Jerome Frank and his allies within the AAA moved to stop further evictions without cause, FDR and Henry Wallace, the secretary of agriculture, decided to dismiss the young reformers from the AAA. This was done in the interest of political expediency, for the New Deal political coalition was heavily dependent on cotton-state spokesmen in Congress who served the interests of southern landlords. Vorse saw the defeat of Frank as the final clear sign that the New Deal would mean only reform, not deep social change. The New Deal has been "all washed up since the 'purge,'" she wrote Matthew Josephson in February.[11]

Yet in 1935, both liberal government and the labor movement were to undergo revitalization. Over the summer, Congress passed several of its most far-reaching reform measures yet. One of the first to become law was the Wagner Act, which allowed workers to select union representatives through majority vote, and restrained employers from discharging union members, fostering company unions, or committing other "unfair labor practices." The Wagner Act spun through to victory in both houses in July. Then, in the fall of 1935, at the stormy AFL convention in Atlantic City, the modern American labor movement was born, its entry into life forever symbolized by the right-hand punch driven by the mine workers' John L. Lewis into the face of the carpenters' president, William Hutcheson. That scuffle on the floor of the convention was followed by the formation in November of the Committee of Industrial Organization as a rival organization within the AFL. Led by Lewis, the union leaders of the CIO committed themselves to an all-out and immediate effort toward industrial organization of the workers in the largest American industries.

Eight months before the CIO was formed, Vorse accepted a government position. Hired by her old Village friend John Collier, the controversial New Deal commissioner of Indian affairs, she became publicity director for the Indian Bureau and editor of *Indians at Work*, the Bureau's in-house, biweekly journal. During his tenure as Indian commissioner from 1933 to 1945, Collier vigorously attacked the belief that Indians should be assimilated into white society. His reform goals aroused strong opposition from various business interests, as well as from some Indian groups who did not favor Indian communal segregation and return to a tribal heritage.[12]

Collier offered the job as editor to Vorse at the very appealing salary of thirty-two hundred dollars. Agreeing to begin work as soon as she finished her autobiography, she was officially appointed to the Office of Indian Affairs in late February 1935. Under her direction for the next twenty-one months, *Indians at Work* propagandized for Collier's reform ideals, castigated his opponents, and featured articles from anthropologists, lawyers, and conservationists that dealt with all aspects of Indian life. As editor, Vorse made several trips west to Indian reservations and gatherings where she reported the achievements of the bureau and lauded the effect of Collier's reforms on Indian culture, education, and economic development.[13]

She received a leave of absence from her post as editor in November 1936. According to FBI records, her personnel file in the Interior Department indicated that "she had been cited for inefficiency" prior to her resignation in July 1937. The full story of Vorse's departure from government work, however, is considerably more interesting. Her exit was influenced by the denunciation of her before Senate and House committees on Indian affairs. She and her colleagues on Collier's staff were smeared as "Christ-mocking, Communist-aiding, subversives bent upon finding a back door entrance for the establishment of Communism in the United States of America, and supplanting of the Stars and Stripes with the red flag of Moscow."[14]

Being singled out for redbaiting was hardly a new experience for Vorse by 1936. She had been named by several radical-hounding police forces, legislative committees, and intelligence agencies during World War I and after. The Lusk Committee, founded by the New York legislature in 1919, listed her "seditious" associations. The Bureau of Investigation of the Department of Justice had tracked and recorded her political and literary activities between 1919 and 1922. Her name also appeared on the well-publicized 1928 "blacklist" of the Daughters of the American Revolution, where she was described as "a Communist" and banned as a speaker before DAR gatherings.

Elizabeth Dilling's private publication of *The Red Network* in 1934 was perhaps the single most irresponsible—and most humorous—example of anti-Communist propaganda in this period. Aiming at the "Communistic" New Deal, Dilling listed 460 organizations and 1,300 persons as American members of the international Communist conspiracy. Vorse, as well as most of her close friends, along with a host of liberals like Jane Addams, John Dewey, and Eleanor Roosevelt, were featured in Dilling's book, complete with each individual's connection to "Communist" organizations and activities. The few journals that reviewed *The Red Network* in 1934 treated it as a howler, some even recommending it as an inexpensive and accurate guide to the people and groups most concerned with social justice in the United States. But Federal Laboratories, Inc., a chemical munition firm serving strikebreakers, with a 60 percent share of the domestic tear-gas market and distribution rights to the Thompson submachine gun, at once recognized the value of Dilling's work; the firm distributed a copy of *The Red Network* to prospective customers. Initially, however, Dilling's book was recognized by most for what it was—an anti–New Deal diatribe favored only by the far-right fringe. Yet, by 1938, when redbaiting again became respectable in the halls of Congress, Dilling was hailed as an incontestable authority to support congressional attacks on the civil liberties of political dissenters. Beginning with the reign of Martin Dies and the House Un-American Activities Committee (HUAC), American political leadership legitimized the activity that would come to be called McCarthyism.

Only three weeks after her appointment to the Indian Bureau, Vorse attended the hearings of the House Committee on Indian Affairs that questioned Collier about his connection to the American Civil Liberties Union, cited by the committee member from Montana as a group seeking to "protect the Communists in their advocacy of force and violence to overthrow the government." The committee also heard Alice Lee Jemison, spokeswoman for the American Indian Federation and a major critic of Collier and the Indian New Deal. Jemison branded Collier an atheist and red. For evidence, she presented poems Collier had earlier written in praise of Isadora Duncan. A year later, in hearings before the Senate Indian Affairs Subcommittee, Jemison and her associates in the American Indian Federation named seven members of Collier's staff, including Vorse, the one woman listed, as "admirers" of the ACLU and charged "that there can be no doubt that the purpose of the present group in control of Indian Affairs is to establish 'communism' in the United States."

Five months later, Vorse left the bureau on a "leave of absence." Two of the six males named by Jemison also left the service then. Perhaps, as a sixty-two-year-old woman, Vorse was easily expendable. The evidence shows that Jemison believed Vorse more vulnerable to charges of leftist association than were the four males named, all of whom remained on the government payroll after 1937. When Jemison next appeared as a witness before HUAC in 1938, she gave little attention to these four men but testified at length regarding Vorse's reputation as a "well-known, left-wing labor agitator and writer" who "while in the employ of the Federal Government . . . published a book . . . in which she recounted her twenty years of work and association with William Foster and other Communists . . . including her third husband, Robert Minor, at one time Communist candidate for President of the United States, now a member of the central committee."

Two years later, Jemison lamented before the House Committee on Indian Affairs that "back in 1935, 1936, 1937, and even as late as 1938, most people laughed in your face if you talked about subversive activities, particularly communism." But times were good for right-wing red chasers like Jemison by the end of the thirties. In June 1940, Jemison was allowed two days to recite before the House committee an expanded version of her 1938 HUAC testimony recounting Vorse's "subversive" activities and associations since 1912. Jemison concluded that "there is a surprising similarity of language in the terms used [in Vorse's autobiography *Footnote to Folly*] to describe the peasants of Italy taking over the land of the property owners and seizing the factories which she witnessed [in fact, Vorse neither witnessed nor discussed this in her autobiography] and the language used by Commissioner Collier to explain his 'organized communities' and other parts of his program." [15]

In December 1941, although Vorse had left government employment three years before, Director J. Edgar Hoover instituted an FBI investigation of her possible violation of the Hatch Act, which prohibited government employment to those who sought to overthrow the government. The FBI inquiry relied on a search of the HUAC file, which held twenty-seven index cards under Vorse's name. Much of HUAC's "investigation," which was based solely on Dilling's book, was faithfully copied into FBI files as "Security Matter-C," a designation that marked her as a "Communist" and "potentially dangerous to the internal security of the United States." In 1944, she was assigned a Security Index number; this ensured that the FBI maintain a listing of her current address so that she could be found and quickly arrested in the event of a "national emergency." Thus did Vorse's brief employment in the Indian Bureau reap totally unexpected results. Once trapped within the FBI filing system, few citizens escaped, no matter how unjustly maligned. Although largely unrecognized by Vorse, this predicament would profoundly affect her future opportunities as a journalist.

=====

It was not the red smear alone that influenced Vorse's exit from government employ. Her course was also determined by a request for help with publicity from John Brophy and Len DeCaux, two leading officials of the newly formed CIO. Mary had reached that stage in life when a rising sense of the chill of exclusion had made the writing of an autobiography seem appropriate. She found the invitation to reenter the center circle of labor activists irresistible, and the attention paid her by CIO leaders immensely gratifying.

In late 1935, John L. Lewis made a calculated decision to draw on the energy and dedication of his former left-wing critics to spark the creation of the CIO. He appointed his socialist foe John Brophy—who had challenged Lewis's autocratic control of the United Mine Workers in the 1920s, often working with Communists to do so—as director of CIO organization. Brophy immediately hired the talented, British-born, left-wing journalist, Len DeCaux, another former dissident in the UMW, as CIO publicity director. Like Brophy and DeCaux, Vorse had taken the side of the progressive faction in the fight within the miners' union. She had shared the common left attitude toward Lewis, who functioned as a Coolidge–Hoover Republican and champion redbaiter during the twenties. Now this powerful man Lewis was taking the lead in a principled and courageous stand against the ossified AFL leadership in his drive to organize the mass-production industries. His cool nerve and self-confidence dramatized the aspirations of millions of workers.

"Who gets the bird—the hunter or the dog?" was Lewis's oft-quoted reply to David Dubinsky, who remonstrated with Lewis about the wisdom of using so many Communists and independent leftists in the early days of the CIO. Lewis understood his need for committed activists as he moved toward that confrontation with superior force in which labor had usually come out the loser. Lewis also believed that the left activists needed him as much, or more, than he did them; he was supremely confident that he could use them to achieve his own goals. Lewis needed militant, experienced organizers and staffers, people who would work for little or no money and whose reward was personal achievement and the realization of social goals. Most of these who stood outside the AFL in the 1930s were radicals, either Communist or non-Communist. His own UMW staff was little help, for it was loaded with mediocrities—the result of the consolidation of his dictatorial control over his associates in the 1920s. Shortly after the CIO struggle got under way, young and capable new leaders rose from the rank and file, but the first teams to go into battle for the industrial union movement in 1936 were usually composed of the scarred veterans of the Brophy–DeCaux–Vorse variety. The only reason Lewis did not use more of them was that there were no more at hand.

DeCaux first approached Vorse on July 9, 1936. Prior to his job with the CIO, DeCaux had been the Washington representative of the Federated Press, the labor news service Vorse had helped to staff after the 1919 defeat in steel. He knew Vorse as a politically trustworthy journalist, the author of *Men and Steel*, and the foremost labor publicist. Brophy and DeCaux visited her Washington apartment often in early July. Perhaps they were lonely for good talk, talk that went on until late into the night. They ate her meals, and drank, and talked of Lewis and his motives. In that brief moment of left-to-center unity in the CIO's first year, DeCaux recalled it was like "light after darkness . . . seen by the red and rebellious, now playing their full part in what they held to be a great working-class advance against the capitalist class. There was light, and a heady happy feeling in the solidarity of common struggle in a splendid common cause." Vorse left on July 19 for the Pittsburgh area, returned briefly to report to DeCaux at the CIO headquarters in Washington, and then left for a second tour of the steel towns of Pennsylvania and Ohio in early August. She was gleeful to be back at "real" work, she wrote Dos Passos.[16]

Within a few months, Vorse would become conditioned to the sight of hundreds of determined union members meeting in open assembly, but on this first field trip to report the formation of the CIO, she could not shake for one moment an incredulous sense of wonder. The mass meetings she saw in 1936 seemed nothing less than miraculous, so sharp was the contrast to her memory of the steel towns seventeen years before, when she had visited workers' homes where every knock on a door meant terror, and women looked out at her through a crack with frightened, drawn faces. Now she was met at the train station by a knot of smiling workers' wives who had been sent to greet her from a CIO headquarters office on the thirty-sixth floor of a Pittsburgh skyscraper. She moved, at first, as through two worlds simultaneously, one real before her eyes, and the other insistently shadowed by ghosts.

Take the meeting at Braddock, in a sunny park, where thousands stood —men and women, girls in bright summer dresses and little boys with caps in hand—and bowed their heads for a full minute of silence in honor of their priest, Father Kazinsci, with whom she had shared so many gray hours in 1919, when not even two workers could have stopped to talk on the streets of Braddock, without fear of beatings, or worse. Now there was Father Kazinsci standing on a high platform, his head all white, still saying the old words: "Have courage. Join the union. Only through unity have you strength." And beside her, applauding, were four black steelworkers wearing CIO pins, the descendents of the black workers who in 1919 had been brought in large numbers as scabs.

Or take the two friendly state troopers she met in Aliquippa, who would not be riding down workers in the streets with three-foot clubs raised over their heads, but who had been sent to ensure law and order by a state whose lieutenant governor was a former union miner. Of course there were still the company spies and "stoolies" in the steel towns, and plenty of rumors about the tear gas and machine guns being purchased by the steel mills. But the old fear was missing. Twenty-five hundred volunteer and two hundred paid organizers operated openly, and from Ohio to West Virginia, every vote for a New Deal ticket was a vote for the CIO. All in all, it was a peculiarly significant trip for her in that summer of 1936, a weird fusion of past and present. She summed it up: "There is an awful power and might in steel, but there is an awful power and might in this age-old drive for freedom. It is like a force of nature irresistible as a tide; it recedes, but it does not die." [17]

Back in Washington in August, Vorse enjoyed a week's visit with Jo Herbst. Herbst had made a final split from John Herrmann the year before, at his furious insistence, and she, like Vorse, yearned to believe that it was her own political and intellectual integrity, colliding with the rigid faith of a Communist husband, that made the break inevitable. She and Vorse also clung to the resentful knowledge that a more politically compliant woman had walked away with their men. Vorse had admired Herbst's 1935 "Cuba on the Barricades" series in the *New Masses*. She wanted to hear more about Herbst's dangerous meetings with the Cuban guerrillas resisting the powerful U.S. sugar interests, which helped the Fulgencio Batista regime consolidate its dictatorship.

And of course the two women discussed the New York literary quarrel then consuming a vast amount of the time of a set of Communist and non-Communist writers, who were all aglow over the supposedly vital political significance of the literary debate over "proletarian realism," a tiff from which Herbst had just retreated in revulsion. The literary wars of the New York critics had flared up when the Communist Party had shifted into its Popular Front period in 1935. The Communist attempt to build an antifascist alliance with bourgeois radical writers had foundered on the party's tendency to endorse art for its political line, a propensity heatedly denied or confirmed according to one's place at any particular moment in one literary faction or another. The relation of all this literary tussle to revolution was murky, but inconsequential, Vorse and Herbst agreed. They felt so partly because as activists they scorned the never-ending talk of self-absorbed cultural radicals who would never visit a picket line or a guerrilla stronghold in the mountains of eastern Cuba, and partly because as women thinkers and writers, *they* were inconsequential to the raging literary combatants in New York. It is not difficult to imagine the look exchanged between the two when Herbst told Vorse how when the Communist organizers of the conference of the League of American Writers belatedly recognized that they had a *Negro* (it was Richard Wright), but no *woman* on the program, they popped Herbst up on the platform at the last minute before the solemn opening ceremony began.[18]

In November 1936, Vorse left Washington to report the AFL convention in Tampa. For years she had ridiculed the stodgy AFL chieftains about their annual junket to the Florida sun. This year, the CIO unions, representing over one-third of the federation's total membership, were absent from the convention. The remaining craft-union forces obediently voted to make the suspension of the CIO unions official. The only surprise of the meeting was when Republican William Hutcheson, who headed the powerful AFL unit of carpenters, announced that he was so shaken by FDR's landslide election that he could not travel to Tampa.

In common with most CIO supporters, Vorse hoped for an accommodation with the AFL. David Dubinsky of the International Ladies' Garment Workers Union was the most ardent peacemaker on the CIO Executive Board. He asked Vorse to observe the meetings of the carpenters at Lakeland, Florida. Vorse received more detailed instructions by telephone from the ILGWU vice-president, Julius Hochman. To judge from her final report, she was asked to gauge the strength of industrial unionism sentiment within Hutcheson's union, for which Hochman paid her a welcome hundred dollars.[19]

After the conventions, Vorse traveled to Key West for a visit with Katy and John Dos Passos who had promised her "a dandy house and plenty of room."[20] Eighty percent of Key West's citizens had been on relief in 1934 and the governor had considered moving the entire population to Tampa. Now it was a New Deal boom town, with Federal Emergency Relief Administration money flowing through, and artists and authors painting murals and writing guidebooks. The town still had its rowdy and irresponsible charm, complete with Ernest Hemingway. "I would stay here much longer," Vorse wrote Ellen, "if things weren't so exciting out in the world."

By January 20 she was headed north toward Detroit, pulled there by that uncanny sixth sense for news that invariably brought her to the center of action.

Chapter 16

Labor's New Millions

When CIO organizers began moving into Detroit, their prime target was General Motors, the largest manufacturing corporation in the country. A series of wildcat sit-downs in late 1936 pushed leaders of the United Auto Workers toward a strike for which they did not feel ready. On December 30, GM employees sat down and occupied two body plants in Flint, Michigan—Fisher One and Fisher Two. The most crucial CIO battle of the 1930s had begun.

On January 11, with below-zero weather outside, GM turned off the heat inside Fisher Two. That night a battle between police and workers raged for three hours, the police firing buckshot and tear gas, the strikers heaving coffee mugs, bottles, nuts and bolts. The victory of the UAW over the fleeing Flint police survived in union legend as the "Battle of the Running Bulls." Unaccustomed to the use of violence ending in *union* victory, conservatives blanched and hysteria flared. The Catholic bishop of Detroit proclaimed that Soviet planning was behind the sit-down strategy —a kind of red "smoke screen for revolution and civil war," he warned.[1]

Michigan's Governor Frank Murphy, just elected in the New Deal landslide, sent the National Guard into Flint, but refused to use the troops in the usual manner as strikebreakers. Murphy ordered GM not to deny heating, water, or food to the strikers. The state troops, many of them sympathetic to the strikers and led by an experienced officer who had once been an auto worker, restored order around the plants.

Vorse reached Detroit ten days later. She went directly from the train to meet Carl Haessler, chief of the Federated Press and publicity director for the Flint strikers. During their drive to Flint Haessler filled her in on the fast-moving events. They arrived at UAW headquarters in the crowded Pengelly Building, social center and staging ground for the Flint battle. A stream of men and women pushed purposefully in and out its dingy door and up and down its narrow wooden staircases twenty-four hours a day. Pairs of union guards checked credentials at every bottleneck. A first aid station, transportation center, picket captain's room, kitchen, and reading room were always full.[2]

That evening, back in Detroit, Vorse and labor reporter Louis Stark of the New York *Times* traded information about union strategy, their meal periodically interrupted by new reports of company violence against CIO organizers. But conditions in Michigan in 1937 were quite unlike those on the Mesabi Range in 1916, or around Pittsburgh in 1919. Attacks against unionists were well reported in most major newspapers. Exposure of GM labor espionage hurt the company's public relations effort. As one national magazine observed, GM "was in no spiritual shape to fight an honest holy war."[3]

On January 28, Vorse visited a picket line in Detroit and attended an evening union meeting in Hamtramck. Her hope that the CIO, aided by the New Deal government, might at last readjust the old political and economic scales, overflowed during the Hamtramck gathering at her first sight of the Women's Emergency Brigade of Flint. Ten women wearing red tams and red armbands with "EB" lettered on them in white, filed onto the small triangular stage in the Dodge union hall. They waited quietly, while the audience listened to reports from picket captains and local organizers. Then the chair turned to introduce the women. They had come from Flint, he said, to tell the women in Detroit how to organize, because, the chair grinned, "they say the men don't tell us anything." A ripple of laughter rose from the audience, anticipating fun. One slender, dark woman rose to speak.

> We came over here expecting that you would have an auxiliary [of women] twice as large as you have, but I expect we have had more to do in Flint. Our Women's Emergency Brigade is ready for action day and night, we take food over to the sit-down strikers in the plants and we are on guard to protect our husbands. We can get fifty women together at a moment's notice, we expect and are ready for any and all emergencies.

Vorse learned that the Emergency Brigade was a unit of the Women's Auxiliary in Flint. Women's auxiliaries to male unions were not uncommon, even before the formation of the CIO. But the Women's Emergency Brigade was an entirely new idea: 350 women were pledged to place themselves between the strikers and any attacking police, company guards, militia, or vigilantes. The women on the stage described the origins of the Emergency Brigade. The initiative had come from Genora Johnson, a twenty-three-year-old mother of two. During the fight on January 11, when police gathered their forces for a final assault on the sit-down strikers, Johnson asked for permission to speak from the union sound car to the hundreds of spectators watching from behind the police lines. Taking the microphone, Johnson blasted the police as cowards who were willing to shoot unarmed men. She called for women in the crowd to break through police lines and come forward to protect their men, warning them that if the police were cowards enough to shoot men, they would probably shoot defenseless women too. At first a few, then many, women responded to her plea, soon followed by others, then scores of men and women who placed themselves between the police and the embattled strikers. On January 20, Johnson formed the Women's Emergency Brigade, ready for the next skirmish. She declared: "We will form a line around the men, and if the police want to fire then they'll just have to fire into us."

Listening to the women talk, Vorse knew that here was her CIO story. She would tell the story of the Women's Emergency Brigade, so easily overlooked by male reporters intent on following union leaders and reporting confrontations among the great. "I have never seen the splendid organization and determination of the Women's Auxiliary of Flint," Vorse wrote in her journal. "The Emergency Brigade is destined to make labor history in America, for there has never been anything like it."

The next day Vorse moved her baggage to Flint. She was surprised to find her thirty-six-year-old son, Heaton, there; he had found a job as a stringer for the Federated Press. On the evening of January 31, she and Heaton attended a packed union gathering in the Pengelly Building. The word was out in Flint. Vorse learned there would be an attempted sit-down in a Chevrolet plant the next day, the same day on which Judge Paul V. Gadola was to hold hearings to determine if he should grant the GM petition for an injunction that would expel the strikers from Fisher One and Two.

The next morning she was up very early. A mass meeting had been called to organize a march to the courthouse where the injunction hearings were to be held. In mid-afternoon, unionists waiting at Pengelly were told they were needed at once at Chevrolet Nine, where a sit-down attempt was in progress. When the union supporters arrived, closely followed by reporters and newsreel crews, fighting had already begun in the plant. Vorse watched as members of the Women's Emergency Brigade marched single file toward the building. Under their heavy coats they concealed long clubs made of wood. She later recorded the memory of one Brigade member:

> We got the call there was trouble down at Chevrolet no. 9. We were having a meeting of the Emergency Brigade up at the Women's Auxiliary. We went down as fast as we could. There was a big crowd gathered in front of the plant. People were fighting outside and they were fighting inside the plant. Someone yelled. "There are thugs and company police beating up our boys." Tear gas was coming out of the plant. We formed in a line and marched right ahead. We carried the American flag before us. Of course we got gassed but we had been gassed before, nothing was going to stop us. We were going to protect our husbands. There would have been a worse fight if we hadn't come. Seeing us march along with our flag kind of made them stop.

Several hundred Chevrolet police had been alerted by a company spy to the sit-down attempt at Chevrolet Nine. Using clubs and tear gas, the police entered the plant and drove the workers toward the rear of the huge building. Through the windows, shadowy figures could be seen battling in eerie silence behind the glass. The Emergency Brigade members began to swing their clubs and break the windows to let fresh air into the gassed unionists inside. Jumping up to reach the high windows, the women smashed the panes of glass, one after another, while another group of women fought off policemen who were trying to stop them. But by 4:00 P.M., the workers inside the plant emerged defeated. They went back to the Pengelly Building, along with members of the Emergency Brigade who had not been arrested, to wipe the tear gas from their eyes and get first aid.

Slowly, the great crowd massed outside Chevrolet Nine sensed the truth. They learned that the UAW leadership, with perfect timing, had created this diversion at Chevrolet Nine as a way of drawing the company police away from Chevrolet Four, the real objective of the union strategists. As the story spread, reporters and spectators hustled several hundred yards to Chevrolet Four, the more important plant, where all Chevrolet engines were produced.

Genora Johnson was one of the few people who had been told the real plan. Following the instructions given her, she strung a lean line of Emergency Brigade members across the entrance to Chevrolet Four. When city police sought to enter the gap, the Brigade women locked arms and ignored police orders to move. For a precious half-hour, Genora Johnson and the brigade held the police back, for the officers were reluctant to attack unarmed women. Johnson and her crew attempted to reason with the policemen, desperately playing for time. The action of the women was a crucial contribution to the unionists who were then fighting hand-to-hand inside Chevrolet Four. By 5:30 P.M. the union gained control of the plant and effectively stopped the production of Chevrolet automobiles. During the next few hours, assisted by hundreds of union men from Detroit and Toledo, the strikers barricaded the entrances to Chevrolet Four with heavy metal moved into place by cranes. Meanwhile, the Emergency Brigade members who had retreated to Pengelly reappeared, marching single file down Chevrolet Avenue, still carrying their American flag. Following instructions from Johnson, who spoke from a sound car, several hundred Emergency Brigade women set up a revolving picket line outside Chevrolet Four. Over and over they sang "We Shall Not Be Moved."

Mary's joy at the sight surpassed all imaginable limits.

Although Vorse was up most of the night, she rose early on February 2. Judge Gadola ordered the evacuation of Fisher One and Two the following day. The injunction also forbade all picketing and strike activities and levied an enormous penalty on the lands and possessions of UAW officers and sit-down strikers if they failed to obey the order. Reasoning that it was not they but the employers who were defying the law by their refusal to honor the Wagner Act, the strikers decided not to move. Their telegram to the Michigan governor read: "We fully expect that if a violent effort is made to oust us many of us will be killed and we take this means of making it known to our wives, to our children, to the people of the state of Michigan and of the country that if this result follows from the attempt to eject us you are the one who must be held responsible for our deaths."

February 3 was, in the words of the historian Sidney Fine, "the day when the Flint strike came the closest to erupting into civil war."[4] Expecting that the injunction ordering the expulsion of the strikers would be enforced, UAW leaders urged their locals in other towns to send as many men as possible to Flint. By dawn, the roads leading into the city were clogged with hundreds of men responding to the call. A crowd of ten-thousand gathered around Fisher One. It included about seven-hundred women wearing their red and green tams. By chance, February 3 had been designated as Women's Day in Flint. Women's Auxiliaries from the surrounding cities sent their members to join the parade through Flint, which ended at Fisher One in mid-afternoon.

A tremendous demonstration occurred just before the injunction deadline. Singing pickets, six abreast, carrying clubs and pieces of metal, circled the plant, while strikers cheered from the factory windows and union sound trucks methodically called for the people to remain calm. When word came that there would be no attempt to expel the strikers, the mass gathering exploded in celebration. A jubilant victory parade moved through downtown Flint, ignoring traffic lights.

Vorse was scheduled to speak on "Labor's Heroines" to the mass meeting in Pengelly that climaxed the Women's Day parade and demonstrations. "Mrs. Vorse has firsthand experiences to tell of labor conflicts in American history in which such figures as Mother Jones, Fannie Sellins, Mother Bloor and other fighters took a leading part," the announcement read. Although the meeting was scheduled for eight o'clock, the great hall was full by six. The women in the auxiliaries made brief speeches, telling the wide span of their activities: picketing, child care, food preparation, fund raising. The high point for Vorse came when all the women from Detroit stood up, held up their right hands, and took an oath to protect union members at all times and in all emergencies. The women spoke of political action too. "A little while ago there were few women interested in union," Genora Johnson told the crowd, "but they learned through the auxiliary they have power. The workers are going to learn they have political power . . . and when they do we'll elect every county and state official." In her press dispatch, Vorse wrote: "A new vision to work for. A new life for workers. It might be the Emergency Brigade has started it." [5]

On February 5, Josephine Herbst joined Vorse in Flint to report the labor war. Assisted by Dorothy Kraus, chair of the UAW food committee at Flint, Vorse and Herbst began an ambitious project—the writing of a play for the entertainment of the strikers. It was to be a Living Newspaper style production, in which a cast of eighty—the actors, the workers playing themselves—would enrich the skeletal script by their own interpretations and impromptu contributions. Entitled *Strike Marches On*, the play portrayed the scenes of the Flint sit-down, preceded by a dramatization of the speedup. Vorse persuaded Morris Watson, vice-president of the American Newspaper Guild and managing producer of the Living Newspaper project of the WPA's Federal Theater Program, to serve as producer. On February 9, *Strike Marches On* went into rehearsal at the Pengelly Building, with eager workers helping with costumes, scenery, and lighting. [6]

As it turned out, the first showing of the play came after the strike ended. On the scheduled date of the first performance, GM signed an agreement with the UAW. Under pressure from the federal government, resolute union officials, and Governor Murphy, GM conceded defeat and agreed to reemployment of all strikers and a six-month grace period for the UAW to organize without fear of company interference within seventeen struck plants. The strike settlement of February 11 was perhaps the most significant union victory in American history. It cracked the industrialists' front against unionism and opened the way for the sensational growth of the CIO, modifying the structure of American politics.

That afternoon, Vorse joined the huge crowd gathered to greet the sit-down strikers emerging from Fisher One. A parade line formed, headed by the victorious strikers, the Women's Auxiliary, and the Emergency Brigade. Led by two drummers and a drum major they marched toward Chevrolet Four and Fisher Two.

Invited by a gesture from the strike leader Bob Travis to join the union delegation, Vorse walked with him into Fisher Two. "They were all sitting and waiting for us," she wrote, "dressed in clean shirts, neatly shaved with their bundles in their hands ready to go. They asked us to go through the plant and see in what [good] order they had left it. . . . I stood in the windows looking at the street toward Chevrolet Four. I saw the militia step aside and the crowd surged up. It was now dusk." The Fisher Two men emerged to cheers, and the inevitable labor songs. The men from Chevrolet Four next came out, met by their wives and children. In the dim light, Vorse jotted in her notebook:

> Everyone was singing. Great calcium lights went off and illumi-
> nated the crowds of cheering people. . . . By now [the crowd] is
> bright with confetti, people are carrying toy balloons, the whole
> scene is lit by the burst of glory of the photographers' flares, the big
> flags punctuate the crowd with color. . . . Men and women from
> the cars shout to the groups of other working people who crowd the
> long line of march. "Join the union. We are free!"[7]

She remembered she was due at the Pengelly Building to put the play on, but the streets were so packed with people she could barely fight her way through. At the entrance to Pengelly she found it was impossible to move up the stairs. The auditorium was filled. Loudspeakers were erected to address the crowd of thousands outside. Almost two hours late for the opening of her Living Newspaper production, Vorse pushed to the back of the Pengelly Building and began a perilous trip up the fire escape. She arrived just as the cast was assembled, waiting for *Strike Marches On* to begin. She found Morris Watson persuading some of the workers' wives who were actresses in the play to stay. The women had not seen their striking husbands in forty-four days, and were all for bolting. Vorse took a position near the stage, to prompt the actors if they forgot their lines.

In the confusion and noise, she could not see or hear much, except to know that the jubilant workers acting the play "added detail, made it their own." Two thousand auto workers and their families applauded at almost every line of the production.

"You ever heard of property rights?" asked the man on the loudspeaker.

"You ever heard of human rights?" the audience roared in unison with the actor.

The celebration dance at the Pengelly Building was interrupted by Bob Travis in the early hours of February 12. He announced that forty or fifty men were needed at once in Anderson, Indiana, where a large mob had surrounded a UAW victory meeting in a downtown Anderson theater. The unionists and their families in the theater, including Victor Reuther, asked Travis to send reinforcements. Nine men in Flint who owned cars were selected; four men were assigned to travel with each driver.

Vorse's son Heaton decided to join the flying squadron on its trip to Anderson. He had only a moment to find her in the packed hall and to tell her goodbye before he left. Less than twenty-four hours later, Vorse received a midnight call. At first she thought the message that Heaton had been seriously wounded in a shooting in Indiana was a bad joke. Finally convinced, she took the next train to Anderson.

Heaton and the caravan from Flint had arrived in Anderson to find that the anti-union mob surrounding the theater had dispersed with the coming of daylight. That afternoon, Heaton and several carloads of Flint unionists drove to a seedy tavern on the edge of town where, they had been told, several unionists were being manhandled. In an apparent ambush, the owner of the tavern began shooting as soon as they got out of their cars. Nine unionists were wounded. Heaton had eighty shotgun pellets in his legs. On February 13, Anderson was placed under martial law. Heaton and nineteen others were arrested by the National Guard while the tavern owner remained free to boast of his marksmanship. "Violence and murder are in the air," Vorse wrote Carl Haessler on February 16.[8]

For the next month Vorse remained near her son, oblivious to national events. Outside the hospital room a soldier stood day and night, guarding his prisoner. Heaton underwent two leg operations. At first it seemed he would easily recover, but in that preantibiotic era, his infection spread. After the second operation he became feverish and pale. The doctor advised that his leg might be amputated. The odor of the hospital room reminded Vorse of the smell of the boys she had seen dying in hospital wards in France. She endured that terrible time of waiting alone in her dimly lit hotel room, after the hospital closed each night, with no friends or family there to share the anxiety, unable to sleep. She had never felt so alone. After several long weeks, Heaton slowly began to recover.

Because of Vorse's prominence and her important union and journalist friends, Heaton's shooting received wide press attention; Walter Winchell addressed the injustice on several radio broadcasts. According to the UAW attorney, the state eventually dropped all charges against Heaton and the other unionists because no one "was too anxious to try these men, in light of the fact that the perpetrator of the shooting affray has not been indicted up to this time."

The national publicity brought a deluge of letters from friends. Elizabeth Gurley Flynn wrote, "We are living in great days—dreams coming true. I feel sorry for people . . . who are living in the past and can't see the CIO and what it means to American labor . . . [for the left] can't go on forever on poor reputations and dead organizations." Katy Dos Passos, conscious of Vorse's chronic need for funds, assumed she must need help: "Feel very proud. . . . We send much love to you dear. . . . Do you need money? Can always raise money for our talented, beloved auntie whose triumphs and troubles are shared by your loving Katy."[9]

Vorse returned to Detroit to report the consolidation of CIO strength. The Flint example set off an explosion of 447 sit-downs, involving over 400,000 workers in 1937, not only in the auto industry but in every imaginable group, from dogcatchers and textile workers to lumbermen and dime-store clerks, as millions of men and women roared, "CIO! CIO!" On March 2, John L. Lewis announced to an amazed public that mighty U.S. Steel had conceded to the CIO—prior to any strike—and signed a collective bargaining agreement. "What the A.F. of L. had failed to accomplish in half a century the CIO had achieved in three weeks," the historians Melvyn Dubofsky and Warren Van Tine wrote. U.S. Steel came to this dramatic shift partly because the Democratic landslide in November made it unlikely that the steel industry could rely, as in the past, on the power of the state to smash a national steel strike, and partly because the corporation did not wish to risk the loss of large profits anticipated from the armaments contract then being negotiated with Great Britain—

but mostly because a minority of militant workers within the labor force had reshaped, for the moment, at least, American economic and political reality.[10]

The sit-down tactic brought tremendous power to the rank and file. Management hesitated to attack these strikers physically for fear of damage to plant and machinery. The sit-down tactic compensated for the lack of a mass union membership base within most factories. Workers maintained high morale during a sit-down, since there was no need to endure the cold or danger of a picket line, or to watch helplessly as strikebreakers were brought through the picket lines under armed escort. A sense of worker solidarity was heightened during a sit-down: workers cooperated inside, while families and supporters organized outside to provide food and information. Inherent in the notion of the sit-down is the revolutionary idea that workers who have seized the factories might also seize the means of production for more far-reaching social goals. Although substantial gains were often made by the workers during the wave of wildcat strikes, many CIO officials voiced opposition to unsanctioned worker actions, which hampered the union leaders' effectiveness in negotiating with management.

Coming at a time when FDR was pressing for reorganization of the Supreme Court, the wave of sit-downs also frightened political conservatives. In the Senate, the La Follette Civil Liberties Committee's hearings on employers' espionage tactics were only partially successful in countering the media propaganda blitz against the "hoodlums" and "Communists" who led the CIO. In the House, Martin Dies of Texas prepared his assault on organized labor that would culminate in the establishment of HUAC the next year. The anti–New Deal redbaiting campaign was well along by the summer of 1937 when the CIO began a long and violent struggle against the independent steel concerns known as Little Steel. Vorse's coverage of the Little Steel War in Ohio would bring her the widest national acclaim she had yet received as a labor journalist. It would also mark the moment when her long career as a reporter entered a steep decline.

The bloody battle that the CIO's Steel Workers' Organizing Committee (SWOC) waged against the Little Steel companies in the spring and summer of 1937 resulted in eighteen deaths and hundreds of injuries. Conservative national forces effectively countered the New Deal's support of organized labor and significantly slowed the momentum of CIO organization. Little Steel's heavily financed propaganda campaign convinced many Americans that SWOC and the CIO were dominated by revolutionaries intent on violent disruption of economic life.

Youngstown, Ohio, was the heart of the Little Steel strike, which covered seven states and brought out ninety-thousand strikers in the first major strike in the steel industry since 1919. On June 19, Vorse attended a meeting in the countryside near Youngstown. Arriving back in the city in the late evening, she was told that several workers had been injured at a battle outside Republic Steel's Stop Five. The fight occurred on the day that a group of female sympathizers and wives of the Republic strikers had assumed picket duty in observance of "Women's Day" on the picket lines. At the end of the day, several women and children sat down to rest a few feet inside the company's property line. Reports of the incident differ, but the majority of journalists agreed that Captain Charles Richmond ordered the women to move their chairs off company land. The women refused to move fast enough to please Richmond who had suffered their taunts all day and was in an ugly mood. One of the policemen fired a tear-gas grenade that fell near the feet of a woman holding a four-month-old child.

Several hundred furious strikers in a nearby field ran to aid the women. They rushed the police, throwing stones and waving clubs. The police force retreated into an underpass near the gate, firing a barrage of tear gas as they went. During the next two hours, the fighting grew more fierce. Several hundred deputies and police rushed to the scene, where about seven-hundred angry strikers and their families and friends congregated. Firing came from both sides, although observers reported that the first shots came from the company guards in the Republic plant. Two workers were killed by gunfire and at least twenty-two men and women were injured by gunshot wounds.[11]

Vorse came down to the Stop Five area with Scotty O'Hara, the SWOC organizer from Homestead, Pennsylvania. "All was quiet," she recalled. "The streets were perfectly empty. We passed a group of pickets without trouble. I said to Scotty, 'Am I cramping your style?' He said, 'No, come on, everything is all right.'" Suddenly a truck containing about twenty deputies drove toward them. She heard several shots. "At the sound of the rifles I turned to run, and two men fell at my feet, and suddenly I too was on the ground, with blood running down my face. One man groaned. The other lay still. I learned the next day that Jim Eperjessi, a fifty-seven-year-old Hungarian, one of the men who fell in front of me, had been killed by the bullets." Vorse was taken to the hospital with a head wound and received several stitches in her forehead.

The next day, most of the nation's large Sunday newspapers featured an Associated Press photo of Vorse with headlines proclaiming "Shot in Youngstown." The dramatic picture showed blood streaming down her face and splattered over her ruffled white blouse. Conflicting reports from reporters, observers, and local Youngstown officials and citizens make it impossible to determine with certainty the nature of her wound, but it does seem probable that she cut her head as she dived for protection from flying bullets or buckshot. She several times spoke of the source of her wound as a ricocheting bullet, both publicly and in her diary, but in her description of the shooting scene in *Labor's New Millions* she artfully phrased the description of her injury in vague terms: "Scotty O'Hara also sprawled on the ground, and I thought he had done so to get out of the way of the bullets. I had better do the same thing, I thought, and the next I knew, I was lying on the ground myself near one man who was groaning and another who lay motionless." Vorse was not seriously injured; wearing a head bandage, she addressed a workers' rally in Youngstown the next day. But at sixty-three, Mary Vorse was labor's new national heroine.[12]

Vorse's injuries won her astounding attention from several groups of fresh admirers. She described one union rally to her daughter: "I am rapidly becoming a legend among the miners and steelworkers. Scotty O'Hara who was with me [at Youngstown] tells the story better and better every time. This is what it's gotten to be at meetings he speaks at: 'And I lifted her up—our Mary. She was bleeding like a stuck pig. "Are you hurt, Mary?" I sez.' "No, Scotty," sez she. I'm not. They can cut out me eye but they can't cut my heart out of the strike.' It goes over big. I expect to be known as Mother Vorse to the steelworkers. I can see it coming." Meanwhile, the Federated Press, notorious for its low or nonexistent salaries, took the unprecedented step of forming a special fund for keeping her in the field. John Hammond donated the initial seventy-five dollars.[13]

The Communist Party, ever alert to public relations in the Popular Front era, also discovered Vorse's new appeal. The party previously had made no real attempt to woo her into joining the League of American Writers, organized in 1935. She now appeared as a bright star to party leaders. Vorse had attended the league-sponsored Second Congress of American Writers held in New York in early June, and received no special notice there, but after the Youngstown shootings, the report of that congress proudly spotlighted her wound "by a vigilante bullet." In July, the league executive secretary wrote Vorse she was "horrified to hear about the shooting" and reported that the league had voted to make her a member: "Membership application is enclosed." Two months later, the league again hustled Vorse to join their ranks. Myra Page offered Vorse an invitation to speak to a group of league writers in New York in December. Perhaps anticipating a rebuff, Page added with hesitance, "I know you have to be careful and I appreciate the reasons for it." [14]

Even the FBI paid new attention to her, increasing its surveillance of her activities. Yet Vorse was probably saved from the worst effects of government persecution by the intervention of one of the most conservative Congressmen in Washington. Allen T. Treadway from Massachusetts, whose long tenure in Congress (from 1913 to 1945) made him the ranking Republican member of the powerful Ways and Means Committee, had a special fondness for Vorse, his first cousin.

His tolerance of Cousin Mary's misguided propensity to sometimes stray into areas where reds congregated is well illustrated in his response to her injury at Youngstown. He told the House that Vorse, "my nearest relation, aside from my own immediate family," had become another innocent victim of the violence instigated by the hoodlums led by John L. Lewis and the CIO, all "aided and abetted" by FDR and the Democratic administration. A discreet but impatient call from Congressman Treadway to the FBI was sufficient to lessen, at least temporarily, any FBI interest in her case. [15]

None of the sudden acclaim seemed more remarkable to Vorse, however, than the attention showered on her by Ernest Hemingway. When Vorse traveled to Key West in the spring of 1938, Hemingway, who had always ignored her during her trips to the Keys, now sent his wife, Pauline, to fetch Vorse and bring her to his house. Receiving Vorse as he reclined in bed, he lauded her writing as "clear and cool." Vorse was at first flattered: "No one is better than he is at his best as a conscientious craftsman," she preened herself under his praise. Four days later, she had grown tired of his adolescent strutting and vision of True Masculinity. Hemingway— a man who took immense pride in killing fish—bored and annoyed her. She was miffed that his notice of her rested solely on his belief that she had demonstrated manly courage under fire. "Now suddenly I am in the Hemingway inner circle," she muttered to her diary in March. "All because I got a scratch on the puss. The long years in which I have been in the labor movement, have been in danger and served with devotion, when I was arrested, mobbed, kidnapped—all that didn't mean anything. Because I happened to get shot it did. Last night I read [Hemingway's] *To Have and Have Not* with amazement—a very juvenile performance." The next evening, listening to Hemingway's bluster, she scornfully noted: "Ernest thinks war is glorious." [16]

Hemingway's belated attention to her did bring one nice dividend. Through his influence, she was allowed to rent for a pittance a spacious home on the water within the Key West Navy Yard. She was sure she would "never again have anything so perfect for a writing place."[17] That spring she completed *Labor's New Millions*, her story of the formation of the CIO.

Published in 1938, it recreates the high drama of worker struggle from the first CIO strike to the consolidation of an organization nearly two million strong in less than two years. The overriding theme of the book is the role played by organized labor in realizing the most basic ideals of American democracy. She examines the history of union busting, the manipulation of the media and public opinion by well-financed employer organizations, and the successful new organizational techniques evolved by the CIO. She praises the CIO's welcome to black workers and highlights the contribution of women to labor victory. Throughout, Vorse emphasizes that it was not the New Deal government, but the massed strength of thousands of militant workers, that served as the crucial driving force to expand democracy and force a more equitable relationship between employer and employee.

The other predominant theme of *Labor's New Millions* is the nature and purpose of the red hunt. Falsely accusing unionists of being radicals was the employer's favorite weapon long before the Communist Party was formed, Vorse knew, citing incident after incident from before World War I. Throughout the book, Vorse presents convincing evidence, in instance after instance, strike after strike, of how the old red bogey was trotted out to confuse the public, weaken the union drive, and falsely brand the New Deal and the CIO as Communist dominated. She does not deny the presence of Communists in the CIO; she simply denies the predominance of their influence, and refuses to discuss either their limited or potential power.

Labor's New Millions is frequently cited in labor histories along with Benjamin Stolberg's rival account, *The Story of the CIO*, also published in 1938.[18] The free-lance journalist Stolberg, like Vorse, is critical of union busting. But nearly half of Stolberg's book focuses on the CIO as an organization in grave danger of subversion by Communists. Stolberg's work sounds obviously dated and biased today, in a way Vorse's book does not, partly because she does not discuss the various factional leaders within the CIO. History has changed many of Stolberg's red villians into heroes of anticommunism. His work was heavily publicized by the AFL and conservative business and political groups. Vorse's more measured appraisal of the CIO and communism could not serve the needs of the day in the same way that the sensational "exposés" of the increasing number of anti-Communist specialists like Stolberg could.

Vorse knew that CIO Communists were greatly outnumbered in the labor movement by traditional trade-union leaders. She believed that since Communists were so precariously dependent on the good will and tolerance of CIO leadership and the mass of unionists, Communist organizers would be dropped from the labor movement the moment they lost their usefulness or overreached accepted bounds. She felt that the leading party functionaries, many of whom she had known for years, were no threat either to capitalism or to democracy, for they were ineffectual leaders of an essentially undemocratic and foreign-based movement, which as constituted could never hold a mass appeal for American workers.

Vorse was also sure that the historic red hunt was not motivated by any actual threat of the Communist Party to capitalist hegemony, but was rather the prime means used by conservatives to discredit labor successes and progressive reform. She would not join that effort, no matter what the consequences to her pocketbook and popular reputation. This conviction best explains why she ridiculed and scorned the Communist left in her private writings and conversations, while refusing to attack American Communists in her published work. Of course, this decision meant running the risk of being branded as a "Communist" by the right and even a "fellow traveler" by non-Communist liberals and leftists, despite her early rejection of Bolshevik dictatorship. The example of the Soviet Union had never been the center of her political universe. Rather, it was her own radicalizing experiences and her recognition of the social construction of the suffering of the poor that determined her stance as an independent democratic socialist. Vorse's public political stand was already an anachronism, as out of fashion during the economic recession and New Deal fallback of the late 1930s as it had been during the Red Scare and conservative retrenchment of the 1920s.

But if Vorse's political perspective can be justified by historical hindsight, if Labor's New Millions still reads well today with its ever-fresh vision of expanded justice, still one cannot avoid a sense of incompleteness in the work, a kind of studied simplicity, which sometimes brings it nearer to propaganda than to art. The complex history of labor, with its intricate relationships and contradictions, recognized in her private writings, is not relayed in her book. The reader is instead told a simple story of capital versus labor, the rich and powerful versus the people. Although this tale is not false, it is less than whole. In her desire to protect the beleaguered

CIO, Vorse does not risk the suggestion that any failure of the CIO might be self-imposed.

In her public analysis of the Little Steel defeat, so crucial to the slowing of CIO progress, Vorse only briefly discusses SWOC's failure to provide the worker education and publicity essential to winning a strike. She does not mention the serious inadequacy of the relief provided by SWOC to strikers and their families. Another defeating factor was SWOC's rigid top-down hierarchy, which damped worker spirit and initiative. Vorse addressed this factor in typically polite fashion: "The organization has been built so rapidly in the eighteen months of the S.W.O.C.'s existence that there has not been sufficient opportunity for the development of leadership within its ranks." [19]

Perhaps she went this far in her public criticism because she was still stinging from Bruce Bliven's rebuke to her in the fall of 1937. Bliven, an editor of the *New Republic*, wrote her a stiff note: "Several of us in the office were quite disturbed about the marked difference between your article on the steel strike and your discussion of it when we were at lunch. I think a very valuable service can be rendered to the CIO by criticizing its tactics when they need criticism. I am sure it is doing them no service in the long run to argue publicly that everything is rosy, when you know privately that things have been pretty badly mismanaged." [20] Vorse was sixty-four years old in 1938 and the political climate was changing. Her encounter with Bliven indicates that if she had not yet lost her writing talent, she had lost her sense of political discretion, another sign, perhaps, of her aging in the eyes of others.

Without question, the years from 1938 to 1942 are the nadir of her biography. There was collapse on every front—personal, professional, financial, political. In many ways this time of retreat was for her similar to the decade of the twenties, but with one important difference. It would require infinitely more courage to recover and begin anew when nearing seventy, than at age fifty. [21]

First, there was the family trouble. Through much of these four years, Vorse was so obsessed with family concerns that momentous national and world events appear in the gloom-filled pages of her journal as accounts of radio or newspaper reports, as though only the most agitated tones of the newscasters or the blackest of headlines were capable of breaking into her dismal trance. As the woes of her immediate family accumulated, Vorse found it more and more difficult to discern what portion of sorrow sprang from chance and circumstance and what proceeded from her own creation. One great loss was the death of her daughter-in-law in January 1938, from an infection following a minor operation. Even after Sue Vorse's separation from Heaton the year before, she had remained a kind of daughter substitute. For many years after Sue's death, Vorse longed to be with her, to share a thought, a sight, a burden.

Vorse's anxiety over her two older children heightened in the late 1930s. When Heaton remarried, Vorse so disapproved of his new wife that she broke off contact with him for several years.[22] If such cold rejection seemed vastly out of character for Vorse, who had for decades played the long-suffering mother, it paid a dividend in ending a felt financial responsibility. Ellen and her artist husband, Jack Beauchamp, lived in Vorse's Provincetown house during the depression years of the late 1930s. Vorse hated their quarreling and heavy drinking. Whatever the reality, the household on which she broods in her diary of this period is presented as of nightmarish quality—the constant "rows" between shifting participants in various combinations of conflict, the shouts and dramatic exits by one person or another, followed by the tearful returns. To complete the misery, first Jack, and then Ellen, was so ravaged by alcohol as to become tubercular in 1939. Both required care in a sanitorium for many months.

Overwhelmed by medical bills and general family expenses, Vorse tried to grind out a few lollypops, but sold only two during five years. For the first time in two decades, she learned to function without the help of a literary agent, an indication both of her limited output and the agents' consequent lack of interest in her work. "Every lollypop I ever wrote has been a coffin nail in my reputation," Vorse wrote in her diary in 1940. One of her last attempts to earn an income from the sale of light fiction to the popular magazines brought her a welcome large payment of four hundred and fifty dollars that year. But the emotional price she paid for this "whimsical tale of Negro life" had grown higher than her economic need: "I can't stand anymore cuteness about Southern tragedy," she wrote in her diary.[23]

In 1942, Vorse published her sixteenth book, the last of her career, a lively history of Provincetown spanning the years since her arrival there in 1906. Judged by the New York *Times* as a "full-charged and beautiful book," *Time and the Town* sold well. Yet in her chosen beach home, where she had raised her family and resided for thirty-five years, she had failed to create the kind of secure community she would have liked to occupy in old age. Her natural aloofness and political incompatibility kept her apart from the town's inner circle of notables, especially its respectable womenfolk. Most Portuguese residents of Provincetown did not find her life style, politics, or lack of religious beliefs appealing; many resented her literary descriptions of their "dark-skinned beauty" and "foreign" way of life.

Despite her many years in Provincetown, and her abiding love of the town, she was not really an integral part of the community. Half regretfully, she wrote in her diary, "I can imagine nothing more arrogant than the way I have lived my life with a complete disregard to the opinions . . . of all the comfortable people of the town. . . . I remember how shocked I was when I discovered that . . . the dentist's wife was an interesting woman in her own right."[24] Just as in Amherst, she both scorned and coveted inclusion in an environment she romantically conceived as united in its essence, while at the same time she took hurtful pride in exclusion.

As the Depression deepened in the late thirties, she was forced to borrow money from friends like Edmund Wilson, Sinclair Lewis, John Dos Passos, and Cornelia Pinchot. Through most of the thirties she was unable to pay her mortgage or property taxes. The management of the Provincetown bank and her brother Fred Marvin interceded several times to save her house from repossession. Begging and borrowing, she squeaked through one dispiriting financial crisis after another.

Although she attended several CIO and Amalgamated conventions, Vorse all but withdrew from labor reporting from 1938 to 1942. For a woman who had been in the thick of the CIO battle—conferring with John Brophy and Len DeCaux, monitoring AFL meetings for David Dubinsky, marching alongside Bob Travis into the Flint factories to bring out the sit-down strikers, receiving injuries on the front lines in the Little Steel War—the sudden shift from active participant to sideline observer was startling in its swiftness and finality. Her changed position cannot be explained by her advancing age or her preoccupation with family concerns alone, for she would demonstrate her physical and mental vitality in future years, and it seems most probable that it was the absence of meaningful work that led to her obsession with family problems, rather than the reverse. Her loss of journalistic opportunity and status was the result of external events she could not control: the slowing of CIO momentum, the factionalism that rent the unions, and the successful conservative attack on liberalism and radicalism within the labor movement and without. Vorse foundered in confusion for a long while, while seeking new direction, although, in fact, she would never recapture the esteem and influence that had once been hers.

The new political environment also affected the CIO chieftains. David Dubinsky returned his International Ladies' Garment Workers Union to the AFL in 1938, ostensibly because of his fear of Communist influence on the CIO. John L. Lewis and Sidney Hillman were also ready to move against the Communists, a decision based as much on political expediency and common-sense public relations as on anti-Communist beliefs. Lewis removed John Brophy and Harry Bridges from their CIO positions in 1939; Philip Murray purged Communist organizers from SWOC. In August 1939, when Stalin and Hitler signed their Non-Aggression Treaty, the party's credibility was irreparably damaged by its brazen flipflop from praise of FDR to denunciations of New Deal officials as war-mongering, Wall Street imperialists. This zigzag shattered the Communist unionists' reputation not only among left intellectuals and CIO leaders, but also among politically aware rank-and-file unionists as well. Thus, even before the war began, or the party line shifted again when Hitler invaded the USSR, the influence of the left within the CIO was drastically weakened.[25]

These events had an inevitable impact on Vorse's standing as a labor publicist. On the one hand, she found that she was now honored as an engaging old-timer, a relic of the glory days of labor's struggle. Thus, when she showed up at the press table during the Amalgamated convention of 1938 (having traveled there with Len DeCaux who was not to be purged from CIO office until 1947), Vorse wrote her children: "Sidney Hillman came down from the platform and shook both my hands and told me how glad he was to see me and sent down word that I was to be the guest of the convention and invited me to the luncheon the board was giving for Lewis. . . . I wasn't allowed to buy meals or anything for myself and they begged me to stay longer."[26] On the other hand, she was publicly denounced as a Communist before the House Un-American Activities Committee as well as by the largest mass circulation magazine of the period, the *Saturday Evening Post*.

On August 12, 1938, HUAC opened its first formal hearings. The next day, John Frey of the AFL named "280 organizers in C.I.O. unions, under salary, who are members of the Communist Party." Vorse was number eighty-six on Frey's list:

> Mary Heaton Vorse, directing organizations of C.I.O. women's auxiliaries. At one time she was alleged to be the secretary of William Z. Foster. She wrote her red memoirs while publicity

agent in the Indian Bureau in United States Department of Interior. Reported on leave from Department of Interior while operating for C.I.O. She has just published a book which is strictly C.I.O. in character and she was one of the active "red" leaders at the 1936 Tampa A.F.L. convention.

Frey's diatribe was heavily publicized, even though he offered no evidence to support his charges. Three days later, the delusionary right-winger Walter S. Steele, editor of the ultraconservative *National Republic*, began his testimony before HUAC. He assured the Congressmen that Communists had infected hundreds of American organizations, including the Camp Fire Girls. He named Vorse as among "45 leaders" of the John Reed Clubs, who were "engaged in revolutionary activities, either in propaganda or agitation and organizational work." Alice Lee Jemison, who accused Vorse and other members of the Indian Bureau of being Communists, was the third witness to smear Vorse before HUAC in 1938, and again before another House committee in 1940.

In early 1941, Benjamin Stolberg published a scurrilous attack on Vorse and several other non-Communist leftists sympathetic to the CIO in the *Saturday Evening Post*. In faithful imitation of HUAC style, Stolberg found a few real reds in the labor movement and then proceeded to smear as "Stalinists" anyone associated with them at any time in the past who did not practice his kind of ritualistic anticommunism. Stolberg praised HUAC as "the most competent research organization in the Government on subversive activities," and charged that Vorse's *Labor's New Millions* was a "Communist version of the CIO," published by a house whose list read like a "Bolshevik Five Foot Shelf." [27]

Certainly these attacks had a considerable influence on public opinion and many publishers. Vorse was troubled enough by Stolberg's accusations to write her friend Gardner "Pat" Jackson, a crusading liberal journalist who had been branded in Stolberg's magazine article as "a Stalinist busybody in Washington," to inquire what could be done to protest Stolberg's libelous journalism. Branded as a red journalist, Vorse was obviously a liability to labor's publicity efforts. This was clear even to the small group of Provincetown citizens who in 1939 let her know that they did not want her assistance in Washington with their planned town recreation project because two of the town leaders on the project committee scorned her as "a red." [28]

The events of the late 1930s left her without a commitment to any political faction. She agreed with Lewis that labor should not tie itself to the Democratic Party, and favored his suggestion of a third-party farmer–labor alliance. Like Lewis, she was highly critical of FDR's assignment of massive defense contracts to employers who blatantly violated the Wagner Act. Yet she deplored Lewis's refusal to join the antifascist coalition and was appalled by his endorsement of the Republican candidate for president in 1940. At the CIO convention that year she observed—this time from the sidelines—one startling event after another: Lewis's resignation as CIO president after his appeal for FDR's defeat had been rebuked by the votes of labor; the Communist CIO faction's vote in favor of an anti-Communist resolution that placed Communists and fascists in the same category, a vote, furthermore, that had been supported by party leadership. Labor's political world was topsy-turvy. She returned home "in a shell-shocked state."[29]

Vorse had been committed to the destruction of fascism since her observation of Hitler's Germany in 1933, a position sharply in contrast to her earlier feminist-based pacifism. She abhorred the isolationist mood of many Americans and the failure of the Western democracies to provide aid to the Republican forces fighting Franco-led fascists in the Spanish Civil War. After the Munich settlement, she correctly predicted that "the two dictators [Hitler and Stalin] will come to terms to limit the British Empire. . . . I feel as though the people who have been soaked in the Marxian dialectic are living in a former century. That is all over now. All the talk of collective security was antiquated Bunk . . . as was the Popular Front. . . . For what Germany is aiming at is not 'revision' or justice or *lebensraum*, but a rearrangement of the world as we know it. This has been . . . proved by the words of Adolph Hitler and [stated] by various . . . socialist theoreticians, but it is still not believed by the majority of Americans."

In the four months prior to Hitler's invasion of Poland and the advent of World War II, she reported events in Europe for the *New Republic*, the New York *Times*, and the North American Newspaper Alliance. She traveled through France, Germany, and Switzerland and to Belgrade and Budapest between April and September of 1939. "It is not by chance that I am here," she wrote in her diary. "It is by some deep inner necessity. . . . I couldn't help coming—and when I got here and the familiar sights of Paris closed around me I knew why I had come. *I had come to defend France.* It was so absurd, an old woman like myself come to save France that I laughed out loud. And then it didn't seem so funny because I am part of the strength of France. I am one small atom of her combined power. And there was another reason for my coming, not so pure. It was that the corruption of the passion for news is such that one would rather die than miss anything, literally rather die—"[30]

Vorse sailed home from Europe in September 1939, a week after war began. At sixty-five, she felt an understandable urge to flee what might become an actual battleground at any moment, although as it turned out, the deceptive quiet of the "phony war" would stretch another six months before Hitler began his western offensive.

Vorse was also distressed because she had experienced an inability to gather news during her assignment to prewar Europe. For the first time in her life she admitted the incalculable but pernicious effect of age on her journalistic opportunities. During the past few years she had slowly become aware, with increasing anger, of the unfamiliar difficulties she now faced when gathering information or gaining access to news sources, or when attempting to charm her way through barriers to research. As a younger woman reporter, she had been an interesting sexualized novelty to many of those who manned the doorways to news gathering. Vorse had instinctively used her feminine skills to enchant or manipulate in aid of her search for a story. But now her inquiries were apt to be greeted with no interest, or, more often, with the excessive and distant politeness due a motherly figure. She faced suspicion that there was something unbecoming in a woman of her age still in quest of news, that she might even be a little daft, or at the least, eccentric, and thus a potential nuisance. Now she fully realized the impact of advancing age on the seriousness with which she and her work were greeted by the masculine-dominated worlds of war, politics, and diplomacy.

All these factors drove her home from Europe, but as soon as she arrived in New York she suffered a nervous collapse as serious as the one of 1928, aggravated by her regret that she had ignominiously left wartime Europe and thus "missed the story of my life. I should have stayed in France. And maybe even died there." Every front-page war story she read that was written by a reporter whom she considered inferior to herself sent her into new spasms of guilt and self-fury: "This remorse at having missed my best chance in life will follow me always and I shall never get over it. . . . My place given up—and the anguish that I felt against myself welled up again and followed me even into my sleep." She threw up black clots of blood. In this troubled time, old friends offered her refuge, money, and affection. Wealthy John Gilbert Winant, the New Deal ambassador to Britain, stunned her by his offer to finance a month's vacation in Cuba, "just because he thought I was tired," she wrote. In Havana, in the late fall of 1939, she rested in grateful solitude, regained her health, and rebuilt her emotional defenses.[31]

She brooded about how to regain her standing as an author: "So many years out of the market makes my position only a little better than a beginner," she moaned. "While the whole world in which I live is being torn up," she wrote, "so is my own private life." She reread her diaries of the past fifteen years—"a painful examination into my relations with my children." The exercise brought her as close to self-analysis as she could comfortably manage: "My daily notes . . . make a pattern of me escaping family—swamped again—escaping again—neither refusing to be involved [in their lives] nor resolving the difficulties of two generations."[32]

Soon after the entry of the United States into the war, she went to New York in search of a war assignment, knowing that "in the field, moved by events, I write well, otherwise I don't." Suddenly the economy was booming, jobs were plentiful, and the dreadful Russian Communists had become America's allies. Suddenly the publishers and editors did not seem to mind Vorse's reputation as a leftist. From the New York *Post* she received a large advance for a series of stories on American war workers, especially women workers.

She was sixty-eight years old, with a war ahead of her and a postwar reconstruction to report. This was a story Mary Vorse would rather die—"literally rather die"—than miss. She happily began her "last lap," as she called it then, a final surge of active reporting that would last for seven years, take her all over the nation, down to Mexico, and back to Europe for two years of work abroad.

"Oh God let me write like an angel," she entered in her diary.[33]

Part Six: 1942-1966

May we [Heterodoxy members] prove to be women whose opinions advance a mile with every whitening hair, acquiring also them with a certain equanimity, poise, and wide tolerance which are the natural results of an enlightened consciousness. May we discard the caution of youth as year by year we have less and less to lose, therefore less and less that we need fear risking, thus accumulating with time the elderly winters of rashness, recklessness, and a certain splendor of generosity. May increasing age be full of noble illusions always longing for fresh adventure, and ever standing ready to pick out upon high enterprises . . . illustrating by our lives that gray hairs are the banner of adventure.

— Heterodite Myran Louise Grant, 1920

Chapter Seventeen

The Last Lap

For her wartime mission, Vorse set out in 1942 to report the impact on American workers of the total mobilization of the home front. For almost one year, she traveled through the nation's war-production centers, reporting her findings in newspapers and on the radio. Her articles have been described by the author of a recent labor history of World War II as among the most insightful pieces of social history written during the war years.[1] She analyzed the source of labor's unrest, portrayed the blight of racism in the land, and described the problems faced by millions of women workers. Her critical social commentary reads well today, but was deeply at odds with American propaganda of the forties. Still, if nearing seventy was teaching her anything, it was that with age came a self-assurance that lessened the cost of nonconformity.

Vorse first offered her study of wartime labor to Alfred Knopf in September 1943. Within a week she had a polite no. In November the book was returned by Harper & Bros., Harcourt and Brace, Appleton, and Doubleday. The rapid series of rejections meant the manuscript was not even scaling the first barriers to serious consideration. In December, the book was refused by Random House, Holt, and Norton. For the first time in thirty-five years, and after the publication of sixteen books, she could not interest a publisher in a completed manuscript. Her confidence shattered, Vorse took to her bed for three weeks. She consoled herself with the knowledge that wartime publishing did not favor the realistic picture she had created: "From here on, I wonder who will read my pieces. I see them beating against the vast indifference of the country." Fortunately, she could not know then that her eighteenth manuscript, a dull study of the Consumers' League, would also fail, and that her nineteenth one, a feminist satire, would be unthinkable heresy to publishers during the 1950s.[2]

At age sixty-nine, she stumbled, mourned her loss, and recovered, yet something loose and romantic now crept into her writing, especially her fiction. Forceful women or discontented heroines were distinctly out of fashion in the women's magazines, and she could not master a new formula. Her labor work also suffered from her failure to move as fast as history did. It was as though she were so weighted with the horror of pre–New Deal labor wars that every sign of worker advance after the war appeared more glorious than it actually was. Too much of her future labor journalism would be enveloped in sweetness, her critical analysis obscured by breathless awe at the wonder of picket lines unmolested by state policemen or company-bought private armies. Vorse would continue to write as if union activism were still the piercing edge of social change, even after union leaders had entered a mutually profitable truce with Cold War corporate America. She might have moved on, to reflect on the meaning of business unionism as part of an ongoing historical process. She did not, and in her work it was the difference between surviving intact as a radical intellectual and becoming a respected anachronism.

The war years did bring one welcome change. When prosperity ended the Depression in a matter of months, Ellen and Jack moved to Montana, Heaton and his wife into an apartment of their own. Her youngest, Joel, who had worked as a radio script writer, became a correspondent with the Coast Guard. She vowed never to become stranded in family financial responsibilities again, a promise that events, and lack of extra money, allowed her to keep.

Living in Washington, Vorse enjoyed for the first time in her life a circle of friends composed entirely of women, most of them much younger than she. Members of the group—including Hilda Worthington Smith, Kathryn Lewis (the daughter of the famous labor leader), Jo Herbst, Fleeta Springer, and Ann Craton Blankenhorn—ate and drank together, saw plays and exhibits, attended meetings, and shared ideas and their work lives in shifting combinations that brought two or three of them together almost every night.

The anti–New Deal right in the capital had discovered the electoral value of reducing all modern history to a death dance between communism and the Republic. On May 21, 1942, the red chasers hit close to home; a furious Jo Herbst burst into Vorse's apartment to announce that she had lost her job with a government agency where she had prepared radio transcripts for transmission abroad. No reason for her sudden dismissal was given Herbst, but it was clear that it was related to a "loyalty" investigation of government employees by the FBI, in turn a product of the anti-Communist campaign that began to roll in the first months of FDR's war administration. Unable to determine the specific charges against her, Herbst could not prove to be false what she did not know to be alleged. Herbst and Fleeta Springer were the first of many close friends of Vorse's to suffer denial of civil rights in the war years and after because of past or present leftist beliefs.[3] The progressivism of thousands of Americans in the 1930s was fast on its way to becoming the sin of the 1950s.

Vorse's new group of friends in the capital indicated her growing alienation from the older literary circle centered about Provincetown. Dos Passos, in particular, had turned so far to the right after 1940 that Vorse maintained her connection to him more out of loyalty to their shared past and because of her love for Katy, than out of tolerance of his political transition. Vorse felt that even Edmund Wilson momentarily succumbed to a version of anticommunism that she saw as an attempt to make a simple morality play out of the tangled disorder of history, as well as a threat to future world peace and civil liberty in the United States. "Socially . . . it's a desert [in Provincetown]," she wrote Herbst. "Charles Walker and Bunny [Edmund] Wilson and his wife [Mary McCarthy] were over together with some friends and the talk about Russia was unbelievable. Bunny pontificates more and more. . . . I am feeling very low. . . . And intellectuals here are so worked up concerning Russia . . . that no real conversation is possible, even among themselves. All such talk ends in a brawl. . . . In these momentous days one needs good talk. . . . Do write me, Jo."[4]

In the spring of 1944, Vorse won an assignment from Fawcett Publishers to report the political situation in Mexico, where she lived for the next year, returning to Provincetown only for the summer season. Her small income, fattened by the sale of several pieces to the *New Yorker*, would stretch further in Mexico. The exotic crew of writers and artists in Mexico City, centered about the painter Diego Rivera and the writer Anita Brenner, seemed more intent on their art and loves than on politics. Vorse found the delightfully free and slightly mad political environment a relief from the reactionary backlash at home.[5] With all her children now self-supporting, it was her first lengthy vacation from writing since Bert Vorse's death thirty-four years before. But even though she was now seventy-one, she never once thought of the Mexican interlude as retirement.

Several months before the war ended, Vorse began her campaign for an overseas job to report events in postwar Europe. She applied to the largest nonmilitary intergovernmental operation in history, the United Nations Relief and Rehabilitation Administration, founded by forty-four nations in November 1943 to provide economic and medical assistance to the invaded countries devastated by war. Her experience seemed made to order for the dazzling opportunity UNRRA offered her to travel and write. For the magnificent salary of twenty dollars a day, she was hired to produce pamphlets describing UNRRA efforts in Greece, Yugoslavia, Czechoslovakia, and Italy.

It was without a premonition of disaster that she returned to the Publicity and Information Division for a more detailed discussion of her responsibilities as an UNRRA staff member. The director explained to her with deep embarrassment that after a long conference with others, he had decided she was too old for the job; he feared she might become ill or die abroad. "Now age leapt out at me," she wrote. "I who had been secretly proud of never doing anything about my looks, wished that I had the moral support which a youthful appearance can give a woman, a woman who has for instance dyed her hair an encouraging red, who has had her face and neck lifted, and bright shining caps put on all her teeth." Finally, UNRRA found the proper formula to resolve its dilemma; she would travel under military orders as an official war correspondent. (Although she had trimmed seven years off her age on the UNRRA application, she may have been, at seventy-one, the oldest war correspondent traveling under U.S. sponsorship.)

Only her passport picture would remain to remind her of her trial in obtaining the UNRRA job, she wrote, "for no bride has ever done her hair more carefully for her wedding than I did mine for this picture. I have had other passport pictures which made me look a halfwit or a criminal, and others that gave the impression of a hatchet-faced woman of hale middle age. But the picture that peers at me from my [1945] passport is the face of a thousand schemes and compromises—an old, old, crafty face."[6]

Vorse probably never knew that she was then the object of an intense FBI investigation. It is impossible to know the exact information or incident that excited FBI interest. The crucial documents from her case file were so heavily censored prior to their release under the Freedom of Information Act as to obscure completely the purpose of the federal inquiry. In March 1944, just as Vorse entered Mexico, the FBI's Boston Field Office initiated an investigation under the category "Security Matter—Communist," a code to describe persons "considered potentially dangerous to internal security." The new evidence against her included interviews with confidential informants. One reported that she was "a misguided liberal," not a Communist. Another more favored by the FBI was armed with a list of Vorse's activities and affiliations during the period from 1920 to 1942, including the testimony given against her before House and Senate committees, and a report that a German-language magazine published in Moscow had referred to her as "a reliable revolutionary." This informant insisted that Vorse was "a Communist agitator . . . directing the organizations of Women's Auxiliaries of the CIO."

In November 1944, J. Edgar Hoover directed that Vorse be assigned a Security Index number as a "native born Communist," thus ensuring that she would be taken into custodial detention in the event of a national emergency. The Security Index and plan for detention without right of habeas corpus were unknown to the public, Congress, or the judiciary. Vorse's placement on the Security Index, with all its frightful consequences, was reached in typical FBI fashion—through brief, sloppy investigative tactics, based on hearsay and guilt by association, and supported by secret witnesses unknown to the accused.[7]

Hoover's skillful public relations created the popular myth of an incorruptible and above all, effective, FBI. In fact, numerous FBI investigations of "subversives" are known to have been exceedingly clumsy and inaccurate. In Vorse's case, as in so many others, the ineptness of the FBI inquiry becomes almost comical, as the agents valiantly struggled to locate this dangerous woman, Mary Vorse, "alias Mary H. O'Brien," the newly designated threat to the internal security of the American people.

First—after an unsuccessful weeks-long surveillance of her old apartment in Washington—FBI agents thought to ask the Provincetown postmaster for her forwarding address. Thus did they easily locate her in Texas where she was visiting her sister-in-law during the Christmas season. When Vorse reentered Mexico in February, the FBI learned her hotel address in Mexico City, but soon lost her trail once again. Although the Boston office suggested to FBI headquarters that further investigation was not warranted, Hoover insisted that her Security Index be maintained. In June 1945, while Vorse was in New York negotiating for the UNRRA job, Hoover asked the American embassy in Mexico City to locate her and ascertain the nature of her Communist activities. His letter described her as fifty-five—a mere sixteen years off. Five more letters were exchanged between the embassy and Hoover. Vorse had meanwhile sailed for Europe en route to her UNRRA assignment.

Undaunted, the FBI maintained hot pursuit of her cold trail. In December 1945, the Boston Field Office learned that Vorse had an APO address; Boston suggested that the New York Field Office might wish to check with the War Department to see if Vorse was in the armed forces. The search was delayed several weeks because her case was inadvertently directed to the New Haven, Connecticut, office. Three months later, the FBI in New York advised Hoover that Vorse might be located through the embassy in Rome. In April, the embassy informed him that she was not to be found in Italy, even though Vorse was at that time working at the UNRRA office in Rome. Toward the end of May, the FBI reported her living at a Washington, D.C. address, although she was actually visiting her son Joel in London.

Meanwhile, an agent in the Boston office reviewed the case and became suspicious. One can see his computations on the pages of Vorse's file, as he attempted to figure her approximate age using the various inaccurate figures for her birth date—1881? 1883? He obviously became disturbed at the thought of chasing after this aged woman and directed the New York office to determine her age. New York reported their failure to locate her birth records.

Suddenly, after thirty-two months of failure to find her, the Boston Field Office stated its renewed determination to close the case, in belated recognition that "there was little or no legally admissible evidence to prove the subject to be a member of the Communist Party and to have knowledge of the aims and purposes thereof." In fact, the office had acquired no additional evidence of any kind since the items obtained when she was originally assigned a Security Index number almost three years before. It seems likely that the Boston agents decided to drop the case when they determined that Vorse was in her late sixties (she was actually seventy-two). This time Hoover, too, was ready to throw in the towel. On January 15, 1947, FBI headquarters, still not sure of her location, also closed the case, placing her hefty dossier of over two-hundred pages in the general "investigative case file," where it would remain until the next FBI intrusion into her life in 1949.[8]

———

As UNRRA publicist, Vorse traveled through Greece, Yugoslavia, and Italy during 1946, visiting isolated villages, destroyed cities, and displaced persons camps to translate into human terms the impact of UNRRA on the lives of ill, hungry, and desperate people. She also published a series of articles on political and economic conditions in Greece, Italy, and

Germany in *PM*, as well as in major outlets like the New York *Times*, the Washington *Post*, the Boston *Herald*, and the St. Louis *Post-Dispatch*.[9]

For the first time in twenty-five years, Vorse found herself free of immediate financial and family worries. The Provincetown house had been rented; she traveled and lived at government expense, while earning a generous salary from UNRRA. As a young woman, she had longed for just such an opportunity. Now she relished the chance as much as ever, but soon learned to her dismay that loss of physical energy gravely limited her ability to produce quality material.

She noted another big difference. She was alone much of the time during her thirteen months with UNRRA, isolated from other staff members who treated her with the sometimes polite—often cruel—indifference offered to the aged by the very young. It was not an easy adjustment for Vorse who was long accustomed to deference as a distinguished writer. She learned anew how growing old changed the world's perception of her. The knowledge that older women were treated differently from aging men rankled. "That is why sergeants' eyes bug out to see [my] grey hair under a field cap . . . when grey-haired colonels are thick as cranberries in a bog. Even in Washington with the government being run by the well-along in years, and the high places starred with active men in their seventies, an older woman causes remark." Whereas no one thought to congratulate older generals, Congressmen, or corporation executives on not being in their dotage, well-meaning young secretaries in Rome felt free to remark on her astounding ability to get about. Vorse felt "perpetually reminded" that she was "approaching the grave . . . that tomorrow—or shortly thereafter—there will be no more work."[10]

Separated from UNRRA in January 1947, Vorse spent eight months traveling and writing of postwar conditions in Germany, France, and England for the New York *Times*, the New York *Post*, and the *Cape Codder*. Without distinction, this work presents superficial accounts of the operation of the American military government. Her political concerns are revealed only in letters to her friends. She told Jo Herbst and Ann Craton Blankenhorn of her disgust at the failure of denazification. Most worrisome to her was the general hatred of the Soviet Union she encountered in Western Europe. Vorse had realized at once that "since the atomic bomb fell on Hiroshima . . . all values had changed with fission. We are now in a new world." Yet despite entry into a vastly new era of human history, the world was dividing into two hostile forces, each billing itself as an absolute good in battle with absolute evil. In such a conflict, accommodation with the enemy was unthinkable, and hence nuclear war inevitable. "I believe that both Russia and ourselves have forced a stream of misunderstandings," Vorse wrote Jo Herbst from Frankfurt in 1947. "What was a trickle fed by a thousand irresponsible statements, a thousand lies, has now become a current swelling on to the abyss of war . . . in which the nations are equally enmeshed and for whose starting we are equally guilty . . . if blind people who set off a deadly machine by chance can be called guilty. . . . How can one write of anything else but fighting for the basis of a lasting peace? What's happening here dwarfs anything else." [11]

That summer Vorse visited Joel in London and met her infant grand-daughter. Turning toward home after two years abroad, she seemed to know she was seeing Europe for the last time. "Anyway," she wrote, "I've enjoyed every moment and if I were to die tomorrow I couldn't but rejoice at having had such an absorbing last spectacle of the world." [12]

Just as over a quarter of a century earlier, Vorse returned from Europe to an American postwar Red Scare. As the United States and the Soviet Union moved to consolidate their wartime gains and establish or strengthen their respective spheres of influence, a propaganda campaign in preparation for war dominated the politics and economies of both nations. Yet many Americans who feared atomic destruction did not support a global defense or a fight to the death against communism. Others, like Vorse, believed that talk of containing communism did not reflect commitment of Ameri-can policy makers to world democracy, so much as their willingness to strengthen even authoritarian anti-Communist regimes abroad in order to limit revolutionary change. When Henry Wallace voiced criticism of President Truman's foreign policy, Wallace became a rallying point for those liberals and leftists who questioned the U.S. shift to a hard-line Cold War diplomacy.

A real choice was offered to the non-Communist American left when Wallace became the 1948 presidential candidate of the Progressive Party. Although Vorse favored his stand for what later would be called "peaceful coexistence," she could not support a futile third-party effort, which would weaken the Democratic chance for victory. She also felt that Wallace and his supporters were "thinking still in terms of Russia under Lenin's model of 1921. And to hear his followers talk is like going back to the liberalism of that era. It is terrifying, especially as these followers are . . . completely hornswoggled by commies. . . . The Russian dictatorship is not the revolution."

As usual, Vorse did not fit any common political pattern. Devoid of a political home for the remainder of her life, she remained an unrepentant independent radical, even as the American left dwindled into virtual eclipse during the fifties. "It would be a good thing to let it be known how you feel about Wallace," a friend told her. "You know like me you have a record." But Vorse refused to spend her old age "in the fruitless pastime of acting like a turtle engaged in not sticking out its neck. The dumb bunnies [in the intelligence agencies] have no doubt long since got me docketed, and I intend to talk with whomever I want to—and be seen and go with whom I choose." She had made up her mind on a few subjects—one, that the most important goal in the nuclear age was to keep the peace; some area of agreement must be reached with the Soviet Union. A second opinion—made easier for her to embrace because she had no family to support and no waged position to protect—was that one must fight the redbaiters: "Everybody seems afraid today for fear someone will call them a commie. . . . You can lose your job because you were seen going with so and so —[but I believe] being a pro-fascist is worse than being a communist."[13]

Vorse soon demonstrated her resistance to anti-Communist crusaders. En route to Mexico in 1949, she visited in Los Angeles with her reporter friend Margaret Larkin who had married Albert Maltz in 1937. As one of the famed "Hollywood Ten," Maltz had defied the House Un-American Activities Committee in 1947, was blacklisted as a scriptwriter, and eventually went to prison for contempt of Congress. Vorse was "burned up over the evil form of censorship" that banned the production of Maltz's work, but she also found it hard to talk with the Maltzes. As Communist sympathizers, Maltz and his wife "seem to be living in a world of illusions," Vorse wrote Herbst from California. Still, that Vorse was willing to stay in Maltz's house during the period his conviction was under appeal shows her courageous determination not to be intimidated during the Cold War red scare, despite her vulnerability to blacklist as a writer. The witchhunt led by the committee that President Truman once called the "most un-American thing in America" had achieved virulent influence by 1949. Her association with Maltz and Margaret Larkin definitely placed at risk Vorse's own ability to find publishing outlets. She was fulfilling her promise to "see and go with whom I choose," no matter how popular the inquisition against free speech and free thought might be.[14]

During her last years as an active journalist, Vorse attended CIO and UAW conventions as often as she could manage. There she could count on recognition by the union leadership, public accolades, and always a complimentary room and meals. A convention meant dinner or coffee with the old-timers of the labor movement, shared memories of having been part of a stirring human effort, political conversations so heated it seemed that the fate of the nation was at stake, introduction to the admiring young who knew her work. All this brought a sense of relatedness—a confirmation of her choices in the world. When the union greats on the stage spoke her name into the microphone, paid notice to her presence in the great crowd, she could feel again the thrill of vital involvement in a magnificent endeavor. "When I went to greet [Philip] Murray at the cocktail party," she reported to her diary in 1951, "to my astonishment he said he saw me in the audience, then turning to delegates . . . he went on, 'This is the darling of the labor movement. We all love her. You must join me on the platform, make free of the platform.' . . . I was amazed at his fond warmth. It is in this way by the various people in the labor movement knowing me that I get my laurel crown placed on my head, as much by the obscure big steelworker [who is] Murray's bodyguard, as by Murray himself." [15]

Trapped as a relic in the American political reaction of the fifties, she was on hand to see the purging of much of the left from the CIO in 1949 and 1950. She feared that without a strong radical faction within the CIO —the last remaining dissident group of any consequence within the nation —there could be no significant opposition to challenge the government's abuse of civil liberties or the country's growing militarism. Vorse found the scenes of the 1952 UAW convention so painful that she left the meeting early: "[The convention] degenerated into something monotonous and dreary, of a union which has no vital healthy opposition. . . . Not only that but . . . the State Dept. wobbles due to the attacks of McCarthy. . . . Government has passed into the hands of reactionaries . . . [and] everybody is engaged in building bombshelters." [16]

Another kind of vacancy depleted her life. Over a period of five years, she lost her oldest friends. The first to die was Hutchins Hapgood. A harder blow came when her sister-in-law Josie suffered a fatal heart attack in June 1947, while Vorse was in Europe. In September, just as Vorse returned from London, Katy Dos Passos was killed in a grotesque automobile accident on Cape Cod. Her head was nearly sliced off in the collision, and Dos Passos lost his right eye. Susan Glaspell was the next to go, ten months later. Vorse helped to nurse Neith Boyce, whose death followed in 1951. Finally, Vorse must have felt the news of Robert Minor's death the next year. "These steep stairs I climb slowly," she wrote in her diary. [17]

As the years progressed, Vorse also worried about money. After the war, she sold only a few articles to the high-paying journals; her work for the labor press or for small journals like the *New Republic* and the *Nation* paid very little. Renting out rooms in her Provincetown house was not enough to sustain subsistence. In the long spells between sales, Vorse relied on monetary gifts from professional organizations or a grateful labor movement. She received her first such payment in 1952 from the Artists' and Writers' Relief Fund of the National Institute of Arts and Letters and the American Academy of Arts and Letters. The next year the United Auto Workers sent her an unspecified sum. In 1954, the Sidney Hillman Foundation sent five hundred dollars in "deep appreciation of your pioneering efforts and your many achievements." In the 1960s, Vorse grew more dependent on monetary gifts, which were often accompanied by tender best wishes and recognition of her earlier struggle and sacrifice on behalf of workers.[18]

In her mid-seventies, a wondrous change came about in Vorse's life. Her long, aching concern over family relationships dwindled and finally disappeared. Although he had little money, Heaton seemed happy enough in his life as a writer and musician. Joel had a successful career as a television producer and director in New York. When Ellen divorced the artist Jack Beauchamp in 1948, she did not return to Cape Cod, but worked at a series of service jobs in the West. Her decision to join Alcoholics Anonymous marked a complete reversal in Ellen's life style. As she conquered her alcohol addiction, she also found a new stability and contentment through religion. In 1951, Ellen married the attorney Frederick "Archie" Boyden and lived with him until her death in an automobile accident in the 1970s.

Vorse's relations with her children had always been intense, more egalitarian than parental. In her last years, the old wounds healed. She lived long enough to enjoy her children's middle-age maturity, and she was richly graced with their love and respect. In the twenty years before Vorse's death, Ellen wrote her several times each week, long, newsy letters filled with warmth and concern. After all the countless, heartbreaking scenes of battle, reconciliation with Ellen seemed a miracle. Now, in classic fashion, it was time for the daughter to play the part of nurturing parent, and for the aging mother to assume the role of coddled child. Vorse could also count on the steady and loving attention of her sons. The children customarily returned with Vorse's grandchildren to spend several weeks of their summer vacation in Provincetown each year. Now—at last—Vorse had the time to prepare their favorite meals, settle down to animated political conversations, play with her grandchildren, quietly relish her children and their companionship.

For over forty years Vorse had been tortured with the belief that her greatest failure in life was as a mother. Now, near the end of her life, she saw that as untraditional as her children were, they were also clearheaded social thinkers who greatly admired her accomplishments. She was uncommonly proud of their commitment to progressive politics. Heaton, as highly political as herself, wrote for the local newspaper. (In the 1980s, Heaton would appear as one of the twelve "witnesses" in Warren Beatty's movie *Reds*, the story of John Reed and the Greenwich Village crowd.) Vorse's younger son, Joel, received the National Brotherhood Award in 1960 from the National Conference of Christians and Jews for a public service production that discussed restrictive housing practices in the United States. In 1961, Ellen joined a small group of inspired peace marchers who protested the production of nuclear weapons.

Clearly, Vorse's maternal wisdom had not been so frail, after all. Quite unlike herself, her children had embraced their mother's most important beliefs and most cherished values and made them their own. With that knowledge there came to Vorse a serene peace, more meaningful, more precious, because so long denied.

Disillusioned by labor politics and excluded from the arena, Vorse returned to investigative reporting, publishing her last major piece at seventy-eight.[19] Based on six months of research on waterfront crime in New York, the article won national attention. Walter Winchell predicted it would be made into a play. A condensed version appeared in the high-circulation *Reader's Digest*. The story was a grand finale to her forty years as a labor journalist.

"The Pirate's Nest of New York," published in *Harper's Magazine* in 1952, shows Vorse at the height of her reportorial skill. Her tale of greed, murder, courage, and even humor, leaves the reader informed and infuriated. Here one finds documented evidence, complete with names of mobsters who dominated the union local, parceled out the jobs, took the kickbacks, and ran the rackets. Vorse's work, along with that of a few other star reporters like Murray Kempton and Malcolm Johnson, aroused public interest in waterfront crime and its causes and led to the establishment of a commission, which made some reforms. *Harper's* gave the piece a long introduction, praising her as "not only the dean of American labor reporters but also one of the most active and indefatigable. She has been writing for *Harper's* for almost fifty years (since 1906 to be exact) and we don't know any reporter of either sex or of any age who can dig out a tough and explosive story with more energy, imaginative grasp, and human kindness." These were heady words but not so fulfilling as the attention she received at the CIO convention that year: "When people rush up to me and say they have been longing to meet me and that my book has been a turning point in their lives . . . it is like a Turkish bath of ego building. . . . This year they're all saying that I got these crime hearings going through my piece in *Harper's*." [20]

Vorse moved to New York while tracing the connection of waterfront crime to politicians, businessmen, and union leaders. Her son Heaton served as her researcher in areas near the docks where the presence of any woman, much less an elderly one, would have created an immediate sensation. Vorse spent weeks arranging clandestine meetings, talking to dissident members of the gangster-ridden International Longshoremen's Association (ILA), and coaxing friends and widows of murdered men to talk to her about the mob terror that ruled the docks.

Her most adventurous interview was with Anthony (Tony "Bang Bang") Anastasia, hiring boss of the Brooklyn piers, prominent official in the ILA, and brother of the notorious Albert, of Murder, Inc. For years afterward, Vorse loved to describe her meeting with Anthony Anastasia, no doubt embellishing the details as the story grew. She had dressed carefully one morning, put on a demure lace collar and a prim black hat with a long face veil, and gone to his Brooklyn office. She found him in an expansive mood. Perhaps he was amused by the incongruous appearance of this pleasant and seemingly eccentric old lady. Playing the role to the hilt, Vorse fed him adoring smiles. He answered her questions with good humor, despite the worried protestations of an employee who sat beside him. "It's OK, she's harmless," Anastasia assured his companion. Finally, his underling's warnings grew more insistent and Vorse was ushered courteously from the room. Certainly it never occurred to Anastasia that the nice old grandmother who had wandered into his office might be a famous labor reporter. [21]

Despite the triumph of her waterfront story, Vorse's return to Yaddo in 1954 made her feel an outdated ancient. The atmosphere was so strikingly different from her last stay at the writers' retreat twenty-two years before that she could think of nothing else. She wrote a great deal in her diary about what she saw as the younger generation's loss of political content in both their work and their lives. The writer Jeannette Andrews remembered that Vorse often entertained the other residents in the evenings with stories about past labor battles. The other guests may have been less enthralled than Vorse imagined and only listened courteously to an old woman's blissful recitation of lost and better days.[22]

Mary Vorse talks too much, tries to monopolize every conversation, and has lived too long, Ann Craton Blankenhorn wrote Jo Herbst a few years later. "Mary looks ancient, fragile, weak, walks very slowly . . . petulant, nervous and poor . . . still wanting to go somewhere—anywhere—for the sake of going."

> I know she is afraid of being alone, and her need for seeing people . . . is to escape from herself and her fears—old age, illness, no money. But I have decided she has no inner life. . . . Her constant going in her young and youngest days was based on her inability to be alone, even briefly. There is no such thing now as living quietly with books and one's own reflections. . . . She must be here to telephone all and sundry in order to be invited for lunch or dinner —she counts on those free meals to pay her room rent. She is too tired and too feeble to go so much, and she looks terrible. . . . She wants talk and to talk. . . . The hell of it is that is what happens when one lives on and on.[23]

Other reminders of her advanced years were the frequent inquiries from eager scholars. Would she discuss with the researcher her memory of the Provincetown Players? Eugene O'Neill? the Wobblies? the staff of the *Masses*? Then there was the group of efficient archivists, anticipating her death, who wrote to ask about the possibility of acquiring her papers for their university libraries. This pleased her immensely. With an archive, she was assured a special kind of immortality as an important person with a unique perspective. Periodically during the ten years before her death, Vorse spent many months sorting through her boxes of letters, diaries, clippings, manuscripts, culling from the mass only what she could not bear to reveal but leaving most of it intact. Reading through the accumulated data of over sixty years of living encouraged a pensive self-analysis for which she had never made time before. She added corrective notes, cautionary reminders, and illuminating references to earlier materials, carefully dating the new remarks. The bits of paper stashed about her house in nooks and closets took on new significance—the basis for her place in history.

During her last years, Vorse's life assumed a different kind of literary prominence. Her experience was put to symbolic use by two well known authors, John Dos Passos and Murray Kempton. Dos Passos presented her as the character Anne Comfort in his thinly disguised autobiographical novel, *Chosen Country*, published in 1951. Four years later, Murray Kempton wrote a lengthy piece about her in *Part of Our Time*, his study of the radicals of the thirties. Vorse was flattered by their attention to her life, although she feigned an attitude of indifference in one case, and annoyance in the other.

Chosen Country is the first in a series of three novels about American life Dos Passos planned as a sort of sequel to the trilogy *U.S.A.* In the fifties Dos Passos viewed the world as an archconservative. Thus the hero of *Chosen Country*, a fictionalized version of Dos Passos himself, is made sad and wise beyond his years through his youthful brush with radicalism. He manages to escape leftist influence and embraces the American way. Dos Passos wrote the novel as a memorial to his beloved Katy and their life together. He used fictionalized sketches of people he knew to represent strands of American experience. The real-life models for his characters were easily identifiable by those readers who knew Dos Passos well. Beside Katy and John Dos Passos, there appeared their relatives, friends of their youth, and people Dos Passos had met in Paris, New York City, and Provincetown. Dos Passos again showed his fascination with the personality of Mary Vorse. His presentation of Anne Comfort, in a chapter entitled "Footnote on Social Consciousness," is an unmistakable description of Vorse's affair with Robert Minor, who appears in the novel as Carl Humphries.

As a young woman, Anne Comfort knew she wanted a career. She entered an unhappy marriage, lived in pre–World War I Greenwich Village and gave birth to a son and daughter. Like Mary Vorse, Anne Comfort took up the habit of writing in bed and soon became a literary success. In 1914 she, like Vorse, was sent to Europe to write about the effect of war on the civilian population. Having shed her husband, Comfort returned to Europe after the war in the hope that she could "describe the aftermath of war in such terms that people would see the horror and futility of it all."

In Paris in 1919, Dos Passos had observed the meeting and early courtship of Mary Vorse and Robert Minor. In *Chosen Country*, the same scene is replayed when Anne Comfort encounters the American newspaperman Carl Humphries in Paris and falls in love with him at once. Fresh from the Soviet Union and Germany, and afire with revolutionary ideals, Humphries introduces her to a host of French radicals. Comfort pays the bills for Humphries, while he absent-mindedly pockets her change. "Carl walked so fast Anne had trouble keeping up with him. He looked straight ahead and talked in staccato sentences" about the march of the working class, with winded Anne "trotting at his heels. After that night she was only happy when she was with Carl."

Back in Greenwich Village after Paris, Humphries was often away on mysterious political business. Comfort waited patiently for his return and wrote silly love stories, "full of false values, to pay the grocery bills." After the war, her fiction didn't sell so well. Yet "the new radical magazines that came out after the wartime suppressions and the skimpy labor newspapers were delighted to publish her work, but they didn't pay. It all confirmed Anne in Carl's opinion that capitalism was rotten and revolution was the only cure. The trouble was that she had a lot of mouths to feed until the great day came. . . . She was always in debt. . . . When Carl was home it was worse because he insisted on her giving him so much money for the movement." Like Robert Minor, Carl Humphries was egotistical and growing deaf. Soon after his return from Paris, Humphries abruptly dumped Comfort to marry a woman more sympathetic to his politics. In *U.S.A.* Mary French had also been rejected by her Communist lover. But unlike Mary French, Anne Comfort weathers this moment of desertion with some grace. After all, "meetings and the movement took up her life, and of course she had the children and her career."

Once again, as in *U.S.A.*, Dos Passos hauled out the old affair with Robert Minor as the central clue to Mary Vorse's personality. But Anne Comfort's radicalism had no more solid base than her love for Carl Humphries, whose role in the novel is the Communist villain without humanity or intellect. Anne Comfort, a well-meaning do-gooder, worshiped a flawed male deity, who in turn pursued the false God of the Party. In the end, both gods failed.[24]

The slur cast by Dos Passos on Mary Vorse's life was apparent. For him, a woman had no place in politics, radical or otherwise. If she were involved in matters of the world, her activity could only be dictated by a man. If a woman were manless, her political interests could only be compensation for her failure to realize the female destiny through a man. The story of Mary Vorse and Robert Minor was an admirable device to symbolize the betrayal of American idealists by communism, but Dos Passos returned to it for another, more important reason: The tale of Robert Minor's lack of concern for a decent woman, whose only fault was to love him too blindly, is another attempt by Dos Passos to deal with his central trauma regarding the relationship between his own parents. Above all, Dos Passos saw Mary Vorse as he saw his mother—good, brave, weak, and in need of protection from the admired and powerful, but essentially cruel male whom she foolishly loved.[25]

Vorse left no comment in her archival collection about her response to her portrayal in *Chosen Country*. She had seen very little of Dos Passos since Katy's death, and she felt guilty that she had not visited him in the nearby hospital during his recovery from the accident that killed Katy. By 1951, Dos Passos had become so reactionary that Vorse and most of her friends could no longer take his writing very seriously. Perhaps her disdain for his political art helped to soften the anger she must have felt toward him after the publication of *Chosen Country*.

Unlike Dos Passos's portrayal of Vorse, Murray Kempton's use of her life in *Part of Our Time: Some Ruins and Monuments of the Thirties* is not fictionally rendered. It is a direct statement of Kempton's vision of her as one of the few monuments among the ruins. She stands as representative of the American radical, rare in any era, "who dared to stand alone, to whom no man called out in vain, to whom the lie was dishonorable and the crawl degrading."

Published in 1955, *Part of Our Time* is marked by that close attention to the issue of American communism inevitably present in serious political works of that time. But Kempton is no shrill anti-Communist. His book is meant to show the pathos of the lives of those Communists and ex-Communists who were driven by ignorance, desperation, or social conscience into living a lie that finally left them tragic human ruins. Kempton belittles the fear of Communist influence held by HUAC and McCarthy supporters. He argues that American Communists, the dominant radical group of the thirties, were relatively unimportant in furthering the immense change in American society actually produced by fighting union members and New Deal officials. Briefly associated with the Communists himself in the thirties, Kempton concludes: "We were only a part of our time; it was our illusion that we were the most important part, but most Americans knew that we were not, and they were right."[26]

Part of Our Time, now recognized as a classic on the thirties, is a series of perceptive novellas about real-life persons who held a revolutionary view of society in that decade. It is also a roll call of many of Vorse's friends and acquaintances. Gardner "Pat" Jackson, Edmund Wilson, John Dos Passos, Sherwood Anderson, Malcolm Cowley, Albert Maltz, Philip Murray, and Walter, Victor, and Roy Reuther appear, as do other dissidents like Whittaker Chambers, Paul Robeson, Alger Hiss, Joe Curran, and Jim Farrell.

Kempton's portrayal of Mary Vorse is deeply, almost achingly, admiring. In contrast to the Communists he describes, whom he presents as generally without compassion or sophistication, Vorse has been driven by the purest motive of all—the fight for justice: "In all her life, Mary Heaton Vorse has had no involvements which did not lie upon the outermost extremities of love." She represents for him the "rebel girl" of Wobbly imagination:

> The scorned and ragged rebels of the first three decades of the century might logically have considered the thirties a time of redemption in which their survivors would be treated as triumphant saints. It does not appear to have been that way for Mary Vorse, who in any case would hardly have asked so much. . . . Mary Vorse lived on because she found her love young and neither forsook nor was forsaken. For Mary Vorse had joined the avenging army in 1913, because men and women were suffering for its triumph.

"And there will be nothing bitter in her so long as she lives," Kempton wrote. "As Yeats said of another dedicated old lady, she needed upon her difficult road no spur of hate."

Kempton's portrayal of Mary Vorse left her at a CIO convention in 1949, during a coal strike.

> She bore up under all the attentions for three days. Then the things of state were too much for her, and she went back to the coal mines, saying . . . "There's an old fellow in Charleroi I knew long ago in the Wobblies. He always tells me what's going on. I'll have to tell Phil [Murray]; he'll remember him. One of the old fellows, one of the very old ones."
>
> And she was gone to the bus station, her legs a little stiff, her eyes a little rheumy, because she was, after all, seventy-five years old. To have pledged yourself and to have forsaken all others for forty years, to have understood that to love is to abandon sleep and comfort and the ease of age, and to follow, always to follow, the desperate road love sets out for you, such was the limit of the rebel girl's commitment. Mary Vorse sat in her bus as upon a burnished throne.

If Mary Vorse held no great place in men's memory called history, that was her own choice, Kempton wrote. In all the battles she wrote about, there was little about herself in the story. Having "abandoned all sense of profit," she simply followed her hard road, carefully recording "the conversations of persons in trouble," even in her old age "still in the game, talking to the longshoremen the other reporters neglected for a series on the New York waterfront."

Like Dos Passos, Kempton felt compelled to bring up Vorse's affair with Robert Minor, but mentions Minor in only two short references. One sentence reads: "She was married awhile to Robert Minor, then a distinguished cartoonist and afterwards a Communist functionary." The other states that when Vorse attended the 1949 CIO convention, she was so beloved by unionists that "Mary Vorse could have walked into that convention with Bob Minor on her arm, and Philip Murray, the CIO's president, would have been glad to shake his hand."

These references hardly seem to justify the rage Vorse felt toward Kempton for hanging "poor dead Minor like an albatross around my neck," as she wrote in her diary.[27] Her anger was partially a delayed reaction to Dos Passo's attack on her in *Chosen Country*. It was also an outraged protest against the assumptions of a male-made world, which sought to define a woman's life and work chiefly through her relationship to a man.

It was actually not Kempton's book, but Richard Rovere's major review of it in the *New Yorker*, that most infuriated her. In his extensive piece, Rovere crammed into one very long sentence his entire discussion of Kempton's lengthy portrayal of the women characters in *Part of Our Time*. Rovere wrote: "The chilling story of Elizabeth Bentley, the plain, meek, respectable Vassar girl who became the mistress and slavey of a Soviet spy, and the chilling story of Ann Moos Remington, the hard case from Bennington who made her Dartmouth boy friend, the late William Remington, promise that he would never, never be unfaithful to the Communist Party, are told, along with that of Mary Heaton Vorse, a gay and venerable libertarian lady—never a Communist, though once fleetingly associated in matrimony with a man who later became one—of more deeply revolutionary instincts than either Miss Bentley or the former Mrs. Remington."[28]

Was there no end to male arrogance? Did all her years of writing and struggle come to nothing more than that? Would she survive in history as a footnote—an appendage to the lesser life of Robert Minor?

Vorse came to regret deeply her initial rejection of Kempton's piece. At a meeting of journalists following the publication of *Part of Our Time*, she discovered that "since Murray Kempton's book I have become a legend. . . . I am always being introduced as our great (or greatest) reporter." Later, at a union convention, she wrote: "I have a feeling that I have hurt Murray Kempton badly. He meant to pay me the highest compliment he probably could in calling me the Rebel Girl and the descendent of Joe Hill. I am afraid he is right. I went into the labor movement with the singing of the Wobblies in my ears. He meant to give me a little bit of immortality. He meant to clear away the rumor that I was communist—and I didn't even write him a line. . . . Murray will never forgive me and no wonder for not having thanked him for his book and his extravagant words of praise. He has been very cool ever since and didn't ask me to lunch yesterday." A year later she wrote in her diary, "Last night I read over what Murray Kempton wrote about me. . . . Surely no one had a few pages of such tenderness written about them. . . . I had not really read it in context until now. My [original] appalled reaction shows my self-protective coloration. . . . Now I see a skillful apologetic [in the reference to Minor] . . . to put me right as it were. The whole piece is a legend. How sensitive and aware the mind that wrote this."[29]

———

"Mary Vorse had gone on far past her time for going on," Murray Kempton wrote in 1955. That very year, perhaps not coincidentally, Mary Vorse left "the hard road of her choice," which he had described. At age eighty-one, she retired to her cherished Provincetown. She did not deceive herself. She knew this homecoming was the final one. Labor would have to find its way without her presence at the hot spots. The world could rock along without her reporting. As Kempton knew, even though "the chronicles which cover her life span had small room for her name," Vorse "brought to her old age no need for survival. She had been not *in* history but *of* history."[30]

Her retirement was chosen and purposeful. It meant time for reading, for family and friends, for picking and canning beach plums. It promised long summer swims and the slow meandering walks she loved to take over the dunes to the sea. She felt healthy and welcomed the years left for leisure. And she had plans for writing two stories needing to be told— how it felt to grow old and what she had learned about men and women. That would be enough. "The house was mine," she wrote. "With an indescribable feeling of peace I settled back into it."[31]

Chapter Eighteen

Serene Plateau

Vorse filled the slow retirement days with gardening, housework, reading, and meals with new friends, chiefly young people, many of them aspiring artists or writers, who either sought her out or rented one of the nine bedrooms in her house. She continued to write, almost daily for a while, but the old pressure of making a living was lifted from her. Rental income and charity from friends or from labor or literary organizations carried her through. Although she had nothing to spare for extras, she did not feel impoverished, for she had time enough at last to putter, to do nothing at all.

She had enjoyed general good health all her life, partly because she relished strenuous exercise. Until her late eighties, she took long daily walks whenever the weather allowed, about town or out Snail Road to the sea. At eighty-two, Vorse was swimming in the bay near her home. A careless boat driver did not see her in the water. The hull of the boat gave her a smart crack on the head as it skimmed past. The nearly fatal accident did not frighten so much as infuriate her.[1]

The experience of aging intrigued her. More out of habit than intention, she organized her thoughts into a book outline and even roughed out a few chapters. People became "old," she wrote, because younger people treated their elders as incompetent: "I . . . have friends whom I love that I don't see because their quivering eagerness to help me get up, sit down, cross the street, get in a car, prevents any reasonable conversation."[2]

Thinking of the times in her past when she had been most happy—as an art student in Paris, during the summer of 1909 when she broke free from her attachment to Bert, "most of all, the times of hard work"—she knew she would not want to relive those days, because she was now having another experience—that of old age—which she did not want to leave. The youthful vitality of spirit she sustained as an old woman is wonderfully expressed in an entry written early one summer morning in 1964, when she was almost ninety years old.

> One of the strangest things of age is the suddenly glimpsing oneself in the mirror. Here I am, waking with the dawn, feeling like the Valkyrie. . . . Then I watch the houses nearby become incandescent, eager for the day. Unable to keep in the house and making an excuse, [that] I need a breath of air [I go out to] the back of the barn. I toss the branches George has sawed off from the barn into the porch, only coming back because I have to pay the coal man, feeling full of joy and health. Then I catch sight of the dour aging creature in the glass. She walks uncertainly, she is toothless, she has no relation to the way I feel. True, I know I move uncertainly and slowly, but very surely. But the gaiety I feel at the light and simplest outdoor tasks, where is it? There is [instead] this aged creature who has no relation to my feeling of joy in life.[3]

During the early years of Vorse's retirement, the Cold War witch hunt continued to dominate political life. Beginning in the late forties, more than a hundred Communist leaders were indicted and convicted under the Smith Act, for alleged conspiracy to advocate the overthrow of the government. Elizabeth Gurley Flynn, who had joined the party in 1936, was imprisoned for over two years. "Walter Lippmann thinks we're out of the McCarthy woods," Vorse wrote in 1956. "I say not so long as people like Elizabeth are in jail." After Flynn's release, Vorse, at age eighty-five, traveled to New York to meet with her old friend. The two aged rebels, whose political paths had often converged, enjoyed one last spirited evening together.[4]

By the mid-fifties, the American Communist movement that had so affected Vorse's political life was near dissolution. When the government began the arrest of "second-string" party leaders like Flynn in 1951, the party undertook an internal purge and became an underground organization. In 1956, Nikita Krushchev publicly exposed Stalin's crimes. A majority of the remaining American Communists either left the party then or called for democratization of party machinery and freedom from Soviet direction. The Soviet intervention in Hungary was a final blow to the hopes of many party members. By the summer of 1958 the party numbered only about three thousand. As Maurice Isserman so aptly phrased the matter in 1982: "It had taken the Communists a quarter of a century to learn that the American left could not be built on foreign models; that civil liberties and democratic institutions should be at the center of any vision of an American socialist future; and that Marxists had as much to learn from other political traditions as they had to teach about American political realities."[5] This was precisely the lesson Vorse had grasped over sixty years earlier.

In the spring of 1959, Vorse managed one last trip to a strike scene. Boarding a bus, she traveled alone to Henderson, North Carolina, where the Textile Workers Union of America (TWUA) was leading a strike of over one thousand workers, 60 percent of them women. She witnessed again the labor battle she had known so many times, so many years. There was the intransigent employer, the generally hostile state press, the strike-breakers entering the plant under the protection of the soldiers, the angry workers watching sullenly. Once again she toured the workers' houses, was shown the bullet holes in the walls and the probable location of the gun-man when he fired, told the stories of assaults on the union leaders, heard the tales of struggle and defeat. One of her last memories of the South "was of a frightened boy who looked younger than his nineteen years, accompanied by his indignant mother. He had been sentenced to sixty days or *three years* parole for possession of pyrotechnics, in other words, a giant firecracker, illegal in North Carolina, while two strikebreakers whose car was full of guns, which they were about to carry into the mill, received only a suspended sentence."[6]

Vorse received two hundred dollars from the TWUA for her story on Henderson. But the trip to North Carolina at the age of eighty-five proved too strenuous. On her way home to Provincetown, she stopped in Wash-ington, D.C. to visit Neith Boyce's daughter. While there, Vorse experi-enced a stroke that caused the left side of her face to fall and slurred her speech. She did not attempt to write again. When the Alfred Knopf pub-lishing house asked her to write her memoirs of the twenties and thirties, she agreed to do so, but never attempted the task. To her dismay, the stroke affected her memory. She often experienced "a peculiar sense that my brains are sticking to my skull. . . . It actually *hurts* to think."[7]

From the late fifties until her death, Vorse survived on funds from others. Ann Craton Blankenhorn and the reporter Louis Lochner were the greatest help, arranging that Vorse receive grants of twenty-five hundred dollars from the League of Mutual Aid and from the Overseas Press Club. The Amalgamated Clothing Workers and the Authors' League of America sent more than a thousand dollars to assist her in her recovery from the stroke. In 1963, the Correspondents' Fund sent another twelve hundred.[8]

Vorse traveled to the United Auto Workers' convention in 1957 to accept the honorary membership the union awarded her. But when she attended another labor convention in 1961, Ann Craton Blankenhorn was incensed at the expense of the trip: "I am told that old Mary Vorse who last spring looked so ancient and decrepit with a heavy cane . . . revived during the summer . . . and took herself to Miami to the recent convention," Blankenhorn wrote Margaret Larkin Maltz. "Why she wanted to go to . . . a most depressing affair I can't see. How she got there nobody knows. . . . I knew she had the last $150 from the Fund which for the first and last time I sent her in a lump sum, rather than a monthly check. . . . To think that extravagant old gal would use it to go to an unimportant convention because she still considers herself an important labor writer is something."[9]

Fortunately, Vorse's benefactors did not know how she spent the donations sent to her during her last years. Beginning in 1956 she regularly sent a large portion of her tiny income to various civil rights groups in the South. In 1965, one year before her death, Vorse mailed a check to César Chavez and the farmworkers. Her world was stirring again. She had to be part of the process.

When Victor Reuther learned of her need for money he began a campaign in 1961 to elicit the help of UAW officials. The union bureaucracy moved slowly. It was over a year before the officers agreed to send Vorse a donation of a thousand dollars. Because Victor Reuther was reluctant to embarrass her with outright charity, someone suggested that she be given a special award in the name of grateful auto workers, along with an "honorarium" of a thousand. Warming to the idea, Walter Reuther invited Vorse to attend the 1962 UAW convention in Atlantic City as an honored guest. There she would receive the first Social Justice Award, originally conceived to pay her recognition, in a special ceremony at the formal convention dinner.

In May 1962, Vorse entered the UAW Twenty-fifth Anniversary Celebration on Walter Reuther's arm. The assemblage parted to make way—a swirl of applause, smiles, popping flashbulbs. Before the audience of over three thousand people, which included her son Joel, his wife, and Vorse's two granddaughters, Walter Reuther presented her with the golden shield of the Social Justice Award: "With admiration, affection and in thankful appreciation for your years of dedicated and unselfish devotion to the cause of labor and our common struggles to extend the frontiers of social justice. Through your years of writing you have been a continuing source of hope and inspiration to workers as they fought to win fuller and richer lives for their families."

Eleanor Roosevelt and Upton Sinclair were there to share her honor, all faces turned to her, everyone applauding in a long, standing ovation. The photographs show Vorse as a frail woman supported by others, wearing a new brocaded jacket, her large eyes predominant in an aged face lightened and softened by pleasure. She was eighty-eight, now the grand old lady of labor, again the living symbol of a heroic era. The members of the cheering audience fused for that one moment, imposing on her their deeply cherished, bigger-than-life memories of courage, struggle, meaning.

Her acceptance speech was short. "The bucket of life is full," Vorse said simply.[10]

Four more years were left to her. She spent them quietly, fully alert to the last, living with her son Heaton in her beach home. He provided tender care. All her children were safe. Her place in history was secure. Her ideals would survive. Other generations would be rising to defend them.

In the early sixties, Vorse helped to organize a Provincetown protest against the dumping of nuclear waste. In 1963, she testified before a congressional committee in support of the successful effort to preserve the Cape Cod back country and beach in a national park. Two years later, at ninety-one, she began her last campaign. She backed Provincetown's young Episcopalian minister who would be one of the first to march against the Vietnam War. Twenty years after her death, he recalled: "Many church people were horrified by my liberal politics. I knew that Mary Vorse was the intellectual and spiritual giant of the town. The emotional support she offered was very, very important to me at the time."[11]

On June 14, 1966, Vorse arose early. As was her custom, she read the morning newspapers in bed. The daily press reflected the uneasy truce of the time, on the eve of major new confrontations with the old injustice. It was the day that the Supreme Court, under Chief Justice Earl Warren, announced the Miranda decision limiting the power of the police to question suspects in their custody. Leftist students marched in Panama in opposition to new U.S. arrangements for the Canal Zone. Through heavy rains, civil rights demonstrators walked in Mississippi, across bright red, foot-high letters painted on the pavement of Highway 51 which spelled:

"Red [read] nigger and run. If you cant red, run away—KKK." Some of the black leaders called for armed self-defense. In Los Angeles, Ronald Reagan won financial support from wealthy Republicans in his race for the California governorship, and prepared for a fund-raiser party to be addressed by Richard Nixon at the Sports Arena. In labor circles, George Meany and Walter Reuther fought over Meany's opposition to the International Labor Organization Conference, which had elected a Polish Communist to head the session. That day, the National Student Association released a report calling for radical reshaping of college curriculums judged irrelevant and alienating. In 1966 the newspapers still featured a "Woman's Page," which presented menus, society news, and reports of new success in skin care.

The front page of the day focused on the news from South Vietnam. Five hundred Buddhist demonstrators in Saigon, carrying a letter accusing Lyndon Johnson of having turned "deaf ears to our cry for human decency and human rights," burned two jeeps and were halted in their attempt to march on the U.S. embassy by riot police. At Hue, where two monks and twenty youths were arrested, residents placed thousands of small household Buddhist altars in the streets as a gesture of passive resistance to the military regime of South Vietnam's Premier Nguyen Cao Ky.

At noon, Heaton brought her lunch in bed. The Buddhist demonstrations had greatly disturbed her. She and Heaton discussed various options, as she pondered what she might do personally to protest the continuation of the war. Heaton walked downtown in mid-afternoon on some errands. When he returned, he found her still in bed, dead of a heart attack at ninety-two, her morning reading spread about her on the covers.

The funeral was a small affair, for she had outlived her close friends, and lost contact with her colleagues in the labor movement, most of whom were too infirm to travel to Provincetown anyway. Besides, the death of a woman who had lived so long and well as she was not a tragic loss, but a natural event, which one honored best with merely a quiet pause for reflection. Walter Reuther could not attend the last rites, but he sent his representative to Provincetown—the first woman to sit on the UAW executive board—and issued a press release:

> She was one of the great labor writers of all time. While still young, she gave up a bright literary future to devote her great talent to reporting labor's struggles for justice and freedom in this country. At a time when accurate, much less sympathetic reporting was a novelty, she wrote with deep compassion of the human need for working class people. . . . Mary Heaton Vorse was part of the UAW.

This magnificent woman responded to every call for help during the early days of the sitdown. . . . Gentle in manner, Mary Heaton Vorse was a woman of invincible spirit and fearless courage.[12]

Just as she had always planned and hoped for, Mary Heaton Vorse was buried on the cemetery hill above Provincetown, where the beat of the distant foghorn can be heard around the clock. She wanted sea, sky, and earth on her tombstone. The red granite carries carvings of a seahorse and a gull in flight.

Notes and Index

Notes

Archives and Manuscript Collections
and Abbreviations

AJL   Jones Library, Special Collections, Amherst, Massachusetts

AMSS Amherst, Massachusetts, Superintendent of Schools, High School
      Records

CHS   Chicago Historical Society, Chicago, Illinois
 AW   Albert Weisbord Papers
 VBW   Vera Buch Weisbord Papers

CU   Columbia University, Oral History Collection, New York, New York
 MHV   Mary Heaton Vorse

FBI   Federal Bureau of Investigation Case Files, in possession of author
 EGF   Elizabeth Gurley Flynn
 RM   Robert Minor
 MHV   Mary Heaton Vorse

FBI-IR Investigative Case Files of the Bureau of Investigation, 1902–1922,
      Record Group 65, National Archives, Washington, D.C.

FDR   Franklin D. Roosevelt Library, Hyde Park, New York
 GJ   Gardner Jackson Papers

HI   Hoover Institution on War, Revolution and Peace Archives, Stanford
      University, Stanford, California
 ARA   American Relief Administration Papers
 TTCG   T.T.C. Gregory Papers

NMPR	Probate Records and Deed Records, County Courthouse, Northampton, Massachusetts
NPL	Northampton Public Library, Special Collections, Northampton, Massachusetts
NYSL	New York State Library, Albany, New York
LC	Lusk Committee Papers, New York State Committee to Investigate Seditious Activities
PHS	Pottsville, Pennsylvania, Historical Society, Archives
PU	Princeton University, Archives, Princeton, New Jersey
ACLU	American Civil Liberties Union Papers
AB	Arthur Bullard Papers
SC	Swarthmore College Peace Collection, Swarthmore, Pennsylvania
EB	Emily Balch Papers
WILPF	Women's International League for Peace and Freedom Papers
UC	University of California, Archives, Bancroft Library, Berkeley, California
ASWW	Anna Strunsky, William Walling Papers
UNA	United Nations Archive, New York, New York, Personnel File, Mary Heaton Vorse
UV	University of Vermont, Archives, Burlington, Vermont
UVAL	University of Virginia, Alderman Library, Archives, Charlottesville, Virginia
JDP	John Dos Passos Papers
JL	Jett Lauck Papers
WSU	Wayne State University, Walter Reuther Library, Archives of Labor and Urban Affairs, Detroit, Michigan
ACB	Ann Craton Blankenhorn Papers
HB	Heber Blankenhorn Papers
RD	Robert Dunn Papers
CH	Carl Haessler Papers
MVK	Mary Van Kleek Papers
DHK	Dorothy and Henry Kraus Oral History
HK	Henry Kraus Papers
HO	Harvey O'Connor Papers
VR	Victor Reuther Papers
UAW	United Auto Workers Papers
MHV	Mary Heaton Vorse Papers
YUB	Yale University, Beinecke Library, New Haven, Connecticut
NBHH	Neith Boyce and Hutchins Hapgood Papers
JH	Josephine Herbst Papers
MDL	Mabel Dodge Luhan Papers
EW	Edmund Wilson Papers

YUS	Yale University, Sterling Library, New Haven, Connecticut
AB	Alfred Bingham Papers
JC	John Collier Papers
EH	Edward House Papers
HW	Harry Weinberger Papers

Interviews

Jeannette Andrews	Emily Hiebert
Martha Stone Asher	Phyllis Higgins
Justin Avelar	Clingnan Jackson
John Bebout	Dodie Jackson
Jerry Beck	Antoinette La Selle
Fay Blake	Steve Nelson
Betty Bruce	Jill O'Brien
Toby Bruce	Joel O'Brien
Vera Buch	Sally O'Brien
Catherine Cabral	Harvey O'Connor
Angela Campana	Jessie O'Connor
Nea Colton	Myra Page
Grace Cullinson	John Patrick
Sam D'Arcy	Gail Poltrack
Len DeCaux	Ed Salt
Peggy Dennis	Warren Silva
John Dewitt	Helen Tierney
Miriam Dewitt	Ernest Vanderburgh
Joseph Dutra	Heaton Vorse
Sophie Melvin Gerson	Adelaide Walker
Mary Hackett	Isabel Whelan
John Hammond	William Weinberg
Nat Halper	Hazel Hawthorne Werner

Chapter One: Amherst

1. "Deed of Sale," Hiram Heaton, Book 350 (1879), NMPR; Dr. Roger Denio Baker to author, June 30, 1980; the Heaton house was sold after Mary Vorse's father's death to the author Ray Stannard Baker. MHV, "Footnote to History," Boxes 1, 2, WSU-MHV; unless otherwise cited, quotes in this chapter are from this source.

2. Edward W. Carpenter and Charles F. Morehouse, *The History of the Town of Amherst* (Amherst: Press of Carpenter and Morehouse, 1896); Alice M. Walker, *Sketches of Amherst History* (Amherst: Press of Carpenter and Morehouse, 1901); *Essays on Amherst's History* (Amherst: Vista Trust, 1978); for Amherst Woman's Club yearbooks, city directories, Amherst Valuations of Taxes and Insurance, see AJL.

3. Field cited in Robert Conrow, *Field Days* (New York: Charles Scribner's, 1974), 60. Dickinson and Todd cited in John E. Walsh, *The Hidden Life of Emily*

Dickinson (New York: Simon and Schuster, 1971), 146, 24. Dickinson's poem, Number 401, in Thomas A. Johnson, ed., *The Complete Poems of Emily Dickinson* (Boston: Little, Brown, 1960), 191. Also see MHV's view of Amherst in "The Hidden Spring," Box 21, WSU-MHV.

4. MHV, "Conflict," Box 18, WSU-MHV.

5. Mary Adele Allen, *Around a Village Green: Sketches of Life in Amherst* (Northampton, Mass.: Kraushar Press, 1939), 69.

6. Genealogy of Ellen's family in Henry Blackman Plumb, *The Blackmans, Darrows, Bouses, Joneses, Collingses, Stearnesses, Strains, Plumbs, Hydes*, 1894, NPL; MHV, "Family Tree," Box 153, and "Family Legends," Box 20, and Ellen to MHV, Box 73, WSU-MHV; MHV's Application for Membership, Daughters of the American Revolution, November 26, 1899, in possession of author, traces the family tree to a revolutionary soldier who served as representative to the Connecticut Assembly. Ellen's marriage is discussed in the Burlington *Free Press*, October 13, June 2, 1852. "Grassmounte," *Modern Health Crusader of Vermont*, October, November, 1936, 1; and Pauline Burridge, "Glimpses of Grassmounte," *Vermont Alumni Weekly*, December 3, 10, 1930, January 14, 1931; all in UV. For Marvin genealogy, see George Grankling Marvin and William T. R. Marvin, *Descendants of Reinhold and Matthew Marvin* (Boston: T. R. Marvin and Son, 1906). The San Francisco City Directory, 1860–1862, UC, describes Charles Marvin as a liquor merchant.

7. Orlando Pond to Hiram Heaton, August 25, 1904, Box 49, WSU-MHV; Heaton Treadway to author, July 11, 1980. MHV, "New York Childhood," Box 27, WSU-MHV. Throughout her adult years, MHV habitually misstated her correct age. For example, her passport of 1915 gives 1879 as her birthdate, while her passport of 1921 cites the year 1881. Her tombstone in Provincetown, Mass., lists 1882 as the date of birth. The evidence for the correct date of her birth is in, U.S. Census Bureau, Manuscript Census, 1880, Population Schedules, Amherst, Massachusetts; Hiram Heaton to MHV, October 10, 1900, Box 48, WSU-MHV; Amherst High School Records, 1894–1897, AMSS; Daily Notes, Box 86, Hiram to Ellen, Box 46, WSU-MHV, and in Plumb, *The Blackmans*.

8. MHV, Daily Notes, January 1930, Box 81; Daily Notes, 1945, Box 86, WSU-MHV.

9. Ellen Marvin Heaton, "Four Feet on a Fender," Box 40, WSU-MHV.

10. MHV, "Serene Plateau," Box 10, WSU-MHV.

11. MHV, "Older Woman's Leisure," Box 10; Daily Notes, 1926, Box 79, WSU-MHV.

12. MHV, "Three Ages of a Young Lady," Box 32; Ellen to MHV, undated, Box 48; Ellen Marvin Heaton, "Miscellaneous," Box 40; MHV, "Conflict," Box 18; MHV, "Old Age," Box 115, WSU-MHV.

13. MHV, Daily Notes, 1944, Box 86, WSU-MHV.

14. Ellen to MHV, Box 49; Hiram to MHV, Box 49; "Notes on Time and Town," Box 14, WSU-MHV.

15. MHV, Daily Notes, Box 93, WSU-MHV.

16. Malcolm Cowley, *The Dream of the Golden Mountains: Remembering the 1930s* (New York: Viking Press, 1980), 213; Art Young, *On My Way* (New York: Horace Liveright, 1938), 286; Louis Untermeyer, *From Another World* (New York: Harcourt, Brace, 1939), 43.

17. MHV, Daily Notes, Box 93; Time and Town Notes, Box 14; "Serene Plateau," Box 10, WSU-MHV.

18. The writer Josephine Herbst once expressed Vorse's ability to push back disturbing images in her thoughts. Herbst's 1949 short story was a thinly disguised representation of her experience as a summer boarder in Vorse's beachtown home. "Something was lacking" in Vorse, Herbst wrote, something that made Vorse shrink, not just from coming out in active criticism of others which might clear the air, but also from examining the sources of her anger and despair. Herbst recognized the source of Vorse's unexamined fear when she envisioned Vorse imposing upon another the crushing revenge of the formerly abandoned—"who in every disaster first hear their far-off terrified cries for help." See Josephine Herbst, "A Summer with Yorick," *Tomorrow*, June 1949, 31–36. I am indebted to Elinor Langer for this reference. Also see Ann Craton Blankenhorn to Herbst, June 2 and 19, and MHV to Herbst, undated, in YUB-JH, for reaction to Herbst's portrayal of Vorse. MHV thought the short story "witty and amusing."

19. "Vryling Buffum, Long Active As Educator, Dies," Keene *Evening Sentinel*, January 28, 1944; Mildred Dickenson, "The Story of a Tree That Spruced Up," Amherst *Record*, May 13, 1973, in AJL.

20. MHV, Daily Notes, 1926, Box 79; "Serene Plateau," Box 10, WSU-MHV.

21. Ellen Marvin Heaton, "The Odor of Sanctity," *New England Magazine*, 1891, 4:743–760; 5:38–48, 303–309, 470–476.

22. Ruth Bordin, *Woman and Temperance: The Quest for Power and Liberty, 1873–1900* (Philadelphia: Temple University Press, 1981); Barbara Leslie Epstein, *The Politics of Domesticity: Women, Evangelism and Temperance in Nineteenth-Century America* (Middletown, Conn.: Wesleyan University Press, 1981); Karen Blair, *The Clubwoman as Feminist: True Womanhood Redefined, 1868–1914* (New York: Holmes and Meier, 1980). Anne Firor Scott, "On Seeing and Not Seeing: A Case of Historical Invisibility," *Journal of American History*, June 1984, 7–21, gives a broad perspective on the impact of American women's organizations.

23. Cited in Mari Jo Buhle, *Women and American Socialism, 1870–1920* (Urbana: University of Illinois Press, 1981), 66; Carroll Smith-Rosenberg, "The Female World of Love and Ritual: Relations between Women in Nineteenth-Century America," *Signs*, Autumn 1975, 1–29.

24. Peter Filene, *Him/Her/Self: Sex Roles in Modern America* (New York: Harcourt Brace Jovanovich, 1975), 13; Gail Cunningham, *The New Woman and the Victorian Novel* (New York: Barnes and Noble, 1978); Caroline Ticknor, "The Steel-Engraving Girl and the Gibson Girl," *Atlantic Monthly*, July 1901, 105–108; Linda Dowling, "The Decadent and the New Woman in the 1890s," *Nineteenth Century Fiction*, March 1979, 434–453; Sarah Grund, "The New Aspect of the Woman Question," *North American Review*, March 1894, 270–276; Estelle Freedman, "Separation as Strategy: Female Institution Building and American Feminism, 1870–1930," *Feminist Studies*, Fall 1979, 512–530; Carroll Smith-Rosenberg, *Disorderly Conduct: Visions of Gender in Victorian America* (New York: Oxford University Press, 1985), 245–296.

25. MHV, "Grandmother Is a Fraud," Box 21; "Old Age Notes"; "Life Is Real, Life Is Ernest," Box 24, WSU-MHV.

Chapter Two: La Bohémienne

1. Albert Parry, *Garrets and Pretenders: A History of Bohemianism in America* (New York: Dover Publications, 1960); Joanna Richardson, *The Bohemians: "La Vie de Boheme" in Paris, 1830–1914* (Toronto: Macmillan, 1969); Roger Shattuck, *The Banquet Years: The Origins of the Avant Garde in France, 1885 to World War I* (New York: Vintage, 1968); Richard Miller, *Bohemia: The Protoculture, Then and Now* (Chicago: Nelson-Hall, 1977); Lucy H. Hooper, "Art Schools of Paris," *Cosmopolitan,* 1893, 59–62.

2. Germaine Greer, *The Obstacle Race: The Fortunes of Women Painters and Their Work* (New York: Farrar, Straus, Giroux, 1979); Gordon S. Plummer, "Past and Present Inequalities in Art Education," in Judy Loeb, ed., *Feminist Collage* (New York: Teacher's College Press, 1979), 14–21; Linda Nochlin, "Why Have There Been No Great Women Artists," in Thomas B. Hess and Elizabeth C. Baker, eds., *Art and Sexual Politics* (New York: Macmillan, 1973), 1–39; Jo Ann Wein, "The Parisian Training of American Women Artists," *Woman's Art Journal,* Spring–Summer 1981, 42; Christine Havice, "In a Class by Herself: 19th Century Images of the Woman Artist as Student," ibid., 35–40.

3. MHV, "Grandmother Is a Fraud," Box 21; "Hybrids," Box 36; "Art School Story," Box 157; "Newspaper Articles," 1896–1899, Box 36; "Miscellaneous untitled Stories," Box 35, WSU-MHV.

4. Robert MacCameron and MHV correspondence in Box 46, WSU-MHV. His letters to Vorse continue through 1897. On MacCameron, see Charles F. Caffin, "Some New American Painters in Paris," *Harper's Magazine,* January 1909, 284–293.

5. MHV, "Conflict," Box 18; "Footnote to History," Box 1; "Confessions of a College Woman," Box 17; "Lorna Keene," Box 24, WSU-MHV.

6. Cited in Gilman M. Ostrander, *American Civilization in the First Machine Age, 1890–1940* (New York: Harper & Row, 1970), 173. Also see Arnold T. Schwab, *James Gibbons Huneker: Critic of the Seven Arts* (Stanford: Stanford University Press, 1963); Thomas Beer, *The Mauve Decade* (New York: Alfred Knopf, 1926), 154.

7. Charles DeKay, "The Art Students' League of New York," *Quarterly Illustrator,* 1893, 156; W. S. Harwood, "The Art Schools of America," *Cosmopolitan,* May 1894, 27–34; Moses King, *King's Handbook of New York City* (Boston, 1892), 288; MHV, "The Art Student and Successful Work," *Delineator,* November 1905, 940–943, and "The Truth concerning Art Schools," ibid., October 1905, 706–710.

8. William Dean Howells, *The Coast of Bohemia* (New York: Harper & Brothers, 1899).

9. Mary Augusta Jordan, "The College Graduate and the Bachelor Maid," *Independent,* July 20, 1899, 1937–1940; Winifred Sothern, "The Truth about the Bachelor Girl," *Munsey's Magazine,* May 1901, 282–283; MHV, "Miscellaneous Fragments," Box 157, WSU-MHV; Emilie Ruck De Schell, "Is Feminine Bohemianism a Failure?" *Arena,* 1898, 75. A. R. Cunningham, "The 'New Woman Fiction' of the 1890s," *Victorian Studies,* 1973, 177–186, also discusses the Bachelor Girl.

10. MHV, "Miscellaneous Fragments," Box 157, WSU-MHV.

11. MHV, "Grandmother Is a Fraud," Box 21, WSU-MHV.

12. MHV, Sketchbook, Box 154; Daily Notes, 1896, Box 92, WSU-MHV.

13. Albert Vorse, Diary, Box 153, WSU-MHV. Notes and articles on the Peary Relief Expedition in Boxes 45 and 140, WSU-MHV; Robert Keely and G. G. Davis, *In Arctic Seas or the Voyage of the Kite* (Philadelphia: Rufus C. Hartranft, 1893). Hutchins Hapgood, *A Victorian in the Modern World* (New York: Harcourt, Brace, 1939), 372.

14. Albert to MHV, Correspondence, Box 52, WSU-MHV.

15. MHV, Daily Notes, 1932, Box 83, WSU-MHV.

16. Albert to MHV, and MHV to Albert, Correspondence, Box 52, WSU-MHV.

17. See, for example, Albert W. Vorse, "The Play's the Thing," *Scribner's Magazine*, August 26, 1899, 167–178; "An Arctic Problem," Box 43, WSU-MHV.

18. MHV to Albert, Correspondence, Box 52; Theodore Roosevelt to Albert, April 20, 1898, Box 46, WSU-MHV.

19. Amherst *Record*, October 19, 1898.

Chapter Three: Completed Circle

1. MHV, "Seventy-eight Dollar Dress," Box 31, WSU-MHV; Hutchins Hapgood, *A Victorian in the Modern World* (New York: Harcourt, Brace, 1939), 152.

2. MHV, "Village Story," Box 33, WSU-MHV; L. H. Bickford and Richard Stillman Powell, *Phyllis in Bohemia* (Chicago: Herbert S. Stone and Company, 1897), 89–107; James Ford, *Forty Odd Years in the Literary Shop* (New York: E.P. Dutton, 1921), 206–207.

3. MHV, "Forerunners," Box 20, WSU-MHV; MHV, "Bohemia as It Is Not," *Critic*, August 1903, 177–178; MHV, "Grandmother Is a Fraud," Box 21, WSU-MHV.

4. Joseph I. C. Clarke, *My Life and Memories* (New York: Dodd, Mead and Company, 1925), 257–264. In 1901 Bert left the *Criterion* for a position as managing editor of the *New International Encyclopedia*. Bert to Mr. and Mrs. Heaton, December 19, 22, 1901, Box 48, WSU-MHV.

5. MHV, "Miscellaneous untitled Stories," Box 35; "Completed Circle," Box 17, WSU-MHV.

6. See Albert Vorse, "An Arctic Problem," Box 43, WSU-MHV, and *Laughter of the Sphinx* (New York: Drexel Biddle, 1900). The *Critic* of September 1900 has a photograph of Albert in full arctic gear, 197.

7. MHV, "Working Mother," and "Writing for Popular Magazines," Box 34, WSU-MHV; MHV, *A Footnote to Folly: The Reminiscences of Mary Heaton Vorse* (New York: Farrar and Rinehart, 1935), 30; MHV, "Footnote to History," Box 1; MHV to Hiram Heaton, May 20, 1904, Box 49, and Daily Notes, 1925, Box 79; MHV to parents, May 1904, Box 49, WSU-MHV.

8. MHV, *The Breaking in of a Yachtsman's Wife* (Boston: Houghton Mifflin, 1908), 77–78.

9. MHV, "Molasses Seven," Box 26, WSU-MHV.

10. MHV, *Footnote to Folly*, 31; Albert Vorse, "Venice General Strike," Box 44, and "A Gentle Strike," Box 43, WSU-MHV; MHV, "Unusual Venice," *Harper's Monthly Magazine*, November 1913, 890, 893.

11. Bert to Hiram Heaton, January 4, February 4, 1905, Box 49, WSU-MHV. Albert Vorse, "The Husband of a Celebrity, An Autobiography," Box 43; MHV, "Working Mother," Box 34; MHV, "Failure," Box 19, WSU-MHV.

12. MHV, "Miscellaneous untitled Stories," Box 35; "His Irritable Vanity," Box 21, WSU-MHV.

13. MHV, "Working Mother," Box 34, WSU-MHV. Steffens quoted in CU-MHV.

14. MHV, "The Quiet Woman," *Atlantic Monthly*, January 1907, 86, 87. Also reprinted with foreword in E. M. Broner, "Discovering Mary Heaton Vorse," *Ms.*, July 1981, 68, and in Dee Garrison, ed., *Rebel Pen: The Writings of Mary Heaton Vorse* (New York: Monthly Review Press, 1985).

15. Bert to Mary, April 16, 1904; John Hay to Bert, August 25, 1904, Box 49; MHV, Daily Notes, 1925, Box 78; Bert to Mary, 1905, Box 49, WSU-MHV.

16. MHV, Daily Notes, November 28, 1926, Box 80, WSU-MHV. Also MHV, "How I Kept My Husband," *Good Housekeeping*, November 1913, 610–619, featured as "true confession"; and MHV, "Battle in the Dark," Box 15, WSU-MHV.

17. MHV, "The Whimsical Ways of Provincetown Houses," *Country Life*, August 1921, 35–37; *Time and the Town: A Provincetown Chronicle* (New York: Dial Press, 1942), 10, 12; "Affairs of the House," Box 15, WSU-MHV; *Time and the Town*, 31, 32, 33.

18. MHV, *Footnote to Folly*, 32.

19. MHV, Daily Notes, 1945, Box 86, WSU-MHV; Ernest Poole, *The Bridge: My Own Story* (New York: Macmillan, 1940), 171; MHV, "Footnote to History," Box 1, WSU-MHV; MHV, *Footnote to Folly*, 35; Filia Holtzman, "A Mission That Failed: Gorkij in America," *Slavic and East European Journal*, Fall 1962, 227–235; Ernest Poole, "Maxim Gorki in New York," *Slavonic and East European Review*, May 1944, 77–83; Poole, *The Bridge*, 175–176.

20. MHV, *Footnote to Folly*, 34.

21. Interview, Warren Silva, Provincetown, 1980. The teenage driver, Mr. Silva, was able to pinpoint the date of this occurrence because he soon after moved from Provincetown. His memory of the event was still fresh because he was greatly impressed by the intensity of Mary's jealous anger and Bert's chagrin. Also see MHV, "Affairs of the House," Box 15, and "Footnote to History," Box 1, WSU-MHV. Bert to MHV, June 18, 1907(?), Box 50, and April 4, 1907(?), Box 52, WSU-MHV.

22. Martin Bucco, *Wilbur Daniel Steele* (New York: Twayne Publishers, 1972).

23. MHV, Daily Notes, 1923, Box 78; "Carmela Corea," Box 16; Daily Notes, 1925, Box 78; WSU-MHV.

24. MHV, *Time and the Town*, 39, 41; "Affairs of the House," Box 15; "What Age Would You Like To Be?" Box 34, WSU-MHV.

25. *Harper's Bazaar* published the composite novel *The Whole Family: A Novel by Twelve Authors* in 1908. See the recent edition with introduction by Albert Bendixen, published by Ungar Publishing Company, 1986. Also see Albert Bendixen, "It Was a Mess: How Henry James and Others Actually Wrote a Novel," *New York Times Book Review*, April 27, 1986, 28.

26. Dee Garrison, "Immoral Fiction in the Late Victorian Library," in Daniel Howe, ed., *Victorian America* (Philadelphia: University of Pennsylvania Press, 1976), 141–159.

27. MHV, "The March of the Seasons," *Booklover's Magazine*, 1906, 692; "What Makes Men Want to Leave Home," Box 34, WSU-MHV. A nearly complete bibliography of Vorse's writing, compiled by Rusty Byrne, can be obtained from the Schlesinger Library, Radcliffe College, Cambridge, Mass.

28. MHV, "The Confessions of a Young Wife," *Harper's Bazaar*, August 1907, 729; "Confessions of a Young Mother," ibid., March 1907, 212, 218; "The Extra Thousand," *Harper's Magazine*, June 1911, 101–109; "The Staying Out of Jimsie Bate," *American Magazine*, September 1908, 472–477; "The Undoing of Man," *Everybody's Magazine*, March 1907, 403–410; "Your Husband or Your Baby," Box 34, WSU-MHV. "The Casting Vote," *Everybody's Magazine*, January 1906, 22–30; "Chastening of Sally," ibid., September 1909, 390–395; "The Awkward Question," *Harper's Monthly Magazine*, June 1906, 68–75; "Grantham's Limitations," *Scribner's Magazine*, November 1908, 521–532; "Babble of Old Beaux," ibid., March 1909, 369–376; "The Bear at Home," *Harper's Bazaar*, November 1909, 1071–1073; "Breakfast Tables of the World," ibid., May 1910, 298–300.

29. Good examples are MHV, "The Madelon Viera," *Atlantic Monthly*, April 1910, 453–462; "The Perfect Hour," *Harper's Magazine*, September 1910, 505–511; "Confessions of a Young Wife," 731; "The Turn of the Flood," *Craftsman*, 14, September 1908, 607–618.

30. MHV, *The Very Little Person* (Boston: Houghton Mifflin, 1911), 124; "The Confessions of a Young Mother," *Harper's Bazaar*, March 1907, 210–219; "The Shifted Burden," *Everybody's Magazine*, February 1908, 193, 194.

31. MHV, "Audience with a Sultan," Box 112; "Moroccan Story" and "Road to Arzila," Box 113, WSU-MHV.

32. Interview, Heaton Vorse, 1982; Bert to MHV, Box 52, WSU-MHV.

33. Amherst *Record*, June 22, 1910; *Advocate* (Provincetown), June 16, 30, 1910; "Death Takes Two of Family," New York *Times*, June 24, 1910, 7:1. Heaton Vorse believes his father died of a syphilitic infection.

34. MHV, Correspondence, undated, Box 73, WSU-MHV.

35. MHV, "Completed Circle," Box 17, WSU-MHV.

Chapter Four: Crossroads

1. MHV, *Time and the Town: A Provincetown Chronicle* (New York: Dial Press, 1942), 44, 43.

2. Probate Records, Hiram Heaton, Box 383 #34, Docket 10889, 11350; Book 135, 106; Book 139, 22. Ellen's will in Probate Records, Book 126, 4, 16, 1910; Book 170, 215; "Inventory," Box 365 #45, Docket 9605; NMPR.

3. John Duffy, *A History of Public Health in New York City, 1866–1966* (New York: Russell Sage Foundation, 1974); Manfred J. Waserman, "Henry L. Coit and the Certified Milk Movement in the Development of Modern Pediatrics," *Bulletin of the History of Medicine*, 1972, 359–390; Harvey Levenstein, " 'Best for Babies' or 'Preventable Infanticide'? The Controversy over Artificial Feeding of Infants in America, 1880–1920," *Journal of American History*, June 1983, 75–94.

4. MHV, "Infant Mortality," Box 98, WSU-MHV; MHV, "Protection of Nursing Mothers," *Success*, October 1911, 13–14, 24–25; MHV, "Industrial Mother,"

Box 22; "Real Race Suicide," Box 29, WSU-MHV; New York *Times*, January 24, 1910, 6:2; April 16, 1910, 6:5; September 18, 1910, 6:2; June 12, 1910, 6:2; MHV, *A Footnote to Folly: The Reminiscences of Mary Heaton Vorse* (New York: Farrar and Rinehart, 1935), 39.

5. MHV, *Footnote to Folly*, 39–40; Leon Stein, *The Triangle Fire* (Philadelphia: J.B. Lippincott, 1962); Meredith Tax, *The Rising of the Women: Feminist Solidarity and Class Conflict, 1880–1917* (New York: Monthly Review Press, 1980), 235–236; WSU-HB, 7(3).

6. Philip S. Foner, *Women and the American Labor Movement: From Colonial Times to the Eve of World War I* (New York: Free Press, 1979), 428; Foner, *History of the Labor Movement in the United States*, vol. 4: *The Industrial Workers of the World, 1905–1917* (New York: International Publishers, 1965), 313.

7. Melvyn Dubofsky, *We Shall Be All: A History of the Industrial Workers of the World* (New York: Quadrangle, 1969), 227–263; Donald B. Cole, *Immigrant City: Lawrence, Massachusetts, 1845–1921* (Chapel Hill: University of North Carolina Press, 1963).

8. David Brody, "The American Worker in the Progressive Age: A Comprehensive Analysis," in *Workers in Industrial America: Essays on the Twentieth Century Struggle* (New York: Oxford University Press, 1980), 37. Also see MHV, "Notes and Ideas," Box 37, WSU-MHV; and CU-MHV.

9. Interview, Joel O'Brien, 1980.

10. Joe to MHV, February 15, 1912, letter placed in old ledger, Box 36, and MHV to Joe, Box 53, WSU-MHV.

11. MHV, "The Trouble at Lawrence," *Harper's Weekly*, March 16, 1912, 10. Also Joe O'Brien, "Lawrence, 1912," Box 122, WSU-MHV.

12. MHV, *Footnote to Folly*, 8; MHV, "Elizabeth Gurley Flynn," *Nation*, February 17, 1926, 175–176. I am grateful to Rosalyn Baxandall, Flynn's biographer, who has generously shared research information and leads with me. See Baxandall, *Words on Fire: The Life and Writing of Elizabeth Gurley Flynn* (New Brunswick, N.J.: Rutgers University Press, 1987).

13. David Montgomery, "The 'New Unionism' and the Transformation of Workers' Consciousness in America, 1909–22," in *Worker's Control in America: Studies in the History of Work, Technology and Labor Struggles* (New York: Cambridge University Press, 1979), 105.

14. Tax, *Rising of the Women*, 262.

15. Elizabeth Gurley Flynn, "The I.W.W. Call to Women," *Solidarity*, July 31, 1915; Ardis Cameron, "Bread and Roses Revisited: Women's Culture and Working-Class Activism in the Lawrence Strike of 1912," in Ruth Milkman, ed., *Women, Work and Protest: A Century of U.S. Women's Labor History*, 42–61 (Boston: Routledge and Kegan Paul, 1985).

16. MHV, Daily Notes, 1926, Box 79, WSU-MHV; MHV, *Footnote to Folly*, 21.

17. Ray Stannard Baker, "The Revolutionary Strike," *American Magazine*, September 1912, 3019.

18. MHV, *Footnote to Folly*, 18.

19. Ibid., 21.

20. Ibid., 14.

21. Ibid., 40; Marriage License, April 16, 1912, married in Hoboken, Box 145, WSU-MHV.

Chapter Five: Banner of Revolt

1. Alfred Kazin, *On Native Grounds: An Interpretation of Modern American Prose Literature* (New York: Harcourt, Brace, 1942), 168, 165; Henry May, *The End of American Innocence: A Study of the First Years of Our Own Time, 1912–1917* (New York: Alfred Knopf, 1959), 221; Van Wyck Brooks, *The Confident Years, 1885–1917* (New York: E.P. Dutton, 1952), 475; Cook cited in Kazin, *On Native Grounds,* 171; Allen Churchill, *The Improper Bohemians: A Re-Creation of Greenwich Village in Its Heyday* (New York: E.P. Dutton, 1959); Albert Parry, *Garrets and Pretenders: A History of Bohemianism in America* (New York: Dover Publications, 1960); John P. Diggins, *The American Left in the Twentieth Century* (New York: Harcourt Brace Jovanovich, 1979); James B. Gilbert, *Writers and Partisans: A History of Literary Radicalism in America* (New York: John Wiley and Sons, 1968); Arthur Frank Werthheim, *The New York Little Renaissance: Iconoclasm, Modernism and Nationalism in American Culture, 1908–1917* (New York: New York University Press, 1976); Robert E. Humphrey, *Children of Fantasy: The First Rebels of Greenwich Village* (New York: John Wiley and Sons, 1978).

2. Cited in Daniel Aaron, *Writers on the Left* (New York: Avon Books, 1969), 29.

3. Dell cited in Leslie Fishbein, *Rebels in Bohemia: The Radicals of the Masses, 1911–1917* (Chapel Hill: University of North Carolina Press, 1982), 60.

4. MHV, Daily Notes, October 1936, Box 84; "Notes, Time and the Town," Box 14, WSU-MHV.

5. Reed cited in Kazin, *On Native Grounds,* 170; Floyd Dell, *Looking at Life* (New York: Alfred Knopf, 1924), 66; Susan Glaspell, *The Road to the Temple* (New York: Frederick A. Stokes, 1927), 247; Louis Schaeffer, *O'Neill: Son and Playwright* (Boston: Little, Brown, 1968), 345; MHV, *I've Come to Stay: A Love Comedy of Bohemia* (New York: Century Company, 1919), 75–76; MHV, "Greenwich Village," Box 21, WSU-MHV; Anthony Channell Hilfer, *The Revolt from the Village, 1915–1930* (Chapel Hill: University of North Carolina Press, 1969).

6. Joseph Freeman, *An American Testament: A Narrative of Rebels and Romantics* (London: Gollancz, 1938), 233; Bourne in Keith N. Richwine, "The Liberal Club: Bohemia and the Resurgence in Greenwich Village, 1912–1918," Ph.D. diss., University of Pennsylvania, 1968, 77; June Sochen, *The New Woman: Feminism in Greenwich Village, 1910–1920* (New York: Quadrangle, 1972); Sochen, *Movers and Shakers: American Women Thinkers and Activists, 1900–1970* (New York: Quadrangle, 1973); Ellen K. Trimberger, "Feminism, Men, and Modern Love: Greenwich Village, 1900–1925," in Ann Snitow, Christine Stansell, and Sharon Thompson, eds., *Powers of Desire: The Politics of Sexuality* (New York: Monthly Review Press, 1983), 131–152, discusses the inability of Village men to realize the new ideals. Also see Hutchins Hapgood, *A Victorian in the Modern World* (New York: Harcourt, Brace, 1939), 320, and Gerald L. Marriner, "A Victorian in the Modern World: The 'Liberated' Male's Adjustment to the New Woman and the New Morality," *South Atlantic Quarterly,* Spring 1977, 190–218.

7. May, *End of American Innocence*, 310.

8. Freeman, *American Testament*, 249, 228; Hapgood in Churchill, *The Improper Bohemians*, 75.

9. Marie Jenney Howe, "Feminism," *New Review*, August 1914, 441.

10. Mabel Dodge Luhan, *Intimate Memories*, vol. 3: *Movers and Shakers* (New York: Harcourt, Brace, 1936), 143; Howe cited in Judith Schwarz, *Radical Feminists of Heterodoxy: Greenwich Village, 1912–1940* (Lebanon, N.H.: New Victoria Publishers, 1982), 25; Appendix B in Schwarz reprints "Marriage Customs and Taboo among the Early Heterodites," a spoof written in 1919 for the club members. The spoof notes that members of the tribe suspected of taboo were disciplined by the club's refusal to send notice of anarchial, Bolshevik, or pacifist meetings. Two-time offenders were forbidden to serve on the Committee of Arrangements in the coming Revolution.

11. Elizabeth Gurley Flynn, *Rebel Girl: An Autobiography: My First Life (1906–1926)* (New York: International Publishers, 1955), 280. MHV, Daily Notes and Yearly Summaries, and MHV's handwritten list of Heterodoxy members in Box 10, MHV-WSU.

12. Kathy Peiss, "A Great Personal Joyous Adventure: Feminist Ideology of the 1910s and Its Social Context," paper in possession of author. Peiss analyzed the biographies of 60 Heterodoxy women in her list of 100. Also see Schwarz, *Radical Feminists*, 60.

13. Schwarz, *Radical Feminists*, 81.

14. Sara Josephine Baker, *Fighting for Life* (New York: Macmillan, 1939), 182–183.

15. MHV, Oral History, 1957, CU-MHV.

16. Luhan, *Movers and Shakers*, 144.

17. Baker, *Fighting for Life*, 280.

18. Marie Jenney Howe, "Feminism," *New Review*, August 14, 1914, 442; Edna Kenton, "The Militant Women—and Women," *Century Magazine*, November 1913, 13–15. See Nancy F. Cott, *The Grounding of Modern Feminism* (New Haven: Yale University Press, 1987), for analysis of the ideas and influence of the feminists on Heterodoxy and Greenwich Village during this period.

19. Hapgood, *Victorian*, 377; Edward Abrahams, "Randolph Bourne on Feminism and Feminists," *Historian*, May 1981, 365–377; Schwarz, *Radical Feminists*, 81; Ella Winter, *And Not to Yield: An Autobiography* (New York: Harcourt, Brace, 1963).

20. Floyd Dell, *Homecoming: An Autobiography* (New York: Farrar and Rinehart, 1933), 247. Figures from lists in Richwine, "The Liberal Club"; Schwarz, *Radical Feminists*; and Peiss, "Joyous Adventure."

21. Lawrence Langer, *The Magic Curtain* (New York: E.P. Dutton, 1951), 70, 68.

22. William O'Neill, ed., *Echoes of Revolt: "The Masses," 1911–1917* (Chicago: Quadrangle Books, 1966); MHV, "The Day of a Man," *Masses*, May 1912; Inez Haynes Irwin to MHV, Box 53, WSU-MHV; Eastman in *Enjoyment of Living* (New York: Harper and Brothers, 1948), 399. Richard Fitzgerald, *Art and Politics: Cartoonists of the Masses and Liberator* (Westport, Conn.: Greenwood Press, 1973).

23. Eastman cited in Aaron, *Writers on the Left*, 32.

24. MHV, "The Two-Faced Goddess," *Masses*, December 1912, 12.

25. MHV, *A Footnote to Folly: The Reminiscences of Mary Heaton Vorse* (New York: Farrar and Rinehart, 1935), 42; MHV to mother, Box 78, WSU-MHV.

26. MHV to Joe, Box 53, WSU-MHV; MHV, *Time and the Town: A Province-town Chronicle* (New York: Dial Press, 1942), 95, 94, 96, 97; MHV, "Footnote to History," Box 1, WSU-MHV.

27. Cited in Mark Schorer, *Sinclair Lewis: An American Life* (New York: McGraw-Hill, 1961), 638; MHV cited in Grace Hegger Lewis, *With Love from Gracie: Sinclair Lewis: An American Life, 1912–45* (New York: Harcourt, Brace, 1951), 34.

28. MHV, *Footnote to Folly*, 47; MHV, "Freedom for Little Children," *Woman's Home Companion*, October, November, 1913, and February, April, 1914, Box 112, WSU-MHV; Floyd Dell, *Love in Greenwich Village* (Freeport, N.Y.: George H. Doran Co., 1926), 29.

29. Joe O'Brien, "Confessions of a Ready-Made Parent," Box 41; MHV, "Busy Women and Idle Friends," Box 16, WSU-MHV.

30. MHV to Arthur Bullard, February 7, 1913, Box 54; also her series in *National Post*, 1911, Box 36, WSU-MHV.

31. MHV, "Women at Armageddon," *Metropolitan*, September 1913, Box 34, WSU-MHV. Also Joe O'Brien, "Women's Congress," *Colliers*, August 2, 1913, Box 42, WSU-MHV.

32. MHV, "Women at Armageddon," Box 34, WSU-MHV. Gloria Steinem's grandmother from Toledo was also present at Budapest in 1913.

Chapter Six: Women's Peace, Men's War

1. Interview, John and Miriam (Hapgood) Dewitt, 1982; Michael D. Marcaccio, *The Hapgoods: Three Ernest Brothers* (Charlottesville: University Press of Virginia, 1977), 157; Hutchins Hapgood, *Story of a Lover* (published anonymously by Boni and Liveright, New York, 1919), 29, 48; MHV to Hapgood, Box 54, WSU-MHV; Hutchins Hapgood, *A Victorian in the Modern World* (New York: Harcourt, Brace, 1939), 395; MHV to Hapgood, Box 54, WSU-MHV; Boyce to Hapgood, July 23, circa 1912, circa 1911, circa 1916, Correspondence, YUB-NBHH. Boyce wrote Hapgood in July 1913, that Mary was sometimes cross because Joe "didn't work enough." Mary, said Boyce, made Joe's "elopement to go fishing" into "an elegant discussion on the way the world exploited her, etc."

2. Floyd Dell, *Homecoming: An Autobiography* (New York: Farrar and Rinehart, 1933), 254, 170; Susan Glaspell, *The Road to the Temple* (New York: Frederick A. Stokes, 1927) 235–236; Arthur E. Waterman, *Susan Glaspell* (New York: Twayne Publishers, 1966); Hapgood, *Victorian*, 373.

3. Ellen Kay Trimberger, "Feminism, Men, and Modern Love: Greenwich Village, 1900–1925," in Ann Snitow, Christine Stansell, and Sharon Thompson, eds., *Powers of Desire: The Politics of Sexuality* (New York: Monthly Review Press, 1983), 147.

4. Hapgood, *Victorian*, 379–380;

5. Ibid., 373.

6. Interview with anonymous neighbor in Provincetown, 1982.

7. Tresca cited in MHV, *A Footnote to Folly: The Reminiscences of Mary Heaton Vorse* (New York: Farrar and Rinehart, 1935), 55.

8. Boxes 141, 35, 138, WSU-MHV. Also see MHV, "The Case of Adolph,"

Outlook, May 1, 1914, 27–31; Paul Avrich, *The Modern School Movement: Anarchism and Education in the United States* (Princeton: Princeton University Press, 1980), 188, 186.

9. MHV, *Footnote to Folly*, 56, 57; also see MHV, "The Police and the Unemployed," *New Republic*, September 1914, 530–538; Joe O'Brien, "Anarchy While You Wait," *Masses*, May 1915.

10. Justin Kaplan, *Lincoln Steffens* (New York: Simon and Schuster, 1974), 205.

11. Telegram in Box 55, WSU-MHV; Hapgood, *Victorian*, 390.

12. Hapgood, *Victorian*, 385–391.

13. See Blanche Wiesen Cook, *Crystal Eastman on Women and Revolution* (New York: Oxford University Press, 1978), 1–40; C. Roland Marchand, *The American Peace Movement and Social Reform, 1898–1918* (Princeton: Princeton University Press, 1972); Charles DeBenedetti, *The Peace Reform in American History* (Bloomington: Indiana University Press, 1980); Barbara J. Steinson, *American Women's Activism in World War I* (New York: Garland Publishing Company, 1982); International Congress of Women Report, and "Women's Suffrage Notes," and "Hague Congress of Women," Box 132, WSU-MHV.

14. Florence Woolston to MHV, April 6, 1915, Box 132, WSU-MHV. TR cited in Mercedes M. Randall, *Improper Bostonian: Emily Greene Balch* (New York: Twayne Publishers, 1964), 144.

15. MHV, *Footnote to Folly*, 80; MHV to Joe, April 1915, Box 55; copy of Wales's plan in Box 162, WSU-MHV.

16. MHV, ms. in possession of Grace Cullinson, Provincetown, Mass.

17. International Congress of Women, Report, The Hague, April 28–May 1, 1915; International Women's Committee of Permanent Peace, Amsterdam, 1915, 40; Journal of Emily Greene Balch, SC-EB; Series B, Box 1, SC-WILPF.

18. The meeting is described by MHV in *Footnote to Folly*, 79–88, and in Hague Congress of Women, Box 132, WSU-MHV. Also see Jane Addams, Emily G. Balch, and Alice Hamilton, *Women at The Hague* (New York: Macmillan, 1915).

19. Allen F. Davis, *American Heroine: The Life and Legend of Jane Addams* (New York: Oxford University Press, 1973), 226, 232–281; Mari Jo and Paul Buhle, eds., *The Concise History of Woman Suffrage* (Urbana: University of Illinois Press, 1978).

20. MHV, *Footnote to Folly*, 87.

21. MHV's trip through Europe is described in "Getting Arrested," and "Europe, France, WWI," in Box 104, WSU-MHV. Also see MHV, "Picture of the Swiss Women," Box 29, WSU-MHV; and "The Sinistrees of France," *Century Magazine*, January 1917, 445–450; "Les Evacuées," *Outlook*, November 10, 1915, 622–626; *Footnote to Folly*, 90–127.

22. MHV, Box 1; MHV, "Not in Vain," an unfinished novel on worldwide campaign of women to end war, WSU-MHV. Also see Paul Fussell, *The Great War and Modern Memory* (New York: Oxford University Press, 1975).

23. Hapgood, *Victorian*, 392.

24. MHV, *Time and the Town: A Provincetown Chronicle* (New York: Dial Press, 1942), 101; MHV, "The Mirror of Silence," *Harper's Monthly Magazine*, November 1916, 872, 878; MHV, "Destroyers," Box 18, describes the unheeding gaiety of the artistic literary crowd—dancing while the world burns, WSU-MHV. Also Arnold

Goldman, "The Culture of the Provincetown Players," *Journal of American Studies*, December 1978, 291–310.

25. Louis Scheaffer, *O'Neill: Son and Playwright* (Boston: Little, Brown, 1968); MHV, "Playhouse History," Box 29, WSU-MHV; Helen Deutsch and Stella Hanau, *The Provincetown: A Story of the Theater* (New York: Farrar and Rinehart, 1931).

26. MHV, *Time and the Town*, 119–120.

27. Boyce to Hapgood, 1915 Correspondence, YUB-NBHH.

28. *Masses*, January 16, 1920; MHV to Joe in 1914; on Joe's illness, Boxes 53, 54, 58, WSU-MHV.

29. Hapgood to Boyce, Correspondence, November 2, 1915, YUB-NBHH.

Chapter Seven: Down the Road Again

1. MHV, *A Footnote to Folly: The Reminiscences of Mary Heaton Vorse* (New York: Farrar and Rinehart, 1935), 130; Box 154, MHV-WSU.

2. MHV to Whitehouse, February 8, 1916, Box 132; MHV, "Editorial, 1915," Box 132, WSU-MHV. Elizabeth Jordan, ed., *The Sturdy Oak* (New York: Henry Holt & Company, 1917).

3. Sanger cited in David M. Kennedy, *Birth Control in America: The Career of Margaret Sanger* (New Haven: Yale University Press, 1970), 78. Also see James Reed, *From Private Vice to Public Virtue: The Birth Control Movement in American Society since 1830* (New York: Basic Books, 1978); Linda Gordon, *Woman's Body: Woman's Right: A Social History of Birth Control in America* (New York: Penguin, 1977). MHV, "Serene Plateau," Box 10; list of 100 in Box 132, MHV-WSU; "An Endorsement of Birth Control," in NYSL-LC.

4. Glaspell cited in Louis Scheaffer, *O'Neill: Son and Playwright* (Boston: Little, Brown, 1968), 355–356.

5. MHV, Daily Notes, 1925, Box 78; Correspondence, Boxes 55, 56, WSU-MHV. One of Vorse's new admirers was Don Corley, a young architect working with the playhouse group. Much given to solitary leave-takings after early arisings, Corley dropped pillow-notes behind. At August's end, Corley's affection was abruptly transferred to another. "I have been selfish in my own joy, Mary dear," he wrote, "or I would have written last week. Sunday Harriet and I were married. . . . I knew that I loved her when first I saw her, the Wednesday before. . . . I know you will understand, as you always do." Harriet was not so friendly. "I tore your picture to bits and spit vigorously in your face," she wrote Mary, "and I shall do it to you if I see you."

6. MHV, *Time and the Town: A Provincetown Chronicle* (New York: Dial Press, 1942), 121.

7. Allen Churchill, *The Improper Bohemians: A Re-Creation of Greenwich Village in Its Heyday* (New York: E.P. Dutton, 1959), 199–200; MHV, "Playhouse History," Box 29, WSU-MHV; Arnold Goldman, "The Culture of the Provincetown Players," *Journal of American Studies*, December 1978, 291–310. Robert K. Sarlos, *Jig Cook and the Provincetown Players: Theater in Ferment* (Amherst: University of Massachusetts Press, 1982), places the first production of *Bound East for Cardiff* in the last week of July.

8. EGF to MHV, July 24, 1916, Box 55; Tresca to MHV, from jail, Box 56, WSU-MHV.

9. MHV, Daily Notes, Box 78, WSU-MHV.

10. For the Mesabi strike, see John Sirjamaki, "The People of the Mesabi Range," *Minnesota History*, September 1946, 203–215; Philip Foner, *The Industrial Workers of the World, 1905–1917* (New York: International Publishers, 1965); Melvyn Dubofsky, *We Shall Be All: A History of the Industrial Workers of the World* (New York: Quadrangle, 1969); Donald Sofchalk, "Organized Labor and the Iron Ore Miners of Northern Minnesota, 1907–1936," *Labor History*, Spring 1971, 214–242; Neil Betten, "Riot, Revolution, Repression in the Iron Range Strike of 1916," *Minnesota History*, Summer 1968, 82–93. Unless otherwise noted, Vorse's experience on the Mesabi is drawn from *Footnote to Folly*, 132–153.

11. Dubofsky, *We Shall Be All*, 326.

12. Duluth *Labor World* cited in Foner, *Industrial Workers of the World*, 506; also see MHV, "Elizabeth Gurley Flynn," *Nation*, February 7, 1926, 176; Elizabeth Gurley Flynn, *The Rebel Girl: An Autobiography: My First Life, 1906–1926* (New York: International Publishers, 1955), 208.

13. Newsclipping, St. Paul, Box 36, to Women's Welfare League, WSU-MHV. MHV, "The Mining Strike in Minnesota," *Outlook*, August 30, 1916, 1036–1046; Tyler Dennett, "The Other Side," ibid., 1046–1048.

14. MHV, *I've Come to Stay: A Love Comedy of Bohemia* (New York: Century, 1919).

15. Robert K. Murray, *Red Scare: A Study in National Hysteria, 1919–1920* (New York: McGraw-Hill, 1964); Stephen Vaughn, *Holding Fast the Inner Lines: Democracy, Nationalism and the Committee on Public Information* (Chapel Hill: University of North Carolina Press, 1980); PU-AB; MHV, "Czechoslovakia," Box 104, WSU-MHV; MHV, "Debatable Lands in Central Europe," *New York Times Magazine*, July 6, 1919, 7.

16. Vorse was involved briefly with Edward E. Free, a chemist she met in Washington. In 1917, Free asked her to marry him. The affair dissolved when Vorse and Free quarreled over the justice of the IWW arrests. Correspondence with Free, Box 56, WSU-MHV.

17. J. A. Thompson, "American Progressive Publicists and the First War, 1914–1917," *Journal of American History*, September 1971, 383; Allen Davis, "Welfare, Reform and World War I," *American Quarterly*, Fall 1967, 516–533.

18. MHV, "Bridgeport and Democracy," *Harper's Monthly Magazine*, January 1919, 145–154. Vorse's article incensed many prominent citizens of Bridgeport, leading one to claim at a symposium that she "took a taxicab from the [Bridgeport] station and rode out to the nearest sewer and there got her inspiration and facts for her article." William Hincks to MHV, Box 56, WSU-MHV. See David Montgomery, *Worker's Control in America: Studies in the History of Work, Technology and Labor Struggles* (New York: Cambridge University Press, 1979), 127–135, for a realistic judgment of labor's status in Bridgeport.

19. Weyl cited in Stanley Shapiro, "The Great War and Reform: Liberals and Labor, 1917–1919," *Labor History*, Summer 1971, 338.

20. Robert J. Goldstein, *Political Repression in Modern America, 1870 to Present* (Cambridge: Schenkman, 1978), has full bibliography. Also see H. C. Peterson and

Gilbert C. Fite, *Opponents of War, 1917–1918* (Seattle: University of Washington Press, 1957); MHV, "Notes on a History of the IWW," Box 37, WSU-MHV; William Preston, Jr., *Aliens and Dissenters: Federal Suppression of Radicals, 1903–1933* (New York: Harper and Row, 1963); William Preston, "Shall This Be All? U.S. Historians versus William D. Haywood et al.," *Labor History*, Summer 1971, 435–453; Harry N. Scheiber, *The Wilson Administration and Civil Liberties, 1917–21* (Ithaca, N.Y.: Cornell University Press, 1960); Joan M. Jensen, *The Price of Vigilance* (Chicago: Rand McNally, 1968); MHV, *Footnote to Folly*, 160.

21. Reel 271B, OG 357985, 357986, FBI-IR; FBI file MHV, in possession of author, obtained through Freedom of Information Act. Also see David Williams, "The Bureau of Investigation and Its Critics, 1919–1921: The Origins of Federal Surveillance," *Journal of American History*, December 1981, 560–579.

22. Interview, Heaton Vorse, 1986.

Chapter Eight: Footnote to Folly

1. MHV, *A Footnote to Folly: The Reminiscences of Mary Heaton Vorse* (New York: Farrar and Rinehart, 1935), 169.

2. Cited in Arno Mayer, *Politics and Diplomacy of Peacemaking: Containment and Counterrevolution at Versailles, 1918–1919* (New York: Alfred Knopf, 1967), 29.

3. MHV, "Through Sheffield Smoke," *Harper's*, May 1919, 773.

4. Description of trip, speech, and dinner in Edith Bolling Wilson, *My Memoir* (New York: Bobbs-Merrill Co., 1938), 189–190; MHV, *Footnote to Folly*, 187.

5. MHV, "Failure," Box 19, WSU-MHV.

6. MHV, "Footnote to History," Box 2, WSU-MHV.

7. MHV, "Abandoned Lands and Patchwork Quilts," Box 15, WSU-MHV.

8. MHV, *Footnote to Folly*, 198, 201.

9. Merle Fainsod, *International Socialism and the World War* (New York: Octagon Books, 1973); Albert S. Lindemann, *The "Red Years": European Socialism Versus Bolshevism, 1919–1921* (Berkeley: University of California Press, 1974); Mayer, *Politics and Diplomacy of Peacemaking*; Dan S. White, "Reconsidering European Socialism in the 1920s," *Journal of Contemporary History*, April 1981, 251–272.

10. MHV, *Footnote to Folly*, 209, 212.

11. MHV to Selway, March 14, 1918, Box 56, WSU-MHV.

12. MHV, *Footnote to Folly*, 218.

13. Ibid., 223, 224.

14. Cited in Oliver Pilat, *Drew Pearson: An Unauthorized Biography* (New York: Harper's Magazine Press, 1973), 61. Holly Beach reportedly spoke of Vorse as an "international communist organizer."

15. MHV, "Milorad," *Harper's*, January 1920, 256–262.

Chapter Nine: The Left Fork

1. John Dos Passos, *The Best Times: An Informal Memoir* (New York: New American Library, 1966), 77; Dora Russell, *The Tamarisk Tree: My Quest for Liberty and Love* (New York: G.P. Putnam's, 1975).

2. Johns and Freeman cited in Richard Fitzgerald, *Art and Politics: Cartoonists of the Masses and Liberator* (Westport, Conn.: Greenwood Press, 1973), 80, 88; interview, Steve Nelson, 1983; Alan Trachtenberg, ed., *Memoirs of Waldo Frank* (Amherst: University of Massachusetts Press, 1973), 188; interview, Sam D'Arcy, 1984. An enthusiastic and often inaccurate biography is Joseph North, *Robert Minor, Artist and Crusader* (New York: International Publishers, 1956).

3. Minor cited in Curt Gentry, *Frameup: The Incredible Case of Tom Mooney and Warren Billings* (New York: W. W. Norton, 1967), 437; Theodore Draper, *The Roots of American Communism* (New York: Viking, 1957), 123.

4. MHV to Knobby, February 19, 1929, Box 81, WSU-MHV.

5. MHV to RM, Correspondence, Box 59, WSU-MHV.

6. MHV to Selway, Box 56; Credentials, Box 104; Hoover to MHV, May 28, 1919, Box 104, WSU-MHV.

7. MHV, *A Footnote to Folly: The Reminiscences of Mary Heaton Vorse* (New York: Farrar and Rinehart, 1935), 241, 243.

8. Lloyd George cited in George W. Hopkins, "The Politics of Food: United States and Soviet Hungary, March-August, 1919," *Mid-America*, October 1973, 247; Arno Mayer, *Politics and Diplomacy of Peacemaking: Containment and Counterrevolution at Versailles, 1918–1919* (New York: Alfred Knopf, 1967), 367–368; Alfred D. Low, "Soviet Hungary and the Paris Peace Conference," in Ivan Volgyes, ed., *Hungary in Revolution, 1918–1919* (Lincoln: University of Nebraska Press, 1971), 137–157.

9. Correspondence, Box 56; "Footnote to History," Box 2; "Budapest: The Heart of Communism" and "Notes," Box 106, WSU-MHV; CU-MHV; Travel Orders, Gregory to MHV, Box 104, WSU-MHV, instruct MHV to proceed to Budapest and "carry out verbal instructions."

10. MHV, *Footnote to Folly*, 247; MHV, "Footnote to History," Box 2, WSU-MHV; ARA European Operation Papers, Folder, Hungary #2, April–June 1919, HI-ARA; HI-TTCG; Mayer, *Politics and Diplomacy of Peacemaking*, 828.

11. MHV, *Footnote to Folly*, 252.

12. MHV report on Károlyi, Box 106, WSU-MHV.

13. Frank Eckelt, "The Internal Policies of the Hungarian Soviet Republic," in Volgyes, *Hungary in Revolution*, 61–88; Joseph Rothchild, *East Central Europe between the Two World Wars* (Seattle: University of Washington Press, 1974); Andrew C. Janos and William B. Slottman, eds., *Revolution in Perspective: Essays on the Hungarian Soviet Republic of 1919* (Berkeley: University of California Press, 1971). Also see Rudolph L. Tokes, *Bela Kun and the Hungarian Soviet Republic* (New York: Frederick A. Praeger, 1967), 177–189.

14. Gregory claimed credit for the defeat of Kun in a series of articles published in *World's Work* in April, May, and June 1921. Hoover backed away from any definite comment on Gregory's claims. Also see Hopkins, "The Politics of Food"; Murray N. Rothbard, "Hoover's 1919 Food Diplomacy in Retrospect," in Lawrence E. Gelfand, ed., *Herbert Hoover: The Great War and Its Aftermath, 1914–23* (Iowa City: University of Iowa Press, 1979), 87–110; and Edward F. Willis, "Herbert Hoover and the Blockade of Germany, 1918–1919," in Frederick J. Cox et al., *Studies in Modern European History* (New York: Bookman Associates, 1956), 265–300.

15. MHV, *Footnote to Folly*, 272.

16. Gregory to Hoover, April 22, June 4, 1919, in HI-TTCG; Hoover to Wilson, June 9, 1919, Wilson to Hoover, June 10, 1919, in HI-ARA European Operations, Paris, Folder "Hungarian Political Situation," and Simpson to Gregory, June 17, 1919, "Personnel, U-V," HI-ARA.

17. Daily Summaries, 1919, Box 77; MHV to RM, note dated June 21, 1919, located in ledger, Box 36, WSU-MHV.

18. New York *Times*, July 15, 1919, 1:2; also see ibid., June 12, 1919, 5:4; June 15, 14:1; June 16, 15:2; June 22, 3:4; July 1, 15:2; Robert Minor, "The Spartacide Insurrection," *Liberator*, August, September 1919, 22–25, 31–39; Lincoln Steffens, *The Autobiography of Lincoln Steffens* (New York: Harcourt, Brace, 1958), 841–842; Steffens to Hutch Hapgood, December 21, 1919, YUB-NBHH; R. B. Minor to House, June 27, 1919, and House to R. B. Minor, July 25, 1919, YUS-EH. House tells Minor's father he did what he could but was criticized for it. Also see Robert Minor, "I Got Arrested a Little," *Liberator*, December 1919, 28—an inaccurate account of events, probably because Minor prefered to believe that his own courageous integrity and the protest of angry workers, rather than the efforts of American liberals, saved him from trial. Also see New York *Times*, July 4, 1919, 5:2; July 7, 15:7; July 9, 17:5; July 11, 11:2; July 12, 2:7; July 13, II, 1:6; July 15, 1:2; July 16, 12:6; September 30, 21:7; October 11, 13:3; October 13, 12:6; October 19, II, 1:7; October 24, 10:1; October 25, 10:5; and Cases 202 600-1754; 202 600-166; OG 208 369; OG 208 369-A, FBI-RM.

19. Robert Minor to Leo Kaplan, Box 57; also see Box 41, WSU-MHV. Minor's articles are in New York *World*, February 4, 6, 1919. Max Eastman, "Bob Minor and the Bolsheviks," *Liberator*, March 1919, 5–6. The most imaginative judgment is by Albert Weisbord who, after his expulsion from the Communist Party in 1930, decided that Lenin and Minor conspired on the *World* articles so as to mislead the American bourgeoisie and thus hasten withdrawal of American troops, CHS-AW. The general lack of information about Lenin's government or intent brought much attention to Minor's articles. Minor was one of the first American writers to talk to Lenin, who had granted Minor an interview because he knew and admired Minor's work on behalf of Mooney. According to Don Levine, *Eyewitness to History: Memoirs and Reflections of a Foreign Correspondent for Half a Century* (New York: Hawthorne Books, 1973), 65, Lenin was "especially hard on American journalists" after Minor's report in the *World*.

20. Edmund Wilson, *Shores of Light: A Literary Chronicle of the Twenties and Thirties* (New York: Farrar, Straus and Young, 1952), 498.

21. NYSL; Julian F. Jaffe, *Crusade against Radicalism: New York during the Red Scare, 1914–1924* (Port Washington, N.Y.: Kennikat Press, 1972); Lawrence H. Chamberlain, *Loyalty and Legislative Action: A Survey of Activity by the New York State Legislature* (Ithaca, N.Y.: Cornell University Press, 1951).

22. MHV, *Footnote to Folly*, 273–274.

23. MHV to Walter Pettit, August 25, 1919, and Marot to MHV, August 4, 1919, Box 56, WSU-MHV; interview, Joel O'Brien, 1984, who was at the farmhouse when it burned.

24. MHV to Gregory, August 6, 1919; MHV to Gutterson, August 6, 12, 1919; Gutterson to MHV, August 8, 1919, in Box 56, WSU-MHV. Gutterson to Gregory, August 14, 1919, Correspondence, General, A–Z, HI-TTCG. Also see Carl Parrini,

"Hoover and International Economics," and Robert F. Himmelberg, "Hoover's Public Image, 1919–1920: The Emergence of a Public Figure and a Sign of the Times," in Gelfand, *Herbert Hoover*, 183–206, 207–232.

Chapter Ten: Union Activist

1. MHV, Strike Articles and Notes, Box 120, WSU-MHV; David Brody, *Steelworkers in America: The Non Union Era* (Cambridge: Harvard University Press, 1960); David Brody, *Labor in Crisis: The Steel Strike of 1919* (Philadelphia: J.B. Lippincott, 1965).

2. Brody, *Labor in Crisis*, 94; Harvey O'Connor, *Steel-Dictator* (New York: John Day Company, 1935), 102; Robert Asher, "Painful Memories: The Historical Consciousness of Steelworkers and the Steel Strike of 1919," *Pennsylvania History*, 1978, 61–86; Charles Hill, "Fighting the Twelve Hour Day in the American Steel Industry," *Labor History*, 1974, 19–35; Gerald E. Eggert, *Steelmasters and Labor Reform, 1886–1923*, (Pittsburgh: University of Pittsburgh Press, 1981); Melvin I. Urofsky, *Big Steel and the Wilson Administration: A Study in Business–Government Relations* (Columbus: Ohio State University Press, 1969).

3. MHV, *Men and Steel* (New York: Boni and Liveright, 1920), 67; MHV, *A Footnote to Folly: The Reminiscences of Mary Heaton Vorse* (New York: Farrar and Rinehart, 1935), 280. Newdick had worked as a social worker, a newspaperman, and a writer for the Committee on Public Information.

4. MHV, Affidavits, Steel Strike, Box 121, WSU-MHV; David Montgomery, "New Tendencies in Union Struggles and Strategies in Europe and the United States, 1916–1922," and Melvyn Dubofsky, "Abortive Reform: The Wilson Administration and Organized Labor, 1913–1920," in James E. Cronin and Carmen Sirianni, eds., *Work, Community, and Power: The Experience of Labor in Europe and America, 1900–1925* (Philadelphia: Temple University Press, 1983), 88–116, 197–220.

5. Interchurch World Movement Commission of Inquiry, *Report on the Steel Strike of 1919* (New York, 1920) and *Public Opinion and the Steel Strike* (New York: The Interchurch World Movement, Harcourt, Brace and World, 1921); Philip C. Ensley, "The Interchurch World Movement and the Steel Strike of 1919," *Labor History*, Spring 1972, 217–230.

6. MHV, *Men and Steel*, 36, 37, 64–67, 178; MHV, "Slovak Parish," and "Steel" in Box 31, WSU-MHV. In Monessen, after the strike was broken, strikers could not return to work unless they offered an apology to the local Catholic priest who was a friend of the superintendent of the steel mill. John Bodnar, *Worker's World: Kinship, Community and Protest in Industrial Society, 1900–1940* (Baltimore: Johns Hopkins University Press, 1982), 93. Interchurch World Movement, *Public Opinion and the Steel Strike*, 163–220; William S. Haddock to W. R. Rubin, October 17, 1919, Box 120, WSU-MHV; MHV, *Fraycar's Fist* (New York: Boni and Liveright, 1924), 9–32.

7. Interchurch World Movement, *Public Opinion and the Steel Strike*, 71–74; "Interchurch World Movement," in UVAL-JL.

8. MHV, *Footnote to Folly*, 288–289; MHV, Miscellaneous, Box 154, WSU-MHV.

9. MHV, *Men and Steel*, 149–151.

10. Newdick to Mary, December 9, 12, 1919, Box 56, WSU-MHV. Also see William Foster, *The Great Steel Strike and Its Lessons* (New York: B.W. Huebsch, 1920).

11. MHV, "Steel Clippings," Box 120, WSU-MHV; "Behind the Picket Line," *Outlook*, January 21, 1920, 107–109; "Civil Liberty in the Steel Strike," *Nation*, November 15, 1919, 633–635; "Men and Steel," *Call Magazine*, undated; "Steel," in Box 31, WSU-MHV; Interchurch World Movement, *Public Opinion and the Steel Strike*, 132; Robert Murray, "Communism and the Great Steel Strike of 1919," *Mississippi Valley Historical Review*, 1951, 445–466; MHV, *Footnote to Folly*, 293; MHV, Strike News, 1919, Box 121; Steel Correspondence, 1919, Box 120, WSU-MHV.

12. John Dos Passos, *The Big Money* (New York: Washington Square Press, 1961; originally published 1936). Series I, Box 4, "The Big Money," UVAL-JDP. The manuscript notes show that Dos Passos was also thinking of Mary Vorse's later activity at Passaic in 1926, when he mentions that Mary French recovered there after a long slide downward, caused by her lover leaving her for another woman, just as Robert Minor would leave MHV for Lydia Gibson in 1922.

13. MHV, Steel 1919, Notes, Box 120, WSU-MHV; Dos Passos, *The Big Money*, 125, 150–51.

14. MHV, *Footnote to Folly*, 298–299.

15. Harold Josephson, "The Dynamics of Repression: New York during the Red Scare," *Mid America*, October 1977, 131–146. Julian F. Jaffe, *Crusade against Radicalism: New York during the Red Scare* (Port Washington, N.Y.: Kennikat, 1972); Richard Gid Powers, *Secrecy and Power: The Life of J. Edgar Hoover* (New York: Free Press, 1987); Athan G. Theoharis and John Stuart Cox, *The Boss: J. Edgar Hoover and the Great American Inquisition* (Philadelphia: Temple University Press, 1988).

16. Files OG 357986, 202600-1778, 202-600-1768, 208369, FBI-IR.

17. Weinberger to MHV, November 6, 1919, and R. B. Spence to Frank Burke, Department of Justice, November 11, 1919, FBI-MHV.

18. Ann Craton describes her experience in an unpublished autobiography in WSU-ACB; also see Alice Kessler-Harris, "The Autobiography of Ann Washington Craton," edited and with introduction, *Signs*, Summer 1976, 1019–1037.

19. "Authoress Here to Probe Conditions Local Factories," *Pottsville Miner's Journal*, January 9, 1920, in PHS; Ann Blankenhorn to MHV, circa 1965, in possession of Joel O'Brien.

20. Philip S. Foner, *Women and the American Labor Movement: From Colonial Times to the Eve of World War I* (New York: Free Press, 1979), 374–392; "Organizing Clothing Workers in Minerville," January 4, 1920, and "Shirtmakers Hold Mass Meeting at Charlton Tonight," January 15, *Pottsville Miner's Journal*, and "CLU Condemns IWW Organizers Here," January 28, PHS; MHV, "The Five Who Were Fired," *Advance*, January 23, 1920; "Sweatshop of Schuylkill County," Proceedings, Amalgamated Clothing Workers of America, 1918–1920, 165–167; "IWW Agitator's Work Condemned by Labor Body," February 5, 1920, and "Shortage of Orders Hits Factory Hands," February 14, 1920, in *Pottsville Miner's Journal*. The *Journal* gave first-page play to Red Scare hysteria during this period. Also see "Donaldson Strike Case Brings Town to Court Hearing," in ibid., February 20, 1920.

21. Box 5, WSU-CH. Haessler served as managing editor of the Federated Press

until 1956. Also see Gilbert J. Gall, "Heber Blankenhorn: The Publicist as Reformer," *Historian*, 1983, 513–528. I am grateful to Gilbert Gall for an early draft of this article. Also see MHV, "The Amalgamated Clothing Workers in Session," *Nation*, May 22, 1920, 684; Proceedings, Amalgamated Clothing Workers, 1918–1920, 86.

22. Folder 8-2, 7-9, WSU-HB.

23. MHV, "Amalgamated Women of Baltimore," *Advance*, April 21, 1920, 112–113; "Lockout of Women and Children," Box 24, WSU-MHV; MHV, *Footnote to Folly*, 353–354.

Chapter Eleven: Smashup

1. MHV, *Growing Up* (New York: Boni and Liveright, 1920); *The Ninth Man* (New York: Harpers, 1920); *Men and Steel* (New York: Boni and Liveright, 1920).

2. Interview, Heaton Vorse, 1986.

3. MHV, *A Footnote to Folly: The Reminiscences of Mary Heaton Vorse* (New York: Farrar and Rinehart, 1935), 308; Rodney to Burke, March 19, 1920, OG 386207, FBI-IR. Also see R. M. Whitney, *Reds in America* (New York: Beckwith Press, 1924), for typical redbaiting of MHV.

4. MHV, "Sacco and Vanzetti," Box 31, WSU-MHV; New York *Call*, December 27, 1920; MHV, "Sacco and Vanzetti," and Minutes, Executive Committee meeting, November 22, 1920, vol. 228-a, PU-ACLU; *World Tomorrow*, 1921 article, Box 30, and Ann Craton Blankenhorn to MHV, October 26, 1958, Box 72, WSU-MHV; David Felix, *Protest: Sacco-Vanzetti and the Intellectuals* (Bloomington: University of Indiana Press, 1965).

5. MHV to RM, Box 59; MHV, "Daily Summaries, 1920," Box 77, WSU-MHV.

6. Robert Minor, "I Change My Mind a Little," *Liberator*, October 1920, and "Answer to My Critics," ibid., November 1920. After the postmaster general's suppression of the *Masses*, Max Eastman and his sister, Crystal, began publication of the *Liberator*, which reported the socialist movement here and abroad. Also see Leo Caplan to RM, June 22, 1920, in possession of Joel O'Brien, Provincetown. RM to Caplan, Box 57, and RM to Tom Mooney, Box 56, WSU-MHV.

7. MHV to RM, undated 1920, Box 57, WSU-MHV.

8. CU-MHV.

9. MHV to RM, Box 59, WSU-MHV; Daily Notes, Box 78; RM to MHV, September 13, 1919, Box 57, Time and Town Notes, Box 14, WSU-MHV; interview, Heaton Vorse, 1984.

10. Correspondence, August 1920, between RM and LG in possession of Joel O'Brien; RM to Binnochicia (LG), August 11, 1920, Box 56, WSU-MHV; telephone interview with Peggy Dennis, 1984, and interview with Steve Nelson, for impressions of LG, 1984.

11. MHV to RM, Boxes 57, 59; MHV to Elizabeth Gurley Flynn, Box 56; MHV, Daily Notes, Box 78, WSU-MHV.

12. MHV, *Footnote to Folly*, 360–361; Daily Notes, Box 78; MHV, "Men, Some Reflections On," Box 25; passport, Box 145; documents concerning passage in and out

of Germany in June 1921 and January 1922, Box 57, WSU-MHV; YUS-HW, for MHV's will and power of attorney to Josephine Harn, June 7, 22, 1921.

13. See Walter Duranty, *I Write as I Please* (New York: Simon and Schuster, 1935), 107–121. Duranty, correspondent for the New York *Times*, arrived in Moscow about a month after Vorse. MHV, Daily Notes, 1928, Box 77, WSU-MHV; Richard and Anna Maria Drinnon, eds., *Nowhere at Home: Letters from Exile of Emma Goldman and Alexander Berkman* (New York: Schocken Books, 1975), 240–241; Alfred Rosmer, *Moscow under Lenin* (New York: Monthly Review Press, 1972); MHV, *Footnote to Folly*, 362.

14. Paul Avrich, *Kronstadt, 1921* (Princeton: Princeton University Press, 1970); Robert Vincent Daniels, *The Conscience of the Revolution: Communist Opposition in Soviet Russia* (Cambridge: Harvard University Press, 1960); MHV, Daily Notes, March 1928, Box 80, WSU-MHV; Jane Degras, ed., *The Communist International, 1919–1922* (New York: Oxford University Press, 1956), vol. 1.

15. Benjamin M. Weissman, *Herbert Hoover and Famine Relief in Soviet Russia, 1921–1923* (Stanford: Hoover Institution Press, 1974), 8; also see Paxton Hibben, *Report on the Russian Famine* (New York: American Committee for Relief of Russian Children, 1922); H. H. Fisher, *The Famine in Soviet Russia, 1919–1923: The Operations of the American Relief Administration* (New York: Macmillan, 1927); Frank Golder and Lincoln Hutchinson, *On the Trail of the Russian Famine* (Stanford: Stanford University Press, 1927).

16. *Izvetsia*, August 12, 1921, 2:5, researched and translated by Anthony Pasquariello for author. "Soviet Will Get Food," Washington *Times*, August 7, 1921, p. 1, claimed the train would leave Moscow on August 9, with ten American correspondents.

17. MHV, "Russian Pictures," *Liberator*, July 1922; *Footnote to Folly*, 362–392; "Russian Famine," Box 107, WSU-MHV; Duranty, *I Write as I Please*, 122–138, reached Samara a few days after Vorse, as did Floyd Gibbons, "Polyglot Hordes Congest Samara," New York *Times*, August 30, 1921, 5:3; Carl Eric Bechhofer Roberts, *Through Starving Russia* (London: Methuen, 1921).

18. The others were Bessie Beatty, Ernestine Evans, and Helen Auger. Robert W. Desmond, *Crisis and Conflict: World News Reporting between Two Wars, 1920–1940* (Iowa City: University of Iowa Press, 1982), 22–48.

19. MHV, *Footnote to Folly*, 375, 378, 377, 388; MHV to Neith Hapgood, 1921, YUB-NBHH; interview, Heaton Vorse, 1983; MHV, "Profits and Dreamers: The R.A.I.C.," *Nation*, December 2, 1922, 713–714.

20. Emma Goldman, *Living My Life* (New York: Dover Publications, 1970; originally published 1931), vol. 2, 906; Lucy Robbins Lang, *Tomorrow Is Beautiful* (New York: Macmillan, 1948), 201; MHV, *Footnote to Folly*, 382; Goldman, *Living My Life*, vol. 2, 911, and Drinnon, *Nowhere at Home*, 56.

21. MHV, Daily Notes, Box 78, WSU-MHV. Vorse mentions the annulment in 1922 of her marriage to Minor, Box 92, WSU-MHV.

22. MHV, *Footnote to Folly*, 394, 395; MHV, *Second Cabin* (New York: Horace Liveright, 1928).

23. William Preston, *Aliens and Dissenters: Federal Suppression of Radicals, 1903–1933* (New York: Harper and Row, 1966), 240.

24. Philip S. Foner and Sally M. Miller, eds., *Kate Richards O'Hare: Selected Writings and Speeches* (Baton Rouge: Louisiana State University Press, 1982), 333–340; Neil K. Basen, "Kate Richards O'Hare: The 'First Lady' of American Socialism, 1901–1917," *Labor History*, Spring 1980, 165–199; New York *Times* for reports of crusade, March 29, 1922, 8:2; April 30, 1922, 20:3; May 6, 1922, 11:3, and New York *Evening Telegram* for arrival in New York, April 26, 1922.

25. MHV, "The Children's Crusade for Amnesty," *Nation*, May 10, 1922, 559–561; MHV, "Open! The Crusaders Are Here," *National Rip-Saw*, April, May 1922; Cather cited in William Leuchtenburg, *The Perils of Prosperity, 1914–1932* (Chicago: University of Chicago Press, 1958), 272–273; New York *Times*, March 22, 1922, 16:4; also see summation of public opinion in "Amnesty for the Talkers," *Literary Digest*, October 21, 1922, July 7, 1923.

26. FBI-MHV.

27. Interview, Heaton Vorse, 1984. PU-ACLU, 1930, vol. 399, undated news clipping states "The marriage [of MHV and Minor] was a secret one, discovered about 3 weeks later [after their return from Russia]." Minor filed for divorce from his first wife in October 1919, Box 53, WSU-MHV; FBI-RM.

28. David T. Courtwright, *Dark Paradise: Opiate Addiction in America before 1940* (Cambridge: Harvard University Press, 1982); H. Wayne Morgan, *Drugs in America: A Social History, 1800–1980* (Syracuse: Syracuse University Press, 1981); David F. Musto, *The American Disease: Origins of Narcotic Control* (New Haven: Yale University Press, 1973); Nicholas and Lillian Segal Kopeloff, "The Drug Evil," *New Republic*, March 7, 1923, 41–43; Pearce Bailey, "The Drug Habit in the United States," *New Republic*, March 16, 1921, 67–69; "Drug Addicts in America," *Outlook*, June 25, 1919, 315; Peter A. Bryce, "Menace of the Drug Mania," *Current History Magazine*, January 1923, 638–641.

29. John Dos Passos, *The Big Money* (New York: Washington Square Press, 1961), 609, 616. Also Eleanor Widmer, "The Lost Girls of U.S.A.," in Warren French, ed., *The Thirties: Fiction, Poetry, Drama* (Deland, Fla.: Everett Edwards, 1967), 11–19.

30. Interview, Emily Hiebert, 1980.

31. Interview with neighbor, Provincetown, 1984. Name withheld on request.

Chapter Twelve: The Long Eclipse

1. MHV, Daily Notes, 1923, Box 78; MHV to Mary Simkhovitch, Daily Notes, 1927, Box 80, WSU-MHV.

2. MHV, Daily Notes, 1925, Box 78, WSU-MHV.

3. Ibid., 1923, 1926, Box 79, WSU-MHV.

4. Tillie Olsen, *Silences* (New York: Delacorte Press/Seymour Lawrence, 1965), 13, 33.

5. Elaine Showalter, "Literary Criticism," *Signs*, Winter 1975, 459–460.

6. MHV, Daily Notes, 1923, 1925, Box 78, WSU-MHV, says of Linda Gibson, "She had no charity nor did she keep the rules. Her idea was to separate me from RM and to make me as unpleasant in his eyes as possible. I think she was mighty wise."

7. Ibid., 1923, Box 78; MHV to RM, and Griffin Barry to MHV, Box 58, WSU-MHV.

8. Hutchins Hapgood to MHV, cited Daily Notes, 1928, Box 80, WSU-MHV.

9. MHV, Daily Notes, 1923, Box 78, WSU-MHV.

10. MHV, "Drink, a Very Human Document," *Cosmopolitan*, March 1924, 36; Daily Notes, 1923, Box 78, WSU-MHV.

11. MHV, "Why I Have Failed as a Mother," *Cosmopolitan*, September 1924, 46–47. See Nancy Cott, *The Grounding of Modern Feminism* (New Haven: Yale University Press, 1987), 175–213, for a discussion of the criticism of working mothers prevalent in the 1920s.

12. MHV, Daily Notes, 1926, Box 79, WSU-MHV.

13. Ibid., 1925, Box 79, WSU-MHV.

14. Ibid.

15. MHV, "Elizabeth Gurley Flynn," *Nation*, February 17, 1926, 175–176.

16. Selig Perlman and Philip Taft, *History of Labor in the United States, 1896–1932*, vol. 4, *Labor Movements* (New York: Macmillan, 1935), 557.

17. MHV, Daily Notes, 1926, Box 79, WSU-MHV. The host, Lewis Gannett, was a newspaperman and book critic for the New York *Herald Tribune*.

18. MHV, "Passaic," Box 116, WSU-MHV.

19. "United Front Defense for Passaic Strike," *Daily Worker*, April 25, 1926; MHV, "Passaic—The Hell Hole," ibid., February 27, 1926. Also see Boxes 115–118, WSU-MHV, for large collection of material on Passaic strike, including clippings, affidavits, correspondence, *Textile Strike Bulletin*, notes, and draft of MHV's book on Passaic strike.

20. Morton Siegel, "The Passaic Strike of 1926," Ph.D. diss., Columbia University, 1952, 331; MHV, "The War in Passaic," *Nation*, March 17, 1926, 280–281. Also see Paul Murphy et al., eds., *The Passaic Textile Strike of 1926* (Belmont, Calif.: Wadsworth Publishing Company, 1974). Steven R. Irwin, "Conflict Resolution and the Development of Law: The Passaic Textile Strike of 1926 and the New Jersey State Riot Act," senior thesis, 1976, Archives, Rutgers University, New Brunswick, N.J., is sometimes inaccurate but valuable for interviews of strike observers.

21. Interview, Vera Weisbord Buch, 1984; MHV, "The War in Passaic," 281.

22. "Passaic Reviewed," CHS-AW; Michael H. Ebner, "Strikes and Society: Civil Behavior in Passaic, 1875–1926," *New Jersey History*, 1979, 7–24; MHV, "Passaic," Box 116, WSU-MHV; interview, John Bebout, 1984, then a college student at Rutgers University, who often traveled to Passaic to aid the strike effort; interview, Martha Stone Asher, 1986, a strike participant at Passaic, and later a Communist leader.

23. "Outsiders Blamed for Trouble at Passaic," April, 21, 1926, vol. 314, PU-ACLU.

24. Benjamin Gitlow, *I Confess: The Truth about American Communism* (New York: E.P. Dutton, 1940), 371, 372, 16.

25. MHV, "Passaic Strike Notes," Box 118; MHV, "Passaic," Box 116, WSU-MHV.

26. Isabelle Kendig to Forrest Bailey, May 6, 1926, and Bailey to Kendig, May 8, 1926, vol. 310, PU-ACLU; Kendig to Bailey, May 6; Correspondence, Box 58, WSU-MHV, for letters between Kendig, Margaret Larkin, Pauline Clark, MHV, on Washington lobbying effort.

27. *Proceedings*, Seventh Biennial Convention of The Amalgamated Clothing Workers of America, May 13, 1926, 307–309, for speech by MHV to convention, in

Alexander Library, Rutgers University, New Brunswick, N.J. Also "8 New Yorkers to Form Picket Line in Clifton," Passaic *Daily Herald*, May 14, 1926, news clippings on strike in PU-ACLU.

28. Passaic Reference, Box 118, WSU-MHV.

29. MHV, Daily Notes, 1926, Box 79, WSU-MHV.

30. Ibid.; Rosalyn Baxandall, *Words on Fire: The Life and Writing of Elizabeth Gurley Flynn* (New Brunswick, N.J.: Rutgers University Press, 1987), 1–73.

31. MHV, Daily Notes, 1926, Box 80, WSU-MHV.

32. Ibid., Boxes 79, 80, WSU-MHV.

33. Duncan to MHV, Box 58, WSU-MHV.

34. MHV, Daily Notes, 1927, Box 80, WSU-MHV.

35. "Fiance Marries Mary Heaton Vorse's Daughter—Cables for Her Passage Money," New York *Times*, March 31, 1928, 6:4; also see New York *Times*, April 1, 1928, 4:1, and Correspondence, 1928, Box 59, WSU-MHV.

36. MHV, *Time and the Town: A Provincetown Chronicle* (New York: Dial Press, 1942), 220–221.

37. MHV, "The Hole in the Wall," *Parents' Magazine*, January 1929, 14–16, 38, 40–41.

38. MHV, Daily Notes, 1928, Box 80, WSU-MHV.

39. Ibid.

40. MHV, *Second Cabin* (New York: Liveright, 1928); *New York Times Book Review*, November 18, 1928, 30; New York *Herald-Tribune Books*, November 28, 1928, 14.

41. MHV, Daily Notes, 1928, Box 81, WSU-MHV.

42. Ibid.

Chapter Thirteen: War in the South

1. Cited in Liston Pope, *Millhands and Preachers: A Study of Gastonia* (New Haven: Yale University Press, 1942), 159n.; John R. Earle, Dean D. Knudsen, and Donald W. Shriver, Jr., *Spindles and Spires: A Restudy of Religion and Social Change in Gastonia* (Atlanta: John Knox Press, 1976).

2. Theodore Draper, "Gastonia Revisited," *Social Research*, Spring 1971, 5.

3. MHV, "Gastonia," *Harper's*, November 1929, 700; Dan McCurry and Carolyn Ashbaugh, "Gastonia, 1929: Strike at the Loray Mill," *Southern Exposure*, Winter 1973–74, 185–203.

4. *The North Carolina Guide* (Federal Writer's Project: North Carolina Department of Conservation and Development, 1939), 5.

5. MHV, "Gastonia Strike," Box 122, WSU-MHV.

6. Sherwood Anderson, "Elizabethton, Tennessee," *Nation*, May 1, 1929, 527; New York *Times*, April 5, 1929, 10:2; James A. Hodges, "Challenge to the New South: The Great Textile Strike in Elizabethton, Tennessee, 1929," *Tennessee Historical Quarterly*, December 1964, 343–357; Jacquelyn Dowd Hall, "Disorderly Women: Gender and Labor Militancy in the Appalachian South," *Journal of American History*, 1986, 354–382.

7. Cited in Vera Buch Weisbord, *A Radical Life* (Bloomington: Indiana University Press, 1977), 183; Paul Blanshard, "Communism in Southern Cotton Mills," *Nation*, April 24, 1929, 500; interview, Vera Buch [Weisbord], 1984.

8. Paul and Mari Jo Buhle, introduction to Weisbord, *A Radical Life*, xv–xvi.

9. Draper, "Gastonia Revisited," 19.

10. "On Mills—Troubles," Charlotte *Observer*, April 5, 1929, and "Big Innuendo," Gastonia *Daily Gazette*, May 5, 1929, in vol. 367, PU-ACLU.

11. Tom Tippett, *When Southern Labor Stirs* (New York: Jonathan Cape and Harrison Smith, 1931), 86–87.

12. "Wreck Union Office in Southern Strike," New York *Times*, April 19, 1929, 2:7.

13. See newspaper clippings, including Federated Press, in vol. 367, PU-ACLU.

14. MHV, Strike Journal, Gastonia, Box 155, WSU-MHV. Also see Box 156 for clippings, dispatches, notes, and correspondence about strikes in Gastonia and Elizabethton. In my interview with Vera Buch, in 1984, she remarked that she was embarrassed to have the workers read the *Daily Worker*, so inaccurate were its reports of the prospects for victory at Gastonia.

15. Weisbord, *A Radical Life*, 206.

16. MHV, Strike Journal, Gastonia, Box 155, WSU-MHV.

17. Ibid.

18. Weisbord, *A Radical Life*, 218; CHS-VBW in Box 6, CHS-AW.

19. "Action Brought by Leaders of the Loray Strike," Gastonia *Daily Gazette*, May 14, 1929, in vol. 367, PU-ACLU.

20. MHV, Miscellaneous Notes, Box 155, WSU-MHV.

21. MHV, Gastonia, Box 156, WSU-MHV; MHV, "Gastonia," *Harper's*, 707.

22. "Mass Evictions in Mill Strike," Reading *Advocate*, May 25, 1929, in vol. 367, PU-ACLU; MHV, Strike Journal, Gastonia, Box 155, WSU-MHV.

23. MHV, Miscellaneous Notes, WSU-MHV; "Mill Strikers Clash with Southern Police," New York *Times*, April 23, 1929, 48:2.

24. MHV, "Elizabethton Sits on a Powder Keg," *New Masses*, July 1929, 6; MHV, Box 156, WSU-MHV; telephone interview, Sophie Melvin (Mrs. Si Gerson), 1984; letter to author from Broadus Mitchell, February 7, 1985. I am indebted to Rita Heller for this last citation.

25. Weisbord, *A Radical Life*, 219.

26. Daily Notes, 1929, Box 81, WSU-MHV.

27. MHV, "Affairs of the House," Box 15, WSU-MHV.

28. Daily Notes, Box 81; Miscellaneous Notes, Box 156, Correspondence, Box 156, WSU-MHV; MHV to Forrest Bailey, June 11, 1929, vol. 367, PU-ACLU.

29. Edmund Wilson, *The Shores of Light: A Literary Chronicle of the Twenties and Thirties* (New York: Farrar, Strauss and Young, 1952), 497–498. Wilson said the *New Republic* sent a young man to Gastonia who reported back that there was nothing of interest there. Wilson later marveled that the young fellow had been there on the day Ella May Wiggins was killed. Also see Dos Passos to MHV, 1929, Box 60, WSU-MHV.

30. Cited in Samuel Yellen, *American Labor Struggles, 1877–1934* (New York: Pathfinder Press, 1974), 310; MHV, Strike Journal, Gastonia, Box 155, WSU-MHV.

31. Nell Battle Lewis, "Tar Heel Justice," *Nation*, September 11, 1929, 273.

32. See Boxes 155, 156, WSU-MHV, for Vorse's press dispatches and for newspaper clippings on the trial.

33. MHV, "Gastonia," Box 155, WSU-MHV.

34. MHV, Daily Notes, 1929, Box 81, WSU-MHV.

35. MHV, Dispatches, Box 155, WSU-MHV.

36. MHV, "State Orders Arrest in Two Terror Raids," New York *Evening Graphic*, September 11, 1929, Box 155, WSU-MHV.

37. MHV, Daily Notes, September 14, 1929, Box 81, WSU-MHV.

38. MHV, "Songs Live On: Ella May Dies, Mob's Victim," New York *Evening Graphic*, September 16, 1929, Box 155, WSU-MHV; interview, Vera Buch Weisbord, 1984. According to a letter I received from Randal H. Tolbert and Tish Merrill on November 20, 1983, Wiggins was pregnant when she was murdered. Vera Buch wrote me in November 1983 that she believed the puzzling box of "luxury women's clothing," found in Wiggins's home after her death, had been given to Wiggins by MHV. Buch added: "It was a great mistake on [Vorse's] part to imagine that poor despised textile workers coveted these luxuries women have. . . . The gift of it was Vorse's feeling of guilt that she had all these lovely things while the strikers were so dirt poor." No one was ever tried for Wiggins's death.

39. Dispatches, Box 155, WSU-MHV.

40. Cited in Irving Bernstein, *The Lean Years: A History of the American Worker, 1920–1933* (Boston: Houghton Mifflin, 1960), 31. Also see Benjamin Stolberg, "Madness in Marion," *Nation*, October 23, 1929, 462–464.

41. Tom Tippett, "Mill Boss Gloats over Massacre," dispatch to Federated Press, Box 156, WSU-MHV.

42. MHV, "Waitin' with the Dead," *New Republic*, October 30, 1929, 287–288. The *New Republic* paid $50 for this piece, more than their usual rate. Also see "Stirring Rites Held for Marion Victims," New York *Times*, October 5, 1929; and MHV, "Eye Witness Describes Marion Murders," Federated Press release, in vol. 367, PU-ACLU.

Chapter Fourteen: Holding the Line

1. Mary Austin, *Earth Horizon: Autobiography* (New York: Riverside Press, 1932), 279; Dodge to MHV, January 6, 1929, and Austin to MHV, December 31, 1929, Box 59; Austin to MHV, Box 54; MHV, Daily Notes, 1930, Box 81; Daily Notes, 1929, Box 82; WSU-MHV; MHV, "Deer Dance in Taos," *Nation*, August 13, 1930, 179; MHV to Boyce, Correspondence, circa 1929, YUB-NBHH; Henry C. Schmidt, "The American Intellectual Discovery of Mexico in the 1920s," *South Atlantic Quarterly*, Summer 1978, 335–351; MHV, Daily Notes, 1930, Box 81; Ellen to MHV, December 30, 1929, Box 59, WSU-MHV; MHV to Dodge, YUB-MDL.

2. MHV, Daily Notes, 1930, Box 81, and Daily Summaries, 1930, Box 77, WSU-MHV; MHV, "Mexico the Beautiful," *Good Housekeeping*, April 1931, 42–43; MHV, "Mexican Adventure," Box 26, WSU-MHV.

3. Dorothy Day, *The Eleventh Virgin* (New York: Albert and Charles Boni, 1924); Day, *The Long Loneliness* (New York: Doubleday, 1959), 94; William D. Miller,

Dorothy Day: A Biography (San Francisco: Harper and Row, 1982), 211–212; Dorothy Day, "Picture of M-H-V," Box 40, WSU-MHV.

4. MHV, Daily Summaries, 1930, Box 77, and Daily Notes, Box 81, WSU-MHV; Betty Bruce to author, 1980; MHV to Neith Boyce and Hutch Hapgood, 1929, YUB-NBHH; MHV, Daily Notes, 1939, Box 82, WSU-MHV.

5. Edmund Wilson, *The Thirties: From Notebooks and Diaries of the Period*, ed. Leon Edel (New York: Farrar, Straus and Giroux, 1980); interview, Hazel Hawthorne Werner, 1982; MHV, Daily Notes, 1930, Box 82, WSU-MHV.

6. MHV, Daily Notes, 1930, Box 82, WSU-MHV.

7. MHV, *Strike!* (New York: Horace Liveright, 1930). MHV spoke on *Strike!* to Heterodoxy in January 1931; see Inez Irwin to MHV, November 18, 1930, Box 60, WSU-MHV. Carl Reeve, "Gastonia: The Strike, The Frameup, the Heritage," *Political Affairs*, April 1984, 23–31, denies that only women were on the picket line.

8. Roger Baldwin called her novel "an enduring memorial to a great strike," in Baldwin to MHV, November 3, 1930, Box 60, WSU-MHV; Sinclair Lewis, "A Novel for Mr. Hoover," *Nation*, December 10, 1930, 474; Haessler to MHV, Box 59, WSU-MHV.

9. Daniel Aaron, *Writers on the Left* (New York: Avon Books, 1969); Harvey Klehr, *The Heyday of American Communism: The Depression Decade* (New York: Basic Books, 1984); Walter Rideout, *The Radical Novel in the United States, 1900–1954* (Cambridge: Harvard University Press, 1956); Berkshire Conference of Women Historians, Plenary, 1984.

10. EGF to MHV, May 16, 1930, and MHV, Daily Notes, 1931, Box 82, WSU-MHV.

11. MHV, Daily Notes, 1931, Box 82, WSU-MHV.

12. Ibid., September 21, 1931, Box 82, WSU-MHV.

13. Ibid., "England and Germany, 1931," Box 82; MHV, "Ellen Wilkinson Is Dead," Box 19; MHV, Daily Notes, 1931, Box 82, WSU-MHV.

14. MHV, "Reinhardt and Revolution," *New Yorker*, December 26, 1931, 37–39; MHV, "Davis Cup at Zagreb," Box 18; MHV, "Germany, 1931, Notes," Box 105; letters from MHV to Ellen and Heaton, Box 60, WSU-MHV.

15. Telegram, Box 61, WSU-MHV; interviews, Adelaide Walker, 1984.

16. National Committee for the Defense of Political Prisoners, *Harlan Miners Speak: Report on Terrorism in the Kentucky Coal Fields*, ed. Theodore Dreiser (New York: Harcourt, Brace, 1932); "Notes Taken at Harlan County, Kentucky," Box 72, Series I, UVAL-JDP.

17. John W. Hevener, *Which Side Are You On? The Harlan County Coal Miners, 1931–39* (Urbana: University of Illinois Press, 1978), 22; Tony Bubka, "The Harlan County Coal Strike of 1931," *Labor History*, Winter 1970, 41–57; Theodore Draper, "Communists and Miners, 1928–1933," *Dissent*, Spring 1972, 371–392.

18. MHV, Daily Summaries, 1932, Box 77; Daily Notes, 1931, Box 82; Daily Notes, 1932, Box 83, WSU-MHV.

19. Hevener, *Which Side Are You On*, 59; interview, Jessie and Harvey O'Connor, 1982; O'Connor to Bailey, Bailey to O'Connor, January 7, 1932, vols. 549, 550, 570, PU-ACLU. Also see Jessie Lloyd O'Connor, Harvey O'Connor, and Susan M. Bowler, *Harvey and Jessie: A Couple of Radicals* (Philadelphia: Temple University Press, 1988).

20. MHV, Daily Notes, 1932, Box 83, WSU-MHV; Wilson, *The Thirties*, 161.

21. Malcolm Cowley, *The Dream of the Golden Mountains: Remembering the 1930s* (New York: Viking Press, 1964), 68; Alan Trachtenberg, ed., *Memoirs of Waldo Frank* (Amherst: University of Massachusetts Press, 1973), 180–182; interview, Adelaide Walker, 1984; interview, John Hammond, 1984.

22. "Writers Distribute Food," New York *Times*, February 10, 1932, 6:2; MHV, "Harlan County," Box 109, WSU-MHV; Wilson, *The Thirties*, 164; Hevener, *Which Side Are You On*, 79; MHV, Daily Notes, 1932, Box 83, WSU-MHV. Hammond later became the famous record producer and talent scout at Columbia Records who discovered artists like Billie Holiday, Aretha Franklin, and Bruce Springsteen.

23. Wilson, *The Thirties*, 166–167. MHV, "Rendezvous," Box 29, WSU-MHV, is a fictionalized account of her trip to Pineville.

24. Malcolm Cowley, "Kentucky Coal Town," *New Republic*, March 2, 1932, 67–70; Edmund Wilson, "Class War Exhibits," *New Masses*, April 1932, 7; Cowley, *Dream of the Golden Mountains*, 71; Wilson, *The Thirties*, 169, 171, 175.

25. Cowley, *Dream of the Golden Mountains*, 71; U.S. Congress, Senate, Committee on Manufacturers, *Conditions in Coal Fields in Harlan and Bell Counties, Kentucky*, Hearings before a Subcommittee of the Committee on Manufactures, on S.R. 178, 72d Congress, 1st sess., 1932; Wilson, *The Thirties*, 175–176; "Flogged on Way from Kentucky," New York *Herald-Tribune*, February 12, 1932. Herndon Evans, who filed the false report, was also editor of the Pineville *Sun* and then the Bell County correspondent for the Associated Press. MHV, "Harlan County," Box 109, WSU-MHV; "Kentucky Ejection Told to Senators," New York *Times*, February 13, 1932, 15:7; Draper, "Communists and Miners," 387. Wilson, *The Thirties*, 184–185, remembered that after their visit to Pineville, he, Dos Passos, and MHV sat in a New York speakeasy accusing each other of not being far enough left and that Vorse "announced solemnly that she had thought about her Provincetown house being confiscated [by the federal government]."

26. MHV, Daily Notes, 1932, Box 83, WSU-MHV.

27. Yaddo is described in Virginia Spencer Carr, *The Lonely Hunter: A Biography of Carson McCullers* (New York: Anchor Books, 1976); MHV to Ellen, Box 61, WSU-MHV; interview, Heaton Vorse, 1986.

28. Susan Cheever, *Home before Dark* (New York: Houghton Mifflin, 1984), 35; Memoirs, YUB-JH.

29. MHV, Daily Notes, 1932, Box 83, WSU-MHV; Elinor Langer, *Josephine Herbst* (Boston: Little, Brown, 1984); MHV, Daily Notes, 1932, Box 83; Daily Summaries, 1932, Box 77, WSU-MHV.

30. John L. Shover, *Cornbelt Rebellion: The Farmers' Holiday Association* (Urbana: University of Illinois Press, 1965); Lowell K. Dyson, *Red Harvest: The Communist Party and American Farmers* (Lincoln: University of Nebraska Press, 1982); Josephine Herbst, "Feet in the Grass Roots," *Scribner's Magazine*, January 1933, 47; MHV, Daily Notes, 1932, Box 83, WSU-MHV; MHV, "Rebellion in the Cornbelt: American Farmers Beat Their Plowshares into Swords," *Harper's*, December 1932, 3; Herbst to Marion Greenwood, September 9, 17, 1932, in YUB-JH; MHV, "The Farmers' Relief Conference, *New Republic*, December 28, 1932, 183–185; MHV, "Farmers in Revolt," Box 20, "Farmers and Farm Workers, 1932" and "Farmers' Holiday," Box 108, WSU-MHV.

31. Daniel J. Leab, "United We Eat: The Creation and Organization of the Unemployed Councils in 1930," *Labor History*, 1967, 308; Klehr, *Heyday*, 49–68; interview, Sam D'Arcy, 1984.

32. Miller, *Dorothy Day*, 224–225; also see William Miller, *A Harsh and Dreadful Love: Dorothy Day and the Catholic Workers Movement* (New York: Liveright, 1973).

33. "Capitol and Extra Police for Marchers," Washington *Post*, December 1, 1932, 1:6; "Legion to Aid Police on March," ibid., December 2, 1932, 1:1; "DC Ban on Marchers," ibid., December 3, 1932, 1; "Massed DC Police to Meet 3000," ibid., December 4, 1932, 1:4; "DC Warned," ibid., December 2, 1:5; "Marchers Are Hemmed in by Master Police Stroke," ibid., December 4, 1932, 1:1; Cowley, *Dream of the Golden Mountains*, 131.

34. MHV, "Psychology of Demonstrations," Box 29, "Newspaper Articles, Federated Press, 1932–34," Box 36, WSU-MHV; MHV, "School for Bums," *New Republic*, April 29, 1931; Miller, *Dorothy Day*, 225–226; Dorothy Day to author, 1978; Neil Betten, "The Great Depression and the Activities of the Catholic Worker Movement," *Labor History*, 1971, 243–258.

35. Day offended many right-wing Catholics with her stand against the Vietnam War and nuclear weapons, and her support of César Chavez's unionization of migrant workers. Her last years were spent at a Catholic Workers' hospice on the lower East Side.

36. Dan T. Carter, *Scottsboro: A Tragedy of the American South* (Baton Rouge: Louisiana State University Press, 1969); John Hammond, *John Hammond on Record* (New York: Penguin Books, 1977); interview, 1984, John Hammond, who drove to the trial with Vorse.

37. MHV, Daily Notes, 1933, Box 83, WSU-MHV; MHV, "The Scottsboro Trial," *New Republic*, April 19, 1933, 276–278; MHV, Daily Summaries, 1933, Box 77, WSU-MHV; MHV, "How Scottsboro Happened," *New Republic*, May 10, 1933, 356–358.

38. Donald L. Miller, *The New American Radicalism: Alfred M. Bingham and Non-Marxian Insurgency in the New Deal Era* (Port Washington, N.Y.: Kennikat Press, 1979); MHV, Daily Summaries, 1933, Box 77, WSU-MHV.

39. MHV to Joel, May 1933, Box 61; MHV, Daily Summaries, 1933, Box 77; Daily Notes, 1933, Box 83; MHV to Ellen, May 1933, Box 61; clippings and notes on Europe–Germany, 1933, and Economic Program, Box 105, WSU-MHV; MHV to Katy and John Dos Passos, Box 19, UVAL-JDP; MHV to "Bunny" Wilson, June 23, 1933, YUB-EW; MHV, "Berlin Letter," Box 105, WSU-MHV; MHV, "Getting the Jews out of Germany," *New Republic*, July 19, 1933, 256.

40. MHV, "Book Burning," Box 105, WSU-MHV; MHV, "Germany: The Twilight of Reason," *New Republic*, June 14, 1933, 118–119; MHV, "Fires Flare to German Borders—and Beyond," *McCall's*, June 1934, 77.

41. MHV, Russia, 1933, Box 107, WSU-MHV. Also see Sylvia R. Margulies, *The Pilgrimage to Russia: The Soviet Union and the Treatment of Foreigners, 1924–1937* (Madison: University of Wisconsin Press, 1968); interview, Myra Page, 1984.

42. MHV, "Do You Know These People?", *McCall's*, 1934, 35, 25; MHV, Moscow Article, Box 107; Daily Summaries, 1933, Box 77; WSU-MHV; James William Crowl, *Angels in Stalin's Paradise: Western Reporters in Soviet Russia, 1917 to 1937; A Case Study of Louis Fischer and Walter Duranty* (New York: University Press

of America, 1982). Also see William Henry Chamberlin, "Soviet Taboos," *Foreign Affairs*, April 1935, 431–440; Peter G. Filene, *Americans and the Soviet Experience, 1917–1933* (Cambridge: Harvard University Press, 1967); K. A. Jalenski, "The Literature of Disenchantment," *Survey*, April 1962, 109–119; Paul Hollander, *Political Pilgrims: Travels of Western Intellectuals to the Soviet Union, China and Cuba, 1928–1978* (New York: Oxford University Press, 1981).

Chapter Fifteen: Washington Whirl

1. MHV, Daily Notes, Boxes 83, 90, WSU-MHV.

2. Howe cited in Judith Schwarz, *Radical Feminists of Heterodoxy: Greenwich Village, 1912–1940* (Lebanon, N.H.: New Victoria Publishers, 1982), 79; Edmund Wilson, *The Thirties: From Notebooks and Diaries of the Period*, ed. Leon Edel (New York: Farrar, Straus and Giroux, 1980), 390–391.

3. MHV, Daily Notes, Box 83, WSU-MHV.

4. MHV, "Washington Whirl," *McCall's*, June 1934, 16, 130; also see draft in Box 34, WSU-MHV. The note of high glee expressed here was considerably softened by the *McCall's* editors for publication.

5. MHV, Daily Notes, Box 84, WSU-MHV.

6. Susan Ware, *Beyond Suffrage: Women in the New Deal* (Cambridge: Harvard University Press, 1981), 19; MHV, draft "Washington Whirl," Box 34, WSU-MHV.

7. See "Feminine Free Lance," *Time*, December 23, 1935, 51; Robert M. Lovett, "Mary Vorse Remembers," *New Republic*, January 1, 1936, 232; Florence F. Kelly, "A Decade in the Life of Mary Heaton Vorse," New York *Times Book Review*, January 12, 1936, 6; Harold E. Stearns, "Suffer Little Children," *Nation*, January 15, 1936, 80, 82; Edith Walton, *Forum*, June 1936, iv; Beulah Amidon, "News Drama of the Decade," *Saturday Review of Literature*, December 28, 1935, 7; John Chamberlin, New York *Times*, December 16, 1935, 25:1.

8. MHV, Daily Summaries, 1934, Box 78, WSU-MHV; Earl Latham, *The Communist Controversy in Washington: The New Deal to McCarthy* (Cambridge: Harvard University Press, 1966), 101–124, for a thoroughly reasoned discussion of the origins, composition, and function of the Ware group; Allen Weinstein, *Perjury: The Hiss-Chambers Case* (New York: Alfred Knopf, 1978); Elinor Langer, *Josephine Herbst* (Boston: Little, Brown, 1984), 156–157.

9. MHV, "On The Detroit Front," *New Republic*, April 4, 1934, 204–206; Roger Keeran, *The Communist Party and the Auto Workers Unions* (Bloomington: Indiana University Press, 1980), 96–121; Irving Bernstein, *The Turbulent Years: A History of the American Worker, 1933–1941* (Boston: Houghton Mifflin, 1970); Hopkins cited in William D. Leuchtenburg, *Franklin D. Roosevelt and the New Deal* (New York: Harper, 1963), 117; MHV, *Labor's New Millions* (New York: Modern Age Books, 1938), 28–29; MHV, Daily Summaries, 1935, Box 78; EGF to MHV, Box 84, WSU-MHV.

10. MHV, "Textile Trouble: New England on Strike," *New Republic*, September 19, 1934, 147–148. Waldo Frank describes the trip with Vorse to New England in his *In the American Jungle, 1925–1936* (New York: Farrar and Rinehart, 1937), 239.

11. Donald H. Grubbs, *Cry from the Cotton: The Southern Tenant Farmers' Union and the New Deal* (Chapel Hill: University of North Carolina Press, 1971), 3–62;

MHV cited in Matthew Josephson, *Infidel in the Temple: A Memoir of the Nineteen-Thirties* (New York: Alfred Knopf, 1967), 293.

12. Lawrence M. Hauptman, "The American-Indian Federation and the Indian New Deal: A Reinterpretation," *Pacific Historical Review*, November 1983, 378–403; Kenneth R. Philp, *John Collier's Crusade for Indian Reform, 1920–1954* (Tucson: University of Arizona Press, 1977); Lawrence C. Kelly, *The Assault on Assimilation: John Collier and the Origin of Indian Policy Reform* (Albuquerque: University of New Mexico Press, 1983). I am indebted to Professor Kelly for use of his research on Vorse, which he generously shared with me.

13. MHV, "Office on Indian Affairs," Box 114; Harold Ickes to Senator David I. Walsh, March 13, 1935, Box 62; "Helping the Indians to Help Themselves," Box 21, WSU-MHV; MHV, "Our Land," *Good Housekeeping*, July 1935, 38–39; YUS-JC.

14. FBI-MHV; U.S. Congressional Hearings, Before the Committee on Indian Affairs, House of Representatives, 74th Congress, 2d sess., 1936, May 9, April 26, 121–122, 122–124.

15. Box 1, SC-AT; Elizabeth Dilling, *The Red Network* (Kenilworth, Ill.: published by the author, 1934).

16. Kenneth O'Reilly, *Hoover and the Un-Americans: The* FBI, HUAC, *and the Red Menace* (Philadelphia: Temple University Press, 1983), 35; interview, Len DeCaux, 1986; Melvyn Dubofsky and Warren Van Tine, *John L. Lewis: A Biography* (New York: Quadrangle, 1977); Len DeCaux, *Labor Radical: From the Wobblies to the CIO* (Boston: Beacon Press, 1970), 230; MHV, Daily Summaries, Box 78; Daily Notes, Box 84, WSU-MHV.

17. MHV, *Labor's New Millions*, 58; "Organizing the Steel Workers," *New Republic*, August 12, 1936, 13–15; "A Year of the CIO," ibid., November 25, 1936, 106–107.

18. Elinor Langer, *Josephine Herbst* (Boston: Little, Brown, 1984), 185; James Gilbert, *Writers and Partisans* (New York: John Wiley and Sons, 1968). MHV was invited to the First American Writers' Congress, held April 26–28 in New York, but did not attend, although she is listed as a member of the National Council of the League of American Writers. I am grateful to Art Cosinato for this information. Matthew Josephson wrote MHV on February 17, 1935, that he too favored "more political action and less literary criticism," in Box 64, WSU-MHV. Also see Alan M. Wald, *James T. Farrell: The Revolutionary Socialist Years* (New York: New York University Press, 1978). MHV commented on the contribution of anti-Semitism and other manifestations of fascism to the persecution of labor in *We Hold These Truths* (New York: League of American Writers, 1939).

19. Telegram, David Dubinsky to MHV, December 5, 1936; MHV to Julius Hochman, December 13, 1936; Julius Hochman to MHV, undated, Box 64; MHV report to Hochman in Box 127; MHV to Ellen, 1936, Box 63, WSU-MHV.

20. Katy Dos Passos to "Casper" (MHV), undated from Key West, Box 62, WSU-MHV; interview, Toby and Betty Bruce, 1984.

Chapter Sixteen: Labor's New Millions

1. Cited in Frank Cormier and William J. Eaton, *Reuther* (Englewood Cliffs, N.J.: Prentice-Hall, 1970), 86.

2. MHV, "Flint Sitdown Strike," Box 109, WSU-MHV. Unless otherwise indicated material in this chapter on the Flint sit-down is from this source. Also see MHV, *Labor's New Millions* (New York: Modern Age Books, 1938), 67–69.

3. Cited in Sidney Fine, *Sit Down: The General Motors Strike of 1936–37* (Ann Arbor: University of Michigan Press, 1969), 198. Also see Sidney Fine, "The General Motors Sit-Down Strike: A Re-examination," *American Historical Review*, 1965, 260–277; Henry Kraus, *The Many & The Few: A Chronicle of the Dynamic Auto Workers* (Los Angeles: Plantin Press, 1947).

4. Fine, *Sit Down*, 269–270, 279–281; MHV, *Labor's New Millions*, 74–81. Also see *With Babies and Banners*, 1978, documentary film directed by Lorraine Gray.

5. Also see MHV, "The Emergency Brigade at Flint," *New Republic*, February 17, 1937, 38–39; MHV, "What the Women Did at Flint," *Woman Today*, March 1937, 29.

6. Hallie Flanagan planned the didactic plays called Living Newspapers as part of the Federal Theater Project. The first Living Newspaper was censored by Washington authorities in 1935. Before the federal government closed down its program, in June 1939, five Living Newspaper plays reached the stage. See Hallie Flanagan, *Arena: The History of the Federal Theater* (New York: Duell, Sloan and Pierce, 1940). Morris Watson describes the wild rehearsals and delivery of *Strike Marches On* in "Sitdown Theater," *New Theater and Film*, April 1937. Also see Box 109, WSU-MHV.

7. MHV, "Armistice Day Arrives," *People's Press*, February 20, 1937; "Newspaper Articles, 1937," Box 36, WSU-MHV.

8. "Anderson (Ind.) Strike, 1937," Box 94, WSU-MHV; interview, Heaton Vorse, 1986; "Steel, 1936–37," Box 121, WSU-MHV. MHV cited in Fine, *Sit Down*, 316; Claude E. Hoffman, *Sit-Down in Anderson: UAW Local 663, Anderson, Indiana* (Detroit: Wayne State University Press, 1968).

9. Milton Siegel to Harry Poth, February 24, 1937, PU-ACLU; MHV, on Anderson strike, Box 94; Federated Press releases, Box 36; Victor Reuther to MHV, April 5, 1937; EGF to MHV, March 22, 1937; KDP to MHV, March 8, 1937, Box 64, WSU-MHV. The UAW paid Heaton's medical and legal fees.

10. Melvyn Dubofsky and Warren Van Tine, *John L. Lewis: A Biography* (New York: Quadrangle, 1977), 277. Also see MHV, "Steel Signs Up," *New Republic*, May 5, 1937, 375–376; and Melvyn Dubofsky, "Not So 'Turbulent Years': A New Look at the 1930s," in Charles Stephenson and Robert Asher, eds., *Life and Labor: Dimensions of American Working-Class History* (Albany: State University of New York Press, 1986), 205–223; MHV, "Detroit Has the Jitters," *New Republic*, April 7, 1937, 256–258; Box 36, WSU-MHV, contains dispatches MHV wrote in the summer of 1937.

11. Philip Cook, "Tom Girdler and the Labor Policies of the Republic Steel Corporation," *Social Science History*, 1967, 21–30; James Baughman, "Classes and Company Towns: Legends of the 1937 Little Steel Strike," *Ohio History*, 1978, 175–184; Donald S. McPherson, "The 'Little Steel' Strike of 1937 in Johnstown, Pennsylvania," *Pennsylvania History*, 39, 1972, 45–56; Michael Speer, "The 'Little Steel' Strike: Conflict for Control," *Ohio History*, 78, 1969, 273–287. For a different view of the labor conflict see John Shiner, "The 1937 Steel Labor Dispute and the Ohio National Guard," ibid., 84, 1975, 182–195. Also see MHV, "The Steel Strike," *New Republic*, June 16, 1937, 154–156; "The Tories Attack through Steel: Girdlerism in Action at

Youngstown," ibid., July 7, 1937, 246–248; Youngstown *Vindicator*, May 26–June 30, 1937; interviews with Ed Salt, Clingnan Jackson, Jerry Beck, Angela Campana, in Youngstown, 1982. I am indebted to Philip Bracy for sending me the transcription of his interview with Fred A. Fortunato, a Youngstown steel worker in 1937. See Hearings Before Subcommittee of the Committee on Education and Labor, Violations of the Free Speech and Rights of Labor, Hearings on S. Res. 266, 75th Congress, Parts 26–31, July–August 1938, for discussion of the strike and shooting.

12. See, for example, "Johnstown Situation Tense: Mary Heaton Vorse Is Shot in Deadly Youngstown," Boston *Sunday Globe*, June 20, 1937, 1; MHV, radio interview, July 24, 1937, Box 113, WSU-MHV; MHV, *Labor's New Millions*, 144. According to the La Follette Committee investigation, Vorse was treated at the Youngstown Hospital when "struck by a brick or stone." Matthew Josephson in *Infidel in the Temple: A Memoir of the Nineteen-Thirties* (New York: Alfred Knopf, 1967), 415, reports Vorse was grazed by a submachine gun bullet. Murray Kempton describes the incident in *Part of Our Time: Some Ruins and Monuments of the Thirties* (New York: Simon and Schuster, 1955), 216, as: "She was clubbed by a policeman's billy." Professor John C. Tamplin credits the reports of a Youngstown *Vindicator* columnist and the examining physician who said Vorse suffered a head laceration, not a bullet wound; John C. Tamplin to author, August 23, 1984. I am grateful to Professor Tamplin for sharing his research paper, "Mary Heaton Vorse, Journalist: Victim of Strike Violence?" before its publication in *Labor History*, Winter 1987, 84–87. Tamplin also has produced an edited collection of her fiction in his book manuscript, "Lollypops and Bullets: A Mary Heaton Vorse Reader."

13. MHV to Ellen, July 3, 1937, Box 64, WSU-MHV; Marquis W. Childs, "Foreword," in MHV, *Labor's New Millions*, 2–3; Federated Press to MHV, June 20, 1937, Box 64, WSU-MHV.

14. MHV, Daily Summaries, 1937, Box 77; League of American Writers, Box 166; Ellen Blake to MHV, July 6, 1937; League of American Writers to MHV, September 23, 1937; Myra Page to MHV, undated 1937, Box 63, WSU-MHV.

15. "Raps U.S. Aid to Strike in Which Cousin Is Hurt," Springfield *Union*, June 21, 1937; interview, Heaton Vorse, 1986.

16. MHV, Daily Notes, 1938, Box 85; Daily Notes, 1937, Box 84, WSU-MHV.

17. MHV, Daily Notes, 1938, Box 85, WSU-MHV. John Dewey, upon his return from interviewing Leon Trotsky in Mexico, stayed with MHV for a few days in the house within the Navy Yard.

18. Benjamin Stolberg, *The Story of the CIO* (New York: Viking Press, 1938). Also see Edward Levinson, *Labor on the March* (New York: Harper, 1938), which seeks to refute Stolberg.

19. MHV, *Labor's New Millions*, 172.

20. Bruce Bliven to MHV, September 29, 1937, Box 64, WSU-MHV.

21. The description of her private concerns in this period are based on evidence in MHV, Daily Notes, 1939–1943, Boxes 85, 86, WSU-MHV.

22. MHV to Neith Boyce, Correspondence, YUB-NBHH; interview, Nea Colton, 1982; interview, Heaton Vorse, 1985.

23. MHV, "January, 1941 folder," Box 86, WSU-MHV.

24. MHV, *Time and the Town: A Provincetown Chronicle* (New York: Dial Press, 1942), 337; MHV, Daily Notes, 1939, Box 85, WSU-MHV.

25. Roger Keeran, *The Communist Party and the Auto Workers Unions* (Bloomington: Indiana University Press, 1980); Harvey A. Levenstein, *Communism, Anti-Communism and the CIO* (Westport, Conn.: Greenwood, 1981).

26. MHV to Ellen and Heaton, Box 66, WSU-MHV.

27. Testimony of John Frey, Walter Steele, and Alice Lee Jemison in U.S. Congressional Hearings, Special Committee to Investigate Un-American Activities and Propaganda in the United States, 75th Congress, 3d sess., 1936, vol. 1, pp. 96, 121, 561; vol. 3, pp. 2449–2450, 2437–2440, 2487, 1938. See August R. Ogden, *The Dies Committee* (Washington, D.C.: Catholic University of America Press, 1945); Benjamin Stolberg, "Muddled Millions," *Saturday Evening Post*, February 15, 1941, 90.

28. MHV to Gardner Jackson, Box 67; Daily Notes, 1939, Box 85, WSU-MHV.

29. MHV, Daily Notes, 1940, 1941, Boxes 85, 86, WSU-MHV.

30. Ibid., 1939, Box 85; MHV to Dorothy Day, Correspondence, 1939, Box 66, WSU-MHV; MHV, "Europe: Three Capitals," *New Republic*, August 16, 1939, 39–41. Also see her series in the New York *Times* of July 16, 1939, 21:1; July 1939, 17, 4:3; July 23, 1939, 29:1; MHV to Jo Herbst, July 5, 1939, Box 66, WSU-MHV.

31. MHV, Correspondence, 1939–1940, Box 66; MHV, Daily Notes, August 1940, Box 85, WSU-MHV.

32. MHV, Daily Notes, June 1940, Box 86, WSU-MHV.

33. Ibid., 1941, Box 85, WSU-MHV.

Chapter Seventeen: The Last Lap

1. Nelson Lichtenstein, *Labor's War at Home: The CIO in World War II* (New York: Cambridge University Press, 1982), 306, 163; MHV, "Women Don't Quit If —," *Independent Woman*, January 1944, 9: MHV, "Worker's Welfare Is War Work," *Woman's Press*, September 1943, 343–344; MHV, "And The Workers Say . . . ," *Public Opinion Quarterly*, Fall 1943, 443–456. The manuscript of her study of war work is "Here Are the People," Boxes 128, 129; her series of articles for the New York *Post* is in Box 127, WSU-MHV.

2. MHV, Daily Notes, July 1943, Box 86, WSU-MHV; unpublished ms. outline, "Wartown," by MHV, FDR-GJ.

3. MHV, Daily Summaries, 1943, Box 77, WSU-MHV. Herbst was accompanied by Clare Laning when she came to MHV's house the day she was fired. That evening the group commiserated with Mildred Straight. For a complete description of firing of Herbst, see Elinor Langer, *Josephine Herbst* (Boston: Little, Brown, 1984), 245–260, 287–289, 268–276. Langer demonstrates that the author Katherine Anne Porter gave the federal authorities a totally fanciful account, which falsely accused Herbst of serving as a Communist courier. Fleeta Springer would also be affected by Porter's diatribe, when Springer's husband, Robert Coe, temporarily lost his security clearance as a physicist for the Atomic Energy Commission—solely because the FBI interrogators reported him to be the same man as another "Bob" Coe whom Herbst had known in Washington in 1934.

4. MHV to JH, undated letter, YUB-JH.

5. Cordell Hull to Allen T. Treadway, March 25, 1944, Box 67, WSU-MHV; MHV, Daily Notes, 1945, Box 86, WSU-MHV.

6. UNA-MHV, N.Y.; MHV, "Old Age Came to Me," Box 115, WSU-MHV.

7. The FBI Field Office files, containing the raw data that expose the sloppy and often illegal methods of gathering information, were allegedly destroyed by the FBI in the late 1940s. A larger destruction of field-office files began in the early 1970s, just before the Freedom of Information Act went into effect. The Boston Field Office sent me approximately two-thirds of the pages, many heavily censored, in MHV's file, MHV-FBI. The Washington Field Office reported that her file was destroyed in 1972. The New York Field Office, which probably held the bulk of FBI "evidence" against Vorse, reported to me that it possessed no "information identifiable with Mary Heaton O'Brien Minor Vorse," even though I was able to give the New York office the number of her file there, which I had found referred to in other FBI documents. During the Reagan administration FBI files released under the Freedom of Information Act were often censored, to an extreme, as FBI officials made use of notions of "national security" and "classified material" to justify their failure to honor the spirit of the act. These files are so heavily censored that they become all but useless to the researcher, or to the many victims of FBI investigations of "subversives" during J. Edgar Hoover's long reign. My several formal appeals to the FBI to release more information were denied.

8. Building on data collected during the Red Scare of the 1920s, the FBI established a "Custodial Detention List" in 1939. In 1943, the attorney general ordered the termination of this list. Hoover secretly directed FBI officials to continue the program under the new name of Security Index. This list eventually became the attorney general's Portfolio Plan, in operation from 1948 until the mid-1960s. At its peak in 1955, the FBI Security Index included twenty-six thousand individuals.

9. George Woodbridge, *UNRRA: The History of the United Nations Relief and Rehabilitation Administration* (prepared under direction of Columbia University Press, 1950); MHV to Arthur Fletcher, February 6, 1946, Box 68, WSU-MHV. For her writing and notes on UNRRA work, see Boxes 124–127, WSU-MHV.

10. MHV, "Serene Plateau," Box 10; MHV, UNRRA Notes, Boxes 125, 126, WSU-MHV.

11. B. Ashford Russell to Mission Executive Officer, January 14, 1947, UNA-MHV, indicates his disappointment with her work; MHV postwar articles in Box 36; "German Series," Box 20; "Reflections of an American Woman in Germany," Box 29, WSU-MHV; MHV to JH, April 3, July 29, 1947, YUB-JH; Daily Notes, 1947, Box 87, WSU-MHV.

12. MHV, Daily Notes, 1947, Box 87, WSU-MHV.

13. Ibid., 1948, Box 87, WSU-MHV.

14. MHV to JH, April 18, 1949, YUB-JH; Truman cited in Jack Salzman, *Albert Maltz* (Boston: Twayne Publishers, 1978), 103. For a full discussion of Jo Herbst and the Hiss case, see Elinor Langer, *Josephine Herbst* (Boston: Little, Brown, 1984). Pertinent correspondence between Herbst and MHV is in Boxes 68, 69, 72, WSU-MHV, and in Correspondence, YUB-JH. While in Mexico, MHV talked with John Herrmann, Herbst's ex-husband, who had moved to Mexico to avoid questioning by the FBI. To judge from MHV's heavily censored FBI file, and from the surviving

correspondence, the FBI did not attempt to question MHV about her connection to the Ware group. In 1954, Herbst, who had been denied a passport on the grounds she was a subversive, successfully cleared herself from the charge. Herbst asked MHV for an affidavit stating that Herbst had been with MHV in Provincetown during the summer of 1934, the time in which Whittaker Chambers claimed he had developed some film of stolen government documents while staying in Herbst's Washington apartment.

15. MHV, Correspondence, November 1951, Box 69; Daily Notes, 1952, Box 89; Daily Notes, 1949, 1950, Boxes 87, 88, WSU-MHV.

16. MHV to Carmela, Daily Notes, Box 88, WSU-MHV.

17. MHV, Daily Notes, Box 89, WSU-MHV.

18. MHV, Correspondence, Boxes 70, 68, WSU-MHV.

19. See MHV, "An Altogether Different Strike," *Harper's Magazine*, February 1950, 50–57. The State Department admired this article because it emphasized the positive changes the New Deal brought to labor relations. It requested permission to distribute copies to its press officers in Europe, Latin America, the Middle East, the Far East, and Africa for translation and local publication. Department of State to MHV, March 9, 1950, Correspondence, Box 69, and Correspondence, Box 70, WSU-MHV. Also see MHV, "Trouble in Tennessee," *New Republic*, July 10, 1950, 9–11; MHV, "Child Reservoir of the South," *Harper's Magazine*, January 1951, 55–61; MHV, "America's Submerged Class: The Migrants," ibid., February 1953, 86–93; MHV, "The Union That Grew Up: An Informal Portrait of the UAW," ibid., July 1954, 83–88; "Big Steel and the Little Man," *Nation*, June 21, 1952, 603–605; "State of the Unions," ibid., December 5, 1953, 467–468. Walter Reuther to MHV, October 8, 1954, Box 70, WSU-MHV; MHV, "The Pirate's Nest of New York," *Harper's Magazine*, April 1952, 27–37; also see condensed version in *Reader's Digest*, July 1952, 97–101; Vernon H. Jensen, *Strife on the Waterfront: The Port of New York since 1945* (Ithaca, N.Y.: Cornell University Press, 1974); Daniel Bell, "The Racket-Ridden Longshoremen: The Web of Economics and Politics," in *The End of Ideology: On the Exhaustion of Political Ideas in the Fifties* (New York: Free Press, 1967), 175–211.

20. "Personal and Otherwise," *Harper's Magazine*, April 1952, 10; MHV, Daily Notes, 1952–1954, Box 89, WSU-MHV.

21. Interviews, Heaton Vorse, Joel O'Brien, Jill O'Brien, 1986; MHV, notes for waterfront series in Boxes 129–132, WSU-MHV.

22. Interview, Jeannette Andrews, 1982; MHV's experience at Yaddo described in Daily Notes, 1954, Box 89, WSU-MHV.

23. Ann Craton Blankenhorn to Jo Herbst, November 13, 1958, and January 10, 1958, in YUB-JH.

24. John Dos Passos, *Chosen Country* (Boston: Houghton Mifflin, 1951), 226–243. In his early draft of *Chosen Country*, JDP entitled the chapter about Anne Comfort "The Girl on the White Horse." The draft also contains a section showing Carl Humphries' (Robert Minor's) involvement in the Spartacist movement and mentions that the British and French intelligence were after him in Paris in 1919, in Box 9, Series I, UVAL-JDP. Townsend Luddington, *John Dos Passos: A Twentieth-Century Odyssey* (New York: E.P. Dutton, 1980), agrees that MHV was the model for Anne

Comfort. I am the first, however, to show that Vorse was also the model for Mary French in *U.S.A.*

25. Dos Passos was the illegitimate son of John R. Dos Passos, an egocentric, prominent corporate lawyer. His father maintained his mistress, the mother of Dos Passos, for several decades before eventually marrying her. Dos Passos saw his mother as victim, yet also admired his father. Biographers have often described this central tension in the life of Dos Passos as a most powerful force in shaping his life and politics.

26. Murray Kempton, *Part of Our Time: Some Ruins and Monuments of the Thirties* (New York: Simon and Schuster, 1955), 333. Kempton's discussion of MHV is on 214–232.

27. Daily Notes, Box 90, WSU-MHV.

28. Richard H. Rovere, "Ruins and Monuments," *New Yorker*, May 21, 1955.

29. MHV, Daily Notes, 1955, 1956, Boxes 89, 90, WSU-MHV.

30. Kempton, *Part of Our Time*, 215.

31. MHV, "Footnote to History," Box 1, WSU-MHV.

Chapter Eighteen: Serene Plateau

1. MHV, Daily Notes, 1956, Box 90, WSU-MHV.

2. MHV, "The Care and Treatment of the Aged," Box 16, WSU-MHV. During these years she also revised an old manuscript, "Women's Lives," and retitled it "Men: A Gentle Inquiry into Why They Are Not So Hot," Box 25, WSU-MHV.

3. MHV, "Serene Plateau," Box 10, WSU-MHV.

4. MHV, Box 71, WSU-MHV. I am grateful to Rosalyn Baxandall for the knowledge of this last meeting between MHV and EGF.

5. Maurice Isserman, *Which Side Were You On? The American Communist Party During the Second World War* (Middletown, Conn.: Wesleyan University Press, 1982), 255–256.

6. MHV, "Henderson Strike," Box 122, WSU-MHV.

7. Interview, Miriam and John Dewitt, 1982; Henry Robins to MHV, September 30, 1958, Box 72, WSU-MHV.

8. Correspondence, Box 72, WSU-MHV.

9. ACB to MLM, WSU-ACB.

10. Victor Reuther, UAW Convention, 1962, Box 39, WSU-UAW; Walter Reuther to MHV, March 1, 1962, Box 72, WSU-MHV; interviews, Joel and Jill O'Brien, 1984.

11. Province Lands, Box 119, WSU-MHV. MHV was featured in a television documentary on Provincetown, "The Community," produced by National Educational TV in 1965; interview, Ernest Vanderburgh, 1984.

12. Provincetown *Advocate*, June 16, 1966. Also see obituaries, *Newsweek*, June 27, 1966, 83; New York *Times*, June 15, 1966, 47: 4, 5; *Time*, June 24, 1966, 100; *Publishers Weekly*, June 27, 1966, 77.

Index

Ettor, Joe, 56, 108

Farmers' Holiday Movement, 251
Farrell, Jim, 317
Federal Bureau of Investigation (FBI), 70, 118, 267, 269, 287, 302–303, 304–306, 367nn7, 8
Federated Press, 162, 168, 241, 243, 251, 260
Field, Eugene, 4
Filene, Peter, 15
Fine, Sidney, 279
Flint, Mich., sit-down strike (1937), 275–282, 292
Flynn, Elizabeth Gurley, 68, 69, 70, 171, 174, 239, 265, 283, 322; and amnesty campaign, 182; and Carlo Tresca, 203–204; at Lawrence, Mass., textile strike, 55, 57–58; at Mesabi Range strike, 107–108, 110–111; at Passaic textile strike 196–197
Forbes, Beatrice, 68
Foster, William Z., 154, 160, 239, 248, 293
Frank, Jerome, 262, 266
Frank, Waldo, 136, 244, 246, 247, 249, 250, 252
Free, Edward E., 346n16
Freeman, Joseph, 65, 66, 136, 238
Frey, John, 293–294

Gale, Zona, 68
Gastonia, N.C., textile strike (1929), 213–225, 227, 256; trial in, 226–228
General Federation of Women's Clubs, 14
George, Lloyd, 121, 140
Gibson, Lydia, 174, 183–184, 235, 250, 354n6
Gilder, Richard Watson, 37
Gilman, Charlotte Perkins, 13, 68, 70
Gitlow, Benjamin, 201
Glackens, William, 37
Glaspell, Susan, 63, 64, 68, 75, 80–82, 83, 236; and Joe O'Brien, 100–101; and Provincetown Players, 99–100, 106–107; death of, 310
Gold, Michael, 237–238
Goldman, Emma, 67, 136, 180
Gompers, Samuel, 122, 158, 160
Gorky, Maxim, 37–38

Greenwich Village, N.Y.C., 28–29, 47, 62–74
Greenwood, Marion, 249
Gregory, T. T. C., 139–140, 143, 144–145, 149
Gutterson, Herbert L., 149

Haessler, Carl, 238, 275–276
Hale, Robertson, 68
Halladay, Polly, 86
Hamilton, Alice, 88
Hammond, John Henry, 244, 245
Hapgood, Hutchins, 25, 26, 63–64, 66, 71, 75, 80–81, 83, 86–87, 98–100, 102; death of, 310
Hard, William, 158
Harding, Warren, 181–182
Harlan County, Ky., 60, 239–240, 241–248
Harn, Josie, 149, 170, 195, 208, 234; death of, 310
Harriman, Mrs. J. Borden, 48
Harrison, Constance Cary, 23
Havel, Hippolyte, 86, 161
Hawthorne, Hazel, 236
Haywood, William (Big Bill), 55, 57–58, 59, 62, 70, 73, 107, 118, 215
Heaton, Ellen (mother), 5–9, 11–14, 20–21, 30, 47, 125; death of, 44
Heaton, Hiram (father), 5–6, 12–13, 20, 47
Hemingway, Ernest, 256, 274, 287–288
Herbst, Josephine, 249, 251, 265, 272–273, 307, 308, 314, 335n18; and FBI, 302–303, 366n3, 367n14; at Flint, Mich., sit-down strike, 280; and Ware group, 262–263
Herrmann, John, 251, 262–263, 272
Heterodoxy Club, 63, 66–72, 299, 342n10
Hickerson, Harold, 244
Hillman, Sidney, 164, 168–169, 264, 293, 309
Hinkle, Beatrice, 68
Hirsch, Charlotte Teller, 37
Hiss, Alger, 262–263, 317, 367n14
Hochman, Julius, 273
Hollingsworth, Leta, 68
Hook, Sidney, 249
Hoover, Herbert, 129–130, 138, 140, 144, 148, 151, 178

and Lydia Gibson, 174, 183–184; and
  Part of Our Time, 319; death of, 310
Mitchell, Elsa Reed, 244, 247
Montessori, Maria, 75–76, 80
Montgomery, David, 58
Mooney, Tom, 137, 145
Murphy, Frank, 275, 281
Murray, Phillip, 293, 310, 317, 318
Muste, A. J., 264

National American Woman Suffrage
  Association, 14
National Hunger March, 251–253
National Recovery Administration (NRA),
  260–261
National Textile Workers Union, 216, 229
National Woman's Party, 69
New Woman, 14, 20, 23
New York (City) Milk Committee, 48–49
New York City Woman Suffrage Party, 88
Newdick, Edwin, 154, 158
Nordfeldt, Bror, 39
Norris, Kathleen, 105
Norton, Mary T., 261

Oak, Liston, 229, 244
O'Brien, Joe (husband), 61, 74–76, 80–81,
  82–85, 87, 97–102, 107, 125, 137;
  at Lawrence textile strike, 56–57, 59;
  death of, 100–101
O'Brien, Joel (son), 84–85, 105, 106, 114,
  234, 236, 253, 260, 302, 306, 308, 312
O'Carroll, Joe, 86
O'Connor, Harvey and Jessie, 243, 260
O'Hare, Kate Richards, 182
O'Neill, Eugene, 107, 235, 314
O'Neill, Rose, 37
O'Reilly, Leonore, 88, 90

Parsons, Elsie Clews, 68
Passaic, N.J., textile strike (1926), 196–203
Pearson, Drew, 131
Peary, Robert E., 25, 35
Perkins, Frances, 37, 100, 106, 260
Pethick-Lawrence, Emmeline, 90
Pinchot, Amos, 106
Pinchot, Cornelia, 292
Platten, Fritz, 127–128
Plotkin, Abe, 165–166
Poole, Ernest, 37
Potter, Grace, 68

Provincetown, Mass., 35–36, 39–40,
  81–87, 97–100, 106–107, 225, 236,
  291–292, 294, 320, 321, 325, 327
Provincetown Players, 63, 75, 80, 99–100,
  105–107, 161, 314
Putnam, Nina Wilcox, 68

Rauh, Ida, 68, 106
Red Scare, 147, 148, 161–162, 165
Reed, John, 114, 118, 135, 196–197,
  257; and Greenwich Village, 63–64,
  312; and John Reed Clubs, 294; and
  Provincetown, 97, 98, 106–107
Reuther, Roy, 317
Reuther, Victor, 317, 325
Reuther, Walter, 317, 325, 326
Rivera, Diego, 235, 303
Robeson, Paul, 317
Robinson, Herbert, 131
Rodman, Henrietta, 64, 66, 67, 69, 71, 72
Rodman, Selden, 254
Rogers, Lou, 68
Roosevelt, Eleanor, 261, 266, 325
Roosevelt, Franklin Delano, 264, 294–295
Roosevelt, Theodore, 26, 38, 51, 88

Sacco–Vanzetti case, 171–172, 202
Sand, George, 29
Sandburg, Carl, 73
Sanger, Margaret, 53, 56, 67, 106, 148
Schechter, Amy, 216, 225
Schneiderman, Rose, 51
Scott, Leroy, 37
Scott, Miriam, 37
Scottsboro Boys trial, 253–254
Scudder, Vida, 59
Shaw, Anna, 77
Shinn, Anne O'Hagan, 68, 106
Siegel, Morton, 198
Simms, Harry, 245, 246
Sloan, Dolly, 37
Sloan, John, 37, 72
Smith, Hilda Worthington, 261, 302
Smith, Jessica, 262–263
Soule, George, 254
Springer, Fleeta, 260, 302, 303
Steel strike: of 1919, 149, 154–160, 271–
  272; of 1937, 284–286, 290
Steele, Wilbur Daniel, 39, 43, 74, 99–100
Steffens, Lincoln, 26, 34, 59, 63–64, 85,
  106, 145, 262

≡ American Civilization

A series edited by Allen F. Davis